Natural Spirituality

A Handbook for Jungian Inner Work in Spiritual Community

Revised Edition

Joyce Rockwood Hudson

www.ChironPublications.com

Interior and cover design by Cornelia G. Murariu
Printed primarily in the United States of America.

ISBN 978-1-63051-448-8 paperback
ISBN 978-1-63051-392-4 paperback
ISBN 978-1-63051-393-1 hardcover
ISBN 978-1-63051-394-8 electronic

Library of Congress Cataloging-in-Publication Data

Names: Hudson, Joyce Rockwood, author.
Title: Natural spirituality : a handbook for Jungian inner work in spiritual community / Joyce Rockwood Hudson.
Description: Revised Edition. | Asheville, North Carolina : Chiron Publications, 2016. | Includes bibliographical references and index.
Identifiers: LCCN 2016044603 (print) | LCCN 2016045335 (ebook) | ISBN 9781630513924 (pbk. : alk. paper) | ISBN 9781630513931 (hardcover : alk. paper) | ISBN 9781630513948 (E-book)
Subjects: LCSH: Spirituality--Christianity. | Jungian psychology--Religious aspects--Christianity. | Wisdom--Religious aspects--Christianity. | Psychology, Religious. | Individuation (Psychology)--Religious aspects--Christianity.
Classification: LCC BV4501.3 .H821837 2016 (print) | LCC BV4501.3 (ebook) | DDC 248--dc23
LC record available at https://lccn.loc.gov/2016044603

Cover art: “Inner Wilderness” by Betty Beshoar

In memory of
Susan Cardwell Hurt
(Known to many as Susan Kingsley)
1946–1984

*Her death brought us not only sorrow
but also the saving grace that
set all this in motion*

When the Lord has given you the bread of suffering and the water of distress, he who is your teacher will hide no longer, and you will see your teacher with your own eyes. Whether you turn to right or left, your ears will hear these words behind you, "This is the way, follow it."

Isaiah 30:20–21

Nature is the mistress, the soul is the disciple; what the one has taught, or the other has learned, has been delivered to them by God.

Tertullian, Christian writer, c. 200 AD

Contents

Preface

OUR WORLD IS IN TROUBLE, and we all know it. Climate change is already hurting us, and this is just the beginning. Terrible upheavals of populations, economies, and polities lie ahead, and none of our leaders—in politics, religion, journalism, or business—are up to the great challenge that is bearing down on us. Few, if any, can even name the underlying problem, for this requires a way of thinking that is not yet familiar to the general populace. But at the leading edge of wise thought in our time, there is a growing awareness that the human race as a whole has grown dangerously one-sided toward the masculine energies of life—toward technology, power, action, and pursuit of the ideal—and that this has come at the expense of the feminine energies of life—nature, process, reflection, and acknowledgment of the limitations of reality. Our masculine one-sidedness has come to seem like the norm for human consciousness, and a different balance cannot yet be imagined by most people. But humanity is equally masculine and feminine, and so should our consciousness be.

If an imbalance toward masculine consciousness is the underlying problem of our time, the answer to the problem is self-evident. We need more attunement to nature, process, reflection, and the limitations of reality. We need to wake up to the feminine energies of life. We need to invest ourselves in them and bring them back into balance with our masculine energies. But how do we do this? Who can show us the way to this new orientation of our fundamental perception of life? Our politicians, economists, and journalists could be of help in this if they themselves were being truly led, but they can hardly be expected to be in the vanguard of such a profound transformation in human consciousness. It must necessarily be the world's religions that lead us forward, for this transformation has to do with our souls, our psyches, our depths. Human consciousness is fundamentally shaped by our understanding of the divine. Unfortunately, however, our foundational religions, especially in the Western world, have to a large degree lost sight of and lost interest in the fact that a balance of masculine and feminine consciousness is central to a healthy and whole spiritual life. Nor, at this point, do they have much of an idea of what such a balance would look like, for they have little idea of what the feminine side of divine reality actually is. In the wake of the Enlightenment and its accompanying Scientific Revolution, almost all knowledge of the feminine manifestation of the divine has been lost, as masculine consciousness has pushed it out of greater human consciousness and all but completely usurped its place.

This book is an expansive guide to restoring the balance of masculine and feminine consciousness to our healthy and whole spiritual life as human beings. Informed attention to dreams and synchronicity is the most natural and direct approach to the feminine divine. And the best way to inform our attention to these naturally occurring elements of spiritual life is through a rudimentary knowledge of the basics of Jungian psychology. This book offers these Jungian tools in clear language and shows how to use them to make sense of our dreams and synchronistic experiences. At the same time, it emphasizes the importance of retaining our connection to the masculine divine as we take up our new connection to the feminine divine.

Jungian inner work can and must be done individually, but it is also greatly enhanced when brought into spiritual community, whether such a community be situated inside or outside an institutional setting. Natural spirituality dream groups can be formed anywhere—in homes, yoga centers, places of worship, coffee houses, or wherever people of faithful heart and intent might gather. The original edition of this book focused primarily on dream groups in churches, but in the almost two decades since it was first published, the spiritual-but-not-religious segment of our population has grown significantly and now has as much, if not more, potential for fostering natural spirituality dream groups.

Consequently, this new edition has been expanded in content and tone to include the world of the spiritual but not religious. Christians will still be comfortable here, but so also will their brothers and sisters of other faiths and those who have left all institutions to find new paths in a less constricted spiritual world.

For those who are familiar with the first edition, this revised edition contains a few significant changes. In Part One, *Nature and Spirit*, Chapter One, "Beginnings," has been revised somewhat, and Chapter Two was retitled "Is Inner Work Really Necessary?" and is almost entirely new. Part Two, *Jungian Spiritual Tools*, is largely unchanged except for the omission of the first edition's "Carl Jung and Christianity" chapter, much of which has now been folded into Chapter Fifteen. In the remaining chapters in Part Two—"Consciousness," "The Unconscious," "The Language of the Unconscious," "Dreams," and "Synchronicity"—small changes have been made, though more at the level of tweaking than revision. The same applies to the chapters in Part Three, *The Individuation Journey*. These chapters, which are essentially unchanged from the first edition, are "The Opposites," "Masculine Wholeness," "The Beatles and the Masculine Quaternity," "Feminine Wholeness," and "Psyche and Eros and the Feminine Quaternity." In addition, a new chapter, "Types, Quarters, and Stages of Life," has been added to Part Three. In this new material, the masculine and feminine quaternities are joined together with Jungian typology and the Myers-Briggs personality types to reveal a dynamic model that illuminates the distinctive stages of life for each of the sixteen types. As was true with the masculine and feminine quaternities in the first edition, the description of these particular archetypal patterns in the human psyche is original and appears for the first time in this book.

The last two chapters of the first edition have been entirely replaced by two new chapters, which have been put into a new Part Four, *Inner Work in Spiritual Community*. Chapter Fourteen, "How To Start a Dream Group," now draws on many more years of experience than the how-to chapter in the first edition and is, therefore, a much more valuable guide for organizing dream groups, whether in places of worship or in the greater community.

Chapter Fifteen, "Does Jungian Inner Work Belong in Church?" is a new combination of material that was originally published in two chapters of the first edition, "Carl Jung and Christianity" and "Individuation as Church Mission." This has been placed as the final chapter so that it can be skipped over easily by those who are not interested in matters specific to Christianity.

In the appendices, Appendix A, "Find Your Type," is new. It contains a very short but surprisingly effective test for determining one's Jungian psychological type, which is now commonly called our "Myers-Briggs" type. It also contains a fairly extensive description of each of the sixteen types, which is a great help for determining whether a test result is actually a good fit or not. Appendix B, "A Liturgy for Dream Groups," is also new. It contains the liturgy that is used in my own dream group for opening and closing our gatherings, and it can be freely copied and distributed by any who wish to do so. Appendix C, "Natural Spirituality Resources," has been carried over from the first edition, but it has been updated.

I find it gratifying that *Natural Spirituality* has enjoyed significant sales for almost two decades. The number of people who are expanding their consciousness to include the feminine divine is steadily growing. For this we can all rejoice, for the goal of human consciousness must be, *has* to be, that the feminine side of our consciousness be brought into full balance and equality with the masculine side of our consciousness. An intrinsic component of this goal should be that these two sides of our inner and outer reality do not compete with each other but join together in effective union. Collective consciousness changes as a result of cumulative changes in the consciousness of individuals. This book is a handbook for expanding consciousness at the individual level in order to help bring about a much needed expansion of our collective understanding of what human life requires of us in order to be healthy, whole, and in balance with the natural order.

Joyce Rockwood Hudson
Frankfort, Kentucky 2016

Part One

Nature and Spirit

Chapter One

Beginnings

In the fall of 1991, I offered to teach a course on natural spirituality at the Episcopal church I had been attending in the university town of Athens, Georgia. Though the content was to be based largely on Jungian psychology, I coined the term "natural spirituality" to distance the subject matter from clinical and secular contexts and to emphasize its rightful place in the life of any intentional spiritual community, including the church. Natural spirituality refers to a manifestation of the divine in creation that in biblical times was called Wisdom. It is an aspect of God that our scientific materialism has pushed out of religious awareness in the Western world, and yet this Wisdom, or natural spirituality, has always been with us, an ever present reality in every human life, whether noticed and attended to or not.

I am the daughter of an Episcopal clergyman. By both my nature and upbringing, I have always been positively oriented toward the church, finding nourishment for my soul in liturgical rites, hymns, and the rich imagery of the biblical tradition. But when I was in my late thirties, seven years before I offered to teach this course, a series of events overtook me which shook the foundation of my rational and religious understanding of the very nature of life. At the time, I was a successful writer with four published books. I had just completed a long historical novel for which I did not yet have a publisher. My husband of sixteen years, a university professor of anthropology, was also a writer, renowned in his field. We were satisfied with our lives and had no idea that we had come to a turning point.

The turn began with a visit from family friends: two women, who were around my own age, and their three children, ages five to eight. They were from our close circle of friends in my husband's hometown in Kentucky, where we had a summer home. It was now early February and our friends had driven together to Florida to visit the two women's respective parents. Our home in northern Georgia was their overnight stop on what was supposed to be their return trip.

We had a pleasant visit, lingering long around the dinner table, catching up on news. One of the women, whose name was Susan, was an actress of considerable accomplishment. What she especially wanted to talk about that evening was what had happened between her mother and her on the last day before she left Florida. She had a history of strained relationship with her mother, whose strong spirit was powerfully oriented toward church and family. As a successful actress, Susan was living a life very different from her mother's. She felt estranged. Her work required her frequent absence from home, sometimes for months at a time, during which time her two children remained behind in the care of their father. Although her family was doing well, Susan felt guilty and assumed negative judgment from her mother.

So it was that she was especially pleased with the time the two of them had spent together just the day before. She had taken her mother to the movies to see *Terms of Endearment*, the first time in years her mother had been to a movie theater. *Terms of Endearment* was about the relationship between a grown daughter and her mother. The daughter, who is herself the mother of young children, learns that she has incurable cancer. Together with her mother, husband, and children, the heroine faces her death and takes her leave of life, knowing that her family is strong and will be able to carry on without her. Much of the film's drama is centered around the heroine's mother as she comes to terms with the death of her child.

This movie inspired a conversation of deep healing between Susan and her mother. In telling us about it, Susan kept reiterating that they had never before had such a satisfying conversation, that they had never before met each other with so much understanding and love. Her mother had told her that a mother always loves her child as tenderly as if it were a babe in arms, no matter how old the child becomes. Susan told her mother that she felt guilty about her own mothering of her children because she was away so much. Her mother told her that she must not feel that way, that her children were turning out beautifully, a joy to their grandmother, and that Susan was a fine and worthy mother. This blessing from her mother was, for Susan, an especially precious treasure. Throughout that evening and the next morning, she kept bringing it out and looking at it again.

The February day on which our friends arrived had been warm and pleasant, but in the evening rain began to fall. Later, while we slept, the temperature dropped and the rain turned to snow, and beneath the snow, the rain-drenched ground became a field of ice. The morning dawned clear and cold—much colder than we had expected. Our water pipes were frozen. The roads were covered with several inches of snow, with ice beneath. But the sun was bright, and by midmorning, the road in front of our house was completely clear. Traffic was moving again. Our friends loaded up their car, and we waved them off toward home.

Twenty minutes later the phone rang. There had been a wreck. Another car had slid on a shaded patch of ice and collided with our friends head on. Susan had serious internal injuries, though everyone else was only shaken up. Susan had been taken to the large hospital near the university. The others were received at a smaller hospital closer to where the wreck had occurred.

My husband went to be with Susan while I brought the others home. Susan was taken into surgery. Back home, we waited, not knowing if she would live or die. For several hours we clung to hope, but then I began to think about what had happened between her and her mother—the two of them watching that particular movie and the reconciliation that had followed. It was too perfect. I could see that the end had already been arranged: Susan was going to die.

This realization caused a major shift in the ground of my being—a veritable earthquake. This did not come simply from the fact that my friend was dying. That was a tremendous shock, but even more of a shock was the realization that life could be this way—that Susan and her mother could live their last day on earth together as meaningfully as such a day could possibly have been lived, and yet neither of them had had the slightest idea that she was about to die.

As I reverberated from this stunning recognition and began to let go of my hope that Susan would live, a second powerful inner event took place. I suddenly saw vividly in my mind's eye a newspaper page, more than half of which was taken up with an obituary for Susan, including her picture. It was very clear, no mistaking what it was. I began to cry. At this same time, my husband called with news that Susan had just died.

This tragedy marked the end for me of the world I had always known and that everyone around me seemed only to know—a world in which the human mind is the highest source of knowledge and human will is the greatest purposeful power, religious statements ascribing higher knowledge and power to God notwithstanding. That world of ordinary consciousness did not allow for purposefulness in such events as Susan's last day with her mother. In the modern intellectual world, that day would be defined as a coincidence, an amazing one perhaps, even a blessed one, but only a coincidence. Since no human mind had designed it, it had not been designed. It just happened to turn out well.

Similarly, in the world I was leaving behind, it would be said that my vision of Susan's obituary just happened to coincide with the time of her death. By what mechanism could it be otherwise? The explanation from that world would probably be that the vision was my imagination at work, along with a repressed realization that she was too badly injured to live. This despite the fact that through several previous hours of anxious waiting, I had *not* imagined her death, much less her obituary, and it was only right at the time she actually died that the image intruded itself into my mind's eye.

As for myself, I knew more absolutely than I had ever known anything that these events were not merely coincidental. And so I was left stranded alone on the shore of a new world, a world in which a reality greater than any human reality orchestrates mercies to accompany tragedies, a world in which spiritual gifts flow copiously from death, not simply in a vague, ethereal way, but in a real, embodied way. On that tragic and transforming day, I realized that I was standing more directly in the presence of the divine than I had ever thought possible, that all of us were, and that the meaning of God's presence in our lives was more all-pervasive than even the church had ever taught me it could be. I knew on that day that I had been changed forever by my experience of this truth and that I could never go back to the old world of more limited vision and understanding. And yet at the same time, I wanted to go back because I did not know how to go forward into the new world.

A New Way of Thinking and Perceiving

Thus began a profoundly unsettling time for me. For a year I struggled alone to get my feet back under me, to return to "normal," which to me at that time meant the life I had been living before the wreck. But that life was never to return. I was caught in the throes of a spiritual transformation, and I was as helpless against it as Paul was helpless on the road to Damascus.

Although my traditional religious background did not help me *understand* the spiritual transformation that overtook me, it did prepare me to meet it in the right way. Because of my deeply-rooted spiritual heritage, I was able to stand strong in my trust that this storm was, in fact, coming from God and that God would not abandon me. I knew also that wherever this experience was leading me, I would have to go there, however terrified I was of what God's intentions for me were. In that year following the wreck, every area of my life became unsettled and seemed to be called into question. What did God want of me? Was I supposed to leave my marriage? Give up my writing? Those were my greatest fears. Although neither outcome came to pass, I did have to open myself to major adjustments in both those areas and in every other aspect of my life.

The greatest change asked of me, however, was a change in *thinking and perceiving.* If the world is such that Susan's last days could be orchestrated as they were, how is a modern mind to grasp that reality and think about it? It was here that the church failed me. No clue came from that quarter. It was only when I stumbled across the autobiography of Carl Jung, about a year after the wreck, that I began to gather up the tools I needed to make the fundamental change in my understanding of the world that was necessary to regain my footing.

The problem with which I was struggling was what to do with the increasingly unshakable realization that natural life in this world has more behind it than simple cause and effect. There is *meaning* woven into it. There was meaning in Susan seeing that particular movie with her mother, meaning in the inner image of the obituary. Ever since the day of the wreck, I had continued to see meaning in the world itself, and by this, I do not mean general and abstract meaning—as in, God made the world and loves it and works in mysterious ways—but very personal and specific meaning. A door would slam as certain words were being spoken. What were those words? I would notice them and think about them and see that something of importance to my own life was being emphasized. An image would arise in my mind as I was driving down the road, or perhaps a line from a song. What was that image or that line? I would catch it and think about it and understand that something was being hinted at. Dreams would come tumbling darkly in the night, punctuating the patterns of meaning I was struggling to patch together in waking life.

What to do with all this? I knew I was not losing my mind. I was not hearing voices or having hallucinations or saying irrational things. Nor was I becoming dysfunctional in my outer life. But inside myself, I was having a terrible time. I had no cognitive framework for this new way of perceiving. Neither the ordinary intellectual world in which I lived with my university professor husband nor the traditional religious world in which I participated as an active church member was broad enough to include this expanded reality.

What I found in Carl Jung's autobiography was a man with a powerful intellect and a deep religious awareness whose frame of reference took in the kind of experiences I was beginning to have. He too lived with heightened meaning. Here, at last, was someone who would have been able to understand me, had he been alive and accessible. Carl Jung had words and concepts for the new world I had entered. He himself was one of its earliest modern explorers and had led the way in describing its features in modern terms. He was both scientific and religious, intellectual and soulful, rational and nonrational, without contradiction. I immediately searched out more of his writings and read them intensely, gathering up his concepts to equip myself for my new spiritual journey.

Carl Jung was my mentor and guide for this journey. Most people have a more embodied guide—an analyst or some other person who has made the journey ahead of them. But in my ability to navigate those dark waters alone, with only a man's printed words to help me, is the indication of the fact that this spiritual journey is indeed a *natural* one. It unfolds from the human psyche in a generally predictable way, although in its particulars and in its outcome it is altogether different in each individual life.

I did, however, have a flesh-and-blood counselor for a very brief period of time—for six weeks to be exact. After I had been reading Jung's writings for a few months, my inner experience intensified, bringing with it a gripping anxiety. One night as I was getting into bed, I thought to myself that I had better make an effort the next day to seek some outside help. Immediately the name of the priest at the Episcopal church I was then attending flashed into my mind. I did not *think* it—I had not had time to. It came of its own accord, with its own energy, and I was glad to accept it as a suggestion of a person who might be helpful. Although the anxiety attacks made me worry that I could actually lose my sanity, I was very reluctant to turn myself over to a psychiatrist, fearing that my experience would then be dealt with in purely psychological terms. I felt that at the heart of my struggle was the challenge to open myself to God and the new direction God was trying to give me, and I needed to be able to talk about it that way and have it understood in those terms. Jungian psychology would not have precluded this, but there were no Jungian analysts nearby.

It is to the credit of the modern church in the 1980s that the priest I went to see had some psychological training and was familiar with the fundamental concepts of Freud and Jung. He understood the terminology I was using and the basic nature of my crisis. He was comfortable with giving value to dreams and was also willing to puzzle with me about how much meaning there might be in the intensified outer events that were surrounding my inner journey. He was frank in acknowledging that he had never been through a similar "confrontation with the unconscious," as Jung might have phrased it, but he recognized from the literature the nature of my experience and knew that it was good.

He knew I was going through a psychological process that is comparable to a shaman's initiation and which in the literature of analytical psychology is called a "creative illness." It is a serious event, but if the ego is not shattered by it, this life-changing process provides a rite of passage into the healing world of psyche and spirit and imparts to those who are called upon to endure it a significant gift for the healing of souls. Because of the ego strength my counselor perceived in me, he was able to assure me that I was not going to lose my sanity and that I would come out on the other side of this crisis changed and more solid. He was a great help to me as a steadying presence in this most tumultuous passage in my journey, a time I look back on as "when I was in the abyss."

It seemed at the time most unfortunate that this priest was in his last weeks in our parish. He had accepted a call to a church in another state, and after I had seen him for six weeks of regular sessions, he was gone and I was on my own again. I had come through the worst of the swirling passage, however, and was back on firmer ground, learning now to live in this new world of perception into which my journey had led me.

A New Room in the Spiritual Community

As I look back, I can see that it was a good thing that I had no more outside help than I had—no other Christian clergyperson nor any Jungian analyst to lay words and explanations over my experience. I had to put together for myself a new cognitive framework, shaping it from my inner material, using Jung's writings as my primary source of intellectual understanding and the Judeo-Christian tradition as a touchstone to keep me grounded. Whatever new truth I was coming to, I knew it had to be congruent with the old truth of my world. It had to fit with town and country life in the American South, where churches and synagogues are the centers of religious life. In the late twentieth century, it was these institutions of traditional religion that carried the wisdom of the ages, conserving it and passing it on to each new generation, however imperfect that effort might be. It was to these centers that one went to talk forthrightly about matters of the soul and to participate openly in spiritual activity. These religious centers in the modern world preserved an ancient discourse, and my new discourse had to mesh with that. Otherwise, my spiritual life would be disconnected and irrelevant, too airy and grand, or too dark and submerged, to be lived in the outer world.

In the early years of this journey, I had a difficult time fashioning a correspondence between my private spiritual experience and life in the community. My most persistent error was to try to interject my new understandings into traditional discussions and activities, both in the university community and in the church. That this was not effective in secular life is not surprising, but neither was it useful in church life, not even in study groups, where issues of all sorts were open for discussion. I never met any hostility in the church: people were always polite, sometimes interested, and now and then intrigued. But they were unable to take in what I was trying to say. It took a long time for me to become reconciled to the fact that this new way of seeing is not for everyone, at least not in its full measure. The fact is that for the majority of people there are other valid spiritual paths that are sufficient for their needs.

And so after several years of futile effort, I grew wiser and learned to be quiet. I began to keep my inner life to myself and to accept church life for what it was, without asking for more.

It is frequently the case that when you stop trying to get the thing that you especially feel you need and reconcile yourself to living without it, it finally comes to you. One evening I was participating in a discussion group in which the question was asked of us: "What is it that you need from this church that you are not getting?" I seriously debated whether or not to answer truthfully, so much had I given up on the possibility of ever having what I really wanted. But I decided that here of all places I should be honest, and so I told the group that what I was not getting from church was an opportunity to talk about my spiritual life in the terms in which I experienced it.

Evidently my moment had come, for people were interested in this and wanted to know more about it. I tried to explain that the traditional language of the church was not broad enough to take in my experience of the spirit of God flowing into me through my everyday natural life, through dreams, intuitions, and ordinary events, all of which take on a divine quality when you really begin to pay attention to them. A number of people replied that they would like to broaden their spiritual framework in this way, but that I would have to teach them how to do it. Again, it is to the credit of the modern church that at this point in the discussion the priest who was present said to me, "It sounds like you have a gift that is not being used."

It was with his encouragement that a few months later I put an announcement in the church newsletter offering to lead a seminar on "natural spirituality." I explained: "The focus of the seminar will be on learning to recognize the unfolding of our individual spiritual journeys in the ordinary events of our lives, including our dreams. We will explore basic Jungian concepts of consciousness and the unconscious; the phenomenon of synchronicity, or meaningful coincidence; and aspects of our masculine and feminine natures. The interconnection of natural spirituality and Christianity will be emphasized." The seminar would meet one night a week for twelve weeks. There would be required reading. Participants would have to buy their own books, but there would be no other charge. Enrollment would be limited to twelve.

I was not at all sure that there were twelve people who would be interested in taking the seminar, but I knew I wanted no more than that number since I was uncertain how people would react to this material. I wanted a group small enough to allow me to stay personally connected to each participant in order to give a guiding hand where it was needed. I was surprised and pleased when more than twelve people wanted to participate, and with the overflow, I started a list for a repeat seminar the following spring.

The content of that first seminar was similar to what is contained in this book. In the first part, I laid out the basic concepts of Jungian psychology as tools for recognizing and dealing with the natural spirituality that flows through all of life. In the second part, I surveyed some of the issues that are raised when natural spirituality begins to be attended to in a person's life, especially the problem of reconciling the opposition between the masculine and feminine principles. And in the last part, I examined the connection between natural spirituality and Judeo-Christianity, the spiritual tradition in which so many of us in the Western world have our roots.

The seminar was received differently, of course, by the different participants. About a third of the group had come out of curiosity and at the end of the seminar their curiosity was satisfied—natural spirituality was interesting, but it was not particularly for them. Another third connected more enthusiastically, but they did not feel ready at that time to embark on deep journeys of their own.

The remaining third were greatly stirred up. Their lives were at a point where they needed this deepening, and they came to this material like persons who were hungry. Most of these were strongly spiritual people with deep roots in the church, faithful members for whom traditional religion still had meaning but who were no longer being completely fed by it. Essential nutrients were missing, and these they now recognized as being present in their own dreams and intuitions and in meaningful events of their lives.

The problem now was how to appropriate this new food, since the symbolic language of the divine can be so difficult to understand. As we neared the end of the seminar, this group began to get anxious. “What will we do when the seminar is over?” they asked. “How can we go on from here? Now we know that our dreams are important, but we still don’t know how to interpret them.”

Thus began the Journey Group, which became the heart of the natural spirituality program in this church. Almost every week since that first seminar ended more than twenty years ago, the journey groups (there are now two) at Emmanuel Church have met to help their members puzzle out the meaning of their dreams and significant life events. New participants have joined as the introductory seminar has been repeated, with the same pattern usually prevailing: about a third of the seminar graduates come into a journey group and begin the hard but rewarding task of connecting with the deeper levels of their souls. This task entails not months but *years* of commitment, and the personal change and growth that result are amazing to see.

Natural spirituality has become a rich room added to this particular spiritual community. Those who participate in the dream groups find that this deeper experience of the divine does not diminish traditional church experience, but rather enhances it. As their journeys progress, the true meanings of traditional teachings emerge spontaneously from the depths of their individual souls. A truth arising from one’s own soul in connection with one’s personal life experience has a much stronger effect than the same truth read in a book or heard from a pulpit. When truth comes to us in this way, we can say with Carl Jung, “I don’t need to believe. I know.”[1]

1 References for all quotations can be found in the NOTES at the end of the volume.

What Exactly Does "Natural Spirituality" Mean?

This book grew out of the original natural spirituality class and contains much of the content of that twelve-week course. The initial spiral-bound, copy-shop edition of the book was published in 1998, followed by the first trade paperback edition in 2000. As it spread out into the greater world, the book took with it its particular use of the term "natural spirituality." This phrase, of course, could have many meanings, but it is used here with a specific meaning that has both a primary aspect as a noun and a secondary aspect as an adjective. At the primary level, "natural spirituality" refers to the living presence of the divine that *permeates all of life* and expresses itself in every aspect of unfolding life, both inner and outer. Once we have grasped the existence of this subtle, natural reality, it follows that we should pay attention to it as we tend our spiritual lives. Those who pay attention to it want to talk about it, and "natural spirituality" is simply a handy, blanket term for that to which we are paying attention.

This particular meaning was all I had in mind when I first offered the class. But this primary meaning as a noun immediately produced a derivative adjective. The class about natural spirituality became the natural spirituality class. The dream group that grew out of the class, though formally named the Journey Group, began to be referred to as the natural spirituality dream group. The overall program in the church that contains both of these became the Natural Spirituality Program. As the book spread into the world, natural spirituality programs were started in other churches, with natural spirituality classes and dream groups. There is now even an annual conference called the Natural Spirituality Regional Gathering. These two particular uses of "natural spirituality," the primary use as a noun and the derivative use as an adjective, have taken on a life of their own.

To clarify the meaning of the term when used as an adjective, it might help to note the difference between a natural spirituality dream group and a purely Jungian dream group, such as might be found under the umbrella of a local Jung society. The natural spirituality framework seeks to awaken people to the divine aspect of the flow of life and to give them Jungian tools for understanding it and integrating it *without losing sight of its explicitly spiritual nature*. The original natural spirituality class was taught in an Episcopal church, and so the explicitly spiritual context in the class was Christian, just as it is in this book, which grew out of the class. But a natural spirituality dream group's spiritual context for paying attention to the divine in the flow of life could be any of the world's valid and healthy religious traditions. A purely Jungian dream group, on the other hand, is much less likely to maintain an explicitly spiritual emphasis. Its emphasis instead will be more purely psychological, and its references to religious traditions will be primarily intellectual, in the vein of comparative religion.

"Natural spirituality" as an adjective, then, means Jungian inner work in spiritual community. This, however, is by no means the only term that can be, and is being, applied to such work. Wherever this particular term is used in this way, this book is usually somewhere in the background. As a term for Jungian inner work in spiritual community, "natural spirituality" may or may not last for the long run, but for now, it is convenient and somewhat widely understood.

Out Into the World

Much new life has flowed from that first class I taught in 1991. As a result of this book's use in introductory classes, natural spirituality programs have been, and continue to be, established in many churches around the country. At the same time, viable spiritual centers of all kinds are growing up outside institutional religion, and natural spirituality dream groups are adding rich rooms to these communities as well. The result is a two-pronged movement of natural spirituality out into the world.

On one prong, church dream groups continue to spread. Those who join them stay in them for years while still participating actively in other aspects of congregational life. Dream groups do not compete with "regular" church. Indeed, some people in church dream groups say that it is the availability of dreamwork at their church that keeps them from drifting away from the institution.

On the other prong, natural spirituality dream groups outside institutional religion also continue to arise. For those who are in these groups, the weekly dream group itself often becomes a primary link to their life with God. A natural spirituality dream group opens and closes with an explicit invocation of the divine. The form varies, but the purpose is always the same: to consciously acknowledge that dreamwork is spiritual work and that it brings to those who engage in it a significant experience of the divine, both in their individual lives and in the life of the group. Many people outside institutional religion find natural spirituality dream groups to be a satisfying and life-enriching form of spiritual community.

This book, then, is meant to help make it possible to build new rooms for spiritual community both inside religious institutions and outside them, according to people's needs. At the same time, it is also meant to illuminate the realm of natural spirituality for persons who are traveling alone. It contains the material that I have found to be most useful in preparing people to look at their dreams and the meaningful events of their lives in a way that is both rationally informed and centered in a healthy consciousness of spiritual reality.

Chapter Two

Do We Really Need Inner Work?

On the night after I first conceived the idea of teaching a class on natural spirituality in my church community, I had this dream:

> *I am in a church setting, which seems mostly to be the Catholic Church. There is a lot of activity, and there are people—women, mostly—sitting in what are school desks more than pews. There is a bishop there whom I know and love as a friend, although he is not particularly in touch with his wholeness. He is going among the women to lead them individually in prayer, which he does in a rather severe manner. I see it most clearly when he comes to a childhood friend of mine, now a mature, independent, working woman. She wants to pray for a friend, and so the bishop comes to her and holds her arms tightly against the desk in what is supposed to be a prayer position, forcing her to pray with him in this particular, rigid way. She will not have it. Pulling free of him, she gets up and goes off a little way and takes another seat away from him.*
>
> *I go to the bishop, who is sitting now in an actual pew, and sit down in the pew behind him. Leaning forward, I put my hands lovingly on his shoulders*

> *and say quietly into his ear that if that had been me, I would have gotten up, too. He is hurt and sad and puzzled. The old way of the church is not working anymore with modern women.*
>
> *Then I am somewhere else in this church setting and see a group of white-robed clergy passing through the room. They are austere old men, lacking in wisdom and determined to hold their power. There is a colorless whiteness about them, a pallor. The congregation is thinning out as people are giving up on the church and turning away. There are almost none but old people left in the congregation, mostly old women.*
>
> *Somewhere in this last part of the dream, the understanding is given that my role is to help bring color into the church.*

Whiteness and color. Masculine and feminine. This was the symbolism chosen by the dream. Whiteness for the spirit of the old men in the traditional church. Color for my natural spirituality work. In earth's prism, the white light of heaven breaks into the rainbow colors of natural life. It is the same light—unified above, broken open below.

So, too, does the life of the divine have more than one manifestation. The spirit of heaven is its masculine aspect, as powerful and dependable as the sun, as ordered and unchanging as the stars. We experience the heavenly spirit in the strength and courage that come to us when we make the effort to rise above our daily problems, to align our minds with a more eternal perspective, and to act on nobler principles. It draws our attention upward and makes us aware of something higher than ourselves.

The spirit of earth, on the other hand, seems to flow into us from below as a part of the life of our bodies. This is the feminine aspect of God, and in it are seeds of wisdom and guidance. As fertile and many-faceted as nature, it teems with life and moves and changes with time, its myriad forms ever evolving. We experience this natural spirit in dreams and waking visions, in emotions and instinctual energies, and in the actual events of life itself.

These two aspects of the divine are universal. They appear in one form or another, in varying degrees of consciousness, in all the major religious traditions. The masculine side of the divine draws us upward toward the eternal truths that transcend human life, taking us through the mind and intellect on its way to the transcendent. Upon engaging the mind on its upward course, the masculine spirit generates ideas; but there it often gets stuck. Meditation and contemplation are meant to free us from an overly tight hold by the mind, allowing us to ascend with the rising masculine spirit to the higher, truer realm of the eternal divine, where the timeless reality of oneness and love can be perceived beyond the mind's understanding. Until the mind is transcended, ideas about the divine tend to dig in and fortify themselves, and this gives rise to the battle of ideas that we see in religious conflicts all over the world. If the masculine side of the divine could reach its final, transcendent destination in worldwide human consciousness, it would unify the world. But as long as it remains stuck in the realm of ideas, it will continue to be more divisive than unifying.

The feminine aspect of the divine, on the other hand, tends by its very nature to unite all religions at an elemental level. This is because it expresses itself through nature, through the life of the earth, and in doing so it speaks in a universal, symbolic language. The feminine spirit is always present in the natural unfolding of life, and it is always talking to us, whether we are listening or not. It expresses itself through our bodies, and the language of the body is the same everywhere. It expresses itself through dreams, and dreaming is natural and universal. It expresses itself in the world around us through synchronicity, or meaningful coincidence, and the natural occurrence of such phenomena in the unfolding of life is the same everywhere. When I perceive synchronicity, I perceive it just as a tribesman in Borneo or a Taoist in China would perceive it. This earthly manifestation of the divine, this recognition of a teaching and guiding Wisdom in the natural life of the world, fits whole cloth into all the great religions. People who cannot agree on religious ideas can talk together in harmony all day about the wonders of God in their dreams and synchronicities. Simply on the basis of unifying the world's religions, there is a great need to bring the feminine aspect of the divine to higher consciousness.

Jungian inner work is one of the best approaches in today's world for raising our awareness of the feminine aspect of God and integrating it into our spiritual lives in a healthy and productive way. Because the essence of Jungian inner work is engagement with the feminine divine, it, too, can be folded into any religion. Already there are books that put Jungian inner work together not only with Christianity but with Judaism, Buddhism, Daoism, Sufism, and so on. (Some of these are listed in Appendix C.) In a single book, however, we cannot cover every possibility. Because Christianity is the religious tradition I know best, this book focuses on this particular tradition as a viable religious context for Jungian inner work. My hope is that readers who follow other traditions, or mixed traditions, will receive this discussion in the spirit of unity that the feminine side of God makes possible, for the gist of how to pay attention to dreams and synchronicity applies to everyone. And if our particular and varied ideas about the divine can be given less than the highest place at our inner tables, if we can allow ourselves to transcend them to the even higher realm of eternal oneness and love, then we can be united on the masculine side of our spirituality as well.

Too Much Whiteness, Too Little Color

Let's go back to my dream of the Catholic Church and the old white men determined to hold their power. The idea that had come to me during the day before the dream was that maybe I should offer to teach a class on Jungian inner work at my church. The feminine divine immediately responded to this idea with a major dream, one that I still remember vividly in all its details. Curiously, the dream set my proposed work in the Catholic Church, not the Episcopal Church. What did that mean? Clearly, the meaning was not literal. I was not in the least inclined to go down the street and offer my class to the Catholic Church instead of to my own home church, and the dream did not seem to me to be suggesting that I should. So instead I sought the *symbolic* meaning by asking myself what my *associations* are with the Catholic Church. In other words, if you say, "Catholic Church," what comes to mind for me? The first thing that comes to mind is the church catholic, the universal church before the Protestant Reformation. And in that same vein, the core of church tradition as it has been continuously developed through the whole history of the church. In short, the 2,000-year tradition of Christianity. That, to me, feels like a fit for what the dream might be addressing. It clicks.

So if that is the meaning, at least on one level, of Catholic Church in this dream, then the dream is saying that in the 2,000-year tradition of Christianity, the masculine side of spirituality has become dominant over the feminine. Here we are assuming that the men in the dream symbolize masculine consciousness and the women symbolize feminine consciousness. This is usually the case in dreams, although in outer life men and women each carry both kinds of consciousness. In this dream, the arms of the feminine are being held down by the masculine and not allowed to participate in spiritual expression. We are given to understand that the feminine consciousness of practicing Christians used to put up with this, but as today's feminine consciousness matures through access to education and the workplace, it no longer tolerates being excluded from religious expression. The woman in the dream gets up and moves away from the bishop. Feminine consciousness in the Christian world is voting with its feet. It is distancing itself from the church of today because of the church's one-sided masculine expression of spiritual practice. Women have always been the mainstay of the church. But now, says the dream, most of the younger women are leaving and the pews are emptying out. Only old women, the ones who were raised in the old way, remain.

The dream shows the more thoughtful masculine leaders to be mystified by this. They have no idea what the problem is. The less thoughtful masculine leaders do not even ask the question. They are digging in, holding on to their old ideas with all the power at their disposal, which is great. I, the dreamer, note the colorless whiteness of their faces—the pallor of old men who are no longer channeling the flow of life. And not only are their faces white, so are their robes. They are clad as servants of the heavenly divine, the masculine spirit of oneness and love that emanates from the eternal white light of heaven. But their pallid faces and grim devotion to power tell us they have gone too far into whiteness. They are in service only to the aspect of God that reigns in heaven and not at all to the aspect of God that suffuses the life of the earth. And yet they claim to serve the living Christ, whose very essence is the *union* of masculine heaven and feminine earth. As I watch them, the higher knowledge that sometimes comes directly in a dream tells me that my role is to help bring "color" into the church. The assumption given is that "color" is the answer to the problem being portrayed by the dream. Evidently, in offering natural spirituality to the church, I will be bringing it "color."

Color as an Archetypal Symbol of the Feminine Divine

This dream was the first time I had ever encountered color as a symbol of the feminine divine. I had never before come across this in waking life. Since this dream, however, I have on occasion seen this same symbolic language occur independently in the dreams of others. This means that this symbol is *archetypal*: it arises from a deep, universal level of the unconscious and presents itself without regard to whether the one experiencing it has ever heard of it or not.

The second time I encountered color as a dream symbol for the feminine divine was in a book I read a year or two after my own dream. Unfortunately, this was twenty years ago, and I can no longer recall the book's author or title. Only because of its correlation with my dream do I remember this particular passage. I do know, however, that the author was a woman, that the book was about the divine feminine, and that this passage came early in the book as the author was telling the story of how she became interested in this subject. She told of attending seminary at a respected institution of one of the mainstream Christian denominations. Immersed in the curriculum's dense theology, with its high-flying intellectual ideas about the heavenly divine, she began to feel oppressed. The overly intellectual course of study did not square with her own more down-to-earth experience of God. In the midst of this inner conflict, she had a dream. In the dream, *she is walking along the sidewalk near her seminary. Suddenly a ball of rainbow-colored light comes rolling past her from behind and goes out ahead, taking a different course from the one she is on. She turns away from her original destination to follow the colorful ball of light.* Upon waking, she recognized the ball of rainbow-colored light as the living spirit for which she had been longing. She withdrew from seminary, and from then on she dedicated her studies and her writing to the part of God that was missing in seminary: the neglected, feminine side of the divine.

The next time I encountered the symbol of color used in a dream in this way was in my own church dream group. The dreamer, who has given me permission to tell her dream, is a high school Spanish teacher and the wife of a Methodist minister. At the time of the dream she had taken the natural spirituality class and had been in the dream group for perhaps six months. This was in the early years of my natural spirituality work, and I had not at that point told her or any others about my dream of whiteness and color in the church. In the dream *the dreamer is in a Catholic Church, standing on a balcony looking down at a group of clergy gathered below. There are female clergy in the group as well as male, all fully vested for a service that is about to begin. The women, who appear to be equal in rank to the men, are wearing beautiful vestments of radiant colors. Each woman wears a solid color, and all the colors are different. Only the vestments of the women are so vividly colorful. The vestments of the men are not emphasized in the dream. Presumably, they are all the same color, although nothing about this comes through upon waking.*

This was not a dream about the ordination of women, at least not at the personal level. Dreams only come to bring new understanding to the consciousness of the dreamer, and the ordination of women has long been integrated into Methodist consciousness: there have been women among the Methodist clergy since the days of John Wesley in the eighteenth century. Nor, at the personal level, was this a dream about the outer-world Catholic Church, where there are no women among the clergy, nor were there about to be in the 1990s, when this dream occurred. The dreamer had no personal involvement with the Catholic Church and no reason to be dreaming about their ordination struggles. Rather, the dream was helping her integrate into her consciousness the new life of the divine that she was coming to know through the attention she was now giving to dreams, synchronicity, and other expressions of the feminine side of God. The message in her dream was essentially the same message I had received in mine: natural spirituality brings equality to feminine spirituality in traditional Christianity and fills the church with "color."

"Color" in the First Christian Community

Given the insistence in these dreams on the importance of "color," or the feminine side of God, to the healthy life of the church, we might ask what happened to "color" in Christianity. Was it there in the beginning and lost over time, or was it never there at all?

If we can avert our gaze from the 2,000 year development of Christian tradition and look directly instead at the writings of the New Testament, we can see Christianity in its primal form. And what we see there is a spiritual community that knows all about the feminine side of the divine and balances it well with the masculine side. Especially in the gospel of Matthew, the book of Acts, and the letters of Paul, it is made clear that this community pays attention to dreams and visions. It notices synchronicities. It watches for the lively movement of the spirit among its members and opens itself to fluidity and change. At the same time, it keeps itself connected to the eternal truth of the heavenly, masculine nature of the divine as received through its time-tested religious tradition. It does not do one or the other, but rather it does both.

For example, in Acts 10 and 11, we have a detailed report of how the first Christians learned that they must open their movement to non-Jews as well as Jews. This required a major adjustment in consciousness, for their religious tradition, in order to protect its unique monotheism from being dissolved into the surrounding polytheistic cultures, had long defined non-Jews as a dangerous source of spiritual contamination. Not only were Jews forbidden by Jewish law to marry non-Jews, but neither were they to eat with them nor visit in their homes. Therefore, it was not at all obvious in the beginning that Judaism's Jesus movement was meant to be extended to non-Jews. Although Jesus had drunk water drawn from a well by a Samaritan woman and had been willing to go into the home of a Roman officer to heal the man's servant, he had evidently not foreseen the expansion of his movement beyond Judaism. Or at least he had not talked about this with his inner circle, of whom Peter was one. It took Peter's experience of a teaching from the feminine divine, after Jesus' death, to open his consciousness to this new development. The teaching came as a series of dreams, visions, and synchronicities.

It started with a dream or vision that came to Cornelius, a Roman centurion. We cannot say for certain that this was a dream rather than a vision, or a vision rather than a dream, because the Greek word that is used, *horoma*, can mean either one. As in Jungian inner work, the people of biblical times regarded dreams and visions as essentially the same: each brought messages from the spiritual world, and it was the content that was important, not the degree to which one was awake or asleep when the content arrived.

So Cornelius had a dream/vision that told him to send for a man named Peter who was visiting at a certain house in another town. Cornelius was duly impressed by this inner event and sent three of his men to invite this man Peter to come to his home. The next day, while the messengers were still on their way, Peter happened to go up to the sitting area on the roof of the house where he was staying, for some time of solitude and prayer. While there he had a dream/vision: *A large sheet, filled with every kind of animal, is lowered by its four corners from heaven. A voice says, "Kill and eat." Peter replies in effect, "No, I can't do that. I never eat animals that our law has declared unclean."* But the voice replies,

"What God has made clean, you have no right to declare unclean." This exchange is repeated three times and then the sheet is drawn back up into heaven.

Peter returned to full consciousness and was still on the roof pondering the meaning of what had happened when Cornelius's men knocked at the door downstairs. The synchronicity of this chain of events was soon apparent. The men invited Peter to come visit Cornelius in his home, which for a devout Jew like Peter would be the same as being invited to eat forbidden animals. So Peter put two and two together and accepted the invitation. Upon arriving at Cornelius's house and going inside to meet with all the friends and neighbors who had gathered there, Peter explained to them why he, a Jew, was willing to come into a Roman home. "You know it is forbidden for Jews to mix with non-Jews," he said, "but God has made it clear to me that I must not call anyone unclean. That is why I made no objection to coming when I was sent for.... I now understand that God has no favorites."

This account of how Peter's consciousness was expanded in this way would be completely believable to anyone in a natural spirituality dream group of today, where such experiences are recounted routinely. In both cases, dreams are taken seriously, their meanings are pondered, and the hints that come from them are put together with meaningful developments in outer life. For people in today's natural spirituality groups, just as in the time of Peter, this attention to feminine as well as masculine spirituality brings new understandings and an ever closer walk with God.

In Peter's day it was not just he and a few others who put great stock in such teachings, but so did the entire community of early Christians. When he got back to the Jesus-movement headquarters and reported that he had baptized a houseful of Romans, they were horrified. "You did what?" But then he told them the whole story, and the book of Acts repeats it: Cornelius's dream/vision, his own dream/vision, the synchronistic knock on the door, the putting together of two and two to make the decision to go, and the unmistakable presence of the Holy Spirit when he met with the Romans. And so, given all this, he baptized them. "Oh, okay then," said the others, in effect. "Clearly God is leading us in this. It looks like we're supposed to include non-Jews." And thus does the feminine side of God play her unifying role in helping to resolve clashes of ideas.

This inclusion of the feminine side of God in original Christianity is also clearly evident in the New Testament letters of Paul. There we find the idea that in the living Christ both the masculine and feminine principles, heaven and earth, are joined into one unified expression of Godhood. In a letter to the Corinthians Paul notes that the Christ we know is no longer the outer-life Jesus but a manifestation of the divine that is perceived with the inner eye, as he himself perceived it on the road to Damascus. "Even if we did once know Christ in the flesh," he writes, "that is not how we know him now." For Paul, the living Christ is synonymous with the Holy Spirit and with Wisdom, the feminine aspect of God known through Hebrew scriptures. This presence of God as Christ/Holy Spirit/Wisdom is alive and at work in the whole of the natural world. In his letter to the Colossians Paul writes, "There is only Christ. He is everything and he is in everything." He tells the Corinthians, "The Spirit reaches the depths of everything." And to the Ephesians, he speaks of Christ as "he who fills the whole creation."

What Happened to "Color" in Christianity?

A thorough account of Christianity's attitude toward dreams through the whole of its history can be found in Morton Kelsey's well-researched book *God, Dreams, and Revelation.* In it, we learn that openness to the feminine side of God was strongly present in Christianity for at least five hundred years, and it faded gradually in the following centuries until it was firmly eclipsed by scientific rationalism in the 1800s. Before this rather recent eclipse, the writings of prominent Christians frequently mentioned dreams and visions as important channels of communication from God. And yet in today's mainstream church, excluding the occasional rare exception, attention to dreams and visions is no longer considered a normal part of Christian life. Synchronicity is seldom noticed or given much value. Reports on the latest lively movements of the spirit are no longer solicited from individual members as a regular church activity, as was done in the first Christian communities. Rather, the attention of the traditional church in the modern era is directed almost exclusively toward established ideas about God based on scripture and theological tradition, while the ongoing murmurings of the divine in the colorful unfolding of life go largely unnoticed and unheard. This is not to say that this is true of every individual person, nor of every individual congregation, but it is true of the institutional church as a whole.

What happened, then, to "color" in Christianity? A completely related and relevant question would be, what happened to "color" in Western European culture? This is a big-picture question in search of a big-picture answer. And so we start with the fact that for the last five thousand years, and especially for the last two thousand, the development of Western consciousness as a whole has been aimed at overcoming the limitations of *nature* through the development of *rational thought and ideas.* Here the fundamental dichotomy between "color" and "whiteness" can be seen as the tension between the colorful life of nature, including its Wisdom, which belongs to the feminine principle of human consciousness, and the lofty purity of the high-soaring life of the mind, which belongs to the masculine principle. In present-day parlance, the struggle between these two principles of consciousness on the stage of history is often spoken of as the matriarchy versus the patriarchy.

Although the masculine principle has now become overly dominant in Western consciousness, it is important to understand that it was a late-comer in the development of human consciousness, and it, therefore, had some catching up to do. We modern *Homo sapiens*, the ones who produce art and religion and complex tools, have only been around for about 50,000 years, and for most of that time the feminine principle of nature, with her cycles and rhythms, was dominant over the masculine principle of pure mind and ideas. For tens of thousands of years, the physical demands of natural life required most of the attention and energy that humankind had to give, and very little was left over for the life of the mind. Ideas during that time changed very, very slowly, as evidenced by the extreme infrequency of innovations in tools and other artifacts. Only with the advent of writing, around 3,000 BCE, did the life of the mind begin to gain enough purchase to rise from its subordinate position and begin to assert itself as a pure activity. With it came monotheistic religion. The one God above all. The head over the body. Mind over nature.

The masculine principle, subordinated for so long to the feminine principle, was due an equal place in human consciousness. To achieve this, it had to have some time of focused attention in order to get established and developed. And although important feminine values were gradually lost in the process, the balance in Western culture, until recent centuries, was not completely one-sided toward the masculine, and the overall effect was a gain. We needed, for example, the masculine principle's stepped-up technological ideas to give us some relief from the overpowering demands of unmitigated physical nature so that we could have a life expectancy of longer than twenty-five years. We also needed the fundamental core of the masculine principle's religious aspect, the knowledge that above the churning and swirling of our limited, physical life on earth there is an ultimate, eternal reality of oneness and love. We needed to know that not only is this the primal source from which we come and to which we return but that its principles of oneness and love, of mercy and justice, are meant to be lived on earth, and that when we align ourselves with them, life goes better.

We needed, in other words, for the masculine principle of pure mind and high ideals to gain enough strength in human consciousness to take its rightful, equal place with the feminine principle of the harmony and balance of natural life, including the natural life of the psyche. But as with most developments in consciousness that finally break through into the light and begin to gain strength, the masculine principle in Western culture did not know when to stop. Unless the mind pays heed to nature's laws of harmony and balance, it can see no limit to itself. It does not know that the compensatory laws of nature absolutely dictate that as one aspect of consciousness grows, the opposite aspect must necessarily diminish and that the health of the whole will always suffer when opposite aspects get out of balance. For the last hundred years or so this inexorable truth has begun to assert itself ever more clearly, as life under the overly-dominant masculine principle has hit its limits and is now becoming more destructive than productive. Global warming, for example, is a direct result of nature being devalued and disregarded by the mind's technological advances.

What happened to "color" in Christianity? With the arrival of the Age of Enlightenment in the 1600s, the bid for complete power by the masculine principle began to gain traction, and in the following centuries, its dominating effects spread into every aspect of Western culture, including Western religion. The accompanying Scientific Revolution championed a rational materialist outlook that eventually came to reject any kind of inner knowledge that could not be proven "true" by scientific observation of the physical world. As Christian thinkers were caught up in this intellectual movement, they began to lose sight of what Paul meant when he said that the living Christ "fills the whole Creation." The domain of Christ was narrowed. Through faith in metaphysical reality, where science could not go, it could still be said that Christ was in heaven with God, and also in the hearts of men, and perhaps, metaphysically, in the bread and wine of the Eucharist. But Christ was not *in* nature. Nature was the province of science. Nature was hard, physical, material reality, separate and apart from spirit and under the dominion of the mind. It became impossible to think that there could be any kind of meaning in it, any intention for humankind, any Wisdom that could deliver specific messages or guidance. Dreams? Neurological firings. The way the brain processes detritus from the previous day. How could they be anything more? As scientific rationalism took hold and grew in the Western world, it became increasingly unacceptable to recognize a spiritual dimension in the natural world or to say that there was any mystery there. In Christianity, such an attitude came to be regarded almost as superstition or even pantheism.

The Turning Point: Quantum Physics and Depth Psychology

At the dawn of the twentieth century, however, the solid, mechanistic world of scientific rationalism began to give way, undermined not by theology or philosophy but by science itself. With Einstein's theory of relativity and with the discovery of quantum mechanics, physical reality has turned out not to be so solid after all. It has been discovered, for example, that the smallest particles of matter actually consist only of waves of probability *until they are observed*, at which point they become discrete and actual. This means that human consciousness is somehow involved in the manifestation of reality. No physicist claims to understand this. The concrete, fully explainable material world of scientific rationalism continues to exist at the everyday, practical level of life, but deeper reality is now known to be less straightforward. The mind cannot completely comprehend it. There is mystery in it.

While the world of physics has been discovering that the comprehensible physical world arises from an incomprehensible physical matrix, the world of psychology has been coming to a similar conclusion about the psychic world. At about the same time Einstein was introducing the theory of relativity, Sigmund Freud was ushering into general awareness the idea that beneath the known realm of human consciousness there exists in each of us an unknown realm of the *unconscious*, a dark, psychological arena where truths and realities that belong to us live outside our awareness and interact with our conscious lives in ways we do not realize. The "Freudian slip" is one way the unconscious shows itself, as when a man unintentionally refers to his wife as his mother, revealing an unconscious psychological truth. In searching for a more readily accessible door to that dark realm, Freud turned to dreams and raised them up from the dustbin of our awareness, where the dominating masculine principle had tossed them, and pointed out their value as "the royal road to the unconscious."

Sigmund Freud was not a religious man. Born in 1856, he was steeped in the scientific materialism of that century and did not believe there was any mystery beyond the physical foundation of our being. He was dedicated to the idea that "God" is an illusion, an infantile wish for an eternal parent. For him, there was no such thing as spirit. The driving force of life was sexual energy, which he called libido.

Freud believed the unconscious to be a repository of unfulfilled wishes stemming from our experiences in the first three years of life, a time of preconsciousness which is to the individual what prehistory is to humankind. The most troubling of these preconscious experiences, according to Freud, were sexual in nature—more specifically, they were infantile incestuous desires. Due to their unacceptability, they remained repressed in the unconscious, where they lived darkly, intruding back into conscious life under cover of disguise. Anything that threatened to bring them to light was also repressed.

Eventually, repressed wishes could create a neurosis, which could be treated by analyzing the unconscious. Through psychoanalysis, the door to the unconscious could be opened and its contents examined and integrated into consciousness. The troubling phenomena of the unconscious could thereby be dissipated and the mind's dominion over the dark realm reestablished. One of Freud's most important tools for this was the analysis of dreams, which he viewed primarily as disguised statements of sexually-based fears and desires.

It took courage to put forth these ideas in the first decade of the twentieth century. A young Swiss psychiatrist, Carl Gustav Jung, was one of the first to embrace Freud's work, recognizing its value and welcoming the boldness of its assertions. Since early childhood, Jung had struggled with powerful personal experiences of the unconscious. He knew instinctively that such experiences had meaning, but nowhere in the literature of philosophy and science could he find the concepts he needed to construct an adequate intellectual framework for understanding them. In Freud's concept of the unconscious, Jung recognized a key building block for his own formulations. In 1906 Jung joined forces with Freud, accepting the older man as his mentor and helping him spread the psychoanalytical school of psychiatry from Vienna to the international community.

But there was an essential difference between these two psychiatrists. Unlike Freud, Jung had a deep awareness of the spiritual dimension of life. He came by this naturally, as his father and eight of his uncles were clergymen. Religion was a core element of life for him, and Freud's insistence that the underlying energy of life was always sexual, whether disguised or apparent, ran counter to Jung's own experience and understanding. He knew the unconscious to be an autonomous aspect of nature that is much more complex than Freud realized. And from his own experience, he knew very well that the unconscious cannot be dominated by the mind. It can, however, be related to in a fruitful way by a well-developed mind that is respectful of its mystery. As Jung came into his professional maturity, the difference in their basic understanding of the unconscious grew larger as an issue between the two men, until finally, in 1913, they parted company over it. From that point on, Jung developed his own school of thought concerning the nature of the unconscious.

For Jung, the energy of life flows to us in a broad spectrum that ranges from fundamental physical instinct to sublime spiritual awareness. It comes to us from the unconscious, which is not merely a dumping ground for repressed personal reality. Instead it is, in fact, the very source of consciousness and life: everything that is conscious in us was first unconscious. The unconscious is by its very nature unknowable. Yet contents from that unknowable realm arrive regularly in consciousness, and by observing this natural process we can gain some insight into the unconscious. Even more importantly, by paying close attention to the effects of the unconscious on our conscious lives, we can learn about ourselves and God. For as Jung discovered, first in his own life and then in the lives of his patients, when we relate to the unconscious in the right way, it becomes our teacher. It speaks to us in our dreams and waking visions, in our emotions and intuitive glimmers, and it also speaks in the outer events of life itself, a phenomenon that Jung himself named synchronicity.

From Jung, we learn that what matters most is *how* we relate to the unconscious. Although the unconscious is a part of nature, the right way of relating to it does not come naturally. In the first place, its language is symbolic, and real effort is required to learn to understand it. For this, we need our now well-developed masculine principle of intellectual study and analytical thinking. But it is not enough simply to understand the unconscious. It also requires a *moral* response to its teachings. If we are to have a fruitful relationship with it, we must take its truths seriously and integrate them into our lives in a real way. For this moral requirement, we need the masculine principle's devotion to the higher ideals of the human spirit, which is precisely why Jungian inner work goes best when partnered with the core teachings of traditional religion.

Jung gives us a modern way to recover the respect for the feminine divine that was once present in traditional religion. When we engage with the teachings of the unconscious with informed intelligence and moral responsibility, we find ourselves following the path that the ancients called the Way, which leads us into harmony with life and helps us find our unique place in it, including the particular way in which each of us can best serve it. In setting forth on this astonishing path, we discover the age-old secret that all of life, waking and sleeping, is rich with the teaching and healing spirit of the divine.

While the times in which we live are presenting us with seemingly overwhelming problems, they are also giving us new means for meeting their challenge, including the gift of Jungian psychology. Although Jungian inner work in spiritual community is still new, it is gradually taking hold and growing as the twenty-first century unfolds. By engaging in this work, we heal the split between spirit and nature in our basic experience of the divine. We integrate "whiteness" and "color." We bring the masculine and feminine principles of life together into a fruitful union. And if on a widespread basis, we can each balance our individual consciousness in this way, then there is hope for the consciousness of humankind as a whole. For what else is the consciousness of humankind but a great tapestry woven from the myriad threads of individual consciousness?

Part Two

Jungian Spiritual Tools

Chapter Three
Consciousness

Our consciousness does not create itself—it wells up from unknown depths. In childhood it awakens gradually, and all through life it wakes each morning out of the depths of sleep from an unconscious condition.

Carl Jung

The fundamental concern of Jungian psychology is the dialogue between consciousness and the unconscious. Before we can think about the nature of the unconscious and the dialogue it seeks with us, we must have a clear understanding of consciousness itself. Though all of us experience consciousness, few of us have ever stepped back and given it a hard look. Carl Jung spent years thinking about what consciousness is, and his work helps us to understand it more objectively.

According to Jung, consciousness is our awareness of ourselves and the world around us, our understanding of things, our conception of what life is. It is not synonymous with what truly is, but is merely our perception, our grasp, our construct of existence. It is, however, all that we know, all that we have. It is our terra firma, our grip on reality, developed little by little through the years of our life. It is the kingdom of our ego, and the finer and more varied the land of this kingdom and the stronger and healthier the ego that reigns over it, the better equipped we are to deal with the unknown, infinite, eternal sea of the unconscious which surrounds us.

Consciousness begins when we first connect one thing with another, when we first "know." Those first moments of consciousness, however, like so many afterward, fall back into the unconscious and do not remain a part of our long-term ego consciousness. Ego consciousness begins with our first *memories*, dim, wispy, and isolated. Those memories are important just because they are remembered, as their energy was strong enough to keep them with us and make them the first stones in the edifice of our conscious life. When we examine our earliest memories for their symbolic content, we find hints of what are to become the major themes around which our individual lives will turn.

My own first memory, for example, is from a few weeks before my third birthday. I had awakened from a dream about a giant mouse that was dressed somewhat like Peter Rabbit in a blue jacket and red pants. The dream mouse was not altogether unfriendly, but its large size was disturbing, and I woke up to get away from it. When I opened my eyes, I saw it standing in the darkness beside my bed. This was much more disturbing than the dream itself, and yet I kept my wits about me. I remember thinking to myself that sometimes when you think you have awakened, you actually have not, but if you do something intentional, then you really will wake up. So I very deliberately turned my head and looked into the darkness on the other side of my bed. There, too, was the giant mouse! I was certain now that I was awake, and yet the mouse was still there! That was too much for me, and I screamed with so much fright that both my parents remembered it ever after. With my cry the dream mouse vanished, and the veil between the inner world and the outer world fell back into place.

Thirty-five years later that veil lifted again in the personal crisis that awakened me to the reality of the unconscious. This time, there were no dream images crossing over into the outer world, but rather the outer world itself began in a certain way to take on a quality similar to the inner world. It could be read symbolically in the same way a dream could be, and it produced meaning through noteworthy coincidences.

My reaction was similar to when I was three years old: I first tried to shake off this disturbing perception, and then, when it would not go away, I was overtaken by fear—anxiety attacks. This time, however, I did not cry out for help. I stood and faced the new reality until I gradually became accustomed to it. My ego consciousness—my sense of myself and my grip on outer reality—had become strong enough to allow me to forge a conscious bond with the inner world of the unconscious without being overwhelmed by it. From that time forward the inner world and the outer world have co-existed for me without such a firm division between them, a development that has had central importance in my life and was prefigured by that earliest memory.

By the time we are four or five years old, our first isolated memories have usually given way to a steady stream of conscious contents. For me, this transition to continuous memory was marked by a move my family made from the western suburbs of Chicago to a small town in southern Georgia around the time of my fifth birthday. I remember the long car trip—taking Dramamine pills crushed up in spoonfuls of honey—and the motel where we stayed while waiting for our furniture to arrive. I remember the house we moved into, the sidewalks and neighborhood and the nearby fields. I have a continuous, solid sense of my life from then on, whereas before that car trip I remember only isolated incidents that float freely in time and space.

Even after continuous memory begins, we retain in consciousness merely a fragment of our total experience. Consciousness is limited. It can only hold so much. In order to concentrate on one thing, we must let other things go, and even that upon which we concentrate eventually falls into the unconscious as future life supersedes it. Many contents that were once conscious return to consciousness through memory, but many others never do.

A good way to think about the limitation of consciousness is to stop, look up, and think about what your consciousness contains at that particular moment. You cannot do that and continue at the same time to read what I have to say about it, which in itself shows the limitation of consciousness and the kind of problem it continually presents to us.

When you do take a moment to look up, the demonstration will be more dramatic if you do not move your head. The only part of the physical world of which you will be conscious will be what you are able to see, hear, smell, taste, and feel. If there is a spider crawling up the back of your chair, you will be unconscious of it. If it crawls onto your neck, it will enter your consciousness. You will also have as a part of your consciousness whatever thoughts you are thinking, feelings you are feeling, and any fantasies or intuitive glimmers that might be arising in your inner world. You might want to bring back into consciousness something that happened yesterday, but to do that you will have to let your awareness of the present go dim—you may even need to close your eyes. And if you really want to know what is happening on the back of your chair, you will have to turn your conscious attention away from what is going on in front of you to get up and look around behind you.

The Four Functions of Consciousness

Not only are we unconscious of most of what goes on beyond the range of our senses, but even much that goes on before our very eyes does not reach our consciousness, or if it does, it falls right back out again. How many times have we laid something down and a moment later had no idea where we put it? We were so dimly conscious of what our hands were doing that our own act fell immediately into the unconscious.

Furthermore, there are whole *categories* of reality that might become conscious if we noticed them but that we do not notice, or only barely so, because of our particular makeup as individuals. When I reminisce with my two sisters about our childhood, it is a marvel to discover what they have carried with them all these years that I never picked up at all. One of them remembers physical details—how things looked, where things were, what different people's outward characteristics were. The other one remembers the feeling tone of our world, where there was warmth and relationship and where there was a chill. I myself remember what was going on beneath the surface of things, psychological subplots of which the others often had little or no awareness.

This difference in conscious orientation was described systematically by Carl Jung in terms that have been so widely accepted that they are almost commonplace today. He determined that there are four functions of human consciousness—*sensation, thinking, feeling,* and *intuition*. These are the gateways by which unconscious contents enter consciousness. Each of us has one of these as our primary function, with the other three following in descending order. Beyond the four functions, there are two basic attitudes by which our consciousness is oriented—*extraversion* and *introversion*—and each of us is by nature aligned more with one than with the other. The relative strength in us of these six different factors determines our psychological type.

Jung devoted much of his early career to discovering and describing the four functions and two attitudes of consciousness, seeing in them a key to understanding some of the basic differences among human beings. The inner journey is both a journey of self-discovery and a journey toward reconciliation with those with whom we share our lives. To understand that there are basic, describable variables in the ways human beings experience conscious reality helps us come to know ourselves as individuals who are fundamentally different from those around us, while at the same time it helps us to be more tolerant of differences in others.

Many people are familiar with Jung's typology through having taken the Myers-Briggs Type Indicator or one of its several variants. These are diagnostic questionnaires which can reveal a person's psychological type through the answers to such questions as, "When you look at a landscape, do you tend to (a) notice details or (b) take in an overall impression?" As will become clearer from the discussion below, the choice of "a" suggests that a person has a strong sensation function, while "b" suggests strong intuition.

It is possible, however, to determine your own type without a formal diagnostic tool by simply thinking about yourself in light of the four functions and two attitudes. Although this can be surprisingly difficult to do, it is worth the attempt in order to begin to grapple with the question of how you as an individual experience conscious life. (In the back of this book you'll find some help: Appendix A offers a quick and easy tool for finding your type.)

It was Jung who coined the terms *extravert* and *introvert.* Today almost everyone has some notion of these opposing personality types. We usually think of extraverts as convivial and outgoing and introverts as shy and withdrawn. While this is more or less true in the broadest sense, there can also be shy extraverts and convivial introverts. According to Jung, a more accurate way to think about the dichotomy is in terms of which way a person's energy flows—outward toward the objective world or inward toward the subjective world. An even simpler measure is to ask whether one tends to be energized by mingling with other people, as extraverts are, or drained of energy by it, as introverts are.

Generally speaking, extraverts, with their attention on the world outside, are the ones who do most to maintain the structure of outer life, while introverts, with their attention on what is going on inside themselves, are the ones who are most dedicated to the realms of creativity and spirituality. At the farthest extremes, the extravert concentrates so much on the world outside himself that he loses his inner reality, while the introvert becomes estranged from outer reality through too much fascination with the inner world.

The principle of opposing tendencies is similarly present in the four functions, which, according to Jung, are actually two pairs of opposites. One pair, *sensation* and *intuition*, has to do with perception, and if a person is very strong at one end of this pole, he will be very weak at the other. Sensation is perception through our physical senses. It tells us that something in the outer world *is*. People who are strong in sensation have an affinity for concreteness and facts. They are especially well tuned to the physical manifestation of life and have a strong sense of the here and now.

Intuitive perception, on the other hand, comes not through the physical senses but through the inner eye and ear. People with strong intuition sniff out things beneath the surface, sensing connections and patterns that are not manifestly apparent. They know in ways that seem impossible, or at least spooky, to a person with a strong sensation function. Intuition glimpses possibilities.

Whereas sensate people tend to get stuck in present reality and have a hard time realizing that things could ever be different, intuitive people have difficulty living in the here and now. They are always running ahead with their intuition toward a more promising future, impatient with the slow development that reality requires.

The other pair of opposites, *thinking* and *feeling*, are described by Jung as judging functions. These provide a basis for decision-making, whereas the perceiving functions simply register what is there without regard to good or bad, logic or illogic. Thinking makes its judgments on the basis of logic, while feeling judges value. All of us tend to judge more with our heads or our hearts, and if we are strong at one end of this pole, we will be weak at the other. Intellectuals can be bloodless and cold in a way that is incomprehensible to a feeling person, whereas a feeling person can be so illogical and unreasonable that a thinking person can hardly bear it.

Thinking is the function that tells us *what* something is. It ponders, analyzes, solves problems rationally, and creates abstractions. It takes place in our heads and brings with it a degree of separation from the life of the body. The feeling function, on the other hand, has to do with evaluation, which should not be confused with emotion, or affect. People with feeling as their first function have a highly differentiated scale of value by which they continually assess the acceptability of things—to what degree something is good or bad, moral or immoral, beautiful or ugly, right for the moment or wrong for the moment, and so on.

Because we tend to think of feelings as emotions, it can be difficult to understand exactly what the feeling function is as Jung described it. When I was preparing to teach about the four functions for my first natural spirituality seminar, I was given a dream which helped me understand this function more clearly:

> *My husband and I are traveling in our car. We arrive at a town which we know is a four-hour drive from home. It is early evening.*

> *"Perhaps we should get a motel for the night and drive home tomorrow," I say.*
>
> *This angers my husband, who feels I am insisting that we do so. But I am not insisting. I explain to him that I make decisions by "trying on" each possibility and then noting what it feels like. It is with my feelings that I am able to choose the right course. I can only do this, however, if I seriously try on each alternative. Then I go with the one that feels best.*
>
> *I have some difficulty explaining this to him, since he is a thinking type and feeling is his weakest function, but eventually I succeed.*

Not only does this dream illuminate the feeling function in its introverted form (my own feeling is introverted), but it also shows the value of Jung's typology for helping us understand the difficulties we all have in relating to each other. Ever since I dreamed it, I have been more mindful of the way in which I make such alternative testing statements to my husband. If I remind him at the outset that I am not yet committed to whatever suggestion I am trying out, things go more smoothly between us.

Ranking the Four Functions

The four functions, then, are a combination of two pairs of opposites. Sensation and intuition are the poles of the perceiving axis; thinking and feeling are the poles of the judging axis. All four functions are available to each of us, although they do not operate in us with equal degrees of consciousness. They are ranked in a hierarchy of awareness that is based not on choice but on natural endowment. Individual ranking can be diagrammed in the form of an equal-armed cross, with one axis representing the perceiving functions and the other one the judging functions (Fig 3.1).

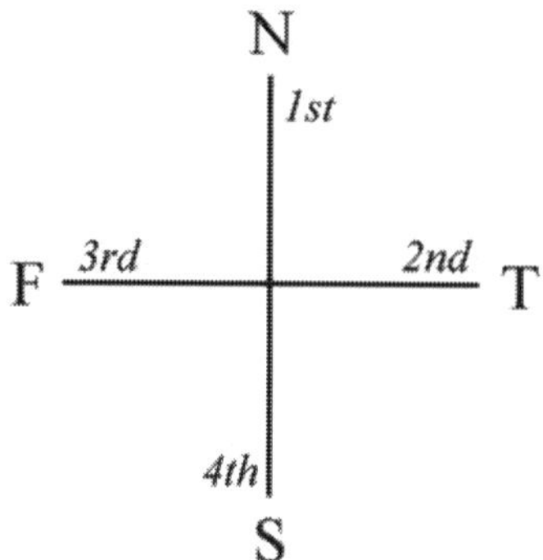

N = Intuition; T = Thinking; F = Feeling; S = Sensation

Fig 3.1. The Four Functions

The first function, which can be any of the four, is placed at the top of the cross, highest in consciousness; the second strongest function is placed on the right, which is also a position symbolically associated with consciousness; the third is on the left, which is symbolically associated with the unconscious; and the fourth is at the bottom, symbolizing its place in the depths of the unconscious. Because the functions are pairs of opposites, the strongest function (the one at the top of the diagram) determines which one will be the weakest (the one at the bottom). And in the same way, the second function determines which function will be in the third position. If intuition, for example, is a person's first function, sensation, at the other end of the perceiving axis, will be that person's fourth and weakest function; and if thinking is second, feeling will be third.

When we try to think about ourselves to determine how our functions are ranked, we often run into difficulty. Complications in our particular situation can obscure things. It is sometimes easier to determine our first function by considering which function is weakest, since another function might seem so near in strength to our first that it is difficult to decide between them. This is especially true for introverts, who tend to meet the world with their second function rather than their first, which is reserved more for their inner life.

To use myself as an example, it was only by looking for my weakest function that I was able to identify intuition as my first function. Thinking is my second strongest function. But as sometimes happens with lesser functions, second-ranked thinking received more development in my early years than did first-ranked intuition. Thinking, therefore, masqueraded as my first function.

Ordinarily, it is our first function that undergoes the most development in childhood since it is the mode of functioning at which we are best, and thus it is usually the one with the most payoff for us. But there can be a family bias, or even a cultural one, against our primary function, so that we are pushed to develop one of our lesser functions in its place. No matter how well we do with this substitute function, however, so long as we have not developed our actual first function, we will always operate at a disadvantage and be a little off our true mark, never rising to the fullness of our own strength.

In my own case, as with most intuitives, especially introverted ones, I had the problem of our society's strong cultural bias against intuition. This bias was even stronger in the 1950s, when I was a child, than it is today. There was no model in the greater culture for introverted intuitive functioning and very little comprehension of it. Nor was there much correction for this in my family. However, thinking was a strong function in my family, and since thinking was my second function, I followed the family pattern and developed that as my primary mode of consciousness. Intuition, my natural strength, remained undeveloped and semiconscious, although it still had a great deal of power and manifested itself in an active fantasy life. I have more memories of being alone on the playground lost in my fantasies than I have of playing with other children. In the sensate world, I was miserable. I was slow to learn to ride a bicycle, clumsy at jumping rope, and got nauseated on swings and merry-go-rounds.

In compensation, I became good at thinking. I did well in school and had interesting conversations with other thinkers, graduated with honors from college, and married a college professor. Despite all this, however, I never found an official place for myself in the thinking world. I lacked the drive to dedicate myself to a thinking path such as teaching or graduate school. Instead, I hooked up my college degree in anthropology with my orphaned intuition and wrote novels for young people that were set in the traditional culture of the Native Americans of the early South. Although I was successful at writing fiction, I never considered it to be an intuitive enterprise. I was only conscious of myself as a thinking person, and thinking dominated my work. My intuition was there in my ability to imagine a story, but it was still operating in semi-darkness.

This lack of recognition of my natural strength in life contributed in large part to the midlife crisis I have already described. At the heart of that crisis was intuitive functioning forcing its way into my conscious awareness and demanding to be recognized and integrated. Thinking had usurped the throne long enough. In an inner struggle that lasted for several years, intuitive functioning pushed thinking back to its rightful second place.

So strongly developed had my thinking function become, however, that for several more years I continued to stop now and then and ask myself whether thinking or intuition is actually my first function. I could never decide this with certainty until I looked at my third and fourth functions and asked: Which is weakest in me, feeling or sensation? While I know I am not particularly strong in the feeling realm, I am at least competent there. I have learned to be aware of feeling and I often decide things on the basis of it. Sensation, on the other hand, has always been dim and probably ever will be dim. It is difficult for me to pay attention to the physical world around me and experience it in a vivid way. Every now and then, in a moment of grace, my senses come fully awake and I see, hear, smell, taste, and feel everything, or at least it seems to me that I do. But this only lasts a few moments before the normal vagueness sets in again. There is no doubt that sensation is the weakest function for me, the one deepest in the unconscious. That means that intuition is indeed my first function, thinking is my second, and feeling is third.

Integrating the Four Functions

In a life fully lived, one open to inner guidance, growth, and change, each of the four functions is eventually integrated into the total personality (see Chapter Thirteen). Their hierarchy of relative strength, however, remains unchanged. The first two functions will always be the most differentiated and powerful in a worldly sense. They are the ones we use for competition against others. The third and fourth functions, on the other hand, with their deeper connection to the unconscious, will always be more primitive, slow, and simple—but also potentially more profound and God-centered.

Our first function comes to us most naturally and is usually the one that dominates our personality from our earliest years. However, it takes the inclusion of the second function to give us both a perceiving and a judging function, and we need both kinds if we are to get very far in the world. The second function, therefore, usually also undergoes at least some development in the first half of life.

There is little initial impetus, however, for developing the third function. It does not give us an obvious competitive advantage in a worldly sense since we are not very good at it by nature. An even greater stumbling block is that it brings with it the problem of reconciling opposite modes of consciousness. This is because the third function is the polar opposite of the second function. In order to use both the second and the third functions, we must resolve within ourselves the conflict between either thinking and feeling, or sensation and intuition. The use of two opposite functions creates such an inner conflict that it can only be resolved by moving to a higher level of consciousness that includes both ways of judging or perceiving. Growing to a higher level of consciousness, however, is always painful and difficult. Therefore, while the third function does operate in the first half of life, it does so in a largely unconscious, or shadowy, way. It is not integrated into greater consciousness until the second half of life, if at all.

Although Jung did not put it this way, I find it useful to think of the first two functions as "power" functions and the third one as the "salvation" function, which only comes into conscious play when we have become exhausted from trying to use our power functions to win the world for ourselves. When that approach to life has played itself out, our salvation is to turn to our third function, which in turn brings with it our fourth function. In turning to these neglected parts of ourselves, however, we have to accept new ways of perceiving and judging life. This is always a defeat for our power functions, which are required to step back and give up some of their energy and truth.

A feeling of defeat also comes from the fact that our third and fourth functions are more primitive—less differentiated and sophisticated—than our first two functions. But it is precisely because of this quality of greater unconsciousness that when we turn to our third function, we are led down to our earthier, simpler self and toward our deeper truth.

It is through our third function that we gain access to our fourth function, which is so deep in the unconscious that we cannot bring it directly to the surface and put it under our conscious control. Because of its place in the depths, the fourth function, which is the least valued and the most overlooked, is the one that is closest to God. It is like the insignificant baby born in the lowly stable behind the inn in the darkest time of the year. When we turn to our third function and consciously make room for it in our life, it brings with it, clinging to it from the depths, that fourth, "divine" function, which comes as grace and completes our life, not in an ideally perfect way, but in a way that is just right for the individual that we are.

In my own case, for example, my power functions are intuition and thinking. With these, I can have deep glimmerings and "knowings" about the unconscious and easily spend all my time and energy spinning them into theoretical frameworks, with little regard for what is truly important and valuable for life and even less regard for the physical reality around me. Who cares what my house looks like, or what I wear, or what I eat, or whether the garden has been weeded? Who cares whether real people in real life can understand my complicated insights and make use of them or whether they even need them?

It is a constant struggle for me not to go out too far in this direction. What brings me back when I lose my center is a growing difficulty in functioning. Something in me rebels. A mood sets in—vague discontent at first, or if that is ignored, a more notable stress. If I still fail to realize the problem, a physical symptom will arise to slow me down or stop me. When I finally halt and turn my attention to what is wrong, it is feeling that can give me the answer.

I must stop intuiting, stop thinking, and feel where I need to be and what I need to be doing. What *feels* like the most important thing? To rest. To sit with the cat. To go somewhere. To do something or see someone. To wear this sweater with these pants, and these earrings—they feel just right. To go into the kitchen and cook something, a particular something with particular ingredients that *feel* like the one and only right thing for this day.

My feeling brings the sensate world to me in a way that is ordinary and yet touched with beauty and meaning that reverberate in my soul. Feeling puts me on God's path, brings me to my center. With that, my intuitive thinking comes down to earth and simplifies. Because it is now sharing its energy with my weaker functions, it has to slow down and operate at a lower level. This brings it into accord with the reality of the world in which I live and makes it more effective than it was before.

This process would look quite different in persons of different types and even in others of my own type. Each of us must find our individual way, but the basic principle of going to the third function for centering and salvation will always be the same.

Stages of Life

It is one thing to talk about integrating a new function, or making any other change in consciousness, but it is quite another thing actually to do it. Consciousness undergoes constant revision on our journey through life, or at least it wants to be revised. There is an inner pressure for revision and change, for growth toward complete realization of individual potential. Yet at the same time, there is an inner conservative force that resists change. Present consciousness always feels threatened by whatever future consciousness is trying to break through, no matter how beneficial the new reality promises to be. This resistance serves the positive purpose of making sure that the hard-won consciousness of the past is not completely swept away by whatever new consciousness is trying to arise. The tension between the pressure for change and the resistance to change is what makes the transition from one stage of life to the next so difficult.

In order for each new stage of life to be truly realized, there must be a change in *consciousness.* Outward, physical change is not enough. The two most fundamental changes required of us come, first, at adolescence, when we must move from childhood to young adulthood, and, second, at midlife, when we are supposed to move from young adulthood to mature adulthood. Not everyone makes a successful transition in adolescence, and even fewer meet fully the challenge of midlife. Carl Jung considered the time of childhood and young adulthood to be the "first half of life," and mature adulthood and the transition to it to be the real business of the "second half of life."

Each of the three stages of life—childhood, young adulthood, and mature adulthood—has its own primary source of consciousness. Throughout childhood, that source is the family. A child's reality is defined by her family's reality. Whatever consciousness rules the house also rules the child. Whether she embraces it positively or sets herself up in opposition to it, it is still the family's consciousness that has the most influence on how she sees the world. The family, however, is not her only source of consciousness. School, media, other children, adults outside the family, and striking life experiences all make their contributions. So, too, does the unconscious itself.

Children are naturally open to the unconscious, especially when they are very young. That is where spontaneity, imagination, and the amazing "wisdom of a child" come from. In imagination and play, in dreams and fantasy life, and in a child's thoughtfulness and reflection, important truths come to light regarding both the child's development and destiny and the general situation of the family. These contents from the unconscious are usually couched in symbolic language and are not often recognized as particularly meaningful by the child or his parents. Very powerful experiences of unconscious contents, however, may stay with a child and have a lifelong effect on his understanding of the world. Big dreams, God experiences, and deeply fascinating play activities often become foundation stones of consciousness and are referred back to time and again in later life.

As a child gets older and his ego consciousness grows stronger, he gradually loses his openness to the unconscious. This is bemoaned by that part of us that would resist the adolescent transition to young adulthood, but this loss of natural connection to the unconscious is necessary for the consolidation and focusing of the child's emerging personality. The same ego strength which helps an adolescent consolidate consciousness at the expense of the unconscious also helps him move away from the family toward the greater world. In order to make a place for himself in life, the young adult must get in step with the world and assimilate its ways. He must learn to construct reality as the world constructs it, with sharp, rational thinking, and he must familiarize himself as much as possible with the shared knowledge of his time. The high school and college years are meant to help a young person prepare himself in this way.

The layer of consciousness added in young adulthood is primarily a collective one. A young adult lives as a member of the herd, whether it is the mainstream herd or a countercultural one. The contents of consciousness come primarily from peer groups, from television, the internet, and books, from work and its focus, from relationship experiences, and from significant life events.

The dual engines driving this stage of life are instincts and ideals. Young adulthood is a time when nature demands that her needs be met, and she supplies the sexual drive, the power drive, the parenting instinct, and other forms of the earthly spirit that flow into the young adult from the depths of his being and help him perform the tasks necessary to reproduce and sustain life. From the realm of the upper spirit come the high ideals of youth, some of them inherited from the young person's family, some breathed in with the air of his time. They inspire him and spur him on. Young adulthood is the time of the hero. Its success depends upon the strength and development of the ego.

If a young adult is fortunate enough to have a parent or mentor who has made a connection to the wisdom of the unconscious, he can begin at this stage of life to become aware of the unconscious in a new way that takes the place of his lost childish connection with it. With rare exception, this more mature awareness of the unconscious is something that can only be taught, for it requires a conscious framework of understanding. When a young adult is able to begin to be aware of the guidance that comes from his inner processes, he will be able to make his way through the first half of life in a more balanced way. It is important, however, that he does not go overboard in this direction and try to substitute inner knowledge for outer effort. The balance of attention in young adulthood should be on the outer world.

The more usual time to awaken to the deeper wisdom of the unconscious is at the midlife turn, which typically begins sending out its first signals between the ages of thirty-five and forty, although this sometimes happens earlier or later. The strength of the signals varies greatly, bringing some people to a grinding halt and fazing others not at all. The midlife call to a change in consciousness may elicit an immediate positive response, or it may be put off for years by various dodging maneuvers, even until death.

Whether it arises from within as a vague dissatisfaction and unease or from without as the traumatic events of a full-blown midlife crisis, the aim of the midlife turn is to make us break our identity with collective reality and begin to know life from the voice of Wisdom within ourselves. This is the process Carl Jung refers to as *individuation.* It requires a new kind of thinking and reasoning that allows a dialogue with one's inner processes and the discovery of one's individual truth. In this stage of life, new contents of consciousness begin to come in large part from the unconscious, which brings a return of the spontaneity and wonder of childhood. Unlike childhood, however, there is now a strong ego consciousness to reflect upon the natural flow of unconscious contents and draw meaning from them.

When a constructive dialogue with inner processes begins before midlife, it is either because there is an individuated adult already present in the young person's life or because there has been a developmental crisis which has forced the young person to go out and find a mentor, usually a professional counselor. In either case, the young person is led by her inner processes toward the goals of the first half of life, whereas a person at midlife or beyond is led toward the goals of the second half of life. Many people do not open up to their inner processes until they are well into the second half of life, even into old age. Many others never open up to them at all.

The process of individuation, once consciously engaged, is never-ending. It goes on for the rest of our lives. But the tumultuous intensity that initiates individuation at midlife and is similar to the tumult of adolescence, lasts about as long as adolescence does. This is a difficult time, but also a rewarding one. There is suffering as one is led to sacrifice the instincts and ideals of young adulthood, and with that the primacy of the ego, but there is also a deep joy and satisfaction in realizing the richer existence of life lived under the primacy of the guiding God-center within. As the individuation process evens out into mature adulthood, it leads us to our most particular and most effective contribution to the human community, ushers us into a meaningful old age, and gradually prepares us for death by shifting our focus from things temporal to things eternal.

Consciousness is the business of our life on earth. Our challenge is to allow it to arise continually from the darkness of the unconscious, to nurture and protect it when it is new, and to let it die and give way to new reality when it has seen its time. The ever-developing consciousness that we gain through this process is what makes us solid and real, and most importantly, it is what makes us *human.*

As conscious beings, we must remember this as we begin to learn about the unconscious. The unconscious is vast and full of mystery, but it is not human. It is good to open ourselves to the unconscious if we have the strength to do so. It is good to listen to it and take promptings from it. But it is also right that we contend with it, that, like Job standing up to God, we state our position over against it. Our relationship with the unconscious is meant to be a *dialogue.* As carriers of consciousness we have the responsibility, small as we are, to stand up to the great unconscious and say to it, when we need to, that what it is asking of us is too painful or too blissful for the human life that is ours, that it must take account of our humanity and help us find a way that we can bear.

God, in fact, is not the unconscious itself. God is all that is, both conscious and unconscious. In order to most fully reflect God's reality in our lives, we must stand firmly in our human consciousness and from that vantage point open ourselves to dialogue with the unconscious.

Chapter Four
The Unconscious

Just as conscious contents can vanish into the unconscious, other contents can also arise from it. Besides a majority of mere recollections, really new thoughts and creative ideas can appear which have never been conscious before. They grow up from the dark depths like a lotus.

CARL JUNG

JUNG'S OBSERVATIONS OF the effects of the unconscious on conscious life convinced him that the dark realm of the unconscious is not a mere absence of consciousness. Rather, the unconscious has an autonomous reality of its own, and whether we are aware of it or not, it is engaged in a dynamic relationship with consciousness.

Jung also knew, however, that by its very nature the unconscious cannot be known. All that we claim to know about it is but inference drawn from its effects on consciousness. Just as no physical model can be constructed to illustrate Einstein's four dimensional universe and no words can adequately describe the quantum reality of subatomic particles, so no picture or words can adequately portray the true nature of the unconscious. Yet we must make an attempt to get some grasp of it, no matter how inadequate that may be, for it is only by trying to understand the unconscious that we can become more conscious of its dialogue with us.

The unconscious portrays itself symbolically in dreams, visions, art forms, and in life itself using many different images. Some of the most common of these images are water in all its forms, underground realms, wild places like forests and jungles, and great beasts like whales and dragons. Noah's flood, Orpheus's journey into the underworld, Joseph Conrad's African journey into "the heart of darkness," Jonah's ordeal in the whale, and St. George's fight with the dragon are all symbolic images of encounters with the unconscious.

Although the unconscious is not located in space—it is beyond space and time—it often seems to us, as we struggle to put into words our experience of it, that it is somehow *underneath* our physical reality, or *within* that reality, or that it somehow *surrounds* us. Concrete models can be made of it for explanatory purposes, but none can capture it. In putting forth such a model one must always say, "It is as if ..."

I find it helpful to think of the unconscious as if it were an infinite realm beneath the surface of consciousness. While the unconscious in this model is all one undifferentiated, continuous reality, consciousness rises from it in discrete units (Fig 4.1).

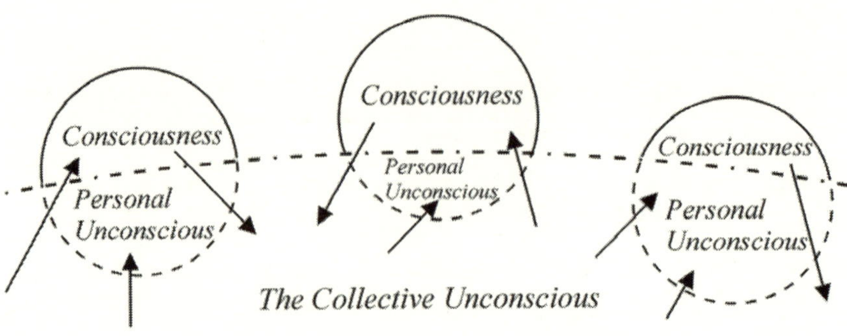

Fig 4.1. The Unconscious

According to Jung, each individual person carrying his own bit of consciousness experiences the unconscious on two levels. Jung referred to the first and most accessible of these levels as the *personal unconscious* because its contents are personal to us, as they are part of our individual, temporal lives. In our personal unconscious is everything that *could* be in our consciousness but is not. It is like a basement or a closet in our house where things accumulate in a dusty clutter and from which we avert our eyes.

In the personal unconscious are all those contents that once were conscious but have fallen away due to a lack of energy. If we make an effort to remember them, we can bring many of those contents up from the unconscious into the light again. Some of the contents in the personal unconscious, however, can never be retrieved through memory because they entered that realm subliminally. These are events and details of our life that our senses registered at such a low level of energy that we never consciously noticed them. We often encounter them as if for the first time as elements in our dreams, fantasies, and artistic expressions.

The personal unconscious also contains those aspects of our life that we have repressed—truths that we have not wanted to know or have not been strong enough to handle. All of us relegate some of our truths to the darkness of our being by refusing to be conscious of them. They are a large part of the reason that there is something in all of us that would rather not open the door to the unconscious, even when we believe in theory that it would be beneficial to do so. We all have aspects of our lives that we do not want to see. Each of us has a *shadow*, a part of ourselves that is inconsistent with the light side we consciously cultivate and try to present to the world.

Our shadow parts are not so much the unsavory things that we know about and consciously keep hidden from others, but rather they are truths about ourselves that our own psychological processes keep hidden from ourselves. *We* are the ones who are most in the dark about our own shadow. Some parts of our shadow are obvious to everyone except ourselves, while other parts are so well disguised that almost no one can discern them. Our shadow includes both inferior aspects of our personality that we are unwilling to see because they are unacceptable to us and superior aspects that we have not yet discovered and claimed.

Among the inferior aspects that everyone finds hard to own are unconscious instinctual drives such as power-seeking, sexuality, and parenting. Instincts are an integral part of us and only belong to the shadow when they operate unconsciously. It is, for example, when we think we are being generous and noble in a situation but are operating instead from an unacknowledged power motive that our shadow is present; or when we believe we are behaving innocently with another but in fact have an unrecognized sexual agenda; or when we think we are relating equally to a peer but instead are playing mother or father; or when we take the other side and play the child.

Every individuation journey includes the revelation of unconscious instinctual behaviors. They are always present, but because they are unconscious we cannot discover them by sitting down to think about them. Usually, it does not even help very much to have them pointed out to us by others. It is through life that we learn about them. The teachings of life that lead to the fullest realization of them come when we turn a positive face toward the unconscious and open ourselves to its contents by taking note of our dreams and looking for meaning and lessons about ourselves in our outer life experiences.

Other inferior aspects in the shadow that none of us wish to see are those that belong to the weaker departments of our personality—the unstarred, unpracticed parts of ourselves, those opposite our gifted selves. They often have to do with our third and fourth functions. These inferior parts of ourselves threaten our self-confidence, and so we try to live as if they do not exist. But if through our dreams and the events of our lives we are led to acknowledge our weaker parts and bring them forward into conscious life, we find that these dark aspects of ourselves contain a sparkle of gold.

Creativity comes from the unconscious, from the same realm as the shadow. When we face our shadow, we make contact with God's creative spirit. As the divine does its work in us and moves us to new expressions of life, we find that our inferior aspects are bound to superior aspects that are also hidden in our darkness. In accepting our own rejected truth, a part of our being that was gray and dead-seeming is transformed into colorful vitality. The shadow, when claimed, paradoxically brings gifts, authentic qualities like strength, beauty, leadership ability, tenderness, incisiveness—qualities that hitherto we only pretended to have or else never believed could be ours at all.

Until we are able to claim our shadow qualities as our own, we see them only in others, where we have unconsciously projected them. Whenever we have strong, obsessive feelings—positive or negative—about another person, something unconscious is present and is being projected. A quality of our own is being seen not in ourselves, where we cannot see it, but in the other person, who may or may not actually possess it.

Thus there may be certain people—in our family, at work, at church, in the news—who strongly affect us by drawing our irritation, anger, and outrage or else our praise, admiration, and devotion. Often the other person possesses the despised or admired characteristic in an exaggerated form, which makes it easy for us to see it "out there" and hard for us to see its subtler version in our own selves. If it were not a quality that in some way belonged to us, we would not be so strongly affected by it. We could look at it with clear eyes, see it for what it is, and turn away and go about our business. But when projection is involved, we get caught by what we see "out there," and until we stop to reflect upon it, we cannot disentangle our feelings from it nor recognize that the cause of our agitation is in ourselves and not in the other.

The Collective Unconscious

Strong affect in general is an indication that an unconscious content is present. When we are angry, frightened, moved to tears, filled with love, or otherwise overtaken by emotion, a truth hitherto unknown has come toward the surface and is available for recognition. If we are aware of this, we can follow the emotion down into its depths and bring to consciousness what we find there, thus strengthening our individual reality and becoming more whole and fully human. Otherwise our emotions simply possess us. They play themselves out in eternal patterns that lead us blindly into situations which unfold like Greek or Shakespearean dramas, and when all has passed we are none the wiser—no growth in consciousness has occurred.

Those eternal patterns that arise in us, either to be consciously integrated or to take possession of our lives, come not from the personal unconscious but from the second, deeper level of the unconscious, the *collective unconscious.* Here are unconscious contents within us that have not come from our life experience. The collective unconscious is the eternal realm beyond time and space. In it is everything that has ever been or seeks to be in human consciousness, past, present, and future. It is the source of our being. We emerge from it when our life on earth begins, draw our energy and vitality from it while we are here, and return to it when our time is over. All life is connected to it, and through it all life is interconnected. Because of our link to it, we sometimes receive intimations of the future or know, without being told, about events that are occurring elsewhere, as sometimes happens at the moment when someone of special significance to us dies.

The patterned effects that come from the collective unconscious are called *archetypes* in Jungian terminology. They are the themes and motifs that drive and shape our human lives. We can see them depicted most clearly in myths and fairytales, where they have been crystallized into some of their purer forms. The Greek gods and goddesses, for example, are images of archetypal aspects of life that belong to each of us. So are fairytale kings and princesses, youngest sons and only daughters of millers and woodcutters, and non-human motifs like lost rings, wise frogs, and golden slippers. Archetypal contents arise from the collective unconscious in universal symbolic patterns that appear in our dreams, thoughts, fantasies, and art forms, as well as in the elements of our outer lives, whether or not we have ever seen or heard of them before.

Archetypal effects come to us along a continuum that ranges from the physical and instinctual to the psychological and spiritual. For example, the "mother" archetype is physically manifest in the person of our actual mother. Because of the archetypal effect behind it, our relationship with our mother is highly patterned and predictable, although each mother-child relationship also has a unique and individual manifestation. It is the archetype that produces the eternal aspect and the circumstances of temporal life that produce the individual aspect. The mother archetype is present in an instinctual form when we mother our own children. It begins to move toward the spiritual end of the continuum when we extend mother-love to the children of others, and it is present in psychological form when we mother ourselves, especially when we gain wisdom about the unconscious and allow ourselves to be nurtured and led by it.

Besides the direct and obvious manifestations of the mother archetype, there are myriad other forms in life that carry the mother's archetypal attributes of nourishing and protecting, enclosing and containing, fostering growth, and inspiring awe and devotion—as well as the dark attributes of smothering, seducing, poisoning, and devouring. Thus, for example, we encounter "the mother" in the church, the university, and the community hall, in the Virgin Mary, Mother Nature, and the Holy Grail, in the plowed field and the enclosed garden, in the Holy City, and in the shaded grotto. In her dark form, "the mother" is present in the conjuring witch, the ensnaring spider, the devouring beast, and the yawning grave.

Although archetypal effects may be present in any and all forms of life, the forms themselves are not the actual archetypes. The archetypes precede existence, having themselves no form, but only a tendency to form. They remain forever in the collective unconscious from whence their effects come, imbuing life with the images and actions expressive of their particular qualities. The degree to which an archetypal effect is experienced as fascinating or gripping is based not on the thing that seems to carry that quality but on the experiencing individual and his relationship to the underlying archetype in the collective unconscious.

The archetypes in the collective unconscious are the divine energies of life. They belong to the living reality of the unconscious, which is autonomous and beyond our control. Because the archetypes in the unconscious are larger than we are—more sublime and more terrible in their eternal aspects than human life can carry—they can distort our lives or even destroy us if they get too strong a grip on our personality. And yet we cannot live authentically without them, nor do we have the power to keep them away. They arise unbidden within us. Our task is to stand up to their turbulent effect on our lives, to recognize that they and we are not the same, and to become consciously related to them rather than unconsciously possessed by them.

One of the archetypes, for example, is that instinct that makes us want to be on the top of the heap. I call it the Zeus archetype, after the Greek god who ruled from Mount Olympus, although it could also be called the king archetype or any other name that carries a comparable image. Regardless of what name it is given, this archetype activates that part of human nature that makes each of us think that we know exactly how things in the world should be and that it is our role to direct the world around us to that end. All of us experience times when this archetype takes possession of our personality, making us unpleasantly all-knowing and domineering.

The answer to this it to recognize that it is happening. We can learn that when things go badly in a certain way, it is because this godlike pattern of behavior has arisen in us without our awareness, and our limited, mortal self has become unconsciously identified with it. At moments like this, we must remind ourselves that we are not Zeus. We are not the King. Even an actual king in a worldly sense is not the King in this archetypal sense, for, king or not, he is just a man. If we can cease to identify with the archetypal pattern, we will then be able to form a *conscious relationship* with it and integrate it little by little into the totality of our being, bringing it down to human size as we adjust its demands to the ordinary reality of our life. The Zeus archetype, when we relate to it in a positive way, is a crucial ingredient in our ability to exercise effective leadership.

The Self

The factor that makes it possible for us to integrate the archetypes with all their conflicting demands is the God-center within us, a coordinating center point which is itself an archetype in the collective unconscious. This is the archetype that unites all archetypes into its own comprehensive totality. When a person makes a positive connection to the God-center, the chaos of the unconscious is brought into order, its overwhelming power is subdued, and its images and energies are channeled into that person's life in an individual, just right way that teaches, heals, protects, and leads.

Jung named this unifying archetype the *Self* to emphasize its quality of God within, although he did not mean by this to refer to one's limited human self. His German term *das selbst* is more accurately translated, "the Itself." Jung understood the Self to be the greater reality to which our human lives belong, the Lord of lords that our egos must learn to recognize and serve. It is the screen or gate through which the divine is manifested in human consciousness. When we experience an image or understanding that arises from the Self, it is as close as we can come to knowing the divine, which by nature cannot be fully known. Thus all images and experiences of God arise from the archetype of the Self, including many we might not ordinarily think of as divine.

In my own dreams the terms "God," "the Self," "the Center," and "the Christ" have appeared interchangeably. I take this to mean that the eternal divine, from whom I believe such understandings come, regards them as interchangeable. One dream, for instance, which came in words, not images, said, *"To integrate the Self is to integrate God."* I took this to mean that God is to some extent incarnated in human life when we awaken to the reality of the unconscious, make a positive connection to the Self, and take into ourselves the teachings, understandings, and life experiences that this connection brings.

Another dream I had about the Self also came as directly conveyed meaning, although this time it was illustrated by an image.

> *I see a line running from my viewing point to what I understand to be "the Center." The line extends forward along a horizontal plane to a point on the horizon that I know is only there because it is as far as I can see into the distance, while the actual center point lies beyond at infinity. "Jung gave you your first line to the Center," the dream voice says. I know that this refers to the understandings I have gained from Jung's work.*
>
> *Then the dream shows a second line starting at some distance to the right of the first and also running to the Center, making a triangular area between the two lines. In the dream, I understand that this second line is the church in its present, institutional reality and that this, too, is now in place for me. I know that although this second line pertains more to the outer world, and is, therefore, less profound than the first line, it is essential for providing me a playing field. I understand that the triangular area between Jung and the church is the area of human reality in which it is possible for me to live my life "from the Center."*

Because of yet another dream about the Self that I had had earlier, I was aware even as I was dreaming this dream that it is important that one's life be lived "from the Center." That earlier dream also had, at the heart of it, meaning directly conveyed through words which were accompanied by a simple, visual illustration.

> *I dream of an elderly, old-fashioned woman who is a school librarian. I know that she has no children of her own. She is explaining to us that you have to tell children exactly what to do because, being children, they do not otherwise know.*
>
> *Then the dream shifts and becomes an illustration, as if on paper, of a framework that I know to be an equal-armed cross, although the focus is on only one quadrant and the center point. A line from the*

> *center radiates out through the quadrant at about a 50° angle from one of the arms of the cross. On that arm and on the radiating line are two dots, one on each line, at equal distance from the center. Then the dream shows a line connecting the two dots:*

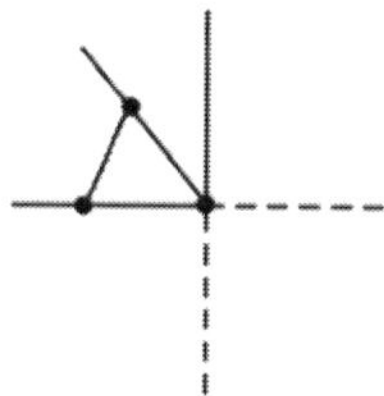

> *A dream voice says, "That is going across," conveying the understanding that it is not good. "God wants everything from the Center," the dream voice says.*

As I understand the dream, the radiating lines with the dots on them have reference to individual lives, and the point being made by the dream is that God does not want us ultimately to receive our understanding of life from other people. We may need this when we are in an early phase of learning, but in the end, God's way is not the school librarian's way. We must be taught and led by our own inner guide, the God-center within us—the Self.

This dream also makes it clear that God and the Self are not entirely synonymous. "*God wants everything from the Center.*" God is greater than the Center, or the Self, and presides over our relationship to it. It is only through that relationship that we can relate consciously to the divine. As the dream I quoted earlier said, "To integrate the Self is to integrate God." Jesus incarnated the eternal, or archetypal, Christ, which is a living image and truth that arises from the Self. The Christ is a particularly accessible symbol of the Self in potential human form, seeking to be known and integrated into human life. Speaking as the Christ, or the Self, Jesus said to his followers, "The Father [the eternal divine] is greater than I." But he also said, "If you know me, you know my Father too."

Like the center point on the horizon in my dream, the Self is as close as we can come to an actual experience of the divine, whose total reality is infinite and thus beyond our powers of perception. Jesus was speaking for the Self when he said: "I am the Way;" "I am the gate;" "come . . . through me;" "believe in me." All of his teachings were about what it is like, and what is required, to have a positive relationship with God through the teaching, healing, and guiding God-center within—which in Jungian terminology is called the Self.

The Dark Self

The very fact that we can have a positive relationship with the Self means that we can also have a negative one. All the archetypes in the unconscious have both a dark side and a light side. I once had a dream that spoke explicitly about the dark side of the Self:

> *I dream deeply of "the negative or dark Christ, also called Self," of what it is. The dream is mostly a mood or perception of a kind of dark energy with this label on it. I am aware of a brooding, turbulent sky. Then I see two doves flying up into the dark heavens, bound to earth by long tethers around their necks. They have flown to the ends of their tethers and are straining against them. I understand the dark Christ or dark Self to be the resentment or protest of the Self against these bonds.*

For me, the dove is first and foremost a symbol of the Holy Spirit, and that is how I understand the image of the doves in this dream. The dream, therefore, seems to equate the Christ, the Self, and the Holy Spirit and to show their dark side to be the resentment of the heavenly spirit—which is a part of the Self, a part of the Christ—against the limitations of earthly life. We see this side of Jesus when he asks in exasperation, "How long must I put up with this generation?" We also see it when he gives way to anger and overturns the tables of the moneychangers, certainly to no lasting avail.

Just as we have the light side of the Self within us, so also do we have the dark side. Something within all of us that is greater than we are resents the fact that the Kingdom has not yet come, that we must live in a world with so much imperfection, that our material life is not as we would like it, that our jobs and marriages cause such difficulty and disappointment, that our children give us as much trouble as they do, that our government at all levels is as corrupt as it is, that the ministers and leaders of our churches have no more awareness of the divine than they do, that nothing is as it should be and would be if the compelling sense of divine perfection that resides in us were realized. This dark resentment, unless balanced by the light, gives rise to evil.

The light side of the Self accepts the limitations of life and willingly sacrifices its own greatness and unfathomable potential for what is realizable in a specific place and time. In doing so, it redeems life on earth bit by bit and step by step. But this does not happen without the accompanying presence of the dark Self. The dream suggests that the dark Self is especially present when a new experience of the Self first comes into awareness. A duality in dreams, such as the two doves, usually indicates an unconscious content that has just entered consciousness, at which point it divides into two, a set of opposites that had been undifferentiated in the unconscious, where all exists in primal unity.

In consciousness, there is always a light and a dark side to everything, a good and a bad, a positive and a negative, just as in subatomic physics a particle is always paired with an antiparticle. When a baby is born, for example, it is a blessed and joyful event; but even the most welcoming parents also have to face the dark side of increased responsibility, curtailed freedom, and the renewal, in this new life, of the cycles of human imperfection of which they are already a part. Post-partum depression registers in a dramatic way the inevitable presence of the dark Self as new life enters the world. Every further development in that new life will bring with it dark moments as the Self continually seeks incarnation and confronts the limitations of reality.

The Compensatory Nature of the Unconscious

Consciously or unconsciously, all the archetypes, including the archetype of the Self, are universally present in every person. An archetype may be experienced one-sidedly with only its light aspect admitted to consciousness and its dark aspect denied, or, conversely, with only the dark side admitted and the light side denied. In either case, life will be imbalanced, and the excluded quality will continually seek to make itself known.

The longer the rejected aspect is kept knocking at the door of consciousness, the greater and more threatening its power will become. But no matter how dark and ugly one may fear it to be, it is one's own truth that seeks admittance through the door of the unconscious. So long as we have a strong ego structure and a conscious connection to the God of heaven and light, our rejected truth will bring redemption when it is faced and integrated. In the end, we come to realize that the unconscious is not an enemy but is, in fact, a valuable source of ongoing, personal truth.

The unconscious always seeks to *compensate* our conscious attitude. If we do not find new understanding in its messages, we have not interpreted them correctly. The unconscious tries to bring to our awareness what is missing and needed for our proper functioning and for the greatest possible realization of our human wholeness. It tries to help us balance the light side and the dark side of life by bringing opposing realities together into a single new reality that is less light than the unbalanced light and less dark than the unbalanced darkness, and yet greater than either of these in its unity and completeness.

Carl Jung once said, "We know that the mask of the unconscious is not rigid—it reflects the face we turn toward it. Hostility lends it a threatening aspect, friendliness softens its features." Some people have turned a hostile face to the unconscious for so long and have become so separated from it, that its contents have become too dark and overpowering to be faced. Such persons live under the threat of a psychosis and for them the unconscious is a real danger. Their best course usually is to leave it alone and to hang on to whatever adaptation to life they have managed to make for themselves.

Many others have not consolidated enough ego strength and moral will to stand up to a direct, unmediated relationship with the unconscious. Their connection to the Self is sufficiently maintained by collective religious experience. They are like the Hebrews at the foot of Mount Sinai: "'Speak to us yourself,' the people said to Moses, 'and we will listen; but do not let God speak to us, or we shall die.'"

Those persons who would be overwhelmed by the unconscious usually have a strong resistance to it—often to the point that they can hardly bear to hear it discussed. Such resistances should always be honored. No one should ever try to harass or cajole another person into opening the door to the unconscious. Those who need a direct relationship with the unconscious will be led from within to seek it. For the rest, there are other valid paths.

A person who is ready to meet the unconscious directly is one who has a strong ego, a well-developed moral sensibility, and the ability to be detached and analytical about his or her own inner processes. He or she must also have a compelling need for inner growth and healing. There is a zone of anxiety through which everyone must pass in establishing a direct relationship with the unconscious. Persons in whom the above qualities and conditions are present are more likely than others to stay the course with courage and not turn back. For those who are called to this path, the light of the Self waits in the darkness to be their guide. In the language of Christianity, this is the light of the eternal Christ, that same light which the darkness cannot overpower.

Chapter Five

The Language of the Unconscious

The unconscious is the only available source of religious experience. This is certainly not to say that what we call the unconscious is identical with God or is set up in his place. It is simply the medium from which religious experience seems to flow.

Carl Jung

Throughout time and history there have been many methods devised for making contact with the unconscious, usually, but not always, for religious purposes. Among these are disciplines of meditation and prayer; vision quests and shamanistic journeys; spontaneous artistic expressions; active imagination, or waking fantasy; and various oracular devices such as the Urim and Thummim of the Hebrew scriptures, the Tarot cards of Europe, and the *I Ching* of China. There are, however, *natural* ways by which the unconscious continually expresses itself in our lives, day and night, without requiring from us any method or device.

The most noticeable of these natural ways is through our *dreams*, which come to us every night, whether we remember them or not. Another noticeable way is through experiences of *synchronicity*, or meaningful coincidence, which occur every day of our waking life, whether or not we are aware of them. This ongoing dialogue with the "Other" is always present. The only question is whether it is noticed, understood to some degree, and consciously integrated into life. It is a process that is so natural that it can always be discovered anew without instruction by thoughtful persons everywhere.

Abraham Lincoln was one such person who, without encouragement from the culture around him, was alert to the natural inflowing expressions of the divine. Many instances were recorded in which he let it be known that dreams and synchronicity were important to him. Of course, he did not know the word "synchronicity." This is the term Jung has given us for the events of life that have a deeper meaning than their mere surface-of-life, physical reality. But Lincoln did not need a special word for this. He understood it when he saw it, as he did on the day of his second inauguration in an event recorded by Noah Brooks, a reporter who was a particularly close friend of his.

That 4th day of March 1865 had dawned cold and gray with drizzling rain. At midday, just before Lincoln made his entrance onto the inaugural platform, the rain stopped. In the company of the nation's leading public officials, Lincoln emerged from the Capitol and took his seat on the crowded platform above the mass of spectators. With solemn ceremony, the sergeant-at-arms of the Senate invited him to step forward to give his inaugural address.

"As he advanced from his seat," wrote Brooks, "a roar of applause shook the air, and, again and again repeated, finally died far away on the outer fringe of the throng, like a sweeping wave upon the shore. Just at that moment the sun, obscured all day, burst forth in its unclouded meridian splendor and flooded the spectacle with glory and light."

The synchronicity of the moment was not lost on Noah Brooks, nor on Lincoln himself. As they were returning to the White House after the ceremony, Lincoln said to Brooks, "Did you notice that sunburst? It made my heart jump."

Lincoln also paid attention to the messages of the night, a trait regarded as peculiar by most people around him in that highly rational age. On the day he died, Good Friday 1865, he told some colleagues about a dream he had had the night before. This conversation took place in a Cabinet meeting in which the topic of discussion had turned to news of the army. The Civil War at this point was essentially, but not quite, over.

Lincoln told his Cabinet secretaries that he had no news, but that he had had a dream the night before which he felt signified that good news would be forthcoming. He had had this same dream several times before, he explained, and it was always followed by a great moment in the war, usually a victory. In this recurring dream, he would be in some sort of indescribable vessel, moving swiftly across a body of water toward an unknown shore. "I had this strange dream again last night," he said, "and we shall, judging from the past, have great news very soon, I think."

The Cabinet members stepped politely around this contribution to the discussion, avoiding an abrupt dismissal of it, but suggesting that the dream's conjunction with major events was probably coincidental or else could be explained by Lincoln's agitated state of mind in times of crisis when such major events would likely be forthcoming. Lincoln put up no argument. "Perhaps that is the explanation," he said and let the matter drop.

But the incomprehension of his Cabinet did not dampen the high spirits with which the dream had infused him. As he rode with Mrs. Lincoln to Ford's Theater that night, she noted a mood of happiness in him that was so strange and unusual that it troubled her. Because of Lincoln's firm belief in his own inner experience, his dream had been able to do its work in preparing him for the moment of his death—for the completion of his journey to the "other shore." This is not to suggest that he had such a specific understanding of the dream, but rather that his general grasp of it was enough to move him to the place inside himself where it seems his God-center wanted him to be for these last hours of his life.

What little Lincoln knew about dreams and synchronicity he had to discover for himself in a world in which such things were not taken seriously except by "old women and by young men and maidens in love," as he himself once put it. He lived just at the end of the rational, mechanistic age, embodying what was best in it and anticipating the new age to come. Sigmund Freud was a nine-year-old boy in Vienna when Lincoln died. Carl Jung would be born ten years later, and Albert Einstein four years after that. Had Lincoln lived a little more than a century later, he could have filled several shelves of his library with easily accessible books that describe systematically the nature of the unconscious and the rudiments of its fascinating but difficult language.

God's Feminine Voice

The natural language of the unconscious is the language of symbol and metaphor. There are occasional instances when it states a truth forthrightly, but these seem to come only when a person is ready to grasp a particular truth, which implies that the cooperation of consciousness is required for the unconscious to be able to make a straightforward statement. Since the purpose of the unconscious is to compensate our consciousness by revealing to us aspects of our truth that we do not already understand, much symbolic and metaphorical expression of an unfolding truth precedes and prepares those rare moments of clarity.

The unconscious speaks to us symbolically because that is the language of life itself. Think of unfolding creation as a manifestation of the divine in picture story. The symbolic language of nature is God's feminine voice, and it requires union with consciousness, which is the masculine principle, in order to be perceived and understood. Human beings are the vehicles through which this process takes place since we are the ones who carry together in our beings both unconscious nature and consciousness. Because consciousness rises out of the unconsciousness of nature and stands above it, somewhat separate and apart from it, consciousness is able to perceive nature with a degree of objectivity and thus is able to *know* it. Without consciousness, life can be lived, but it cannot be known.

It is in our capacity for consciousness that we experience God's masculine spirit, while in the natural reality of our lives we experience God's feminine aspect. In the feminine part of ourselves, we partake of nature, reality, and specificity, while in our masculine part we stand above nature at the level of objectivity, abstraction, and ideal.

The abstract quality of the masculine principle is, in fact, the great problem we have with consciousness. It tends to prefer abstraction and idea to reality. The masculine part of us does not want to be bothered with natural reality. It would rather dream about an ideal world or talk about general principles. It resists limiting itself to the here and now. Although it is able from its objective vantage point to perceive unfolding nature, it does not easily take the next step of valuing natural reality in all its fullness and entering into a true relationship with it.

One-sided consciousness—the pure masculine principle—is such a straightforward, linear process that it has difficulty recognizing that the symbolic expression of life is even a language at all. It dismisses the feminine voice of the divine as nonsensical and irrational. The tendency to this attitude seems to be a condition of consciousness in all human beings, whether men or women, although in general men carry it more strongly than women do.

In its love of abstraction and idea, one-sided consciousness has little patience for the daily unfolding of particular life processes, but this is precisely where the symbolic language of the divine is found. Wherever this language of life is ignored, the feminine principle is closed out. Unless a person gains an understanding of the symbolic language of the unconscious, a full relationship between the masculine and feminine elements of life cannot take place. It is only when there is a true union of the masculine and feminine principles that human wholeness can be achieved and the wisdom of life attained.

Personal versus Collective Symbols

The symbolic language of the unconscious has both an individual and a general aspect, depending on whether the material is coming from the personal or the collective unconscious. In seeking the meaning of an image that comes from the unconscious, we must always begin by asking about our personal associations with that image. If I dream, for example, about a place by the sea, the first question to ask, before looking at the collective meaning of "by the sea," is whether I have any personal associations with that particular locale.

In my life, I have experienced the sea in different places and contexts. Why was this location chosen by the unconscious? For example, sometimes I dream of a place on the South Carolina coast where my husband and I used to vacation with my relatives. I particularly associate it with my mother, who liked to gather our family there. Other times I dream of the blue Gulf waters at Bradenton, Florida, where there is a national park commemorating the landing of the Hernando de Soto expedition in 1539. That expedition was for many years my husband's major research project. Each of these dream locations are "by the sea," but they address very different aspects of my being. Not totally different, however. "By the sea" also has a collective meaning, and these two locales are but variants, albeit important ones, of an underlying, universal human reality symbolized by this general image.

Water is an archetypal motif that almost always refers to the unconscious, the nature of which is symbolized by the nature of water in its every aspect. In the form of the sea, water symbolizes the unconscious as the source of our being, the primal mother, vast and overwhelming, chaotic and beautiful, life-giving, eternal, mysterious, soul-restoring. To be "by the sea" is to be in a place in myself that is close to the unconscious in its primal aspect and thus close to the creative source of my own being.

There are many basic images that almost always carry the same general meanings in everyone's dreams. The collective meanings of the most commonly occurring symbols can be picked up by reading widely in Jungian literature, although no two persons who work with dreams will agree completely on the meanings of even the most basic symbols. The unconscious is too creatively expressive to be caught and nailed down. Individual nuances are always present to forestall the possibility of a pat answer in any interpretation of a dream symbol.

However, the collective meaning of a symbol usually has some light to shed on the interpretation process once the personal associations elicited by that symbol have been reviewed. Over the years I have arrived at my own understanding of the collective meanings of commonly occurring symbols. I offer some of these as examples of the metaphorical nature of the language of the unconscious.

Water, Light, and Earth

In the image of water, for example, many different attributes of the unconscious can be seen. The unconscious flows like a stream or a river in a winding path through the midst of our lives. Like groundwater, it stores itself in the ground of our being, beneath the surface of visible reality. Like a spring, the unconscious emerges clear and pure from an unseen source. Like rain, it periodically pours down on us from above, surrounding us with its presence, merging the heaven and earth of our being and bringing forth new life. Like water piped into our individual houses, the unconscious washes clean the contaminations of our being that we inevitably pick up as we live our daily lives. Like a cool, clean drink of water from a well, it assuages the thirst of our souls. And like the danger of deep water, it can obliterate our individual reality if we do not know how to "swim" in it or if it floods over us with too great a force. We can dip into the watery realm of the unconscious, but we cannot live in it. It is not a human environment.

Light is another symbol that brings a collective, archetypal meaning into our dreams and into the synchronistic events of our waking lives. Light symbolizes consciousness. To "see the light" is to awaken to a new level of consciousness, to realize a truth we have previously been unable or unwilling to grasp. If we dream of being in a dimly lit room or of groping about in total darkness, we are probably being told about a part of ourselves of which we have little consciousness or even, in the second instance, no consciousness at all. The sun is symbolic of the divine source of consciousness in its emanating, masculine aspect, while the moon symbolizes the reflective feminine consciousness of divine Wisdom. Electric lights, on the other hand, usually refer to ego consciousness.

The surface of the earth is the normal physical realm of human life. In dreams, it can symbolize our earthly reality. The region beneath the earth usually symbolizes the unconscious and the roots of things in the past. People often dream of being in a basement or of finding a place in the ground with stairs going down. The world underground sometimes symbolizes death, or the world of the dead, which is itself a reference to the unconscious, where everything from the past still lives. It can also indicate depression, an inner state in which we sink deeply into our earthly energies, growing heavy and inert as we lose contact with our higher spirit. Although a depression is a difficult and sometimes dangerous time in our life, it brings with it the possibility of making a needed reconnection with the fundamental root of our being.

The realm of the upper spirit is symbolized by the air and sky above the earth. This is the world of thought, abstraction, and ideal, of faith and soaring hope, and of heaven. Birds are at home at this level, but humans are not. When we dream of flying like a bird, we are probably being shown that in some aspect of our life we do not have our feet on the ground, that our upper spirit is overbalanced and is carrying us away from human physical reality. A dream of being in an airplane, however, would show an aspect of our life in which we are being carried along by a system of thought or ideals that may not be grounded but at least is a viable human way of going.

Vehicles, Animals, and Children

Vehicles of all kinds symbolize culturally-constructed ways of getting around in outer life. In this context, a car symbolizes an independent way of going, while buses, planes, and trains are collective ways. A dream of driving a pickup truck, for instance, might be a picture of being in our working mode, while riding in a bus might symbolize being carried along by a collective process, such as taking a class. To go on foot is to move through life naturally and individually, without the drawbacks, but also without the benefits, of a cultural system.

Animals in our dreams symbolize instinct, with different species representing different parts of our instinctual life. Cats, for example, usually symbolize a natural aspect of our feminine being. They show us an instinctive part of ourselves that has a strong sense of self-worth, that values being over doing, that is oriented toward inwardness, and that has a streak of wildness that can never be fully tamed. Dogs, on the other hand, represent a masculine instinct for doing, proving, and earning. Dogs portray a life energy within us that is extraverted and that imparts to us a natural social instinct and a preoccupation with competition and hierarchy. This energy helps us delineate and guard our personal boundaries, sets off a warning within us when our space is being violated, and gives us the snarling teeth and fighting spirit that we need to defend what is ours.

When we dream of wild animals, we are dreaming of the primeval nature that lives in the depths of us. A dream of jungle animals, for example, might be a compensation for an overly cultural adaptation to life, reminding us that we are not only cultural beings but also magnificent creatures of earth meant to live in close connection with the natural rhythm of life. Birds are generally symbolic of our higher, spiritual nature. Cold-blooded animals symbolize our deepest, most primal, and least conscious energies. Fish symbolize the living, autonomous contents of the unconscious, which can be fished up and "eaten," or integrated. This makes the fish an apt symbol of the living Christ. The snake symbolizes the energy of life at its most fundamental level, unconscious and instinctual, inhuman but strangely intelligent and purposeful, a source of danger but also of healing and transformation. The snake sometimes symbolizes the unconscious itself.

Another common symbol in our dreaming and waking lives is "the child." We often dream of our own children, or of a child who belongs to us but is not one of our actual, outer-world children, or of a baby we are supposed to be taking care of but have forgotten about and neglected, or of a child who is wise beyond his or her years and knows what to do when we do not know, and so on. "The child" represents something new that is growing in us, something that will come to maturity in the future, something crucial and central to our lives. It might, for example, refer to a significant new relationship, or to an important development in one's working life or in one's spiritual life. There are times, however, when a child in a dream refers not to something new but to something from the past, to an aspect of our own childhood about which we need to become conscious.

At the heart of the symbolism of "the child" is an image of the newly emerging Self. This is what is being emphasized when we dream of a child who is unusually wise and knowing. "The child" in this aspect would be the divine child, God within, incarnated in our own lives both by grace and by our earnest effort to attend to our inner processes and to follow the narrow and dimly lit path of our own true being.

Circles and Squares

There are many other symbols of the Self, including all the many images with which the Christ has been identified throughout the centuries of Christianity. Jesus himself is our most elaborate symbol of the Self, giving us a vivid picture of its qualities when incarnated in a human life. The simplest and most fundamental symbol of the Self, however, is the circle, which when it carries this symbolic meaning is called a *mandala*. Images of roundness that appear in dreams—balls, plates, rings, people arranged in circles, and so on—usually indicate the presence of the archetypal wholeness of the Self. When the center is emphasized, as when a circle is quartered by a cross, it symbolizes the Self as both a unifying and an ordering principle. The flower with its center and radiating petals is a natural mandala and a profound symbol of the Self. Christ is often symbolized by a flower, as is the Virgin Mary, and the lotus is a powerful symbol of the Self in Buddhism. To dream of a flower almost always has a healing effect on one's soul.

The circle symbolizes the Self as it arises spontaneously from nature, within our psyches as well as in the outer world. The sun and the moon are round. So are many fruits, nuts, seeds, and flowers. The eyes of animals are round. All of these symbolize the natural presence of a tendency to wholeness that is carried by life itself. The square, however, which is a constructed form, is also a symbol of the Self, one that points to a cultural aspect of the divine and indicates a human factor that enters into the process of wholeness. Rare natural occurrences of formal line and angle—as in crystals and honeycombs—symbolize the fact that even this tendency to culture has its seeds in the depths of nature itself.

There is a sacred quality to four-squareness. This symbol is found in the Christian cross and in the image of the square-walled city of God in the book of Revelation. There is a human spiritual instinct for squaring off a sacred space within which one can stand in safety to face the power of the divine. It is very common when we are coming into conscious relationship with the unconscious to dream of walking in a square or rectangular pattern—perhaps, for example, around a city block—sometimes repeatedly. Such a dream would indicate that inside ourselves we are shoring up our boundaries, drawing to ourselves human consciousness, tradition, and structure in order to make a safe place in which to stand to receive the potentially disintegrating contents of the unconscious.

In order to safely face the chaos of the unconscious, we must have tools for integrating it, some sort of guidebook from those who have gone before. We need a positive connection to the defining boundaries of human society in order to balance the limitlessness of the unconscious. Jung used the Greek word *temenos* to refer to this archetypal, squared-off, sacred space where a person can meet the unconscious without being overwhelmed by it. A temenos is a well-ordered place of healthy consciousness. Churches carry this deep, archetypal symbol, as do ball fields, courthouses, city parks, and even tables around which we gather for meals or meetings.

A temenos serves the function of bringing chaotic elements into order through a human system of customs, rules, insights, and understandings. When a person who is trying to connect with his or her dream life takes care to use Jungian tools and a religious attitude, he or she stands in the safety of a temenos. To give another example, sometimes when I am suffering one of life's overwhelming and disintegrating pains, I will hear the line of a hymn arise within me. If I get out my hymn book and sing that hymn, I will find that it has just the right words, feelings, and understandings for building a temenos for myself. To sing each verse is to walk around my boundaries, squaring my corners, making a sacred space in which my pain can be integrated and transformed.

Intruders and Bathrooms

As in the archetypal dream image of making a square, much of the symbolic language that arises from the unconscious has to do with the *process* of becoming conscious. It is fairly common, for example, to dream of an intruder coming into our house. This usually symbolizes something yet unknown that is trying to come into consciousness from the unconscious. It tells us that we are being so resistant to a new understanding, to new life of some kind, that it has taken on a dark and threatening aspect. It feels threatening because it is unknown.

When we have a dream like this, we should not be frightened, but rather we should stand bravely and face it, acknowledging that there is something arising in our consciousness that we cannot yet see and affirming that we are willing to come to grips with it. After all, it is nothing more than our own truth trying to get in. It may turn out to be a pleasant truth or an unpleasant truth, but either way, we will be better off when we have found out about it and dealt with it. If we do stand and face it, we may then have another dream that shows it in a less threatening form, perhaps as a stranger whom we meet, a part of ourselves that no longer frightens us but that we still do not know very well. As life continues to bring us new consciousness about this unfolding aspect of ourselves, we might dream of being with a new friend.

Another theme having to do with the process of becoming conscious is that of toilets and bathrooms. These are very common symbols, especially in the dreams of people who are consciously engaged in the individuation process. There are, for example, dreams of not being able to find a bathroom, of finding one that offers no privacy, of a clogged toilet filled with excrement, or of a toilet that is like a throne. The variations are endless. This theme has to do with shadow work, with the need to periodically deal with the darkness, or unconsciousness, that accumulates naturally as a result of living. The regular cleansing of the soul requires solitude and privacy, times of withdrawal from active outer life. Shadow work requires inner work.

Defecation symbolizes a natural process by which we eliminate the residue of life gone by. This speaks of our need to periodically rid ourselves of old attitudes, old relationships, old activities, old passions, old answers to life's questions, and so on. When our dreams show problems with defecation, it is usually an indication that we are having trouble doing our shadow work.

Urination has to do with the natural flow of the unconscious through our individual beings. We are channels for the symbolic images that flow into us from the unconscious and seek to flow out into consciousness through our dreams, fantasies, spontaneous artistic expressions, and deeply felt emotions. The release of these images is private inner work, not meant for public display, but for our own personal growth toward human wholeness. On another level, urination has to do with the flow of life itself, the river of time, the demands of the hour which are constantly changing throughout each day and throughout our lives. Life is a flow of images and experiences in which one must participate in a timely way. It cannot be held back.

These are only a few of the most common symbols through which the unconscious speaks to us. No symbol can be completely or rigidly defined. The fact that it is a symbol means that it refers to a mystery of life that is always just a little beyond our grasp. We can never quite lay hold of the full meaning of our dreams or of life itself as it unfolds before us. We must, however, do the best we can, always holding our constructs lightly, letting further insights rearrange them in our hands, going forward with a conscious balance of understanding and not understanding.

Analogy, Plays on Words, and Repetition

Besides its use of symbols, there are many other definable characteristics of the language of the unconscious. One of these is the frequent use of *analogy*. The unconscious often says to us in effect, "It is as if . . ." For example, I had a dream like this one night after I had been sleeping fitfully with lots of tossing and turning, all the while being vaguely aware that something was trying to come into my dreams that just could not get in. Finally, I awakened a little and said to God, "What is this? What do you want me to understand?" Then I slept again and dreamed:

> *My husband has a groundskeeper working for him to whom he gives a mail-order item that has just arrived, some kind of gardening equipment. My husband asks him not to open the package yet, for there is a similar item coming later and the man will need to choose which one of these he wants to keep.*
>
> *As my husband is telling him this, the groundskeeper proceeds to open the package. My husband again asks him to wait, explaining that the item coming later will have with it neither packaging material nor an invoice and that if this present one is chosen over that later one, this packaging material and invoice will be needed to send the other one back.*

> *The man keeps on as if nothing were being said to him. My husband gets angry and raises his voice and then angrier still as the man continues to ignore him. The growing intensity of anger awakens me, and I feel shaken.*

As I collected myself and felt around for the place in my life where this dream fit, I realized it had nothing to do with my actual husband. I knew it was pointing out that I had failed to listen to a dream that had come to me the night before. I had not allowed that dream to change my conscious attitude. This current dream was saying: *It is as if* you are this groundskeeper and God is your employer trying to give you directions to which you are not listening. The dream took the form of a parable and even used the imagery of biblical parables in which God is shown as the master of an estate and us as the workers. Upon seeing this picture of my stubbornness, I submitted to the message of the previous night and let go of some feelings I had been holding onto concerning something in my outer life. After that, I slept peacefully for the rest of the night.

The unconscious also frequently uses *plays on words* to get its messages across. A dream of someone named Hightower, for example, might have more to do with a haughty attitude or with being too much up in one's head than with any particular characteristics of the person in the dream. We can never be sure where the meaning will be found. In each case we have to try out all possibilities—personal associations, symbol and metaphor, analogy, plays on words—until something "clicks."

The unconscious uses *repetition* to signal importance and to construct themes. If a dream is repeated, we know it is of special significance. Sometimes a particular dream is repeated from time to time throughout our lives until we finally understand the issues that lie at the heart of it. Once a dream has been truly understood, it will not come back again unless we have regressed.

Life events will also repeat themselves until we get their message. We might, for example, find ourselves involved in repeated minor auto accidents for which we are not at fault. When the first event happens we might not think to look beneath the surface of events. But if a second one occurs soon after, we should know that something serious is going on and that we should look around in our life for someone who is "not in control of his vehicle." There might, for instance, be someone in our current life from whom we need to distance ourselves. Or we might look at where we were going when these mishaps occurred. Were we straying unwittingly from the safety of our true path? The repetition means that it is important for us to wake up to a danger that is threatening the integrity of our life.

The unconscious relates to us over time by constructing *themes* through repeated motifs. This happens regularly in dreams, but it also happens in outer life through synchronicity. I might be driving along a country road, for example, and see a cow that has gotten out of its pasture. That would be interesting but not necessarily thought-provoking. If later in the day, however, I ask for directions and am told to go to the Brown Cow Dairy and turn left, my antennae would begin to go up. And if that night I find myself drawn into a conversation about the sacredness of the cow in Hindu religion, I would know I have a theme going. I would at least give some thought to the symbolic meaning of "the cow" and wonder what part of my life this theme might be addressing. Then I would stay tuned for further developments both in my dreams and in outer life. The theme might last only a day or it might go on for weeks. And if I did not draw from it everything that pertained to me, it would eventually come around again.

At any one time, we have several related themes threading their way through our sleeping and waking lives. Every theme common to humankind comes to us at one time or another although some are more central to our individual lives than others. Some of the many possible themes we might be dealing with at any particular time are: balancing the high and the low; finding our vocation; relating in a conscious and balanced way to mother energy or father energy; accepting old age; realizing the spiritual value of being at home without working; accepting the authority of the unconscious; letting go of power; coming down to earth to accept responsible adulthood; healing relationship wounds; accepting the true nature of the masculine or feminine principle; letting go of hands-on parenthood; and so on.

Most themes stay with us for a few weeks or months. As they go out, new ones come in, and all eventually come around again. If we are learning the lessons they offer, their continual cycling through our lives will be a spiral toward the God-center within us, each return bringing a new and deeper level of integration and understanding. Each time a theme comes around, we will feel ourselves in better balance than before, more conscious of what it is all about, and more accepting of the shape of our individual lives. When we are not learning our lessons, our themes will repeat themselves, unchanged, in an endless circle, and each episode of life will only be more of the same old story, going nowhere.

Because the unconscious is a part of nature, *cycles* are intrinsic to its expression. We each have personal yearly cycles, whether we are aware of them or not. Dramatic events bring this to consciousness, as in the inevitable psychic disturbances we experience on the anniversary of an important death or a divorce. But we can also see a less obvious personal cycle if at some random time we look back in our dream journal to see what themes we were working on at the same time the year before. Usually, we will find that at least some of those themes have come around again a year later. Another personal cycle that can often be seen is the nine-month gestation period. If we look back at what happened nine months before an important new development, we often find a noteworthy event in which, through some sort of word, action, or realization of truth, we committed ourselves to new life.

The unconscious also resonates with the great impersonal cycles under which we live, both natural and cultural. Thus we will find our themes tied to the natural seasons of the year, to national holidays, and to our religious calendars. It is good to keep an eye on the many strands of our unfolding story as special days and seasons come around. There is often more being taught to us than we might imagine about the deep meaning in our individual lives of springtime, Independence Day, Halloween, or Christmas. If we have a Christian background, for example, we might dream that it is Christmas in July or Lent in November, telling us that regardless of what is going on for everyone else, the Christ has just been born in us anew or a season of sober introspection is upon us.

The language of the unconscious is the language of mythology and fairytales, of religious rituals and music, of color and number, of kinship, friendship, and enmity, of food, of body and sexuality, of plants and animals, of heaven and earth. It is a universal language, common to all of humankind. Yet, while our souls always know it by nature, our minds do not, and the more highly developed our mind, the more estranged we tend to become from our soul and its natural language.

People in native, pre-modern cultures had the advantage of a more direct knowledge of the language and wisdom of the unconscious, not because they were more conscious than we are but because they were less conscious and therefore more at one with the unconscious. Despite the romantic yearning we sometimes have to be like them, we can never go back to a less conscious state without bringing harm to ourselves, just as we cannot return to childhood or adolescence or young adulthood once we have grown past those stages of life.

Embracing the outer trappings of pre-modern life and religion, therefore, will not remedy our estrangement from the language of our souls. The only viable remedy in our time is to make a conscious effort to learn to understand the language of the unconscious using modern tools that belong to our own time, such as these tools of Jungian psychology. In this way, we can open ourselves to the vitality, healthy wholeness, and natural wisdom of primeval humanity while at the same time remaining true to our own reality as modern persons rooted in a several-thousand-year development of religious and scientific understanding.

Chapter Six
Dreams

The dream is often occupied with apparently very silly details, thus producing an impression of absurdity, or else it is on the surface so unintelligible as to leave us thoroughly bewildered. Hence we always have to overcome a certain resistance before we can seriously set about disentangling the intricate web through patient work. But when at last we penetrate to its real meaning, we find ourselves deep in the dreamer's secrets and discover with astonishment that an apparently quite senseless dream is in the highest degree significant, and that in reality it speaks only of important and serious matters.

Carl Jung

The fullest expression of the unconscious comes to us through our dreams, and, for this reason, the interpretation of dreams is a central element of natural spirituality. Unless we learn to interpret our own dreams, we cannot receive the full benefit of the individuation process. Put in religious terms, unless we learn to interpret our own dreams, we cannot listen with a fully open ear to what God is trying to tell us in our individual lives.

In Judeo-Christianity, the idea that full attention to God includes the interpretation of dreams is strongly supported by a number of passages in the Bible. Among the most striking of these in Hebrew scriptures are the stories of Joseph and Daniel, both of whom are portrayed as men of God who knew how to understand the divine messages in dreams. In Christian scriptures, one of the most dramatic examples is found in the nativity story in the book of Matthew. Five different dreams are recounted in this story, each one crucial to the survival and protection of the Christ child. Four of these dreams came to Joseph and one to the Wise Men. While this is one of the best known stories in the Bible, the fact that almost all of its action depends on dreamwork is almost never mentioned from the pulpit or portrayed in Christmas plays. And yet if viewed with open eyes, we see that it provides clear testimony for the high value in which dreams were held by the first generation of Christians.

The Gospel of Matthew happens to be the very first book of the New Testament, the place where people start when they sit down to read the Christian scriptures. It opens with a lengthy recital of the ancestry of Jesus, after which we are taken straight to Joseph's plight in learning that Mary, his betrothed, was with child. Joseph, an upright man, did not want to disgrace Mary publicly through the legal procedure of nullifying the betrothal, and so he decided to end their relationship informally. "He had made up his mind to do this," Matthew tells us,

> when the angel of the Lord appeared to him in a dream and said, "Joseph son of David, do not be afraid to take Mary home as your wife, because she has conceived what is in her by the Holy Spirit. She will give birth to a son and you must name him Jesus ['Yahweh Saves']. . . ." When Joseph woke up he did what the angel of the Lord had told him to do: he took his wife to his home and, though he had not had intercourse with her, she gave birth to a son; and he named him Jesus.

Matthew then moves directly to the story of the Wise Men who came to Jerusalem looking for the new "king of the Jews," having seen his star rise in the night sky. Pretending a religious interest,

King Herod directed the Wise Men to Bethlehem, the prophesied birthplace, and asked them to revisit him on their way home and let him know exactly where the child could be found. The Wise Men went to Bethlehem, found the Christ child, and offered him their gifts.

> But they were warned in a dream not to go back to Herod, and returned to their country by a different way. After they had left, the angel of the Lord appeared to Joseph in a dream and said, "Get up, take the child and his mother with you, and escape into Egypt, and stay there until I tell you, because Herod intends to search for the child and do away with him." So Joseph got up and, taking the child and his mother with him, left that night for Egypt, where he stayed until Herod was dead.

Matthew goes on to tell about the Slaughter of the Innocents. And then:

> After Herod's death, the angel of the Lord appeared in a dream to Joseph in Egypt and said, "Get up, take the child and his mother with you and go back to the land of Israel, for those who wanted to kill the child are dead." So Joseph got up and, taking the child and his mother with him, went back to the land of Israel. But when he learned that Archelaus had succeeded his father Herod as ruler of Judea he was afraid to go there, and being warned in a dream he left for the region of Galilee. There he settled in a town called Nazareth.

How can it be missed that Matthew's nativity story turns almost entirely upon dreams? It shows Joseph as a man who had deep trust in the divine nature of his dreams and a remarkable willingness to respond to them. People today who have not learned to work with their dreams might find the dream-guidance aspect of this story to be incredible or fanciful, a quaint way the ancients had of talking about the discernment of God's will. But for those of us who pay attention to natural spirituality, the idea that Joseph could have been so closely led by dreams is entirely credible. We, too, are taught and closely led by our dreams. We, too, change our attitudes and alter our paths and take unexpected actions because of the guidance that comes to us in the night. We know what the writer of Psalm 16 was saying when he wrote, "I bless the Lord, who is my counselor, and in the night my inmost self instructs me." And we know what Carl Jung meant when he said, "Every night a Eucharist."

Dreams, when we pay attention to them, are constantly at work offering us daily instruction, guidance, and illumination for the unique individuals that we are. Using metaphors from our own life experience, they address our particular circumstances and help us understand ourselves and our path with God. Dreams show us our truth as it really is—not as our minds think it should be nor as our hearts would like it to be, but *as it truly is*. To walk hand in hand with our dreams is to walk with the spirit of truth, with an understanding that comes to us directly from the realm of the divine.

With this in mind, we might say with all good intention that we do wish to pay attention to our dreams. However, there is a powerful force in us—always in everyone—that is highly resistant to discovering the real truth of our lives. Our minds do not want to give up their own ideas of how things are. Our hearts do not want to give up their own insistence on what is good. This force of unconsciousness often keeps us from being able to remember our dreams. Or if we remember them, it might make us feel too busy to write them down. Or if we write them down, it might keep us from putting our minds to analyzing them. Or if we analyze them, it might make us see them in the wrong terms and miss their meaning. No one is ever free of this resistance to truth; it is a natural defense of the ego's hard-won hold on life. But as we grow in consciousness, our ego gets braver and more trusting of the changes being asked of it by the wisdom of our dreams. The strength of the ego's resistance weakens and its tricks are more easily recognized.

Remembering and Recording Dreams

It is easy to dream, but it is not so easy to know what to do with our dreams. The first challenge, of course, is to remember them. For some people, this is no problem, but for others, it is, especially for individuals who are strongly extraverted. One has only so much energy available for life, and if most of it is going into outer activities, there will not be much left to activate and illuminate the inner world. Usually, however, when we consciously turn our attention toward the dream world, we do begin to remember our dreams. Talking about dreams, reading about them, writing them down, and, if possible, participating regularly in a dream group, will almost always bring dreams to consciousness, although the amount of dream material recalled will vary from person to person.

Some people do well to remember one dream a week, while others regularly remember several dreams from each night. Most of us also experience variation in dream recall in different periods in our lives. A time of trauma and transition can bring heavy dream activity, while a dramatic swing toward outer life involvement can cause the dream world to recede into darkness.

Assuming that we do remember at least some of our dreams, the next question is what to do with them? The first thing we must do is gather them up as we awaken, and for this, there must be time allowed between waking up and getting out of bed. Most dream material slips away very quickly. Outer life activity, even simple tasks like making coffee, will usually dispel it. To counter this, we must lie quietly in bed and gather up what threads and fragments we can catch and go over any story lines we can recall. Conscious thought helps solidify the material and hold it, although much of this will soon be lost if we do not then write it down.

It is very good, therefore, to allow further time in the morning for recording one's dreams. This can be done after we have made our coffee or even later in the day, although the more time that goes by, the more details will be lost and the more the mood of the dream will fade.

Setting aside time in the morning for dreamwork has the same value as taking time for prayer and meditation. I once dreamed about Julian of Norwich, the fourteenth-century anchoress who left us beautiful mystical writings. I dreamed that if she were alive today, she would not live out her spirituality in the same way she did in her day but would live closely with her dreams in a modern way.

Most people keep a separate dream journal, although others record dreams along with other journal material. While it is useful to note down associations we have with the motifs and moods of a dream, it is generally not a good idea to record our interpretations, at least not at length. Initial interpretations are almost always inadequate, and writing them down tends to freeze them, whereas if we carry them along in our minds, we can continue to work with them and readjust them to new insights. Furthermore, while it is very useful to go back from time to time and read through old dreams, it is not very rewarding to wade through the tedious windings and twistings of our old interpretations. Old dreams are like old gems, sparkling and valuable, carrying an abiding truth that we can often see more clearly as time goes on. But if they are buried in outdated musings from the past, we are less likely to want to return to them.

It is essential to index our dreams so that we can later go back and look up specific ones. Sometimes in outer life, we encounter elements that we have dreamed about earlier, sometimes years earlier, and we might want to go back and read that dream again. Often we have a dream that reminds us of one from the past and we might want to compare the two. Or we might want to refresh our memory about an insight that once came to us in a dream. *It is very hard to find a particular dream without an index.* I myself use the last few pages of my journal for this. After recording a dream, I turn to the back and list the date under which I have written and note the key motifs of the dream. It is easy at a later time to scan the index and find the dream I am looking for. Some people give titles to their dreams and use those in their index.

In writing down our dreams, we sometimes encounter the problem of how much to write. We may, for example, get more dream material than we can deal with in a practical way. A night of dreaming is like a net full of fish: we take what we can use and throw back the rest. Even material we do not consciously process does a certain amount of work in us unconsciously. And anything we miss that we really need will come around again, usually in a different form.

If it has been a night of hazy, jumbled dreaming, all we can do is gather up the fragments that we remember most clearly—the most vivid images, the strongest emotions, the most troubling scenes, or the most impressive ones. Often a small fragment yields great meaning all by itself, even when we know it was surrounded by an entire night of dreaming that can no longer be recalled. I always assume that I remember what the unconscious wants me to remember, and if it is only a fragment, it is because that was the most important message of the night.

Sometimes, on the other hand, we might recall endless details that would keep us writing for hours, none of it adding up to much of anything except a picture of confusion and lack of focus. When this is the problem, we can help bring focus to such chaotic dreaming by foregoing the many details and looking instead for what the overall theme might be. We can try to feel what part of our life the whole night of dreaming pertains to. We might also select a few of the most vivid details and look closely at them while ignoring the rest. If we can pull out a thread from an overloaded dream, the next dream might respond to our increase in focus by being more focused itself.

Some dreams feel like big dreams. They come to us with vividness and energy and powerful emotion, sometimes with archetypal material strongly present. These dreams should be reviewed in every detail and thoroughly pondered, although their full meaning may not become entirely clear for weeks, months, or even years to come. If possible they should be written down with all details included. Their energy means that they are important. The biggest of our big dreams are those I call "flagship" dreams. They project the progress of our lives forward for the next year or so, sometimes for the next several years, and in some cases for an even longer span. We are especially likely to get far-reaching flagship dreams when we first begin to pay attention to the unconscious.

There is a discernable difference between these big dreams, on the one hand, and the smaller dreams that lead us day by day through the personal developments the big dreams have projected. Smaller dreams feel less important. Their energy is weaker and they seem to have to do with ordinary daily activity. These we can think through quickly when we awaken, focusing on their stronger points and taking what bits of meaning we find in them. They will add to our understanding of what is currently going on in our lives and give hints and guidance for the immediate future. Generally, if we feel unsettled by a dream, it needs more thought, but if we feel at peace about our understanding of it, we can let it go.

Whether or not we record all of our smaller dreams depends on our inclination and on how much time we have. We can always see more in a dream when we write it down, and ideally, we should record every dream we can remember. On the other hand, we must balance our dreamwork with the legitimate demands of outer life. There is not always time to wring out the last drop of meaning. We can get just as much off balance toward too much inner life as toward too much outer life. There are even times when we may need to restore the balance toward outer life by foregoing our dream journal altogether for a while. At several points in my own journey, I have found it necessary to stop writing down my dreams for rather long periods of time. But even then, I never ceased to think about them every morning and to take what guidance I could from them, and I can still remember many of the dreams that I never recorded.

Interpreting Dreams

The next step in dreamwork is interpretation. Because our dreams are always just a little bit ahead of our consciousness, interpretation is never easy. Many people throw up their hands and assume they lack the knowledge and expertise to do it. But dreaming is a natural process that belongs to every human life. No stethoscope or x-ray equipment is needed to perceive its activity. It is an integral part of us, and that means there is something in us that knows how to respond to it at some level. Just as a person with even the most minimal musical ability can listen to music and derive some enrichment from it, so can even the least gifted dream interpreter gain something from his or her dreams. Therefore, one should approach one's dreams with confidence. The fact is that no other person, however highly trained, can ever understand a dream as well as it can potentially be understood by the one who dreamed it. Our dreams use our own language to talk about our own lives in terms best suited to our own particular consciousness.

What gets in the way of the dreamer's understanding is the resistance that comes from that very state of consciousness that is being addressed. Dreams are always seeking to make an adjustment in the way we understand things, and this requires from us a constant sacrifice of some aspect or another of our personal sense of reality. It is here that a religious attitude can be of more value than an advanced degree in psychology. The more willing we are to enter into the real give-and-take of a dialogue with the divine, the more successful we will be in interpreting our dreams. The more dedicated we are to the triumph of our own ego's point of view, the more likely we are to misinterpret our dreams or to see nothing in them at all.

This is not, however, an either/or situation. There are times when our ego needs to win at the expense of the view from the unconscious. A strong and healthy ego consciousness is the most important factor of all in the total balance of our psyches, for without the ego we cannot function in the world. The ego needs to try to understand and accommodate the unconscious, and it needs to have a willingness to sacrifice its cherished illusions, desires, and outworn truths when it sees that it must do so. But it must proceed with this at its own pace if it is not to crumple and be overrun by the potentially overwhelming power of the unconscious.

This is why it is not important that we understand everything a dream is offering. Sometimes we can handle a lot from the unconscious and other times we can handle only a little. What is important is that we start trying to understand our dreams *as best we can*. When we make this effort, our dreams respond to it by addressing themselves to our developing understanding.

The first rule of thumb in dream interpretation is that the dream is almost always a picture of our own personal truth. We look at the setting of the dream and ask, "What part of myself does this dream address?" If the setting is at the place where we work, the dream may be about our working self. As with all the examples given here, it may be about something else, the situation at work perhaps being an analogy for a problem in some other realm of our life. We always have to feel around for the arena of life to which the dream belongs. It makes sense, however, to start with the most obvious possibility.

With that caveat, it can be said that if a dream is set in a city, it may be about one's cultural self. A natural setting suggests one's earthier, instinctual self. A setting in a church is likely to be about an aspect of one's spiritual self. A fellow dream group member of mine was once dreaming of being in a hotel when, in the midst of the dream, she was explicitly instructed by the dream itself that a hotel symbolizes a situation in life that is temporary, a condition in which we live for a short time and then move on.

I myself used to often dream of being in a vacation house by a body of water. The houses and the bodies of water varied and were seldom the same as any I had known in outer life. For a long time, I had only a vague sense of the part of my life to which this setting referred, but then one night, while dreaming, the meaning clarified itself:

> *While dreaming again about a waterside vacation house, I understand for the first time that this is the theme of the family side of myself, that when you are on vacation you are in your family side, and when you are in your family side, you are on vacation. The dream then moves on to my*

> *hometown and my childhood, and I understand that this, too, refers to my family side. I sense the distinctive reality of the family side, as opposed to the work and achievement side.*

The question we must always ask about the setting, and about every aspect of the dream, is: "What do I associate with this?" And then we must listen carefully to our answers. The process of dream interpretation is very much like solving a mystery. Clues are given that must be sorted out, and some of the best clues come from our associations. We might say, "The setting reminds me of a scene from a show I just saw on television about a mother whose teenage daughter ran away." Or, "It was the town I lived in when I was first married." Or, "This place makes me think of the underground house where Peter Pan and the Lost Boys lived."

Associations like these are clues for us to follow. With the first example, we would go on to ask what part of our life is like that mother whose daughter ran away? Are we having actual, outer life difficulty with a teenage daughter? Or is there an inner problem with our youthful feminine energy? What does the dream say about this problem? It is important always to come back to the dream in this way—what does the *dream* say about it?—rather than move away from it through a chain of associations.

In the second example, our attention would be drawn to the person we were when we were first married. Is the dream saying that in some way we are still that person, that a part of ourselves has not adapted to new times and circumstances? Or perhaps it is saying that some present situation is like a new marriage for us.

In the third example, we would look to see what the dream might be saying about a part of ourselves that, like Peter Pan, does not want to grow up. And we would ponder what it means to live in a home beneath the earth.

Sometimes it is the association we make with the mood of the dream rather than with the setting that tells us what the dream is about. When we feel that the mood of the dream somehow fits a situation in outer life, then that may be the part of our life that the dream is addressing.

In always coming back to the dream from our associations, we are asking what the dream images themselves have to say to us about the arena of life that is being addressed. Is the vacation house shabby and rundown? This would suggest that our family side does not have much "money," which symbolizes psychic energy. Are we lost in the hotel? This would indicate that our temporary situation is so unfamiliar that it has put us into a state of confusion. A dream I once had suggested I was in danger because the church I was attending lacked a basement. I took this to refer to a collective spiritual situation that could be harmful to my spiritual self because it lacked roots in tradition and openness to the unconscious.

This same process of discovery must also be applied to the characters, both human and animal, who appear in our dreams. If we dream of a dog, for instance, what kind of dog is it, and what does that kind of dog suggest to us? Is it a dog we know, and if so, what do we associate with that particular dog? If we dream of a bear, what do we personally associate with bears? What do dogs or bears symbolize in a general way? And then, coming back to the dream, what does the dream tell us about this dog or this bear? With a dream animal, we can always at least know that we are being told something about our instincts.

With human characters, the situation is more complex. When we dream about someone we know but are not in a day-to-day relationship with, we can almost always be certain that we are dreaming about some part of ourselves that this person represents. This is true even when the person is our sibling, parent, or child. To find out what part this is, we ask, "What do I associate with this person? What are his or her defining characteristics? What does he or she represent to me?" Then we look for similar qualities in ourselves.

It is more confusing when we dream about someone with whom we are in an active, daily relationship. Is it a part of myself I am dreaming about? Or am I being told something about this actual person that I need to understand? Often our dreams do help us see the people in our lives more clearly, but even more often a dream is primarily about ourselves—our own mothering part, our own son aspect, our own intellectual self, our overbearing self, whatever that person represents. When a person we dream about is very close to us in outer life, it is especially difficult to see what he or she represents symbolically and to see that the dream is about a quality in ourselves and not about that other person.

This question of inner meaning or outer meaning is one of the greatest areas of ambiguity in dream interpretation. Jung suggests that when the dream is about the people and places of our everyday life, we should try first to interpret it as if it had objective, or outer, meaning. If this fits and seems to click, then we can accept the likelihood of objective meaning, although we should reflect further on the dream to see if it also applies to an aspect of ourselves. But if the interpretation does not fit the outer situation, if the objective meaning does not square with reality, then we should look for a primarily subjective, or inner, meaning.

Sometimes we dream we are with "another person" without knowing who that person is. An unknown person in a dream refers to a part of ourselves of which we are not yet fully conscious. Usually, we know whether the unknown person is male or female, and that in itself makes an important distinction about the part of ourselves to which the dream refers. Any person in a dream, whether known or unknown, who is of our same sex can be seen as a part of our shadow, which is to say it is an aspect of our outer personality of which we are not entirely conscious. A person of the opposite sex, on the other hand, refers to a contrasexual aspect of our inner selves that completes us as whole human beings.

Anima and Animus

Carl Jung understood that every man has a feminine component in his psyche and every woman has a masculine component in hers, just as in the physiological realm each sex carries a minority component of the opposite sex. He called the feminine part of a man's psyche his *anima*, or soul. The realm of the anima is the life of body and soul rather than the life of mind and spirit. A man's feminine component is present when he relates to other people, when he experiences his emotions and feelings, when he tends the limited, everyday reality of physical life, and when he is receptive to the wisdom of nature, including the unconscious.

If he relates poorly to people, if resentment, rage, and sentimentality are his predominant emotions, if he neglects the real in his pursuit of the ideal, if he tramples what is natural and ignores the unconscious, then he will have feminine figures in his dreams—anima images—who have unpleasant characteristics. They may, for example, be dangerously seductive, or blatantly hostile, or perhaps sickly or abused. The parts of a man's feminine self that are more conscious and well-developed will appear in his dreams as positive feminine figures. When an anima figure is an unknown woman, she symbolizes a part of a man's inner, feminine self that he does not yet know. When the dream figure is someone he knows, she represents an aspect of his feminine side of which he already has some consciousness.

Jung called a woman's masculine side her *animus*, or spirit. The animus presides over the life of mind and spirit rather than the life of body and soul. When a woman is speaking her mind or is inspired to action, her animus is present. When she organizes and focuses, when she appeals to high principles, when she reads, writes, and masters objective information, and when she is creatively or religiously inspired, she is experiencing her masculine side. Her animus is also present when she breaks a relationship or keeps others at a distance.

If a woman misses the point when she speaks her mind or digresses interminably, if she is generally disorganized and unfocused, if she is rigidly devoted to political, intellectual, or spiritual principles, if she is seduced away from genuine, grounded life by the lure of an intellectual, spiritual, or creative activity that arises from the collective spirit and thus is not truly her own, or if she breaks relationship destructively or alienates other people unconsciously, there will be unpleasant masculine figures in her dreams who reflect these dark aspects of her animus. The healthy and positive manifestations of her masculine spirit will be portrayed in her dreams by friendly, helpful, and sometimes loving animus figures. Unknown masculine figures will symbolize parts of her animus of which she is unconscious, while those parts with which she has some familiarity will appear in her dreams as male persons whom she knows.

It is important to keep in mind that our experience of the opposite sex is an experience of "the other," which at a deep level symbolizes our relationship with the unconscious, and through that our connection to God. Sexuality, therefore, with all its fascination and power, is linked to our experience of God. This is a difficult fact that wreaks havoc with human life when it is not properly understood. When we are young, the pull of sexuality and romantic love serves the positive purpose of entangling us in life. For the sake of the warmth and comfort of intimate human love, we risk ourselves and make decisions and commitments that establish us, however tenuously, as adult participants in the real world. Even more importantly, a close connection with the opposite sex gives us a preliminary version of a completeness and fulfillment that we are not yet ready to find wholly within ourselves.

Later in life, however, this same sexual energy can have a destructive effect when we take it to mean exactly the same thing that it meant when it came to us in our youth. The pull toward a person of the opposite sex is not always a pull toward sexual and romantic union in the outer world. It is often a pull toward a deeper level of relationship with God.

The image of woman is the image of soul for a man, and when he feels powerfully attracted to a woman, it is at some level a projection of his own soul that draws him. That woman has qualities that reflect the qualities of his soul and that need to be realized within himself. He can come closer to them by relating to her in a positive way, but he cannot make them his own by physically possessing her. Those projected qualities can only come to life within him when he accepts the painful fact that he cannot have them in the form of another person. This sacrifice of outer, physical fulfillment opens the door to a deeper, more spiritual level of relationship to the feminine within, which leads toward human wholeness and oneness with God. The same is true for a woman, who unconsciously projects her own spirit onto the man to whom she is romantically and sexually attracted. He has attributes that ultimately need to be realized in the depths of her own being.

This basic understanding of the underlying spiritual reality of our experience of the opposite sex is necessary if we are to handle wisely the images and feelings of sexuality and love that sometimes come in dreams as well as in waking life. This also applies to same-sex attraction. Is it the real person to whom we are being drawn, or is it a part of ourselves? If human warmth and companionship are lacking in our life and if the person to whom we are attracted is available and suitable, the feelings and images arising from the unconscious may have as their true goal an outer life relationship, possibly a romantic one. But it is just as likely that we are simply being invited to know and love a part of our inner being that wants to become a part of our consciousness.

Everything that belongs in us is first projected out onto the world around us—we always have to see it there before we can see it in ourselves. This means that every new aspect of our anima or animus has to be met initially in a projection onto a person of the opposite sex. It is important to keep this in mind when we awaken from a dream of a sexual or loving encounter with someone we know but with whom we do not have an actual intimate relationship. As we lie there in the warm glow of feeling that has been stirred by the dream, we must remember to ask ourselves, "What does this person represent?"

The Structure of Dream Life

All the images in a dream are important, not just the setting and the characters. The unconscious is very careful with its language. Each image is specially chosen for the nuance of meaning that it carries. It is important, therefore, to pay attention to the inanimate objects in a dream, especially the ones that remain vivid in our memories. Just as with the other components, these should be pondered for our personal associations with them and also for their general symbolic significance. We must ask: What does that bracelet remind me of? Whose car was that we were in? Where have I seen a table like that? What do bracelets, cars, or tables represent in a general way? Sometimes the key to a dream is a seemingly insignificant object or detail that we might be tempted to let go unexamined.

Dreams are not individual and unrelated. All the dreams of one night usually belong together as different views of the same subject. Dreams on successive nights form a sequence, one dream leading to the next. When we are baffled by a dream and have done all we can with it, we can let it go knowing that clarification will be coming to us in the dreams ahead, as well as in the developments of waking life.

Dream sequences form cycles that vary in duration, usually lasting for several months. We become aware of these cycles as we learn to work with our dreams. In the beginning of a cycle, our dreams will be murky, dim, and somewhat chaotic, their settings and the people in them will tend to be unfamiliar, and we will not be able to remember much about them when we awaken. In waking life, we might feel vaguely out of sorts, a bit unfocused and unsure of what we are about.

Then gradually life begins to sort itself out. Our dreams become a little clearer and we begin to recognize their themes. There begins to be a noticeable interaction between dream life and waking life—the two work together to develop our themes and to bring us new understandings. As our dreams grow in clarity, life develops in decisive ways. Sometimes the new understandings culminate in a dream that lays out a relatively explicit picture of what we have come through and what we have learned. I call these "summary" dreams. There will also be events in outer life that add to the feeling that we have come through to something new.

Then for a few days, at most, we feel at peace. Life is in balance. These little respites that come between cycles remind me of how the hobbit heroes in Tolkien's *Lord of the Rings* were always given brief interludes of rest, feasting, and singing in the mystical safety of elven glens after each stage of their harrowing adventure. Like the hobbits, we are never allowed to linger in this restful place for long. Before we know it, another cycle has started. Once more our dreams are dark and murky and our life feels somewhat out of joint as the next phase in our journey begins to take shape.

Giving Dreams Their Proper Weight

As we take up the task of paying attention to our dreams, we must go through a process of learning just how much weight to give them. It usually requires several years to work this out. Those of us who identify very strongly with consciousness and outer life will at first give our dreams too little weight. We will use "nothing but" statements in regard to them: "This dream was nothing but me dreaming about some things that happened the day before." Or, "It was nothing but me worrying about my situation at work." Or, "That dream of someone knocking was nothing but the shade bumping against the window." This is a very common attitude in the beginning.

When we do this, we are interpreting our dreams as if they can only complement or support what we already know. Having not yet truly accepted the fact that it is possible for dreams to bring us new information, let alone that this is their main function, we fail to ask, "What is the compensatory purpose of this dream? What does it tell me that I do not already know?"

It is also symptomatic of undervaluing dreams when we go to the trouble of recording our dreams and yet can never make heads or tails of them, or when we pay attention to our dreams for a while, but then turn away for a long period and reimmerse ourselves completely in outer life. We have not yet had enough experience with our inner life to realize that it is worth the effort to learn its language and to keep up with it every day.

Others of us begin dreamwork off balance in the other direction. In this case, we identify especially strongly with the unconscious and give too much weight to our dreams. Often we try to use our dreams as power tools to know the future or to engineer outer events. On the basis of a dream, for instance, I might call up an acquaintance and say, "I dreamed about you last night. I think that means we need to get together." In fact, the dream probably had nothing to do with that other person but was all about a part of myself. This arranged meeting, therefore, is likely to be empty of any real meaning and purpose and will probably strike the other person as somewhat weird.

Those of us who give too much weight to our dreams have to learn that life proceeds from life, not from dreams. Life has its own reality, with one real moment leading to the next. Dreams do their work on the inside, beneath the surface, helping us understand things more clearly, giving us hints and helpful leads. It is wonderful that we have these marvelous communications from the unconscious, but when it comes to integrating them into life, they are merely factors to be considered, additional aspects to be weighed in and measured against our actual experience of life.

If life opens to what we think a dream is saying, then we can go with it, cautiously. But if life is resistant, it may be because we are not seeing the dream clearly. Or it may be that we do see a truth clearly but that the world around us is not ready to accept that truth. There is nothing we can do about this. We cannot use our dreams as weapons to badger other people into seeing what we see. That never works and only brings us trouble. Life proceeds from life and no other way. A person in touch with her dreams has to learn to walk silently at times as the only one who sees certain realities beneath the surface of her shared life with others.

As for the value of dreams in foretelling the future, it is true that dreams are oriented primarily toward life that is unfolding. What they tell us, however, is the *essence* of what is coming, not how that essence will be made manifest. Dreams of death and of weddings, for example, are usually about inner, psychological developments, although occasionally they are about actual outer-life realities. The problem is that much the same symbolism is used for both inner and outer developments. It is tempting to say, "I know from my dreams that so and so is going to happen." But after a while, we learn that we can never be sure what is actually going to happen in outer life, even though we can get some sense from our dreams about the essence or underlying truth of what is coming.

Some dreams about the future are warning dreams. The essence they show is not what necessarily *will* be but what *could* be if we fail to grasp the reality of our situation. Many dreams are not about the future at all but about what is happening now. Others are about what has already taken place, sometimes in the recent past, sometimes in the distant past. Still others give us a picture of what we fear to be true in order to help us see that it is not true. We awaken from these with our hearts pounding, thinking, "There! It is just as I feared!" But as we try to line ourselves up with the picture the dream has given us, we begin to realize it does not fit the reality of our situation. The picture in the dream is *not true.* Our fears are *not true.* The dream has objectified them for us so that we can see them clearly and measure them against reality.

A Supporting Context for Dreamwork

There is no easy formula for understanding dreams. Some people have a greater gift for it than others. Anyone who is serious about his dreamlife, however, whether he is especially gifted or not, needs to do extensive reading in Jungian psychology, a field in which much has been written for laypeople. The reading list in Appendix C is offered as a starting place for this.

It is also important to have an interested person with whom to talk about one's dreams, even if that person does not understand very much. Telling a dream to someone else does something to illuminate it, whether the other person has anything helpful to say about it or not. It is as if in the presence of another consciousness, our own consciousness can more easily expand and open itself to intuitive insight.

Where it is feasible, a weekly dream group can be of great value in keeping us focused on our dream lives and in giving us help in interpreting our dreams. Others in the group can often show us our blind spots. And by listening to the dreams of others, we learn more than we otherwise would about dream interpretation and the universal themes of human growth and development.

The value of other people when working on our dreams has in it something of what Jesus meant when he said that wherever two or three are gathered together in his name, he will be there. The living spirit of the divine plays a large role in dream interpretation, provided we go about it with a religious attitude, aware that dreams come from the realm of the divine and have to do with the fulfillment of our divinely intended life, which is not necessarily the same life our ego has in mind for us. When that is the spirit in which we are discussing a dream, insights almost always come to the surface once we begin to make our associations with its images. It is for this reason that the best context for a weekly dream group is one that includes an explicitly spiritual component.

I am continually amazed at the process through which clarity arises from even the most puzzling of dreams. Often when a person tells me a dream, he or she has no idea of what it means, and when I hear it, I also have no idea. I wonder to myself how we will ever find anything in it. But then we begin to talk about it. We start at the beginning and look at the setting or the opening situation. What are the dreamer's associations? What does the dream situation say symbolically? Then we look at the characters and the other striking images. We talk about these, and before we know it an element of the dreamer's life has come to the fore and we are beginning to grasp something of what the dream might be saying about it.

We keep talking, looking at the dream this way and that, always paying attention to what the dreamer herself is saying. The elements of the dream lead the dreamer to talk about her life in words that are significant. The way the dream unfolds suggests connections and underlying realities that begin to coalesce for us. Then finally comes the "Aha!" moment when the dreamer feels we have found the key. An important insight "clicks," and she feels satisfied that yes, this is what this dream is saying, now she has seen something that helps. It does not matter whether she has gotten from the dream all that someone else might have gotten. She has gotten from it what she was able to get, and the unconscious can work with that and build on it in future dreams.

This is typically how it goes when we work with our dreams, whether we ponder them alone or talk them over with others. Our penetration into the meaning does not depend solely on human skill and knowledge. The message of the dream comes from the realm of the divine, and the living spirit of the divine participates in our understanding of it. It is necessary that we apply ourselves and do our part in working with our dreams, but in the end, it is grace working in us that makes the difference and helps us arrive at those insights that we are ready to receive.

Chapter Seven
Synchronicity

Since psyche and matter are contained in one and the same world and moreover are in continuous contact with one another and ultimately rest on irrepresentable, transcendental factors, it is not only possible but fairly probable, even, that psyche and matter are two different aspects of one and the same thing. The synchronicity phenomena point, it seems to me, in this direction, for they show that the nonpsychic can behave like the psychic, and vice versa, without there being any causal connection between them.

Carl Jung

I did not learn about synchronicity from Carl Jung. I learned the *term* from him, but the natural reality to which it refers is something I first discovered for myself. This was not an intentional discovery. It would never have occurred to me to look for a manifestation of meaning in the natural world. Rather, the realization of synchronicity forced itself upon me, causing me much anxiety and dread, an anxiety which arose in part from my lack of knowledge that any other modern person understood the world in this way.

My awakening to synchronicity happened gradually over a period of a little more than a year, the first year of my midlife crisis. While I struggled to adjust to the disorienting events in my life during that time, I noticed that little things happening in the outer world seemed strangely meaningful. Birds made dramatic appearances in significant times and places. There were startlingly coincidental meetings with persons about whom I had just been thinking or speaking. Even more disturbing were the objects, places, and circumstances I sometimes encountered for the first time in outer life *after* I had dreamed about them. I did not know how to think about any of this except with the idea that God had something to do with it.

After about a year of these sorts of observations, I found the work of Carl Jung. I did not, however, immediately come across a discussion of synchronicity, for Jung elaborated upon this phenomenon in very few places in all his written works. For most of his life, Jung felt that if he made too much of synchronicity he would be misunderstood and dismissed as a mystic even more than he already was. So at first I found only hints of it. What I did find explicitly laid out in Jung's writings was the notion of the unconscious and the symbolic reality of dreams. Putting this with my experience of strangely meaningful events in outer life, I began to formulate the idea that in a certain sense life itself is like a dream, that it can be read and interpreted symbolically just as a dream can be.

This was still an idea and not true knowledge, but it was leading me close to the breakthrough realization toward which this stormy period in my life was leading. With this, my anxiety intensified, an inner state that my reading of Jung helped me understand. I understood that a new truth was trying to come through from the unconscious and that my ego consciousness felt threatened and was trying to bar the door, thus raising this great anxiety. My old consciousness feared its imminent death, for it was about to be superseded by a new level of consciousness. Although understanding the anxiety did not make it go away, it helped me bear the process. Part of myself could stand aside and watch and analyze while the other part suffered through a psychological death and rebirth, a harrowing baptism in the symbolic waters of the unconscious.

It was at this time that I sought help from the priest at my church. In him I found someone who could listen while I talked about all that was happening to me. Even though he had not been through a similar experience, he was able to comprehend my journey with his intellect and feel it with his soul, and thus he provided crucial support for me in an hour of great need.

This intensified period of anxiety began on the exact day of Ash Wednesday and lasted through the forty days of Lent without resolution, although some progress was made during this time. I was watching my dreams very carefully, and even though I was still a novice at interpreting them, I was able to gain the important realization that I identified more strongly with my father than with my mother and that my feminine being was therefore neglected and underdeveloped. This knowledge was crucial to the process, but it was not the great breakthrough toward which the anxiety was pitched. Another important development during this time was the discovery that my inner processes—my thoughts and emerging understandings and the themes arising from my dreams—were running in tandem with the Sunday scripture readings and sermons. The parallel was uncanny. This heightened my sense of the significance of my journey.

Then on Good Friday the real breakthrough began. Late that afternoon I met my husband at a movie theater to see *Amadeus*, the story of the life of Mozart. This was a troubling time in our marriage. For sixteen years we had been close companions, sharing our thoughts, feelings, and understandings. But now that I was going through this deep water, my husband could no longer understand my experience. I had to keep most of it to myself, which I found to be very difficult. I worried that the change through which I was passing would separate us so much that it would bring an end to our marriage. As it happened, *Amadeus*, with its depth of spirit, was a good film for us to see at this time. We both were deeply moved by it, and it helped us feel connected again, giving us a little respite from our trials.

When we came out of the theater, darkness had fallen. We were in separate vehicles, he in our pickup truck, I in our car, and so we parted for the thirty-minute drive to our home in the country. As I drove out of town onto the rural roads, a spring storm began to blow in, the wind growing stronger and stronger, whipping the trees under a darkened night sky. When the rain finally came, it was a tremendous downpour, a deluge. Though I could barely see in front of me, the shoulder of the road was not wide enough to let me safely pull over and stop. Creeping along, I finally came to a place where the shoulder widened around someone's driveway. There I stopped and waited. I had never been out in such a storm. Branches of trees were blowing across the road before me. Knowing that tornados come in storms like this, I felt grimly that I could die there.

Another vehicle pulled up behind me on what was left of that little wide spot beside the road. I thought how comforting it would be if that were my husband. I imagined running back and jumping in the truck with him and the two of us waiting out the storm together. But I knew how unlikely it was that it would be he since we had not stayed together in the traffic after we left the theater. Anyway, I would get drenched the second I stepped out of the car, and whoever was back there would think I was out of my mind coming up to peer in their window at them. So I sat alone and waited, my headlights and those behind me illuminating the storm.

After a little while, the rain began to let up and the wind dropped. As I pulled back onto the road, the vehicle behind me followed. When I got far enough ahead of it to be able to see it without being blinded by its lights, I saw to my joy that it was indeed my husband. He had been with me all along, following behind in his sturdy truck, weathering the storm with me, even though we each had to experience it separately and alone. Now as the storm passed, he was still with me, following me home.

That event spoke powerfully to me about our marriage in this stormy time. But how did one think about something like that? Was it all just happenstance? Or did God make that storm just to bring that message to me? That idea seemed absurd, much too egocentric to be seriously considered. And yet I knew that the incident had real meaning for me, that the images through which it spoke were just right, and that its message felt like a gift from God. *But how to think about it?* That was the great question for me now.

Although Easter Sunday passed without a resurrection experience, the new truth that began emerging on Good Friday continued to unfold. On the Monday after Easter, I realized that a particular dream about an important personal matter had been repeated in various forms on all the major religious holidays since Christmas. These were the only times I had dreamed this particular theme. I had had one of these dreams on Christmas night, another on the eve of Epiphany, another on the eve of Ash Wednesday, and yet another on Easter Eve. This particular realization hit me especially hard and raised my anxiety to new heights.

I was learning from this experience that the oft-repeated phrase in the Old Testament that the fear of God is the beginning of wisdom means what it says. It means fear, not awe. The realization that God is not an abstract principle "out there" somewhere in a vaguely removed spiritual realm but is actually present in the natural events of one's life, orchestrating those events toward an end one has not chosen and cannot fathom, is truly frightening. It means the end of the ego's illusion of control. It means one's life is not in one's own hands. Someone else is calling the shots.

I wrote in my journal that day: "That business of the dreams and the church holy days is certainly the finger of God on me. That is what has thrown me so. Now I *know* I'm not in control. My intellect doesn't see how I can go on like this, but some other part of me knows that I can."

The next day I went to my appointment with my priest friend. I told him about the dreams lining up with the holy days and about the storm on Good Friday. He did not know how to think about these things either. Having the answers, however, is not the only way to help another person. I also told him of a dream I had had recently about being in a clear, natural pool of water and of dropping something I had been holding in my hand. I dove down deep to the bottom to retrieve it.

"What was it?" he asked.

"I'm not sure," I said. "I think it was a hair comb, the kind a woman uses to hold back her hair."

He looked at me for a moment without speaking. There was love in his eyes and a kind of amazement. Then he ran his hand over his arm. "That gives me chills," he said. We both understood that the dream was a picture of me retrieving my feminine being from the depths of the unconscious.

That moment of human connection, of love, empathy, and understanding, registered deeply in my soul and gave me the courage I needed to stand firm and claim the new reality that was coming through. On the morning after that conversation, I was standing on my back porch when I suddenly saw clearly the new truth.

I knew in that moment that everything around me was in some sense an image of what was within me. Those birds were my thoughts flying by. Those trees were my rootedness. This house was a manifestation of my personality. All was Being. All was God. Within and without, it was all the same. And I knew that everything out there, all of Being, was working to bring me into my own true being. I knew that when I failed to understand things on the inside, the world outside would speak the meaning. I knew what Jesus meant when he said on Palm Sunday that if his supporters were silenced in their celebration of his entry into Jerusalem, the very stones would cry out. I understood that stones *do* cry out, that in its symbolic language the physical world *does* speak. I also understood in that moment that God did not send that storm on Good Friday just for me. That storm was there for *all* the people who experienced it in *all* the different ways it was experienced.

I wrote in my journal that day: "Today I know that all of Being wants me to be. We are all one with all Being. The very stones cry out. They always have. I just didn't hear them."

What followed was two or three weeks of intense synchronistic experiences, a constant flow of messages constellating in the ordinary events of the world around me, a flood that gradually decreased to a manageable level. It was as if the flow of life had been closed off and was suddenly open again, rushing out under the pressure of its impoundment and stabilizing only gradually into a moderate, steady stream. It was a challenge for me to take in this heightened experience, but it no longer felt so threatening, and my anxiety gradually dissipated.

Once I said yes to synchronicity, the worst of my crisis was over. My old consciousness was dead and in its place a new consciousness had arisen that allowed for a more meaningful connection between my inner psychic processes and the physical world around me. I still had to learn how to live with this new ingredient of life, how to balance it with all the other ingredients that were already there, but through my experience of it, I gradually learned how much weight to give it and became accustomed to it.

Synchronistic experiences are now an ordinary aspect of my daily life. I am guided by them in the same way I am guided by the weather or by a hunger pain or by the look in another person's face. To live with synchronicity is to maintain a waking relationship with the unconscious, to be always alert to God's will and meaning and to be guided by that with unusual precision. Synchronicity, once admitted into consciousness, reinforces itself, for one quickly learns that life goes better with it than without it.

The Wisdom of Nature: Mother God

Carl Jung understood synchronicity to be an acausal connecting principle that is present in nature. Through it, events in life are linked not by physical cause and effect but by meaning arising from the unconscious. Synchronicity does not deny or negate causality, but instead it exists alongside it.

For example, my experience with the storm on Good Friday can be thoroughly explained by cause and effect. A warm front met a cold front, and a storm resulted. My husband and I were in separate vehicles because there was not time before the movie started for him to come home from work and ride back into town with me. He pulled into that spot behind me during the storm because he saw my car there and because he, too, needed to get off the road. All of this, perfectly obvious to my rational mind, was never in doubt. But there was more to that event than these mechanical details. There was also a nonrational element involved. My soul recognized a display of meaning, and my mind joined with my soul to process that meaning. My deepest being reverberated with it, and I was changed by it. Causality and acausality, rationality and nonrationality, meaninglessness and meaningfulness existed together in those events, a balance of opposites, neither pole negating the other.

It is significant that my awakening to synchronicity came in conjunction with my awakening to the more personal issue of my own lost feminine being. In a way, my individual problem was a reflection of the larger, collective problem of our time. Since the rise of modern scientific rationalism in the seventeenth century, the Western world as a whole has come to identify more with the "father" than with the "mother." With the seeming triumph of rationality over nonrationality, of mechanistic science over spirituality, of the outer world over the inner world, feminine reality, which has to do with inner life and the connectedness of all things, has, as in my dream, dropped from our hands and sunk down into the depths of the collective unconscious, denigrated and denied. One end of the pole of opposites on which the world is balanced has almost overturned the other, and an out-of-balance, neurotic world has been the result.

This seems to have been an inevitable stage of our human development. Rational and scientific thought had to come into our consciousness and establish itself as a necessary counterbalance to the naive medieval worldview, which was one-sidedly nonrational and spiritual. In the usual way of new developments, scientific rationalism seemed at first to be the ultimate achievement and final answer to life. But inevitably this has proved not to be so. Now we must retrieve the lost value, bring up the denied nonrational element, the feminine reality of the connectedness of all things, and integrate this with the masculine reality of rationality and scientific thought. If we are to be healthy and whole, it cannot be one or the other. It has to be both.

Modern science does not stand in conflict with synchronicity. Twentieth-century physics has shown the universe to be a single fabric, a unified field of energy. Solid objects are not ultimately separate and distinct but are concentrations of energy in the unified field. Time and space are relative. Until they are observed—until they enter consciousness—subatomic particles are only waves of probability, which means that nothing is absolutely predictable but only statistically probable. In such a world there is room for synchronicity, regardless of whether we fully understand it or not. The physicists themselves do not fully understand the phenomena *they* are observing. Despite the best efforts of scientific rationalism, mystery has not been eradicated from life after all.

Although there is a spiritual element in synchronicity, it is no more a supernatural phenomenon than dreams are. Both are natural. Just as most people begin to remember their dreams when they turn their attention to them, so do most people begin to notice synchronicity when they turn their attention to it. Even more than dreams do, synchronicity makes us aware of the divine Wisdom at the heart of natural life. This is the Wisdom of which the Old Testament speaks: "She is so pure, she pervades and permeates all things. She is a breath of the power of God."

In the Wisdom of nature, we rediscover the aspect of God that is "Mother." The words "matter" and "material" are derived from *mater*, the Latin word for "mother." In synchronicity we experience the material world as a vibrant expression of divine motherhood, an aspect of the divine that is present in created life and provides us with nourishment and support both physically and spiritually.

My experience in the storm on Good Friday was like the comforting words of a wise mother: "Don't worry. Go forward with courage through this storm of growth and change. He will stay by you. He will come along in his own way." In times of tumult and change, times when we need a greater wisdom than we actually possess, synchronicity is especially active. Most people have noticed it around the events of a death or at the beginning of a significant new relationship.

There are also times when a synchronistic display of meaning breaks into our complacency, times when we are not aware of any particular issues. At times like this synchronicity tries to wake us up to a mistaken path or to alert us to an unrecognized truth beneath our outward journey. One clear example of the latter occurred in our church one Easter morning. The church was full. Spirits were high. The choir was larger than usual and augmented by trumpets. As we were singing a hymn in the middle of the service, a vase of Easter lilies fell from the altar to the floor. I immediately looked to see what words we were singing at the moment the vase fell: "The Spirit's power shakes the church of God." Seeing those words underlined by God on that Easter morning was a moving, grace-filled moment that few others in the church shared with me, though the event was there for all to see. Most people saw nothing but a mishap—water on the carpet, a glitch in the service.

So much that happens to us is experienced as annoyance when it is actually meant to get our attention in order to alter our course or to teach us something. The key is often to be found in the coincidence between the startling or annoying event and what we are doing or saying or thinking at that same moment. Such manifestations of the divine arise out of nature itself and are fully in keeping with physical laws. The vase of lilies fell because of the vibrations of the music—the pipe organ, trumpets, and voices—and because someone had placed it too near the edge of the altar. The mystery was in the timing. That was where the unconscious revealed itself. In living with synchronicity one learns to accept this nonrational but undeniable aspect of reality. One gets used to the idea that through the Self, the unifying principle that is both within us and around us, God coordinates the life of the world in something of the same way a composer coordinates the many parts of a symphony or a writer ties together the many threads of a book. At the bottom of physical life, somewhere below the subatomic particles, there is this mystery.

Artists of Life

Through synchronicity the physical world not only manifests meaning but it also provides for our physical needs, just as a mother takes care of her children. As Jesus pointed out in his lilies-of-the-field teaching, every day brings its own difficulties and its own solutions. The answer to an immediate problem is always at hand, even though that answer might be that we must submit to misfortune. The question is whether we are open to the answer, whether our conscious attitude is flexible enough for us to recognize and follow the true path of the moment. There is in the midst of the chaos and tumult of everyday life a vital flow that is the true "river of life, rising from the throne of God," and our challenge through the moments of our lives is to recognize it and join with it.

For example, there is an answer to the demands on our time, a way through the hours of the day. Synchronicity gives us hints. The phone call that will not go through may not need to be made. The elevator that is too full directs us to the stairwell where we meet just the person we need to see. The jammed aisle at the grocery store gives us the hint that the meal we had planned, from whose main ingredient we are being blocked, is too elaborate, that the simpler solution that now comes to mind would be better.

Through synchronicity the unexpected check comes in the mail just in time to cover the unexpected dental expenses. The car breaks down near a gas station that has a mechanic on duty. We find the shoes our daughter needs at a bargain price we can afford. A friend happens to call just at the time we are beginning to sink into an emotional quagmire. We uncharacteristically forget our car keys and go grumbling back into the house where we discover we had turned a stove burner to "High" instead of "Off."

Through synchronicity we learn that life has its own Wisdom, much greater than our own, and that to avail ourselves of it, we must be constantly aware and alert. Attunement to synchronicity makes us artists of life, conscious participants in God's creative spirit. With its help, our efforts become more effective, more graceful, more meaningful, more helpful to others, and more satisfying to ourselves. And although synchronicity does not shield us from difficulty and pain, it brings mercy into our dark times in the way events unfold.

There is no method that can be taught for how to live with synchronicity. Each of us must begin to notice it for ourselves and work out our own relationship with it. The vital stream that flows through life is different for each individual, so that what glows with meaning for me in the unfolding of a moment may not mean anything to the person standing next to me. It is the connection to our inner processes that gives meaning to what would otherwise be meaningless.

In working with synchronicity, we must learn how to balance it with ordinary consciousness. Because synchronicity is an expression of the unconscious, it functions as a compensation to consciousness, just as dreams do. Our proper relationship to it is a dialogue, our own consciousness neither overrunning it nor being overrun by it. It is very much like a relationship with a spouse. We supply conscious intent and direction, while synchronicity supplies encouragement, hints, or corrections. We weigh its suggestions and decide for ourselves what to think or how to proceed. If we look to it too much for guidance, we fall into a muddle, for consciousness, as a rule, needs to be strong and to keep charge of itself. But if we fail to take account of it and push on stubbornly against the flow of life, we wear ourselves out and experience difficulties or even tragedies that might have been avoided.

Synchronicity calls us to an attitude toward life that is unceasingly religious in the truest sense of the word. Without it, religious life is reduced to a one-sided affair that depends primarily upon our intentional engagement in prayer, reflection, and good works. While these are important, they are not enough. The natural spirit, with all its dynamic expression, is left out. But when we are open to synchronicity, life itself teems with the presence of God. Synchronicity calls from us careful and constant watching and following, and it can fill us at any moment with amazement and thanksgiving. It is all we can do to keep up with its dialogue and to play our part as servants of the divine in the lively drama of creation.

Part Three

The Individuation Journey

Chapter Eight
The Opposites

IN THE LAST FEW PARAGRAPHS of the Bible, we read:

> "Alleluia! The reign of the Lord our God Almighty has begun; . . . this is the time for the marriage of the Lamb. His bride is ready. . . ."
>
> Then I saw a new heaven and a new earth. . . . I saw the holy city, the new Jerusalem, coming down from God out of heaven, as beautiful as a new bride all dressed for her husband. . . .
>
> The Spirit and the Bride say, "Come." Let everyone who listens answer, "Come." Then let all who are thirsty come: All who want it may have the water of life, and have it free.

With this climax, the Judeo-Christian scriptures come to a close. All who want it may have the water of life, symbol of the unconscious, and have it free. And this is firmly linked with the symbolism of mystical marriage.

What does marriage mean fundamentally? It is the union of opposites, the joining together of the basic polarity of life—the masculine and the feminine—those opposing realities whose differences are never resolved except at a transcendent level of conjunction symbolized by the image of marriage.

When we apply the Jungian tools to our individual journeys and begin to pay attention to dreams and synchronistic experience, we find that the problem of reconciling the masculine and feminine elements of our own lives rises to prominence in the dialogue that comes from the unconscious. The road toward God is a road toward marriage, not in the outer world but within ourselves. It is a road toward a wedding of opposites that seeks to take place in the depths of our own being.

Chinese Taoists understand that Tao, the ultimate source of life, which is both unknowable and undefinable, contains within itself a basic polarity which they call *yin* and *yang*. In the Tao that precedes existence, the opposites are in an undifferentiated state of primal unity. But when Tao manifests itself, primal unity breaks apart into yin and yang, and it is the interaction of these two poles that produces "the ten thousand things," the profusion of life.

There are many pairs of opposites with which we have to struggle in human life: maturity and youth, culture and nature, tradition and innovation, home and work, spirituality and worldliness. The list could go on and on. But Taoism understands that underneath all these varieties of opposition lies the primal opposition of yin and yang.

Yin is associated with femaleness and yang with maleness, but the idea behind them is more complex than this and their basic meanings do not contain explicit gender references. The original written Chinese character for yin signified "cloud" and carried the idea of a dark cloud that overshadows earth and brings life-giving rain. The original character for yang signified a yak-tail and conveyed the idea of a pennant fluttering in the sun. Later a classifier signifying "mountain slope" was added to each. Yin then became "dark mountain slope," and yang, "light mountain slope." Together they convey the idea of a valley with a shaded slope and a sunny slope. This is the valley of life, which has two sides, dark and light, neither of which can be separated from the other.

A pennant fluttering in the sun is a beautiful image of the masculine principle. This is the principle of inspired activity, of high hopes and exciting ideas, of will and purpose, of ideal and perfection, of objectivity, theory, and abstraction. The masculine principle is the principle of heaven, and as such it is free from the constraints of material reality. Reality is only present in the masculine principle as a seed of desire: the pure idea wants to be realized. But for this, it must join itself to the feminine principle of earth and accept the limitations that come with physical being.

When a cloud passes overhead and brings rain for the life of the earth, the pennant's high moment in the sun is interrupted. Wherever darkness is found on earth, something physically real and solid has blocked out or reduced the light of heaven and made a kind of closed in, interior space. That solidity that forms a barrier to the light might be the droplets of water and dust in a cloud, the leaves of a tree, the roof of a cave or a house, or the other side of the earth itself as night begins to fall. The feminine principle is the principle of matter, of solidity and physical reality. It is the principle of the interconnections and relationships that form the complex web of life. It is the principle of nature with its seasons and cycles of birth, growth, and death and its mechanisms of compensation, adaptation, and balance. It is life as it is, healthy or stunted, whole or maimed, easy or difficult, without regard to perfection or ideal but only to overall balance.

The feminine principle is completely absorbed in its own process. Like a cat stalking a bird or a calf frolicking in a field, it is not hampered by consciousness of what it is. It has no outside vantage point from which to view itself, no ideal standard by which to measure itself. And because of that, because the masculine principle is missing, it cannot rise above itself. And yet the seeds of the masculine are present in it. In moments of discomfort or distress, natural life wants to be perfected. Rain-soaked creatures want to be dry. Drought-stricken plants want rain. Parent birds want to keep snakes from raiding their nests. Nature contains this seed of desire to rise above its own limitations. Earth longs for heaven just as heaven longs for earth.

This primal longing and seeking is the image with which the Judeo-Christian scriptures begin. *In the beginning God created the heavens and the earth.* Out of the primal, unknowable, preexistent source that is God comes the first manifestation of Being: the polarity of heaven and earth. *The earth was without form and void, and darkness was upon the face of the deep.* Here is one pole—matter—the realm of physical reality. But there is no consciousness, no idea by which to grasp or know anything in it, no light of understanding by which one thing can be distinguished from another. It slumbers in its own unknowing, its natural processes shrouded in darkness, unseen and unnamed. *And the Spirit of God was moving over the face of the waters.* Here is the other pole—spirit—the dynamic realm of idea and perfection. The primal unity has been broken apart. The two poles show themselves, hovering together, and for a moment each is distinct from the other. Then they begin their interaction. *God said, "Let there be light," and there was light.* The masculine side of God provides the idea, the feminine side provides the substance, and the world comes into being.

This same principle can also be seen in modern physics where it has been discovered that subatomic particles exist only as waves of probability until they are observed. The observing consciousness is the masculine principle. The waves of probability are the feminine principle. Only when they are joined together does the world as we know it come into being.

It is important to understand that masculine and feminine are divine principles of equal value, each with its part to play as a basic component of creation. Their interaction and balance determine the health and viability of life as we know it. As human beings, we carry the opposites within our species as male and female creatures. We also carry both sides of the opposites within our individual selves: each of us struggles to reconcile earthly reality (the feminine) with aspirations and ideals (the masculine). This does not mean, however, that both sexes carry masculinity and femininity in the same way. Ideally, a man carries masculinity on the outside, in his personal identity, and is softened or gentled by femininity as an inner quality, while a woman carries femininity in her personal outer identity and is strengthened or supported by masculinity as an inner quality. This ideal state does not come about automatically, however. To identify oneself superficially with one's own gender is not the same as identifying with the actual properties of that gender principle.

An effort is required to become conscious of the masculine and feminine principles as they exist in our own being, and until we can differentiate between them, they tend to get mixed up. Sorting them out is a difficult task for everyone. It is only because we are conscious beings that we have to grapple with the problem of the opposites. In the rest of creation, this dance proceeds unconsciously. If we were nothing more than unconscious creatures of nature, we would do our part instinctively and the balance of life would automatically be maintained. But as conscious beings, we have a will that can to some extent put us in opposition to nature and threaten the balance inherent in creation. We can align ourselves too much with the masculine principle—women can do this as well as men—and then life as it is begins to suffer at the expense of our excessive striving toward what could be or ought to be. Or we can cling too tightly to the feminine principle, and then life as it is begins to carry too much weight and to swallow up what could be or what ought to be.

The opposites turn in and out upon themselves. A close look at any polarized situation will reveal its converse present within it. Too much masculine striving, for example, will suddenly flip over and show another side—too much feminine holding hiding underneath it. One is lived consciously, the other unconsciously. Nothing is simple and straightforward when it comes to the problem of the opposites.

Our personal relationship to the masculine and feminine principles, to spirit and matter, is reflected in every aspect of our lives—in our physical and mental health, in our material well-being, in our relationships, in our intellectual life, creativity, and spirituality, in our capacity for initiative and our capacity for contentment. If we are to find redemption and resolution for the problems of our lives and live toward the inner marriage to which the way of the divine calls us, we must become conscious of the opposites. We must understand what is feminine in us and what is masculine and allow these two principles to find their right relationship. They cannot be consciously related until they are consciously separated. Each principle must be recognized and honored in its own right. Only then can the two come together in true union.

Physical sexuality is but a small part of our experience of the opposites, much of which takes place in our inner lives and in outer expressions that do not involve sexual intimacy. The full range of human sexuality exists in all of us and is experienced by us in one way or another as we pass through phases of separating and strengthening the opposing principles and then conjoining them. The part of this process that seeks expression through physical sexuality depends upon the make-up of each individual. I once had a dream in regard to the variety of sexual expression:

> *I am shown that there are several sexual packages, so to speak, different ways of being sexual. Each one is suited to certain circumstances, thus allowing us to meet the need to be sexual in a way that goes with the particular person that each of us is. The idea seems to be that different human configurations carry different requirements and difficulties in regard to sexuality. Sexuality itself, the dream seems to say, is not a part of any human configuration but only a package that is compatible with that configuration.*
>
> *Homosexuality is given as an example. It is one of the packages, but it is not a basic human configuration. The basic configuration would be something non-sexual, such as being a Wise Man [see Chapter Nine], who by first nature is more connected to the spiritual aspect of the feminine than to the physical aspect. When this is a man's basic configuration, homosexuality is a sexual package that can fit his needs.*
>
> *The idea is also present that although sexuality at the physical level is not terribly important, everyone needs to spend some time with it. That is why the variety of sexual packages has been made available.*

When we think about the sexuality of our lives, therefore, we should move away from the limited idea of physical sexuality and begin to notice the deeper and more meaningful ways in which our experience of the opposites pervades every aspect of our existence.

Sun and Moon: Symbols of the Opposites

A good way to begin thinking about the opposing attributes of the masculine and feminine principles is to consider the differences between the sun and the moon. As the two principal sources of natural light, the sun and moon symbolize our two principal modes of consciousness. Although some of the world's mythologies have considered the sun to be feminine and the moon to be masculine, it is much more common to find the sun linked to the masculine principle and the moon to the feminine. It is not that one mythology is right and the other is wrong, but rather that different attributes of the opposites appear depending upon the lens through which they are being viewed. Using the more common lens, we can learn much about the polar qualities of the opposites by looking at the sun as a symbol of masculine consciousness and the moon as a symbol of feminine consciousness.

Just as sunlight is hard and bright and moonlight is soft and mellow, so is masculine consciousness by nature concentrated and focused, while feminine consciousness is more gentle and diffuse. Masculine consciousness focuses intently on one thing at a time and carries one overriding idea at a time. Everything else tends to be closed out as extraneous and distracting. This concentration allows accomplishments that might not be possible by a less focused approach. Feminine consciousness, on the other hand, takes in the whole picture, moves easily from one aspect of a situation to another, and holds many strands together without concentrating exclusively on any one part. This is the consciousness that is needed for tending life, for keeping an eye on children, for taking care of the many details of a household or an office, and for maintaining the cohesion and health of a group by noticing the feelings and needs of all the different members.

Both men and women have access to each kind of consciousness. In most cases, however, a man will be healthier and more whole if he meets the world with focused consciousness and cultivates diffuse consciousness as an inner, spiritual quality which balances and tempers his outer way. Similarly, a woman, in most cases, will be more whole if she meets the world with diffuse consciousness and lets focused consciousness arise from within as a spiritual quality that gives her an authority and effectiveness which does not conflict with her feminine being. This same general pattern of outer and inner manifestations holds true for all the properties of the opposites.

Another difference between moon and sun is that moonlight has a melding effect on the world, while sunlight has a differentiating effect. On a moonlit night, distinctions between things are blurred and all are united into one undifferentiated landscape. At sunrise, distinctions begin to return. As the sun drives away the darkness, one thing is separated from another. So too does feminine consciousness weave and connect the many strands of life into a whole, while masculine consciousness cuts and divides the world into separate constituent parts. Masculine consciousness carries *logos*, which Jung defined as "objective interest." The realm of logos is the realm of knowledge and discrimination, of separating and naming. Feminine consciousness, on the other hand, carries *eros*, the principle of relationship and feeling, of interweaving and connecting. Feminine consciousness seeks communion and peace. It says, "We are." Masculine consciousness seeks singularity and says, "I am." Competition and conflict come from this masculine preoccupation, but so does individuality, which carries the possibility of the fulfillment of one's unique, God-given path.

Another difference between sun and moon is that the sun's light emanates from its source, while the moon's light is reflected. The surface of the sun is fiery and projecting, flaring out as it hurls its energy into the universe. The surface of the moon is cool and cratered, receptive to the light of the sun, pocketed with interior spaces. So too is the masculine principle oriented toward outer life and the feminine toward inner life. The masculine is the principle of activity and movement, of dynamic energy. The feminine is the principle of stillness, receptivity, and reflection. The focus of the masculine is on what is outside—outside the body, outside the house, outside in the visible world. On the other hand, the feminine knows the importance of what is inside—inside the house, inside the body, inside the psychic realm, hidden from the visible world. The feminine understands the veiled and secret world where new life grows and develops, secluded and protected until it is strong enough to emerge into the light. Where the masculine sees nothing of importance, nothing that is dynamic and exciting, the feminine sees the slow, miraculous unfolding of what matters most.

Another notable difference between sun and moon is that the sun always shines with the same steady light, while the moon's light is constantly changing. Masculine consciousness shares with the sun this aspect of constancy. Masculine consciousness tends to be either up or down, light or dark, fully engaged or fully disengaged. There is not much in between. This makes it reliable and steadfast when it is operative, but it also gives it a certain inflexibility. Masculine consciousness does not move easily from knowing to not knowing, nor even from one idea to another. It has difficulty with ambiguity, paradox, and compromise. When a shift is required, it tends to collapse instead.

Feminine consciousness, on the other hand, is more comfortable with varying degrees of knowing and perceiving. It knows the limitations on knowing that spring from life itself, and it is guided, rather than stymied, by changing circumstances. Like moonlight, it is able to mingle with darkness.

Sunlight, in contrast, excludes darkness. When the sun comes up, darkness disappears. We are under the light of the masculine principle when we see our goal clearly and move toward it directly, without ambiguity or confusion. This calls for initiative and action, which are masculine properties. When we are aware of the darkness, of the limitations of reality, we are under the light of the feminine principle. In this light, we must feel our way toward an unseen goal. Nothing is completely clear, though the degree of darkness can vary. This calls for the feminine qualities of stillness, discernment, and waiting for gradual development rather than charging ahead.

The Opposites and the Stages of Life

This brief look at the sun and moon does not exhaust their symbolic attributes. Much less have we considered all the many aspects of the opposites as they appear in human life. To learn fully about the opposites, we must pay attention to our own experience of them. Each of us is born with a different mixture of masculine and feminine qualities, with particular strengths and weaknesses inherited from our forebears, each of us with special gifts and special problems in this complicated arena. And yet, although each person is different, there is also a shared human pattern in the general development of the opposites in the course of human life.

Speaking very generally, without regard to variations in the way this pattern is manifested, we can say that in early life—in infancy and childhood—we live in the world of the mother, under the sway of undifferentiated feminine consciousness. In this stage of life masculine and feminine co-exist in an unconscious unity suggestive of the primal unity of preexistence. This is the innocence of childhood when sexuality has not yet become the polarizing and dominating factor that it later will become. In the world of the mother, consciousness is more diffuse than focused, who we are is valued over what we do, gradual development is more important than heroic accomplishment, and imagination and play, which are expressions of the inner world, command more of our energy than do the discipline and achievement required for life in the outer world.

At puberty, the undifferentiated unity of the opposites breaks apart into the separate realities of masculine and feminine. We become more strongly identified with one than with the other. Now we are divided against ourselves, and the tension of that division energizes us. Feeling incomplete, we are driven to seek completion. The containing life of the mother, life as it is, must now be left behind in a bid for life as it could be. This adolescent state of polarity is conducive to masculine consciousness, which begins to gain ascendency as we move toward the outside world, the world of the father. This is a time when hopes and aspirations lead us forward. If we are to have any chance of realizing them, we must develop focus and discipline. Masculine consciousness helps us claim a separate identity as we leave the mother-world. And it gives us the objective interest we need to learn about the greater world in order to make our way in it.

Just as boys, with their masculinity, live under the dominance of the feminine principle in childhood, so do young women, with their femininity, live under the dominance of the masculine principle in young adulthood. This is true whether the masculine principle is manifest in themselves or in a husband upon whose support they depend. Life does not thrive at this stage if the masculine does not take the lead. A young woman, however, can be hurt if the balance at this time goes too far toward the masculine, just as a boy can be hurt at the earlier stage by too great a dominance by the feminine.

At midlife, when support in the outer world has been secured, another change in consciousness occurs. Our outward striving has helped relieve our sense of incompleteness but has not been able to lay it to rest altogether. In answer to this, the feminine principle reasserts itself. Inner life makes a bid to return. But now, because masculine consciousness has been established, it is possible for the masculine and feminine principles to co-exist in a conscious way rather than in the unconscious, undifferentiated way they co-existed in early life. A woman at this stage is called to rediscover her own feminine value and to learn the effectiveness of the feminine way when supported by the masculine as an inner rather than an outer quality. A man is called to discover the value of the feminine world within himself and to find there the balance he needs to bring his outer life to wholeness and peace.

This view of the unfolding of the opposites in human life is a broad and simplistic one. The real picture is much more complex. Later stages begin their development in earlier stages. Earlier stages carry over into later stages. We stumble at transitions and sometimes bungle them altogether. One stage might usurp another. Our life with the opposites is never smooth or ideal.

Much of our work on the opposites is outer work and lies at the heart of our relationships—with mother and father, sister and brother, girlfriend and boyfriend, husband and wife, lover and would-be lover, son and daughter, boss and co-worker, friend and enemy. Even dog and cat have a part to play as symbols of our masculine and feminine instincts.

Inner work on the opposites is done as we struggle with ourselves, with our sense of belonging and being at one with others, with our need to separate from others and make a unique place for ourselves, and then, in later life, as we struggle to reconcile our separate reality with the world as we find it and to shift our energy from our own striving toward furthering the lives of others.

The true marriage of the opposites does not take place until death when we leave the manifest world, which depends for its very existence on the polarization of the opposites. Death is often symbolized in dreams as a wedding, for it is only at death that our inner and outer selves can finally be united in true wholeness. Until then, the limitation of time and space, that inescapable condition of life in this world, breaks wholeness apart into its many aspects and prevents us from having a continuous experience of it.

I once had a dream about this:

> *I am moving through outer space. It is like flying, although I am not aware of flying, just of moving. There is a man with me, a masculine presence. I am not aware of how he looks or of any particular identity, although I know him very well. We are in outer space as I have seen it in pictures. Then we are out of it, beyond it. I look back and see the universe being folded up like a map. I know we have gone beyond infinity. I am aware of the love coming from the masculine presence beside me. He is my lover, my companion in a totally satisfying way, the perfect masculine love for the individual woman that I am.*

> *So this is where this kind of love is, I think to myself. Out here, beyond the universe. No wonder I could never find it back there. There could only be parts of it back there in all the men I loved and in all the men my women friends loved.*

It is interesting that when the dream refers to the parts of my masculine lover in the world of space and time, it includes the men in the lives of my women friends—masculine lovers one step removed. I also find it instructive that the dream shows me to be distinct from my masculine self. He and I are together, each with an arm around the other, but he is not the same as I. He is my Lover, the Divine Lover, the Beloved. My own feminine consciousness is going into eternity firmly linked and completely loved by my own most perfect masculine Companion, a spiritual quality that is greater than myself. He is not surprised, as I am, to see the universe folded up behind us nor to realize that only in eternity can perfect love be found.

For me this dream was a foretaste of the marriage of the opposites, the goal of our journey toward God. It has helped me to be patient with life on earth and to reconcile my hopes and ideals, my desire for perfect love, with human life as it is. In this way, the dream has furthered my journey toward the very goal it depicts, the goal of a perfect union of love between spirit and matter, between heaven and earth.

Chapter Nine
Masculine Wholeness

ISSUES OF MASCULINE AND FEMININE wholeness are so fundamental to human life that they arise immediately in the dreams and synchronistic events of anyone who sets out on the path of individuation. One of the very first dreams that came to a woman who had just joined our church's natural spirituality dream group was this:

> *I ask a woman friend at work to help me pin some lace on my sweater. I am going to be married.*

The friend at work, in outer life, was a recent bride. The dreamer herself had long been married and had raised a family. And yet the dream showed her making an adjustment to her feminine way of being—adding lace, a more conscious femininity—in preparation for an inner wedding with her animus, the true masculine spirit within her.

This is the essence of the individuation process. The unconscious first leads us step by step through our shadow work—a man becomes more effectively masculine, a woman more effectively feminine in the particular way God intended for each of us, individually, to be. The honing and polishing of our masculine or feminine outer being paves the way for fruitful union with our anima or animus—the contrasexual element within. This divine inner marriage gradually rounds us out as individuals, giving us healthy access to both the masculine and feminine aspects of our whole being, enabling us to serve life with more wisdom, love, and effectiveness than we ever before thought possible.

Although this inner-directed process of growth and transformation takes place over a lifetime and is never fully completed, a great deal of progress is made in the first few years of an individuation journey, a time when the individuating person takes a giant leap forward. It is helpful, therefore, to carry in mind at least a rough idea of the elements of masculine and feminine wholeness in order to more easily recognize the themes being raised by the unconscious.

There are many worthwhile books on this topic, a number of which are listed in Appendix C. For a thumbnail sketch of the elements of masculine and feminine wholeness, however, I offer here and in the next four chapters a quaternity-based system of understanding that has arisen in my own consciousness during the course of my journey and has proven helpful to many people with whom I have shared it.

Systems of categorization based on quaternities—or four-part divisions of a whole—are probably as old as mankind itself. A natural product of the unconscious, they can be regarded as thought-mandalas, expressions of wholeness and order arising from the organizing principle of the God-center deep within us.

One of the earliest symbols found in the archaeology of the native peoples of the American South, for example, is the so-called "sun circle," a circle quartered by an equilateral cross. Virtually all Native American groups had elaborate cosmological systems based on the four compass directions, often referred to as the Four Winds. Certain colors, qualities, and spiritual properties were associated with each direction.

In the history of European thought, at least two quaternities figured prominently: the four elements—earth, air, fire, and water—and the four humors, or bodily fluids—blood, phlegm, choler (yellow bile), and melancholy (black bile). Elaborate early theories of physics, physiology, and personality were based on these four-part divisions. The rise of rational, scientific thought put these old systems into disfavor. In the twentieth century, however, Carl Jung reintroduced quaternity-based thinking with his system of the four functions of consciousness—thinking, feeling, sensation, and intuition (see Chapter Three).

Jung's associate Toni Wolff made her contribution to quaternity-based thinking with a four-part division of feminine wholeness. While Wolff's quaternity has a certain value in regard to woman's relationship to man, I have never found it compelling as a useful way to categorize the foundational energies of feminine being, and it played no role in the development of my own version of the feminine quaternity, which will be presented in Chapter Eleven and is based on a different set of categories. There is, however, a rough correlation between the two quaternities, which seem to have been fished from the same waters of the unconscious. Where I have Eve, Scarlett, Sophia, and Athena, Wolff has Mother, Hetaira, Medial Woman, and Amazon. But while the correspondence between the quarters is somewhat recognizable, our descriptions of them and our sense of the fundamental principles that underlie them are quite dissimilar.

Jung himself classified a man's anima, or inner feminine being, into four stages of development, which he symbolized with the figures of Eve, instinctual woman; Helen of Troy, romantic woman; the Virgin Mary, spiritual woman; and Sophia, wisdom woman, the highest of the stages. His treatment of this quaternity in his Collected Works was quite brief, and when I myself first came upon the formulation, it was in a mere synopsis—half a paragraph—in *Man and His Symbols*, a collection of essays by Jung and his colleagues. Even though so briefly described in that synopsis, the truth of his quaternity struck a chord in me—unlike my experience with Wolff's quaternity—and the images of those four women stayed with me as meaningful stages of development in a man's anima. I wondered if they could be applied to woman herself.

My own feminine quaternity did not arise from these thoughts but had a different basis, as I shall presently explain. However, once I began to perceive the qualities of the four quarters that my system was producing, I could see that there was an even closer correspondence with Jung's four stages of the anima than with Toni Wolff's quaternity. Again, we were fishing from the same pool in the unconscious. I therefore incorporated the most basic ideas of his system into mine, using two of his four names for my feminine quarters. Where he has Eve, Helen of Troy, the Virgin Mary, and Sophia, I have Eve, Scarlett, Athena, and Sophia.

More recently, a masculine quaternity has been put forth by Robert Moore and Douglas Gillette, Jungians active in the men's movement of the late twentieth century. Their work became available in published form after I had already developed and begun teaching my own masculine quaternity. Here, then, were two four-part systems of masculine wholeness that had been intuited completely independently. I was pleased to see that Moore and Gillette had arrived at a quaternity that was very close to my own—especially in the names they used. Where they have the Lover, the Warrior, the Magician, and the King, I have the Poet, the Soldier, the Wise Man, and the King. There are some significant differences, however, in the attributes they assign to the four quarters, and they do not rest their four-part division on the same foundation upon which I rest mine. Their system is much more elaborate than mine and claims more for itself than mine does. The fact, however, that there is a somewhat close correspondence between these two independently developed systems seems to me to be a reassuring affirmation of the fundamental truth of this masculine quaternity.

The basis for the four-part division of the masculine and feminine quaternities that I present here is not to be found in any of the quaternity systems developed by others. It is, I believe, a refinement of understanding that makes the quaternities especially easy to grasp and to carry along in consciousness, thereby increasing their usefulness for ordinary people on their individuation journeys. Before presenting the masculine and feminine quaternities separately in all their detail, I will first combine the two into a single human quaternity for the purpose of putting forth the underlying principles common to both.

The Human-Wholeness Quaternity

This human-wholeness quaternity is best thought of as a fundamental duality which is then divided again to form a quaternity. The duality is based on the fact that each of us comes into the world as the offspring of two parents, which means that in a manner of speaking we are each two sons or two daughters. A man is both his mother's son and his father's son, and a woman is both her mother's daughter and her father's daughter. This is true even when one or both parents are unknown.

As our mother's child, we receive our relationship to the feminine realm—to the intimate world of home, self, and psyche, of relationship, nature, and physical being. As our father's child, we inherit our relationship to the masculine realm, which broadly speaking means the outside world, the world of "others," with its issues of power, achievement, and wealth, and of culture and tradition. (Fig 9.1.)

Fig 9.1. Mother-World–Father-World Duality

The second division in the quaternity is based on the fact that "mother" and "father" are each experienced on two distinct levels of reality. Every person is not only the child of a personal father but also of the heavenly Father, the masculine spiritual principle. This is a living reality in each of us, whether we are well related to it or not. Likewise, we are the child both of a personal mother and of Mother Nature, the feminine spiritual principle. The spirit of heaven and the spirit of nature are forces in the world that are larger than we are and to which, therefore, we are subject, giving us a relationship to them of child to parent. (Fig 9.2.)

Personal Father	*Personal Mother*
Spiritual Father	*Spiritual Mother*

Fig 9.2. Mother-World–Father-World Quaternity

Generally speaking, the first half of one's life takes place on the personal level of the mother-world and father-world, a level that could be called the ego's world. When we are young, it is our personal mothers and fathers, and their surrogates, whom we directly experience as powers higher than ourselves. Our task is to grow up to their level, to become what they are and assume their positions of responsibility. When we do that, we ourselves become the mother and the father, no longer the child looking up to others.

This attainment automatically issues in the call for transcendence to the next level, where the Self rather than the ego is central. Again we find ourselves looking up to a higher power, to the divine as eternal oneness and love on the masculine side and as the wisdom of nature, including the wisdom of the psyche, on the feminine side. Again our task is to learn the way of the higher order and to take our place in life as effective carriers of the love and wisdom of the divine. We are called upon, in effect, to grow up to a partnership with God. As Christianity puts it in Jesus' farewell discourse in the Gospel of John, God wants us not as lowly servants who know nothing of God's business, but as friends and confidants.

The following diagram (Fig 9.3) includes some of the aspects of life that belong to each of the four quarters. Although certain aspects of each quarter belong particularly to the masculine or feminine version of that quarter, we all have the qualities of both the masculine and feminine quaternities within our own being, one of them reflecting our same-sex aspect and the other our anima or animus. This is true regardless of our sexual orientation.

Sexuality is one expression of the dynamics between the different parts of the quaternities, and it is as varied as the dynamics are themselves.

Father-World		***Mother-World***	
Personal Father *(Outside World)*		*Personal Mother* *(Home)*	
man	mastery	woman	physical life
will	expansion	love	pleasure
boundary	mind	nurture	play
competition	knowledge	tending	food
ambition	analysis	children	adornment
focus	protection	family	art
discipline	support	intimacy	song
work	fidelity	relationship	self
Spiritual Father *(Heaven)*		*Spiritual Mother* *(Nature)*	
ideals	vision	wilderness	dreams
perfection	order, timing	garden	synchronicity
purity	structure	variety	meaning
justice	hierarchy	life process	solitude
civilization	unity	healing	depth
community	theology	wisdom	inner life
brotherly love	worship	psyche	death
servant leadership	vocation	imagination	transformation

Fig 9.3. Human Wholeness

The Masculine Quaternity

The masculine quaternity begins with the basic dichotomy of father's son and mother's son.

Every man, and every woman's animus, can be seen in these terms (Fig 9.4). Although the divisions of the masculine quaternity are universally valid, the names given to them for the purpose of discussion are arbitrary and necessarily imperfect. The names I present here are simply the ones that seem most useful to me.

On the ego level I call the father's son the *Soldier* and the mother's son the *Poet*. Every man experiences the tension between these two parts of himself, between the "hard man," who can handle himself in the harsh reality of the outside world, and the "soft man," for whom love, pleasure, and the tending of everyday life are important. At the God-centered level, I call the son of the spiritual father the *King*, and the son of the spiritual mother the *Wise Man*. In these two parts of himself a man is divided between the need to play a responsible role in community life and the need to seek the mystery of life in solitude and communion with his soul.

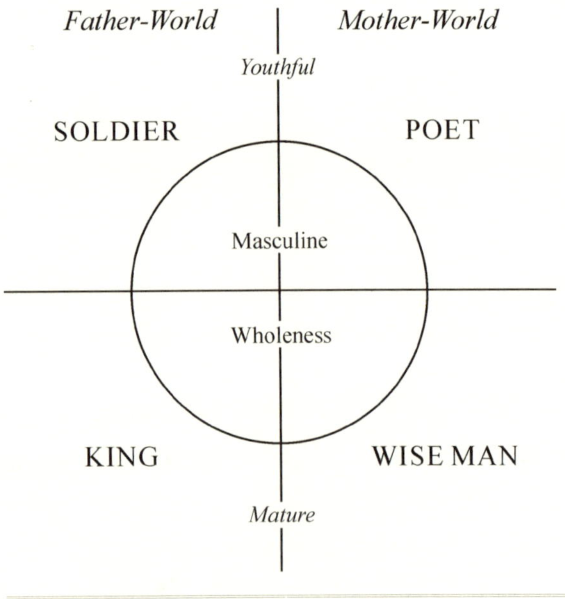

Fig 9.4. The Masculine Quaternity

Every man has a "star" in one of the four quarters. By nature, he might be more a Soldier than anything else, or he might be more a Wise Man. His effectiveness in life, however, will depend on how well he integrates into his conscious being all four aspects of masculine wholeness. A man whose strongest flow of energy comes from the King quarter, for example, but who has not developed the Poet, the Soldier, and the Wise Man in himself, will not be all that a King can be. As we shall see in Chapter Thirteen, our Jungian personality type, based on our particular ranking of the four functions of consciousness, tells us which of the quarters is our "star" quarter. It also reveals the sequence through which we traverse the other three quarters during the course of our lives.

The Poet

Regardless of the variations imposed by the differences in our own star energies, however, every man at the most fundamental level begins life in the Poet quarter. Early childhood takes place in the world of the personal mother. As the son of his mother, a boy experiences his basic relationship to woman and to life, for at a deep, symbolic level woman *is* life. The dominant themes of the Poet quarter are love and the savoring of physical life. Love is so large a part of it that Moore and Gillette name this part of the masculine quaternity the Lover, a term that can be useful when thinking about the quarter, although, in my opinion, it is too limiting. The world of the personal mother is not only the world of love and relationship but also of immersion in physical experience, the zone of life from which come such activities as games and athletics, travel for pleasure, and artistic expressions that distil and heighten the experience of everyday life. The artist, the farmer, the dancer, the chef, and the salesman are among those who might have their star in this quarter. Of all the quarters, this one is the most difficult to nail down with a single name that fully captures its essence. I have settled on the Poet, although it, too, can be an overly narrow term if taken too literally. This Poet does not necessarily write poems. This is the archetypal Poet, the romantic, the lover of woman and of life. He is non-analytical, attending to and expressing the feelings that arise from his experience of life at hand, to which he is keenly attuned. The Poet knows this experience to be valuable for its own sake and loves it and dedicates himself to it as a mother loves her child.

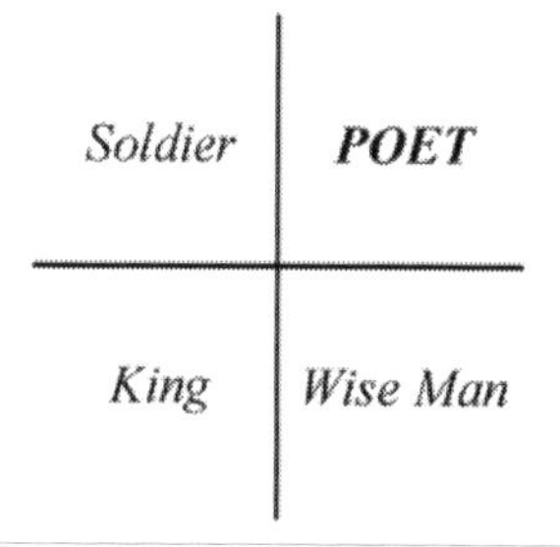

Fig 9.5. Poet Quarter

The Poet as lover has to do with personal and intimate relationship, not with the broad love of mankind, which belongs to the King quarter, nor with the love of feminine Wisdom, which is the province of the Wise Man. The Poet's love is that first experienced with the mother, the love found in home and family, a love based on unity, inclusion, and sharing, not on doing and proving. It is a love centered on pleasing the other and being pleased, on meeting the needs of the other and having one's own needs met. A man whose Poet aspect is healthy can express his feelings to another person. He can embrace another, man or woman, without embarrassment. He can relate easily to his own children. And he can make a stranger feel at home.

A man's connection to his body life comes from the Poet quarter. His body is an important part of his own feminine reality. It is the vessel of his spirit, his "mother" at a deep symbolic level.

Although the Poet and Soldier belong generally to the youthful level of life, and the Wise Man and the King to the mature level, each of the four quarters has within itself a youthful, or instinctual, expression and a mature, or achieved, expression. The youthful expression of the Poet quarter reflects that of the boy in relationship to his mother. The youthful Poet in a man says, "Love me. Please me. Watch me." In his healthy aspect the youthful Poet knows himself to be worthy of love, knows how to take pleasure in life, and knows that that which comes from his own expression of life is valuable.

The mature Poet, on the other hand, no longer needs to be mothered. He says, "I love you. I please you. I watch you." In relationships, he goes beyond emotional gratification to the hard work of love, setting aside his own needs when necessary. He seeks to please others for their sake rather than his own. And he is able to value and nurture the individual life-expressions of others. A balanced Poet is both of these—youthful and mature—in an integrated whole.

As is true with all the quarters, the shadow of the Poet is to be found in its unconscious and unbalanced manifestations. The man who seeks only his own pleasure without regard for others, and the man who seeks too much to please others—both are shadow manifestations of the Poet. So too the man who is obsessed with problems of love and the man who can never commit himself to another; the man who lives always for his boyish dreams and enthusiasms, never facing reality, and the man who is so consumed with reality that he has no time for play.

The list of shadow possibilities could go on endlessly and would include not only blatant manifestations but extremely subtle ones. But no such list would be of much help for anyone on an individuation journey. Through dreams and synchronicity, the unconscious itself teaches each of us in an individual way about the many aspects of our own shadow. This process unfolds slowly over time, as we are gradually able to understand the ways in which we have been off balance and can make the necessary adjustments. While the quaternities are helpful in recognizing our shadow parts as they are revealed to us, this help can only be general in nature. There is no magic formula for shadow work.

The Soldier

Life begins in the Poet quarter with love, pleasure, and play, the gifts of the mother-world—valuable gifts, the lack of which is always crippling. But valuable as they are, they will not carry a man far unless he also receives the gifts of the father-world. He must be able to take his sense of his own worth and potential, which he receives in the mother-world, and turn it into reality in the organized world of competitive interests that lies outside the intimate family circle. In the father-world, the world of "others," nothing is granted unless it is proven, nothing gained unless it is won. Where love counts for all in the mother-world, it is will that counts in the father-world. And will is a quality that is as elusive and mysterious as love itself.

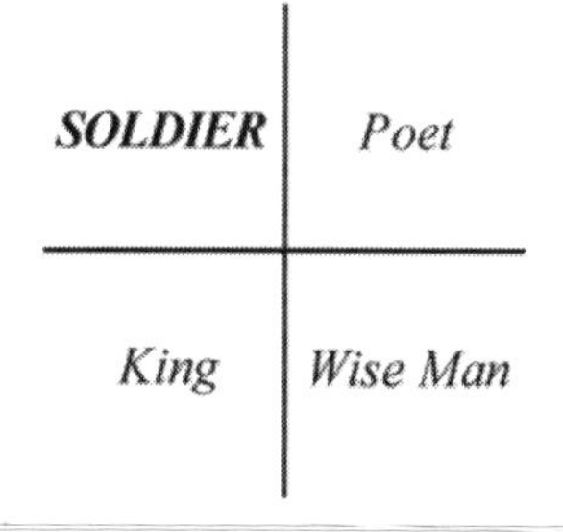

Fig 9.6. Soldier Quarter

The father-world at the ego level is the realm of the Soldier. Here the will is trained and guided with the help and support of the personal father and of father surrogates. In the intimate mother-world, a man can relax and be himself. But if he is to succeed in the outside world of the father, he must learn its ways and adapt himself to its requirements, however foreign and unnatural they may seem. To do this he must gradually gain control of his own will and use it to counter his natural impulse to fall back into the ease and comfort of the mother-world.

The Soldier trains his will into an effective force with which, first of all, he guards his personal ego boundaries. It is the Soldier in a man who must stand up for his separate reality against outsiders and loved ones alike. The Soldier is always on the lookout for the enemy, for anyone who would encroach upon the territory of his being and threaten his sense of who he is. The more a man knows himself, the more effective he will be in differentiating between friendly and unfriendly elements that come toward him, a distinction that is not always obvious.

The Soldier trains his will to work, to accomplish necessary tasks, no matter how difficult and unpleasant. A strong will is required to override the body's natural inclination to stop and rest, to give up, or to take an easier way. A youthful will is not disciplined enough to carry a boy or young man successfully through the difficult requirements of the early stages of life. It is the will of the father, or father surrogates, including the mother's animus, that must make up the difference and supply the needed inspiration, direction, and discipline. A Soldier obeys his superiors, accepting training and mentorship from those who are established in whatever aspect of the organized, collective world he seeks to join. Ultimately he serves the King, the highest principle of that realm.

The father-world of the Soldier and King is the world of consciousness, of ordered reality that has been constructed slowly over time from the creative chaos of the unconscious natural world. It is the structure side of life, a work against nature, difficult to achieve and to maintain. Each life has something new to bring to it. That newness, which arises in the mother-world, must find a way to establish itself in the powerfully conservative world of the father, the constructed world of culture and tradition. It is the Soldier who prepares the way for this by embracing some aspect of tradition and seeking to serve it. To the degree that it is necessary, the Soldier part of a man puts on a uniform and becomes a team player. He learns to march in a straight line, in step with the collective world into which his individual contribution will eventually be absorbed. It is only by engaging in the life of the father-world that a man can find an effective way to make his contribution to it.

There are times, however, when the Soldier must be a rebel and fight against a father-world that has grown dark and is no longer open to the creative contributions that seek to come from the mother-world. There is always some resistance in the father-world to new ways of understanding and doing things. Sometimes that resistance becomes so unyielding that protests and uprisings are necessary. But the rebel must be careful not to become permanently antagonistic to the father-world. The world of the dark father is a distortion, a departure from the true spirit of the father, which seeks to support new life, not to crush it. If a Soldier is always a rebel, standing forever outside the traditional system, feeling hopelessly overpowered by it, railing against it just because it is a system and does not include or go along with everything that he himself is, then he will die with the special gift of his life unrealized. Such a rebellion is actually against the outside world itself and the sacrifices it requires. It amounts to a refusal to leave home and enter adult life.

The Soldier is the part of a man that wields a weapon. If the enemy is starvation, a hoe is a weapon. If chaos is the enemy, a plan is a weapon. A Soldier arms himself with whatever tool enables him to exercise his will upon the world and gain an advantage over the forces that oppose him. A stone spearpoint, a wheeled cart, a windmill, a rifle, a saber saw, a book, a violin, a computer—anything that gives him a competitive edge. The ultimate weapon is the mind itself with its rational, analytic power. The word and the sword are symbolically akin, both able to cut and dissect, to wound and to conquer.

Training, practice, skill, mastery, and craftsmanship fall within the realm of the Soldier. Learning based on established knowledge also belongs in this quarter. Self-worth and natural talent come from the Poet, but it is the Soldier who applies the discipline that is necessary to bring that potential forward against all rivals and establish it in the world.

The youthful Soldier is the one who guards the territory. A boy's task is to defend what is his by natural right. He must be strong enough to maintain his essential being against anyone who would encroach upon it. The mature Soldier expands that territory through training and mastery. Becoming better at what he does, he gains effectiveness in a larger sphere. Both the youthful and the mature aspects of the Soldier are necessary for masculine wholeness.

The Wise Man

In the ego-centered world of the Poet and the Soldier, the basic problem of life is that of the individual in relationship to the human world. In the God-centered world of the Wise Man and the King, the problem is that of the human world in relationship to the divine, a problem that includes the individual's personal role in that greater drama. We do not have to subscribe to a theology that names heaven and nature as divine aspects of life in order to experience them as such. Named or unnamed, the ideal of perfect life (the spirit of heaven) both inspires and oppresses everyone. We are continually called forth by it, and we continually struggle beneath the impossibility of it, unable wholly to satisfy or escape its demands. So too does nature make her overpowering presence felt, though she is noticed more when she blocks and defeats our will than when she moves in accord with it and helps us along. In droughts, floods, and storms, in illness, disability, and death, and in the intractability of human nature itself, we are faced, whether we like it or not, with the mighty power of the feminine aspect of God.

It is the Wise Man who accepts and respects the feminine aspect of the divine. He seeks to understand its wisdom, to learn from it and work with it in its endless unfolding of life on earth. The Wise Man is that part of a man who loves nature, an attitude which draws him into solitude. Whether fishing, hunting, hiking, gardening, or watching a sunset, a true engagement with nature draws a man away from his fellow humans into communion with his soul.

The youthful Wise Man brings masculine consciousness to his experience of nature as a physical phenomenon. He learns the way of things—where the fish bite, when to plant the corn, how to keep a wound from becoming infected, and in what part of the sky to look for the Big Dipper. If he has strength in this quarter, he will go deeper and become a natural philosopher. Drawing analogies between nature and human life, he comes to understand for himself such eternal human verities as: the seasons of a person's life are like the seasons of the year; wherever there is human prey, there will be human predators; individual growth takes time, it cannot be rushed.

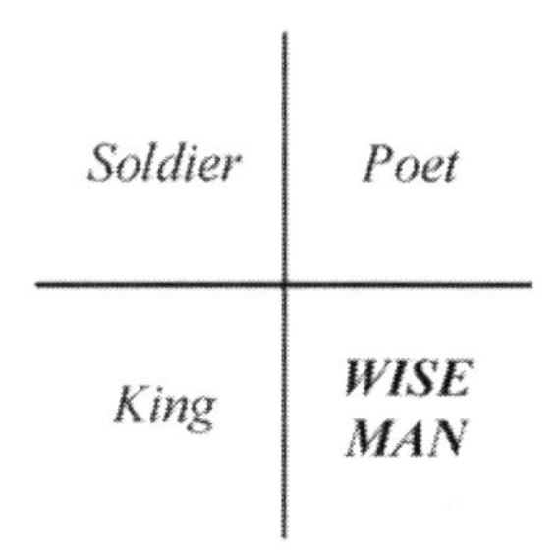

FIG 9.7. WISE MAN QUARTER

The mature Wise Man is the rare individual who goes even deeper and sees *beneath* the physical surface of nature to the divine Wisdom that underlies it. He has awakened to the living spirit of God that uses natural life as the language and process of spiritual growth. At this level, the Wise Man sees in nature not only analogies of eternal truths but also explicit manifestations of particular truths concerning the human drama in which he is presently participating. He understands that through natural occurrences the divine speaks to us personally, guiding us through the moments of our lives. The mature Wise Man pays attention to dreams, synchronicity, and the murmuring undercurrents of his own consciousness. He recognizes the reality of natural spirituality.

The Wise Man uses his masculine consciousness to bring system and order to the feminine truth of the divine Wisdom of nature. The Jungian concepts I discussed in the first part of this book are an example of such a system, perceived and developed by the Wise Man aspect of Carl Jung. Another example is the *I Ching*, the Chinese book of wisdom, an orderly system perceived and constructed by several generations of Chinese sages. The masculine and feminine quaternities as I am presenting them here are a system perceived by the Wise Man in me, an aspect of my animus. Such systems put a grid in front of the natural spiritual process that underlies conscious life, making it possible for us to understand the process more clearly, to work with it more intelligently, and to convey its nature to others.

It is the mature Wise Man who takes the individuation journey, following the feminine Wisdom in himself into the unknown world of the unconscious. He leaves behind his identification with collective consciousness in order to find his own unique truth, submitting to the death of his ego-centered self and experiencing resurrection to a new and more meaningful life centered in God. Once a man has made this journey, he becomes available to others as a guide—a sage, a wise old man. The Wise Man is solitary, off to himself, strongly connected to earth and nature. Community life does not belong to this quarter. This is the side of spiritual life that does not reach out to others, but rather it waits, in the way of the feminine, for seekers to find it. It is a well known aspect of Wisdom that when the student is ready, he will find the right teacher, the one to whom he belongs through a deep and mysterious connection. The meeting of student and teacher is inevitable. Synchronicity brings it about in response to the readiness of both.

The King

Spirituality that is more extraverted and oriented toward community life is located in the King quarter. Here the masculine ideal of perfection seeks realization in human life. This ideal comes from the heavenly divine, the source of all perfection, the Father of all.

The King is that part of a man who, as the son of the masculine divine, is dedicated, consciously or unconsciously, to the heavenly ideal. The last pages of the Bible describe a vision of heaven, an image that can be seen as a symbolic statement from the unconscious about the true nature of the transcendent realm of the divine. In this vision, heaven is described as a holy city where God lives in the midst of humankind, a community in which there is no death and no sadness. The city is perfectly square and is made of gold and precious gems. Rising from the throne of God and running through the middle of the city is the crystal-clear river of life, its banks lined with trees of life bearing fruit in every season. The city is radiant with the glory of God and needs no other light.

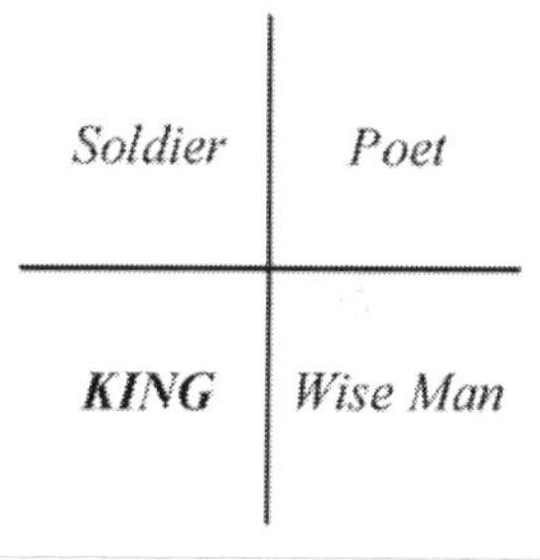

Fig 9.8. King Quarter

The description tells of a perfect union of God and humanity, which includes a perfect union of masculine culture (the square-walled city) and feminine nature (the river and the trees of life). Gold and jewels symbolize the highest earthly values. Radiant light symbolizes the highest spiritual values. The best of heaven and earth are wed. This is a symbolic statement about a potential state of being that can only be fully attained in the eternal realm. And yet it is a potential that lives dynamically within each of us and seeks to find as much expression as possible in our temporal lives.

This drive from within does not come to us in a neat, integrated, and self-explanatory package but rather as a jumbled and unrealistic sense of what life should be. The more unconscious we are of its true and deeper meaning, the more it gives us a powerful desire for its literal realization, for a world in which everyone is always good, bad things do not happen, and we never have to die, which also means we never have to change or be transformed. It fills us with a desire for the highest earthly values—for riches (literal gold and jewels) and for perfect structures (grand houses and magnificent public buildings, perfect families and institutions). We find ourselves wanting literally to sit in luxurious accommodations beside crystal-clear waters and to be served the best fruits of the earth in every season. And we seek the highest plane of spirituality, the ever-present radiance of the heavenly divine, all goodness and light, no darkness.

It is the youthful King in a man who is seized by the ideal and cannot see it objectively or distinguish his own reality from it. The youthful King unconsciously identifies himself with the masculine aspect of God. He feels himself to be the one above all others, the smartest, the fastest, the highest, the best. He expects perfection from himself, from those around him, and from life itself. Whether he admits it or not, the youthful King expects to save the world. His attention is ever drawn to the national and international levels of human life. He knows himself, though unrecognized, to be the best in the country, the best in the world, at what he does or wants to do.

These ideals inspire him and draw him forward into life. They help him find what is best in himself. If he is strong in this quarter, these ideals help the youthful King lead and inspire others. But they also set him up for inevitable disappointment and accompanying feelings of rage and despondency.

The mature King is the rare individual who ceases to identify unconsciously with divine kingship. He no longer feels he is the one above all others—though neither does he feel he is the lowest of the low, which is simply a shadow aspect of the youthful King. The mature King understands who he truly is in his limited human reality, and he knows in the depths of himself, not merely as a high and shining ideal, that it is God who is King of all. The mature King is at one with his kingdom—with earth, nature, and reality. He recognizes the bounded realm to which God has called him, with his particular talents, to be a servant leader. He knows that his role is not to be the savior of the world, but merely to help bring forth in an actual, limited community the best life possible, which is perfect in its own way but not in an ideal way.

The mature King is the culmination of a man's development. Different in quality from the other three quarters, the King incorporates them all and unifies them into a new, transcendent level of life. He has within the kingdom of his own being a Poet who, ideally, loves people and savors the simple pleasures of everyday life; a Soldier who is strong, brave, and disciplined; and a Wise Man who is connected to earth, soul, and meaning.

The King brings order to his world not by force and decree but by the simple fact of being present with his depth and clarity of consciousness and his wholeness of being. He sees how things fit together. He has a sense of timing, of when to move forward into new expressions of life and when to wait for slower elements to catch up. He loves all the inhabitants of his kingdom and sees them with clear eyes, recognizing both the value and the limitations of each and understanding the role each has to play. That love and recognition confer blessing. Order and blessing are the two primary functions of the King.

In the King quarter, inner realities are made manifest in outer life in a way that is healthy for the human community. Civilization belongs to this quarter. Houses and public institutions, manners and mores, customs and rituals—both civic and religious—are manifestations of the King. Charity and religious outreach make manifest the King's blessing.

If the King quarter is too strong or too weak, distortions occur. There can be too much kingly structure and not enough natural chaos, or too much naturalness and not enough structure. There can be too much heavenly spirituality and not enough recognition of earthly darkness, or there can be too much attention to earth's darkness and not enough openness to heavenly light. As with the other quarters, the shadow possibilities of the King are endless.

Few men undergo *conscious* development of both the youthful and mature levels of all four quarters of the masculine quaternity. But whether they are experienced consciously or unconsciously, all four quarters manifest themselves in every human life. Whether these manifestations are for good or ill depends on their degree of consciousness and on the overall balance of the whole.

Chapter Ten
The Beatles and the Masculine Quaternity

THE TRUTH OF THE MASCULINE quaternity and the fundamental importance of the human wholeness it represents are clearly illustrated by an image of it that arose in the second half of the twentieth century with so much energy that the whole world was affected by it. In the two decades after World War II, the value of the father-world was at its height in the hearts and minds of people everywhere. The Soldier, with his courage, discipline, and sacrifice, had saved civilization from fascism. The ideals of the youthful King, a lingering Edwardian ideal of perfect civilization, of all light and no darkness, had a strong, though weakening, grip on the post-war world.

Everyone participating in the collective consciousness of that time was extremely mannerly and constrained. People in all areas of life knew where they fit in the order of things. Every hair was in place, every instinct in check. Families tried their best to give the appearance of perfection, repressing and denying all darkness. Truth had an almost exclusively rational basis. There was little real conversation between men and women. Nature was falling out of the picture as farming ceased to be a widespread occupation. Man was becoming one-sided to the extreme—all father-world, all Soldier and King.

Gone almost completely from collective consciousness was the Poet and the Wise Man, that side of a man that loves woman and Wisdom, that has heart and feeling, that is natural, relaxed, and open to creative play and new expressions of life. Gone was the part of a man that accepts the nonrational and looks beneath the surface of reality to find meaning and guidance, that acknowledges and honors the darkness of life, that accepts death and transformation. Feminine values, half of what it means to be human, had been driven underground.

Into this world in the early 1960s came the phenomenon of the Beatles, an all male rock'n'roll band from the rough port city of Liverpool. Though obviously carrying the masculine toughness of their Liverpool roots, the Beatles had long hair that fell around their faces in a feminine way, a shocking spectacle in the Soldier world of 1963. Their music was hard and driving, and yet joyful and open—a strange and appealing combination of darkness and light. Their personalities were charming and natural, spontaneous, fun-loving and witty, outrageous, and yet in their own way, polite and respectful. Adults and teenagers alike were fascinated by them.

The Fab Four they were nicknamed by the press. John, Paul, George, and Ringo. Even as I write, more than a half century later, most people in the world still know their names. They were the four who were one, the one that was four. Everyone knew that the Beatles could not be the Beatles without each of these particular men. It was the four of them in combination that made them what they were. But although everyone knew that this was true, no one knew why it was true.

Everyone who was open to it could *feel* what it was about the Beatles. It could be felt that they were special, earthshaking, soul-searing, heart-freeing. They meant something important, they brought something desperately needed. Young women especially felt it and screamed and wept in their presence, caught up in an ecstatic joy, seeing something in these four men, hearing something in their music, that belonged to them as women and honored them, something that had been missing in the world and without which they no longer wanted to live. Everyone could feel what it was about the Beatles, but no one could *understand* what it was.

That is the way truth comes in the mother-world—nonrationally, as feeling or deep knowing. It cannot at first be rationally stated. New consciousness must be developed in the father-world before that is possible. For the most part, the new truth that arises in the mother-world is kept inside, held close, treasured, believed in. If conveyed to others it can only be through emotion, art, music, poetry, or mystical language. The truth from the mother-world nourishes the soul. It gives meaning to life, makes it new again and worth living. Awareness of this feminine side of human truth was returning to collective consciousness in the 1960s, and the Beatles were the four-part image of masculine wholeness that heralded that return.

At the height of the Beatles' career, Paul McCartney said of the group, "The thing is, we're all really the same person. We're just four parts of the one. We're individuals, but we make up together The Mates, which is one person....We all add something different to the whole." The Beatles as a single "person" was a Poet personality. Just as every individual whose special strength is in the Poet quarter has within himself all four quarters, conscious or unconscious, so did the Beatles have all four quarters participating together to make them a whole Poet. Because their story was known to all the world, it provides us with the same kind of vehicle that a myth would provide for illustrating the dynamics of the four parts of masculine wholeness.

Before we go on, however, let me take a moment to address those readers who do not have much familiarity with the Beatles and their music. I know from experience that while most readers will find this chapter interesting and fun, there will be others, most of whom were never fans of the Beatles, who will already be feeling resistant to the idea of an entire chapter devoted to them. So if your attention was elsewhere during the time of the Beatles, or if you came along later and never looked back at them, I hope you will stay with us for a demonstration of the underlying presence of the masculine quaternity in this well-documented episode in our collective history. You do not have to know much about the Beatles at the outset—I will give you enough information to bring you along. And you might take comfort in the fact that most other readers will be in the same boat when we get to the Psyche and Eros myth with which I will illustrate the feminine quaternity in Chapter Twelve. There, too, I will catch everyone up as we go along. So think of the Beatles as a myth of which you have heard but about which you know little. By the end of this chapter you will know more, and while you still may not care for their music, you will nonetheless see that it carries, to a degree that is quite amazing, an image of individuation through the four masculine quarters.

Let us turn, then, to the four parts of the Beatles "person," beginning with John Lennon. John was a Soldier poet, a hard man, a man's man. Words and humor were the weapons with which he channeled and tempered the anger and aggression that were never far beneath the surface of his otherwise appealing personality. He himself said that his political advocacy of peace and nonviolence—through his Bed-Ins for Peace with Yoko Ono, for example—was a counteraction to his own violent temper, an attempt to get beyond it. He was the Beatle who was most devoted to the hard, masculine rock'n'roll music that inspired the Beatles' teenage beginnings in Liverpool. It was his tough, brazen energy that led them from obscurity to fame.

John, however, was also the most wounded of the four, having been abandoned by his father essentially at birth and by his adored mother off and on throughout his childhood until her accidental death when he was sixteen. Loss seemed to have been his fate. The uncle who helped raise him had died a few years before his mother, and in the following decade death claimed his closest friend—Stu Sutcliffe, a former Beatle—and Brian Epstein, the Beatles' manager and surrogate father. John's wound was deepest in the realm of the father, which made him a dark, unconscious Soldier, rebellious and antagonistic toward the outside world and given to bouts of paralyzing depression, during which his will would abandon him altogether.

His mother's family, however, in which he had been brought up, had been lively, loving, and well-meaning, if somewhat dysfunctional. That produced a core of love and goodness in John that always came through and tempered the effects of his undeniable darkness. He did not try to deny his darkness but put much of it out for the world to see, which meant that the Beatles as a whole personality did not try to deny its shadow side but faced it squarely and sought to work with it and integrate it. This added much to their depth, complexity, and authenticity.

Although all members of the group were poets, it was Paul McCartney who occupied the Poet quarter in the greater Beatles personality. Melody flowed through him in a natural, unending stream. He was a woman's man, soft and romantic, a true lover of woman. Good relationships were important to him, and he was mannerly and thoughtful toward others. Even though his mother died when he was fourteen, Paul's experience of his childhood was generally a happy one, and his basic outlook on life was positive and optimistic. Because it was difficult for him to see darkness in the world or in himself, he was prone to sentimentality and superficiality in his creativity, and he also tended at times to be covertly mean and manipulative in his dealings with others. John Lennon's dedication to the truth about the hard side of life checked these shadow tendencies in Paul and brought out the best in him as a songwriter and musician. Though John had been the evident leader of the Beatles in their early years, it was Paul who emerged as the leader in the end.

George Harrison occupied the Wise Man quarter in the Beatles personality. He, too, came from a relatively healthy home, where he was the youngest of four siblings and was especially close to his mother. Though younger than the other Beatles, he was from the beginning more self-possessed and thoughtful than the rest. He spoke as if from a higher vantage point, somewhat removed from the fray. His energy was not so ego-driven as that of Paul and John, and he stood back from their competition for supremacy and center stage. Naturally introverted, he preferred solitude to the company of others. It was George who brought the music and spirituality of India to the Beatles. With great discipline, he learned to play the sitar, a difficult instrument to master. He was strongly drawn to Hindu wisdom and became a devoted student of it. Indian spirituality was an interest and orientation that he never abandoned. George was also a dedicated gardener, especially in his later years.

Ringo Starr (born Richard Starkey) was the poet King of the Beatles. Even less ego-driven than George, Ringo was a true "servant leader" in the way he ordered and unified the group musically with his drumming, keeping perfect time, never calling attention to himself, serving every song differently according to its individual nature. True to the King's characteristic of being different in quality from the other three quarters, Ringo joined the group just at the moment the Beatles were moving from the Liverpool stage to the world stage, whereas the others had been together since the beginning. Ringo's very name suggests the symbolism of the Self, of whom the King is a human image. The several rings he characteristically wore on his fingers suggested kingship, as did his enthronement among his drums on a platform above the other three during their performances.

Most important to Ringo's kingship, however, was the depth of love he had for the other Beatles and for people in general, a love that conferred blessing on those around him. The other Beatles responded in kind, loving him more than they loved each other. Ringo was the one thing on which they could all agree. He was the nicest and most decent one of them, the most truly loving. His noble spirit unified them and became their ruling spirit. It is because the Beatles carried this basically decent spirit that the world continues to love them, despite their evident weaknesses and follies.

Ringo's spirit seems to have come from a family life that was fundamentally loving, even though his parents divorced when he was very young and his father went out of his life. Unlike John, he grew up close to his father's family as well as his mother's, and he was particularly close to his paternal grandfather. So while he shared John's wound in the father realm, he also shared Paul's happy family life, including a connection to the father-world. His childhood, however, was marked by two long hospital stays, several years length in all, which served to initiate him into the solitude and depth of the Wise Man's realm. It was presumably from this experience that he emerged with the qualities of humility, loving-kindness, centeredness, and servanthood that belong to the mature King.

By himself, Ringo Starr was not a whole and individuated man. None of the Beatles were. None were authentically God-centered during this period of their lives, not even George with his dedication to Hindu wisdom. But archetypal forces were shaping their experience, making of them an illusion, a living myth for their time. Together they constituted an *image* of wholeness, and together they took a journey that *looked* like an individuation journey. It was because it carried that image that so many people were fascinated by it, although few, if any, consciously understood this. It is only as I have been looking at the Beatles in connection with this book that I myself have come to realize that not only did their personalities and their life together illustrate the masculine quaternity and the individuation journey, but so did their music itself.

Beatles Music: A Dream of Individuation

Like so much artistic expression in the twentieth century, the music of the Beatles is a relatively raw expression of the unconscious and is therefore quite close to dream language. It can be analyzed as if it were dream material. If we follow the music through time as the symbolic expression of the life of this Beatles "person," we can see in it the portrayal of a masculine life that rises from youth to a midlife crisis, discovers the unconscious, and individuates in a journey that passes through each of the masculine quarters, culminating in its fullest expression in the King quarter as it accepts and approaches its own death.

The Beatles' music is dramatically divided into roughly two halves, usually referred to simply as early Beatles and late Beatles. The early Beatles music began in Liverpool and lasted almost to the end of the group's world-touring days in 1966. This was the era of Beatlemania when mobs besieged them wherever they went and the screaming of their fans often rendered their stage performances inaudible. Virtually all their songs in this period were simple teenage love songs set to rock'n'roll music that, though definitely innovative and fresh, was not greatly different from other rock'n'roll music of the time.

As they neared the end of the early period, the Beatles had achieved more fame and fortune than they had ever dreamed possible. As rock stars, they had reached the absolute top. Predictably, this brought with it a crisis of spirit. What next? Like an individual entering a midlife crisis, their music began to show a growing soberness, self-reflection, and even despondency. Then came the song that marks the break between the early and late periods. Its origin reveals the touch of grace that is always offered to a life in need of transformation. The song's melody came to Paul in a dream. He woke up the next morning and went immediately to his piano and played "Yesterday," whole and entire as it had arisen in the night. No other song ever came to him so completely intact.

"Yesterday" was not rock'n'roll. When it was recorded on the *Help!* album, surrounded by rock'n'roll songs, Paul sang it alone accompanied by an acoustic guitar and *a string quartet!* Something new was happening.

Existing consciousness, however, always resists transformation. Their next album, *Rubber Soul*, was a transition album, the old music trying to reassert itself but losing ground to the growing new sound that departed from the usual rock beat and incorporated a greater variety of instruments. The song lyrics were also becoming more sophisticated.

It was the next album, *Revolver*, that marked the true beginning of the late Beatles. With *Revolver* the Beatles went completely beyond the boundaries of rock'n'roll, expanding to a new level of richness and complexity in lyrics, music, and instrumentation. It is this later music that carries the image of a conscious individuation journey, the kind of spiritual journey that takes place when a person discovers and integrates the unconscious.

The Beatles had in fact discovered the unconscious, although not in a legitimate way. Through psychedelic drugs they had artificially broken down their structures of conscious perception, allowing themselves to perceive psychedelically the nuances of spiritual reality that underlie physical reality. Carl Jung was careful to point out that such an approach to the unconscious is almost guaranteed to become poisonous and destructive. The unconscious brings with it a moral obligation to understand it and integrate it into consciousness. Not many users of psychedelic drugs have any understanding of what a moral attitude toward the unconscious would require of them, and even if they did, few would be able to integrate such a large amount of artificially induced unconscious material. The most likely result is a disintegration of personality rather than integration and wholeness. This effect can be seen in varying degrees in the Beatles as individuals, especially in John Lennon.

The music of the late Beatles shows, however, that they did manage to integrate some of the lessons coming to them in that period, at least to the extent that this could be put into song. The unconscious was clearly using them more than they were using it. In a rather amazing example of synchronicity, the four great albums of that period—*Revolver, Sgt. Pepper's Lonely Hearts Club Band, Magical Mystery Tour,* and *Abbey Road*—each carried songs that, when taken all together, were wholly related to a different quarter of the masculine quaternity. Furthermore, the albums appeared in a sequence that followed the masculine individuation sequence of Poet, Soldier, Wise Man, and King.

This certainly was not intentional on the part of the Beatles. They knew nothing at all of the masculine quaternity, which had not yet been formulated by anyone, and they could have had only the vaguest notion, if any, of the process of individuation. Therefore, as I examine these albums through this particular lens, I will not be concerned with what the Beatles *thought* they were saying, but rather I will be focusing on what their songs actually do say to us as listeners. As in dream analysis, these interpretations are to be held lightly, allowing for revisions and further insights, and always with the understanding that it is impossible to grasp all that the unconscious is trying to express.

Revolver: The Poet Quarter

Revolver begins with "Taxman," a song written by George and for which he is the lead singer. (The Beatle who contributed most to the writing of a Beatles song was almost always its lead singer.) In "Taxman" the Beatle Wise Man lays out the hard truth about the steep taxes always demanded by the government. Symbolically, the divine is the government, and when we have made advances on the ego level, the divine demands a payment of energy and attention to the spiritual level. If someone reaches the top, as the Beatles had, the payment demanded in conscious growth is proportionately large. So it is time for the Beatles to pay up. There is a noticeable influence of the music of India in "Taxman," indicating the spiritual turn the Beatles' journey has now taken. But there is also anger in George's voice. The journey is just beginning—he is not yet fully wise. No one at the outset wants to pay the price of individuation. It is only as the journey proceeds that its demands begin to seem worthwhile.

The rest of the album focuses on themes related to the Poet quarter—issues of love and of regression into the mother-world. I will group together the songs written and led by each individual Beatle and look at these groupings separately to see how each of the four masculine parts experiences this journey through the Poet's realm, beginning with Paul, the primary Poet voice.

Paul's first song, "Eleanor Rigby," is the second song on the album, and along with "Taxman," it has a special, flagship quality. Like an initial dream, it sets out the overall problem that this individuation journey is going to address, a problem that sets the Beatles' journey into a wider context than themselves.

There is a real way in which every individuation journey is important for the salvation of the world—more important than collective actions and mass movements. This is because of the true insight and centering that the journey brings to the individuating person, an advance in consciousness which spreads to his immediate environment and out from there in a ripple effect. The outer-life developments which arise from this are sound and lasting, and they help give answer to the challenge of the times in which the individuating person is living.

In "Eleanor Rigby," the Beatle Poet speaks of the loneliness in the world in the 1960s, and he names as loneliest of all a married woman who is lost in a dream world and a priest whose sermons are irrelevant and who lives alone, mending his own socks. Married women, disappointed in the romantic ideal (most of the mothers of those in the Beatles generation), and a father-world whose spirituality has grown sterile through separation from the feminine. The two problems were connected.

Paul's next song is "Here, There, and Everywhere," considered by many to be the most beautiful of his love songs. All the love songs he sings on this album are especially lovely, as befits the Poet's quarter. In this one he sings of a woman whose physical presence makes him a better person. She improves his life so much that he wants her with him always and everywhere. This is a nice sentiment, but few women would actually welcome it as a reality. This Poet needs a relationship with his inner feminine so that he can get along without a woman always by his side.

The Beatle Poet does not yet realize it, but it is in his dependence on the physical presence of a woman that his personal problem intersects the larger problems put forth in "Eleanor Rigby." When a man discovers and integrates the feminine realm within himself—the unconscious—his spirituality deepens and becomes more relevant to life, while at the same time he becomes a better companion to woman, able to allow her a separate reality and to appreciate her depth and complexity. But the Poet will not be able to achieve this integration of the feminine by drawing only on Poet energy. He needs the analytical ability and disciplined will of the Soldier, the Wise Man's openness to the depths, and the King's capacity to pull all these parts together and make them viable in the context of this particular human life.

The Poet's other songs on the album—"Good Day Sunshine," "For No One," and "Got To Get You Into My Life"—show him basking in a sunny, rather shallow, outer-world experience of love; then rejected by a self-possessed lover who no longer needs him, presumably because of his shallow approach; and then finally awakened to his need to find a new way to relate to woman. This individuation journey has brought to consciousness the Poet's issues having to do with the Poet quarter. He has been operating instinctually in this realm, which is his gifted area. The instinctual way served him well in young life, but more is now required. His determined attitude in "Got To Get You Into My Life" is a strong and healthy one that gives us hope that he will do well in meeting the challenge that has been put before him.

The Poet, however, is only one part in four of the "person" that is the Beatles. As we turn to the songs written and led by John, we see that the Beatle Soldier has experiences of an entirely different nature on his journey through the Poet quarter. This variety of experience is true of each of us on our own journeys. As the unconscious unfolds for us the truth about a certain aspect of our lives, we are almost always given a series of dreams and life events which show us the situation from several different points of view, all of which belong to parts of ourselves, revealing the complexity of our total inner experience.

John's first song on the album is "I'm Only Sleeping," a pleasing evocation of what it feels like to stay in bed in the morning, heavy with dreaming, while the world outside bustles about its business. This is an important aspect of the Poet's mother-world—rest, leisure, restoration of physical and mental energy. A Soldier, however, is supposed to be up and at it in the morning, sacrificing his body's needs, if necessary, to do what has to be done. Is this the Beatle Soldier's day off? If not, there may be trouble here. The Beatle Soldier might lack the discipline of will necessary to extricate himself from the powerful pull of the mother-world, which he seems to be experiencing in a sleepy, unconscious state rather than with his eyes open.

John's next song, "She Said She Said," confirms our fears in this regard. He sings of a woman whose conversation with him is going too deep. When she tells him that she knows what death feels like, it overwhelms him and makes him feel crazy. The feminine world is too much for his Soldier consciousness, which does not have a strong enough grip on masculine outer reality to stand firm in the face of what seems like the terrifying nothingness of inner reality. His Soldier mind should be thinking about what she is saying, analyzing it and fitting it into a conscious structure. But he is not up to it. He lacks a structure that can hold it. He speaks of the simpler mother-world of his childhood, where his present consciousness was sufficient. This indicates a tendency to regression, to turning away from the challenge of expanding his consciousness to the point of being able to *relate* to woman and the feminine side of life, instead of falling into it and being carried along by it.

In the rest of the Soldier's songs on the album—"And My Bird Can Sing," "Doctor Robert," and "Tomorrow Never Knows"—we see him break relationship with a woman and then turn to drugs, completing his regression into the mother-world. Instead of getting busy and equipping himself for a healthy conversation between masculine consciousness and the feminine unconscious, the Beatle Soldier has given up, surrendered to the feminine realm. He hopes to remain an unconscious boy, cared for and indulged by his mother, who is no longer a human woman but the unconscious itself, into whose arms he unwisely entrusts himself through mood-altering substances. "Turn off your mind, relax, and float downstream," he sings.

We would be very worried about this "person" that is the Beatles were it not for the strength we have already seen in Paul, the Poet part of the personality. Paul is having troubles in love, but he has taken them in hand and is going forward to meet them, not letting himself be washed downstream, like John, into the cosmic void. The fact is that Poet personalities are characterized by weakness in the Soldier quarter. That is what throws the weight of their experience of life toward cultivating the relationships and pleasures of the mother-world. This can work out well for them if they achieve enough balance in the other quarters. Therefore, while some worry is justified, there is also reason to be cautiously optimistic.

The Beatles were once asked how they were able to keep their psychic balance. George, the Wise Man, answered, "There's four of us, so if one goes a little potty, it's all right." The same is true for everyone. We all have parts of ourselves that are wounded and unhealthy and that are helped along by the parts of us that are sound. Our wounded parts play necessary roles in our personalities and help make us who we are.

As a Poet, the Beatles "person" is basically a youthful personality. His ego parts, the Poet and the Soldier, have the strongest voices, writing and singing the lead for most of the songs. The mature parts—the Wise Man and the King—play strong supporting roles. They are the major instrumental voices—the Wise Man plays the lead guitar, and the King plays the drums. The Wise Man also writes and is the lead singer for a few songs on each album, while the King usually sings the lead on only one song per album, often one written for him by the Poet.

On *Revolver* the Wise Man sees the individuation journey coming and announces it with "Taxman." But he also has issues of his own to be dealt with in the Poet quarter. The Wise Man's energy arises from the side of a man that relates to the feminine principle, but in the Wise Man that relationship is a spiritual one, and this estranges him somewhat from his physical passion for women. All of George's love songs in the early Beatles period show a notable lack of passion. This love problem of the Wise Man rises to consciousness on the *Revolver* album.

His first song after "Taxman" is "Love to You," which has an outright Eastern sound with heavy Indian instrumentation. The Eastern music tells us that the Wise Man is in a decidedly spiritual mode. He says he is awfully busy—with his spiritual life, no doubt—but if this woman wants him to, he will make love to her. Here is his typical lack of passion. But in his last song on the album, "I Want to Tell You," he acknowledges this problem. Singing to a woman, he says that he has so much he wants to tell her. It fills him up when he is not with her, but when he gets near her, it leaves him, and he can no longer find the words. He hopes that in time this will change and he will be able to relate to her more fully. So, like the Poet, the Wise Man leaves this quarter conscious of his problems in love and in search of a solution.

The one song on this album led by the Beatle King is "Yellow Submarine." In surrendering to the feminine world, the Soldier part of the Beatles has abandoned the dry land of consciousness. But the King comes to the rescue with a vehicle to carry the Beatles through their submergence in the unconscious. A submarine is a human way of going through a nonhuman realm. Ringo tells us that the sea through which the Yellow Submarine travels is in the sky. We also note that the music and imagery of the song are happy and sunny. These are indications that heaven is being included in this individuation journey. We can, therefore, be hopeful about its outcome, despite the troubles we have seen with the Soldier.

Sgt. Pepper: The Soldier Quarter

The album that follows *Revolver* is *Sgt. Pepper's Lonely Hearts Club Band.* The very name suggests the Soldier theme. Now we are in the world of the personal father, the competitive outside world of collective consciousness. We have already seen, however, that the Beatle Soldier has regressed into the mother-world. It is not surprising, therefore, that in his first song on this album, "Lucy in the Sky with Diamonds," John describes his outside world as a psychedelic fantasyland with flowers as tall as trees, taxis made of newspapers, and train stations with surreal porters. Instead of seeking a masculine mentor from the father-world, the Beatle Soldier searches through this psychedelic landscape for a magical woman, perhaps feeling she could help him solve his problems.

His next song, "Being for the Benefit of Mr. Kite," is a circus poster set to music. Joining a circus might be the Beatle Soldier's answer to making a living. This could be all right. Poet personalities often support themselves as performers. But there is a question of whether the Beatle Soldier can take on the discipline that comes with any occupation, even one that looks like fun. The antique sound of this song suggests he is still in a state of regression.

The Soldier's next song, "Good Morning Good Morning," confirms that he is not adapting to the dailiness required by life in the outside world. He is, however, at least beginning to face the here and now. He sings of a depressed man going through the motions of life, poorly related to his wife and child, bored with his job, with his town, with everything. And finally, in his last song, "A Day in the Life," he sings of his alienation from the greater world as he reads a newspaper and is unable to see the point of anything in it.

The Beatle Soldier has shown himself to be highly resistant to his own realm of life. The only gain in consciousness he has made in this quarter has been to come back from the world of fantasy and face his depression in the reality of the outside world.

The Wise Man also makes a poor showing in this quarter, although as a basic introvert, whose true home is the inner world, he is not required to shine in the competitive outer world of the Soldier. George's one contribution to this album is "Within You Without You," another song with a strong Eastern sound. In it, he looks at the outside world with introverted eyes and proclaims that all those busy people who are so outwardly occupied with life know nothing of the inner life. They are empty inside, unconscious of true reality, and barren of real love. His tone is preachy. Even though there is some validity to his observations, he nonetheless fails to appreciate the value of collective life. All that busyness (business) keeps the world going. The faithfulness of ordinary people to the requirements of their daily lives has more nobility in it than the Wise Man realizes.

Ringo's one song on the album, "A Little Help from My Friends," gives us a ray of hope in this rather dismal phase of the Beatles' individuation journey. The Beatle King has a willing attitude even though he admits he is not strong in this quarter. Kings do not have ordinary occupations in the outer world, but this King is not above doing his share. If necessary, he will sing for his supper, hoping to be forgiven if he goes off key, trusting that with the help of his friends he will get by.

Three of the Beatles have now sung their parts. The Beatle Soldier is depressed in the competitive outside world of the father. The Wise Man is aloof. The King is willing but in need of help. This puts the weight of the journey on the shoulders of the Poet, who fortunately rises to the occasion. In the opening song, "Sgt. Pepper's Lonely Hearts Club Band," Paul embraces the Soldier theme. The Lonely Hearts Club suggests the organized collective life of the father-world. This particular segment of society is one to which the Poet has evidently been drawn by the love problems he encountered in the Poet quarter.

In his next song, "Getting Better," the Poet tells of several Soldier problems on which he is making some progress. One has to do with the difficulty he has had conforming to a school environment, and the others have to do with controlling his masculine anger and violence. In "Fixing a Hole," he tells us he has taken on the Soldier's task of strengthening his boundaries: fixing a hole in the roof and cracks in the door to keep out disagreeable people. In "She's Leaving Home," he sings of the Soldier's challenge to break out of the mother-world. He puts it in terms of a young woman—his anima, or feminine, relating side—who resolutely and grimly steps out on her own, leaving her distressed parents behind.

In "When I'm Sixty-Four," Paul sings a Soldier's love song about the practical and mundane aspects of long-term marriage. Poets, who are strong on the passionate and romantic side of love, are often weak when it comes to day-to-day commitment. In this song, the Beatle Poet finds in himself a Soldier's fidelity as he asks his beloved if she will share with him the ordinary outcome of love—a house and children, faithful companionship, and mutual support to the end of their days. Finally, in "Lovely Rita," we see the Beatle Poet trying to use his charm to woo a meter maid, presumably to evade a parking ticket. This shows a certain darkness in his approach to the law, although the infraction is not great.

For the most part, Paul has done well enough in the Soldier quarter. Being basically a Poet, he is not as strong as a Soldier can be, but we hope he is strong enough to carry the Beatles forward despite the heavy weight that John's shadow is beginning to exert. In the last song on the album, "A Day in the Life," we see the delicate balancing act of these light and dark sides of the Beatles personality. While John sings about his alienation from the outer world, Paul comes in with a little song within the song and sings of getting up in the morning, combing his hair, and catching a bus, showing an adequate acceptance of life's daily grind. On the upper level of the bus, he handles his boredom by looking out the window and daydreaming. The Poet's soundness balances the Soldier's brokenness, though just barely. The Soldier's failure in his own quarter, however, remains troubling.

Magical Mystery Tour: The Wise Man Quarter

The next album is *Magical Mystery Tour,* and it takes us, as its name implies, into the mystical realm of the Wise Man. Paul opens with the title song, inviting us to join the Magical Mystery Tour, which *wants* to take us away. The unconscious is an autonomous reality which seeks a relationship with us. This is a truth to which our ego consciousness has great resistance, since the ego fears being eclipsed by the much greater power of the unconscious. It tries to hold off the unconscious by denying that it actually has a separate existence of its own. The Beatle Poet, however, has gained strength in the Soldier quarter, and he feels ready now to take on a conscious relationship with the unconscious.

In "The Fool on the Hill," the Poet sings about the wisdom to be gained in the Wise Man quarter, an inner wisdom which seems foolish to people in the outside world. In "Your Mother Should Know" he pays tribute to the wisdom of the mother-world, acknowledging that youth does not know everything and that there is a wisdom of the ages carried by the feminine side of life. In "Hello Goodbye" the Poet sings about the problem of reconciling the opposites, a major task to be accomplished in the Wise Man quarter. It could be said he is coming to terms with the compensatory nature of the unconscious, which says yes when he says no, high when he says low, and goodbye when he says hello.

Then in "Penny Lane" the Beatle Poet is led by the unconscious to revisit his childhood. When a person's individuation journey brings up from the depths long-buried issues from his childhood, it is to help him understand and accept himself as a particular, unique individual who springs from a certain time, place, and set of circumstances. Some of the wounds that have long existed in him can now be healed. Others must simply be accepted. Inherited gifts and tasks must also be accepted. It is these special features of his life that make him the person that he is and none other. In accepting the truth of his life, an individuating person recognizes and honors his individual reality and thereby comes into his true inheritance. The question then becomes, what is he going to do with that inheritance? The Poet sings about this in his last song, which he shares with the Soldier. We will look at that after we have followed the Soldier's progress through this realm.

Knowing the burden under which the Beatle Soldier has been laboring, it is not surprising that John makes a ragged start in the Wise Man quarter. "I Am the Walrus" is all babble and gobbledy-gook. While he was in the Soldier quarter, John failed to develop a disciplined consciousness with which to take this tour of the depths. As a result, the nonrational language of the unconscious now seems to get the best of him. However, it is possible that this nonsensical song actually shows a positive development. Unlike his attitude in the Poet quarter, the Beatle Soldier is no longer protesting against the feminine depths and turning away, nor is he dreamily surrendering. Rather, he hangs in there this time and tries to express what he understands to be coming to him from this foreign realm, however absurd it may seem. Perhaps he glimpses behind it the magical woman he was looking for earlier, the one he hopes may be able to help him. Though it is true that his consciousness is undisciplined, it is possible that his native intelligence will be enough to get him through this encounter with the unconscious.

His next song affirms this positive assessment by showing further progress. In "Strawberry Fields Forever," the Soldier, too, goes down into his childhood, a darker and more troubled world than the Poet's. (Both Penny Lane and Strawberry Fields were familiar places in their Liverpool boyhoods.) In this song, the Beatle Soldier is feeling easier with the strangeness of the inner realm, and he is actually beginning to learn things there. He is sorting some things out.

From this comes a breakthrough in his next song when he sings, "All You Need Is Love." Coming from the Beatles, this is a somewhat naive statement, since love also needs a disciplined will to go along with it. Nonetheless, it does seem that in his brokenness the Beatle Soldier has found his way to something important. Because of his deep wounds in the father realm, the greatest answer for the Beatle Soldier *is* love, even if it is not completely centered and balanced by a healthy will.

The Beatle Soldier has been unable to embrace will, but it seems that he can embrace love. In that, he has finally found at least one sound leg upon which to stand. It is none other than the weak leg of the father-world into which the Beatles were born, the very leg that needs strengthening through more concentrated use. The correction of an imbalance almost always means a temporary imbalance in the other direction. The Beatles and their generation embodied a correction of the world's spirit toward love, away from an overdependence on disciplined will. It was the task of that generation to embrace and retrieve the lost value of love, a task which necessarily entailed letting go of other values that would themselves have to be retrieved by future generations.

This is the way it is with each of us as individuals. Through the process of individuation, we gradually come to realize that we have a specific purpose in life, not so much by choice but by force of circumstance. We were not put on earth to be all things to all people. We can only hope to do a few things well, while many things we can barely do adequately, and at some things we must fail miserably. It is when we can understand and accept the value of our particular, individual strengths that we can also understand and accept our shortcomings.

"Baby You're a Rich Man" is the duet the Soldier sings with the Poet, mixing two songs into one. They sing it after they have visited their childhoods. They ask what they are going to do now that they have discovered who they are. Having become rich with the inner treasure of self-knowledge, they are ready to leave the solitary world of the Wise Man and go out into the active world of the King to make use of what they have gained.

The Wise Man has been more quiet than usual in this quarter, seeming to be already familiar with the territory. He waits for the others, anxious for them to learn their lessons and move on with him to the King's realm, where, perhaps he knows, he himself will finally come into his own. But he is worried about their progress. His one song on this album is "Blue Jay Way." The bird imagery in the title symbolizes the part of the natural spirit that soars away from the earth of the Wise Man's quarter toward heaven and the King's realm of perfected outer life. In this song the Wise Man waits late into a foggy night for the expected arrival of his friends. Though he gave them directions, he fears they have gotten lost. The Wise Man seems to see a problem here that no one else can see.

There are moments like this in every individuation journey. Just when things seem to be going well, a dream speaks of trouble that has not yet shown itself in outer life. Dreams usually project forward in time. They often refer to developments whose seeds are present but that have yet to break through into the light.

The King does not seem to share the Wise Man's concern. Though Ringo sings no song of his own in this quarter, he co-composes an instrumental number with the other three. This is the only song the four of them ever composed together. Its title, "Flying," suggests movement toward the King, as does their unity of effort in composing the song. This balances the Wise Man's concern that the Beatles might be hopelessly lost in the foggy night.

The White Album: A False Move

It turns out, however, that the Wise Man's concern is at least partly justified. The next album to appear is a double album whose cover design is all white, so pure in concept that its minimalist title, *The Beatles*, is visible only in raised relief. Immediately dubbed The White Album by the public, it is the first Beatles album to be met with widespread disappointment. Something has gone wrong. The total effect of the album is ragged, uneven, and undistinguished. There is no unified mood or atmosphere. Few of the songs are deeply pleasing.

The White Album is a false move into the King quarter. The Beatle ego parts—John, Paul, and to some extent George—have become inflated, which is to say, unconsciously identified with the divine, in this case the masculine divine, the One above all. Each thinks he is the best, that he can do what the Beatles do all by himself, entirely in his own way. They are no longer collaborating with each other, but each merely uses the others as a backup band, with little give and take among them as each records his own songs.

In order to understand what is happening, we will have to look more closely at what is actually going on in the real life of the Beatles. This change in perspective comes in with the King, who in his mature phase brings with him earth's reality, an awakening from our unconscious dreams of life to actual life itself. What we see here are real life events that parallel the themes we have been watching in the music.

At the heart of the problem is a major rift that has grown between John and Paul. John was the ego leader of the early Beatles, back when they sang simple rock'n'roll and made albums of unrelated songs that were put together without regard for any connections among them. The new level of music that became the late Beatles arose primarily through Paul's inspiration. These later albums were "concept" albums, characterized by an intentional interweaving of themes, with some of the songs actually linked together, no silence between them. With this and the inclusion of orchestral instruments, these albums seemed to be moving toward a synthesis of popular and classical music.

This called for an expansion of technique, knowledge, and ability—the disciplined work of the mature Soldier. But the demand was too much for John. He could only be a youthful Soldier and defend his original territory. He wanted to go back to their old style. While Paul was taking piano lessons and learning classical music, John turned heavily to drugs. He went along only reluctantly with Paul's leadership through the later albums, dragging his feet and feeling alternately resentful and guilty. The weight he exerted on the Beatles was great. Paul's own Soldier aspect was healthier than John's, and with it, he had carried the Beatles this far. But John's Soldier energy, though dark, was stronger than Paul's, and the downward pull of it was making it increasingly difficult for the Beatles to go on.

The situation came to a head when John fell in love with Yoko Ono. This was a deep and powerful attraction like none John had ever known before. Yoko replaced the Beatles as the center of his life. She was the magical woman he had been looking for, a dark wisdom woman who became the guide for his experience in the Wise Man quarter. She was an avant garde artist whose work was intended to make conscious structure meaningless, in the spirit of "I Am the Walrus." She knew about the wisdom systems that underlie nature and introduced John to astrology, Tarot cards, and the *I Ching.* She helped him grapple with the issues of his childhood and inspired him to believe in love as the ultimate answer to his life. But Yoko was dark in the sense that she, too, was alienated from the father-world, which she viewed as hostile and life destroying. Unwilling to avail herself of legitimate masculine power, she sought to use love and wisdom as means of power, an approach to the feminine that always undermines life.

Following Yoko's lead, John found earth's depths, but with her he was confined to its darkness, unable to open himself at the same time to the sun and sky of collective consciousness and true community. He had made it as far as the Wise Man quarter, but in the end, he could go no further. In one of his better songs on The White Album he sings, "I'm So Tired."

Ringo, the King, actually quit the Beatles during the making of The White Album. Beginning to doubt himself in the face of their disunity, Ringo felt unloved and left out by the other three. The others went after him, reassured him of their love, and convinced him to come back. When he returned, he found they had covered his drums with flowers. On The White Album, the Beatle King for the first time sings a song that he himself has written. Its title was his plea to the others: "Don't Pass Me By."

George sings what is perhaps the most powerful song on The White Album. In "While My Guitar Gently Weeps" he sings to the others that it saddens him to see their love miscarrying to such an extent because he knows how much love is really there.

Paul's best song on the album, the one that most touches the soul, is "Blackbird." In it, he creates a haunting image of a crippled blackbird trying to rise into flight in a night sky. This is its moment, he sings. It must fly despite the brokenness of its wings. This song gives us hope that the inflation of this album will be overcome and a centered experience of the King might still be had.

Abbey Road: The King Quarter

The public's reaction to The White Album made the Beatles realize they had lost their center. They tried to regain it by getting back to their roots and recording an album that was more down to earth, more like the old days in Liverpool when they were of one mind and spirit. But this effort ended in more acrimony than ever. They could not even bear to mix the tapes to make them into a finished album. (*Let It Be*, the album released just after their breakup, was finally pulled together from these tapes.) From this experience, they knew that their days were numbered. The "person" that was the Beatles was dying. Their broken parts were making their reality unsustainable. Without a sound Soldier component, they could not live forward into the next required phase, the King's world of human community.

The Beatles embodied the spirit of a generation. It is the fate of every generation to pass away, hopefully before its shortcomings have undermined the gifts it has brought. With more grace than the generations just before it, the Beatles recognized the end of their time and acquiesced to it. Their journey had brought them face to face with their own death. In full knowledge and acceptance of this fact, they let Paul lead them through one last effort, an album that they hoped would be like the great albums of the *Sgt. Pepper* days, one that would redeem the failure of The White Album. They wanted to show that they could still pull together into one and that, despite their impending death, they really did still love each other. To meet this challenge, even John rose on his crippled wings and flew toward the King, who came to meet him halfway. The album they made was *Abbey Road*, which many consider to be their best. It is the one that reflects the true essence of the King.

The effectiveness of the King does not belong to the ego. It comes from the Self and is only present when we let it be in us without trying to claim it for our own. As so many Christian hymns proclaim, it is the Christ—in Jungian terminology, the Self, the God-center within—who is the true King. Christ the King is an image of earth's reality and heaven's spirit joined together into one. The King within us takes us as we actually are, without idealization, and blesses us—our shortcomings as well as our strengths, our sorrows as well as our joys. He shows us that, despite our limitations, we are perfect for the part we were meant to play in our particular time and place to meet a particular need in the unfolding of the world. This only makes sense when we know ourselves to be one with the intricate web of the human community.

Abbey Road was the street on which the Beatles' recording studio was located. It was their real life kingdom as mortal men. The album cover shows them crossing from one side of Abbey Road to the other, an ordinary street scene, four rather colorful men in London in 1969. The Beatle myth is dissolving into reality.

The music on the *Abbey Road* album has a unified sound, but within that unity, the music is divided into two distinct parts to accommodate the different approaches of John and Paul, a solution that reveals the mediating presence of the King. Side One is for John and is made up of separate songs that have no intended connection between them. (This was in the days of LP records, but the two sides can still be distinguished on digital recordings by the abrupt break at the end of the last song on the original Side One.) Side Two is Paul's and has the connected, rock-symphony style that the Beatles probably would have continued to develop had they been able to go on.

Because this is the King quarter, the symbolic content of this album has a different quality from the albums of the other three quarters. Reality has come in with the King, and the album seems to be about John and Paul as the real individuals who are the ego carriers of the dying Beatles. Because the unification of all the parts is the theme of the King, our best understanding of the album comes from leaving the songs in their given sequence rather than breaking them apart and grouping them according to the separate Beatle voices.

On Side One it seems that all the Beatles come together in spirit to sing a blessing on John's life. He actually asks them to do this in the first song, the title of which is "Come Together." John seems to be asking them to unify in spite of him, or because of him, or for the sake of him.

In the second song, "Something," George surprises us with a beautiful love song about a woman whose movement and smile attract him like none other ever has. "Something in the way you move. . ." The Beatle Wise Man is finally able to give voice to his deep love for a woman. He sings with the passion of a Poet, but also with the Wise Man's ability to leave space in a relationship. With this, the Beatles "person" has become a better lover, a development which goes far to resolve the love problems presented in the Poet quarter. The quality of George's songwriting has also increased enormously, showing that he has integrated the Poet quarter's beauty of expression as well. If we look at "Something" in terms of this being John's side of the album, we see in it John's love for Yoko, which for him was like no other because it reached down to the depths of feminine wisdom. The drumming, especially the use of hollow tom-toms, is particularly compelling in this song, giving us a strong sense of the King's presence. Throughout this album, Ringo is more present in his drumming than on any other album.

The rest of the songs on John's side of the album can be seen as commentaries on his life, the shadow aspects of it as well as the light aspects. The songs are sung without judgment, but also with a clear eye to consequences. Paul sings "Maxwell's Silver Hammer," a cheery song about a serial killer—a shadow side of John—who murders a student, a teacher, and a judge, all symbols of the father-world. In "Oh! Darling," a stirring tribute to John's rock'n'roll spirit, Paul sings of someone who is excessively dependent on his lover and yet must repeatedly assure her that he will not harm her. These relationship problems are consequences of John's rejection of the father-world, and they were mirrored in his life with Yoko.

In "Octopus's Garden," Ringo sings of a free and protected life beneath the sea in the realm of a friendly octopus. As a monarch with a roundness of form, the octopus symbolizes a benevolent but unconscious aspect of the Self. The Beatle King seems to be granting John his own kingdom, an inner one submerged in the feminine realm. It reminds us of John's secluded life as a house-husband in the final years before his death.

John himself sings the last song on his side of the album. "I Want You (She's So Heavy)" speaks of his strong attachment to Yoko, but also of the burden of his life under the domination of the feminine realm. The heaviness of the song seems to reflect the long depressions he often suffered. At the end, there is a protracted and increasingly ominous instrumental refrain that goes on and on and on until it finally ends abruptly, mid-measure. As we listen now to this sudden end, it evokes the image of John's murder in 1980 by a young fan who was more alienated from the father-world than was John himself. In the way of the unconscious, which is not bound by time, it probably does refer to that. John's life, though blessed by the King, will be what it will be.

It is with great relief that we hear George open Side Two with "Here Comes the Sun," another surprisingly beautiful song by the Beatle Wise Man. The sun is a symbol of consciousness and of the King. The Beatles have finally come through into the full daylight of the world of masculine consciousness. This is Paul's side of the album, and in the next song, "Because," John pays tribute to Paul's optimism. He sings of the roundness of the world, the blueness of the sky, and the highness of the wind, all of which move him and lift his spirits just because they are what they are.

Paul, more than the rest, carries within himself the spirit of the Beatles. The remaining songs on his side of the album are connected together in his own creative style and have to do with his life with the Beatles and with the end they now face. He begins with "You Never Give Me Your Money," in which he alludes to the irreconcilable differences that have arisen among them on the business side of their relationship. Then he reviews their lives together, from when they were fresh out of school with no money and no prospects, through their rise to fame, and then to a death—someone has gone to heaven. We think of the death of Brian Epstein, their manager.

In the next song John picks up the story and shows us Paul's shadow, just as Paul showed us John's shadow on the album's other side. We surmise that the "Sun King," of whom John now sings, is Paul trying to lead the Beatles in the wake of Epstein's death. It is obvious from the flatness of their voices that the Sun King's subjects only pretend to be happy with him. In the next two songs, John explains why. He sings of "Mean Mr. Mustard," a mean, low man who stands in contrast to Paul's over-niceness and perfectionism. This is Paul's shadow, poorly hidden beneath his pleasant surface. Whenever Mean Mr. Mustard goes out to see the Queen of England—the ruling monarch—he hurls obscenities at her. So Paul carries in his shadow the same antipathy to the father-world that John carries openly. Then there is "Polythene Pam," a rather bizarre woman with a muddled gender identity who inhabits the sexual underworld. We presume this to be a shadow side of Paul's anima, his inner feminine self.

Paul seems to be strong enough to accept these judgments from the others. His next song, "She Came in Through the Bathroom Window," is vigorous and upbeat. He sings of resigning from the police force (the thankless job of trying to lead the Beatles), of getting a regular job and making a life with an intriguing woman who has burst into his life. We assume this refers to his recent marriage to Linda Eastman and his decision to leave the group and start a new career with her. In "Golden Slumbers" Paul sings a lullaby as if to a dying loved one, poignantly accepting the breakup of the Beatles as a reality that cannot be turned back. "Carry that Weight" seems to be about the burden of the dark Soldier, which all of the Beatles will have to face in themselves when John is no longer present to carry it for them.

Having accepted that, they come to "The End." In this song, Paul makes an important breakthrough by inviting the others to come into his dreamlife. The Beatles meant wholeness to Paul, and if he cannot have these other three parts of himself in his outer life, he would like to have them in his inner life. In this, he opens himself to integration of the essence of the others as parts of his own psyche.

This puts the Beatles' death in perspective and shows why it has turned out to be the goal of their individuation journey. Every outer reality to which we cling must eventually be surrendered in order to be replaced by an inner reality that truly belongs to us and from which we can never again be separated. It was in this spirit that Jesus accepted his own crucifixion, explaining to his disciples that he must leave them in order for them to discover his reality within themselves. It is in this same spirit that we are called upon in our own individuation journeys to let go of outer realities that feel to us as if they are life itself. Death in this context is a painful but transformative process.

The Beatle King responds to Paul's request for inner wholeness with a triumphant drum solo, virtually the only protracted solo he ever played on any Beatles album. After this the Beatles sing their last line, telling us what they have learned about love. Ultimately, they say, it comes down to the fact that what you receive in love is in direct proportion to what you give. "The love you take is equal to the love you make." This, then, is their answer to the problem of loneliness in "Eleanor Rigby." The lonely woman and the empty priest must undertake the task of reconciling life's opposites through the real work of love in order for their own lives to become rich and meaningful.

Paul Is Dead: An Outbreak of Synchronicity

Abbey Road was a huge success with the public. The album's music resonated deeply, although no one yet knew that the Beatles had recorded their last album. Looking back on it with what we now know, we can see that it contains a strong element of farewell, but in the fall of 1969, this was not so obvious. However, the truth of the matter was picked up unconsciously by the Beatles' fans, and it led to the strange "Paul is dead" episode, which was actually an outbreak of synchronistic awareness, although it was not consciously understood in those terms, nor was the true nature of synchronicity correctly perceived.

Immediately after the release of *Abbey Road*, the rumor began to spread among the public that Paul (who, as the Poet, most personified the Beatles) had died in 1966 when the Beatles stopped touring. According to the rumor, a look-alike and sound-alike had secretly been put in his place, for fear the fans would turn away if the knowledge of his death became known. However, the later albums (the individuation albums, from *Revolver* on) were supposedly strewn with clues about Paul's death, as if it were the Beatles' handlers who wanted to keep the secret, while the Beatles themselves wanted to reveal it.

The perceived clues were endless. On the *Revolver* album, Paul was said to be referring to his own death in an auto accident when he sings in "Got to Get You Into My Life" that he made a right turn and found a surprise there. More details about the wreck were believed to have been given in "A Day in the Life" on the *Sgt. Pepper* album. On that album cover, which was now believed to depict Paul's funeral, there is a raised hand, with palm outward, above Paul's head: this was interpreted as the Mafia sign for death. In another picture on that album, Paul stands tellingly with his back to the camera while the other three face forward.

On the *Magical Mystery Tour* album, in the electronically distorted words at the end of "Strawberry Fields Forever," John can supposedly be heard to say, "I buried Paul." (He actually says, "Cranberry sauce.") As the Beatles cross the street in single file on the cover of *Abbey Road*, Paul's presumed stand-in is barefooted while the others have on shoes, supposedly indicating that Paul is the corpse in his own funeral procession. George, dressed in blue jeans, is the gravedigger; Ringo, in a formal suit, is the undertaker; and John, dressed all in white, is the minister. A Volkswagen *Beetle* parked just beyond the crosswalk has a license tag that reads *28*

IF, interpreted as a cryptic reference to the fact that Paul would be *twenty-eight* years old *if* he were still alive. And on and on.

People sensed that something odd had been going on with the Beatles ever since *Revolver*. Because the Beatles carried the image of wholeness, and therefore of the Self, the "Paul is dead" believers projected onto them the Self's use of synchronicity in revealing to us in ordinary daily events the unrealized truths of our own lives. As we have seen, there actually *was* something unusual going on in those later albums—an image of an individuation journey through the four masculine quarters—although the public did not have a conscious framework by which to understand it and describe it.

Not even the Beatles themselves could see the degree to which they and their times were leading the collective consciousness of the world toward the fuller love and wisdom that come from the feminine realm. But they did not need to see the big picture. Because of their basic good-heartedness and their openness to the creativity of the unconscious, these four men from Liverpool proved to be adequate vessels for a truly synchronistic display of a particular image of masculine wholeness, one that stresses the lost feminine side of human life, including the process of individuation. And thus, as is true of any individuating person, the Beatles "person" helped to answer the challenge of his times.

Jung's Liverpool Dream

In light of this analysis of the Beatles, it is interesting to look at a dream that came to Carl Jung at the end of the intense phase of his own individuation journey in 1927. This dream is recorded in his autobiography, *Memories, Dreams, Reflections*, which was published posthumously in 1963, the very year the Beatles were emerging onto the world stage:

> This is the dream: I found myself in a dirty, sooty city. It was night, and winter, and dark, and raining. I was in Liverpool. With a number of Swiss—say, half a dozen—I walked through the

dark streets. I had the feeling that there we were coming from the harbor, and that the real city was actually up above, on the cliffs. We climbed up there. It reminded me of Basel, where the market is down below and then you go up through the Totengässchen ("Alley of the Dead"), which leads to a plateau above and so to the Petersplatz and the Peterskirche. When we reached the plateau, we found a broad square dimly illuminated by street lights, into which many streets converged. The various quarters of the city were arranged radially around the square. In the center was a round pool, and in the middle of it a small island. While everything round about was obscured by rain, fog, smoke, and dimly lit darkness, the little island blazed with sunlight. On it stood a single tree, a magnolia, in a shower of reddish blossoms. It was as though the tree stood in the sunlight and were at the same time the source of light. My companions commented on the abominable weather, and obviously did not see the tree. They spoke of another Swiss who was living in Liverpool, and expressed surprise that he should have settled there. I was carried away by the beauty of the flowering tree and the sunlit island, and thought, "I know very well why he has settled here." Then I awoke.

On one detail of the dream I must add a supplementary comment: the individual quarters of the city were themselves arranged radially around a central point. This point formed a small open square illuminated by a larger street lamp, and constituted a small replica of the island. I knew that the "other Swiss" lived in the vicinity of one of these secondary centers....

This dream brought with it a sense of finality. I saw that here the goal had been revealed. One

> could not go beyond the center. The center is the goal, and everything is directed toward the center. Through this dream I understood that the self is the principle and archetype of orientation and meaning. Therein lies its healing function.

This was a dream about the quarters of the psyche, the tree of life, the center, and the Self, all found in the unlikely setting of Liverpool. It follows the pattern found in all the Wisdom traditions—in the story of Jesus, for example—that new life from God arises in unlikely places and thus often goes unrecognized. Jung received prophetic dreams about World War I shortly before it broke out, and about World War II many years before it occurred. Therefore, while it is remarkable, it is not strange that the dream that confirmed for him the nature of the Self would contain imagery that is linked to the Beatles, that four-part image of human wholeness that arose in the second half of the twentieth century and swept the world before it. It is fitting that on the cover of *Sgt. Pepper's Lonely Hearts Club Band*, Carl Jung's photograph is among those pictured looking on from the crowd.

Chapter Eleven
Feminine Wholeness

THE MASCULINE QUATERNITY of Poet, Soldier, Wise Man, and King belongs to woman as well as man. A woman's Poet must be healthy and in good relationship to her outer feminine being if she is to be playful and artistically expressive. If her Soldier is strong and brave, she will be focused and disciplined. Her Wise Man must be awake and aware if she is to deal consciously and rationally with nature and the unconscious. And when her King is well balanced and sound, she can be an effective leader in the outside world. These aspects of life, however, are not the ones that are most fundamental to her.

Feminine life is of a different quality than masculine life. It is concerned with the human experience of being rather than doing, with personal story rather than public achievement, with life as it is rather than as it is conceptualized, with relationship rather than power, with openness and receptivity rather than defense and conquest, with being at one with the process of life rather than analyzing it and naming it, and with establishing and maintaining the forms of community life rather than with leadership.

The names I use for the quarters of the feminine quaternity reflect this difference in quality. The masculine quarters were given impersonal, occupational names—Poet, Soldier, and so on. But for the feminine quaternity it seems best to use women's names, mythically based for wide application and recognizable meaning, but names that suggest feminine embodiment and personal story.

Every woman—and every man's anima, or inner feminine self—is two daughters: her mother's daughter and her father's daughter (Fig 11.1). At the youthful, ego level of life I call the mother's daughter *Eve*, after the biblical mother of humankind, and the father's daughter *Scarlett*, after the strong-willed heroine of *Gone With the Wind*. Young womanhood is lived in tension between these two sides of feminine being, between the personal mother's world of relationship and the care of physical life, with all its many details, and the personal father's world outside the home, where a woman must establish a relationship with power in order to ensure her own survival. At the mature, God-centered level I call the father's daughter *Athena*, after the Greek goddess who sprang fully grown from the head of Zeus, the sky father. I call the mother's daughter *Sophia*, the Greek name for Wisdom. Here the tension is between that part of woman that is dedicated to the masculine ideal of civilization and high principle and that part that is oriented toward the natural processes and deep meaning of unfolding life.

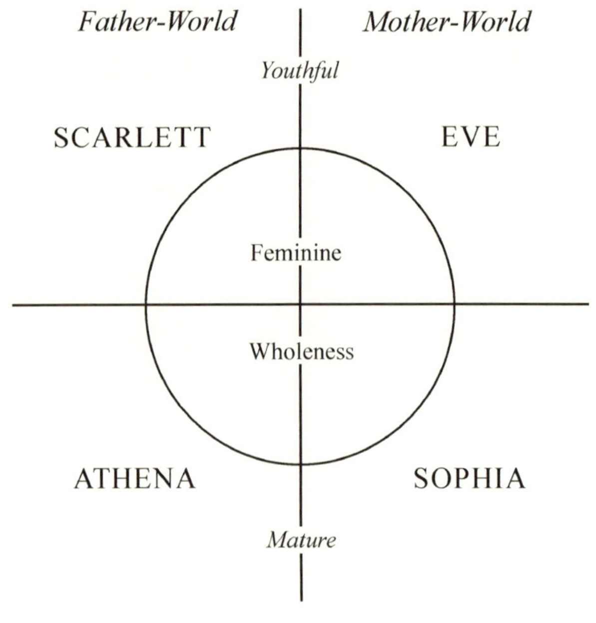

Fig 11.1. The Feminine Quaternity

Every woman has all four of these feminine parts within herself, although by nature they are not present in equal degrees of consciousness. One quarter will be stronger than the others—a woman's "star" will be there. This is the arena in which she will shine most brightly in her life. But all four quarters must eventually be recognized and lived in order for her life to be complete. As we shall see in Chapter Thirteen, our Jungian personality type, based on our particular ranking of the four functions of consciousness, tells us which of the quarters is our star quarter. It also reveals the sequence through which we traverse the other three quarters during the course of our lives.

Eve

Eve is the part of a woman—and of a man's anima—that identifies with the personal mother and is at home at the fundamental level of life that the mother oversees. Eve is woman in her most basic nature, woman as creature, as the vessel of physical life. My own dream voice once said to me, unaccompanied by image: *The important thing about the feminine vessel is that you are never to forget about it.*

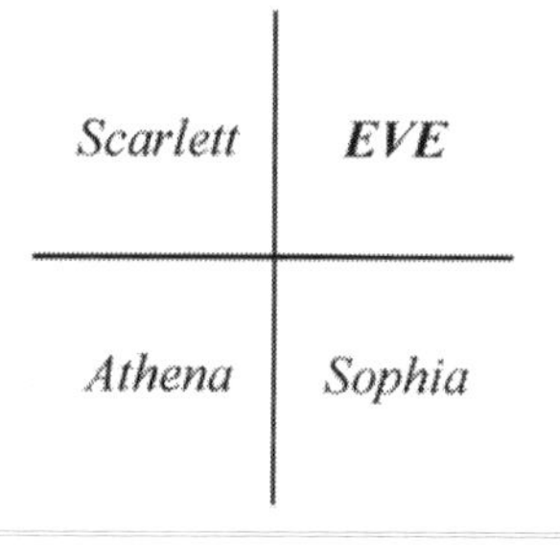

Fig 11.2. Eve Quarter

The requirements and limitations of physical life are easily forgotten, swept aside by our ideas and expectations, our dreams and enthusiasms, and by our aversion to physical exertion—our laziness. It is the Eve in us, the natural mother, who understands and accepts the requirements of physical life.

The essence of this principle is captured in the simple problem of trying to find a jar of mustard in the refrigerator. It is not unusual for a man or a child to open the refrigerator door, take a brief look inside, and then wail helplessly, "Where is the mustard?" It is the Eve in us who knows it is not enough to stand before the open door wishing for the mustard to appear. Eve takes it for granted that time and effort must be spent looking carefully on each shelf, moving larger objects aside in order to look behind them until at last the mustard is located. This might sound elementary, but the fact is that we almost seem by nature to be incapable of accepting the basic physical requirements of life unless the Eve within us is conscious and developed.

Eve is the part of a woman that tends physical life with all its many details. She provides the foundation for life on earth. Without her, a woman will not be healthy and balanced in the other three aspects of her feminine being. To forget about or denigrate Eve is to turn away from the very essence of the feminine principle.

It is in her Eve aspect that a woman maintains relationships through physical connections. Purely spiritual love does not belong to this quarter. Eve wants the real thing, the physical presence of the other. Eve's love is offered with outstretched arms, with a telephone call or a visit, with eyes that caress the reality of the other, with ears that take in the voice, the words, the experience of the other. Her love is a hands-on love, expressed in food, gifts, and other physical ministrations.

Until Eve matures, her relationship with others is the instinctual relationship of unconscious identity. She is one with those she loves. There are no boundaries. The youthful, instinctual Eve lives in and through others, dependent upon them for her experience of life. Her own individual personality is largely unknown and undeveloped. But ironically, to the degree to which she fails to know herself, she will fail to know others, unconsciously seeing them as projections of unknown parts of her own personality and not as the individuals they truly are. The more unconscious she is in her relationships, the more her efforts to meet the needs of others will miss the mark.

The Eve aspect of a woman matures as the other feminine aspects are developed. The mature Eve knows herself as a separate individual. She is not dependent on those with whom she is in relationships, and she is able to recognize their individual needs and the degree of her own responsibility toward them. A balance of the youthful and the mature aspects of Eve are necessary for a woman's wholeness. Without the mature Eve, a woman would be too dependent in her relationships, clinging to and smothering the ones she loves. But without a measure of the youthful Eve, she would be too cool and distant. Some unconscious identification is always present in every deeply felt relationship. It is the permeation of boundaries that provides the warmth of human connection.

Not only must the Eve aspect of every person find a balance between its youthful and mature qualities, but so must Eve be balanced with the Poet, the masculine expression of this same quarter. Both men and women have the problem of balancing within themselves the dual expression of each quarter. Here, the playful, artistic, and romantic activity of the Poet is in direct competition with Eve's attention to the immediate needs of physical life and real relationship. In this same way, the masculine and feminine expressions of life vie for the energy available to each of the other quarters, even as the different quarters vie with each other.

Scarlett

A girl is not only her mother's daughter and heir to the mother-world, but she is also the daughter of her father and heir to his world outside the home. The father wields power in the greater world in order to wrest away from it what is needed to support life in the intimate, noncompetitive world of the mother. The father's daughter is the part of a woman that comes to grips with this necessity of drawing support from the greater world outside the home.

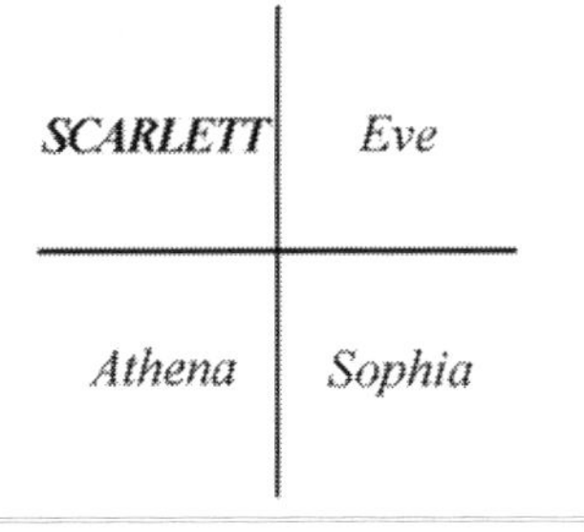

FIG 11.3. SCARLETT QUARTER

The daughter of the personal father is an aspect of woman that has taken a great developmental leap forward in recent times. The modern mythological figure of Scarlett, therefore, is an especially appropriate one. *Gone With the Wind*, the American novel in which Scarlett's character is drawn, was published in 1936 and still registers as the second favorite book of American readers, just behind the Bible. Such a large and longstanding popularity attests to the power of the book's archetypal content and its relevance to its time as this particular aspect of feminine life has arisen to new consciousness.

While the daughter of the personal mother focuses on the needs of others, thereby failing to become conscious of herself as an individual, the daughter of the personal father turns her attention to herself and her own potential for winning recognition and security. From the point of view of the mother's daughter, the father's daughter seems self-centered and estranged from her basic feminine nature of providing love and nurture. Yet every woman has the father's daughter in her, and this part of her is just as necessary for feminine wholeness as is the mother's daughter.

When Scarlett is not consciously present, she is present *unconsciously*, undermining Eve's work in the mother-world with unrecognized motives of self-seeking and competition. An important component of the new feminine development heralded by *Gone With the Wind* can be seen in the way the character of Scarlett consciously and unapologetically embraces her own ego-centered nature. It is healthier to be conscious of one's instinctual ego-centeredness than to be unconscious of it. When it is conscious, it can be directed toward useful ends and checked when it begins to become destructive.

The consciously ego-centered orientation to life that comes from the Scarlett quarter makes a woman more companionable to men, especially youthful men, who carry this quality as their own first nature. It is Scarlett who can relate to a man on his own terms of competitive striving for power and recognition in the outside world. She also relates to him on his own sexual terms through her inborn readiness to make herself into the image of his desires.

In the early chapters of *Gone With the Wind*, Scarlett portrays the youthful, instinctual father's daughter, wielding the power of her femininity to draw support—suitors—from the masculine world. Although she is not particularly admirable in her calculated approach to this, she nonetheless partakes of an aspect of feminine life that is important and cannot be left out of a woman's wholeness.

There is a natural instinct for the masculine to support the feminine. It is based upon the fact that the pure feminine is softer, kinder, less competitive, less active, and physically weaker than the pure masculine. In her feminine being a woman carries the image of soul, an intangible inner reality from which comes the grace, beauty, and loving-kindness of life. As the carrier of soul a woman needs masculine support—from without and from within—in order for this fragile quality to survive in the greater world. If it does not survive, if it is crushed and driven into the unconscious, the world becomes a hard and ruthless place.

The instinct to give and receive masculine support for feminine soul is rooted in the relationship between father and daughter. It begins with the little girl as the "frilly" feminine, an accentuation of femininity that is healthy and instinctual and draws to it the masculine instinct to support it. The frilly feminine forms the foundation for the development in adolescence of conscious sexual attractiveness. Here again, the feminine represents the soul, which seeks to draw men into relationship and connection to life.

Women who miss this development, who were never able as girls to identify with the frilly feminine or, later, with the authentic attracting power of sexuality, often find themselves living lives in which they give support to the masculine world to a greater degree than they receive support from it. In the absence of a healthy measure of masculine support, a woman often tries to become the father, taking on this role in her outer being and growing more and more distant from her own feminine softness and grace. This is an overbalance toward the mature Scarlett, who, as we shall see, develops the masculinity of her own being in order to stand on her own in the greater world.

The instinctual needs of the youthful Scarlett to be soft and graceful and supported by the masculine do not go away just because they have been skipped over. Instead, they appear darkly in the overbalanced mature Scarlett and undermine her strength, making her soft and passive in unconscious and destructive ways, despite her seeming hardness. When such a woman undertakes an individuation journey, her dreams and life experience lead her first to the frilly feminine and unblock her resistance to it. Acceptance of the frilly feminine moves a woman quickly to a conscious experience of the power of her sexual attractiveness, which she then must learn how to handle in a God-centered way. It is only on this instinctual foundation that a healthy mature Scarlett can arise.

The mature Scarlett is the part of a woman who develops her own inner masculine potential to compete and survive in the outside world. Ideally, it is the father who first encourages this development in his daughter, although to do it in the right way, he must be careful not to withdraw support for the soft side of her feminine being—a balance on his part that is not easy to achieve. If the development of the mature Scarlett fails to take place in due course, fate will often step in and try to arrange it by pulling away a woman's outer masculine support in an attempt to force her to find strength and independence within herself.

Through education and training, the mature Scarlett acquires the knowledge, discipline, and skill that are necessary to wield her own masculine power and handle in her own right the competitive reality of the outside world. When this development is balanced, a woman's masculine energy does not take over her outer personality, but rather it comes to her from within, bringing authentic focus, strength, and courage that complement her feminine reality without burying it. Both the youthful and the mature aspects of Scarlett are needed for wholeness—the first to bring a woman the masculine support she needs to retain her feminine softness and grace, and the second to give her strength, independence, and the satisfaction of achievement in the outside world.

Athena

The father's daughter at the higher, God-centered level of life is symbolized by Athena, the Greek goddess who was born fully mature from the head of Zeus. Clothed in armor and carrying a spear, Athena sprang into the world with a war cry. Her father gave her the use of his thunderbolt and shield, conferring upon her the agency of his mighty power. She of all the gods and goddesses on

Mount Olympus stood closest to his throne. Athena was the protector of cities and of the soldiers who fought for them, the guardian of culture and civilization.

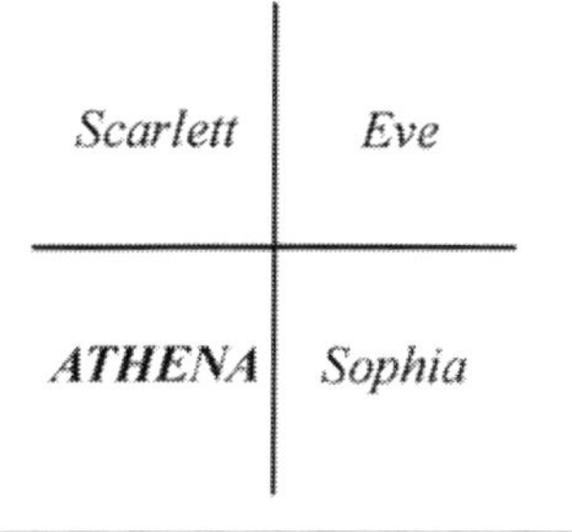

Fig 11.4. Athena Quarter

The Athena quarter has to do with the part of the feminine that strives to give form to the masculine ideal of heaven on earth. The heavenly ideal requires the vessel of physical reality to hold it and give it tangible life. This attempt to shape the components of nature into an expression of heaven's truth is the essence of culture and the basis of civilization.

It is the Athena in a woman, or in a man's anima, who tells us to take our elbows off the table and our shod feet off the sofa, to use the correct fork, to wear clothing appropriate to the occasion, and to make sure our verbs agree with their subjects. The goddess Athena introduced the bridle to humankind. The Athena aspect of woman helps us bridle our natural instincts and turn our energy toward the effort that is required to give the best possible shape to civilization and community life.

The Athena in us invests her energy in libraries, schools, churches, and other public institutions. She helps establish the structures and forms that carry cultural life. She is the teacher, the seamstress, the planning commissioner, the book publisher, the hostess, the nun. She needs her armor, her spear, her warlike determination, and the shielded protection of the spirit of heaven to effect her purpose against the tendency of natural life to return to chaos. Without health in the Athena quarter, civilization devolves.

The youthful, instinctual aspect of Athena can be seen in a woman's preoccupation with perfection of form in her own being, especially in regard to her body, her hair, and her clothes. This preoccupation extends to her house and everything else that she feels is a reflection of herself, including her family, her school, church, neighborhood, and town. It also applies to her personal performance in every situation. *She* is the feminine vessel whose form she feels compelled to make perfect. This very strong compulsion is one with which every woman must contend. The standard to which the youthful Athena holds herself is a collective one. It is also a masculine standard, coming as it does from the outside world. And yet a woman's compulsion to meet it does not come from the collective culture nor from men, but from her own Athena self, an inescapable part of her being that is born of the father's masculine spirit and seeks to serve that spirit with fierce loyalty.

In order to bring the Athena quarter into balance, a woman must develop her other feminine aspects, since all the quarters counterweigh and balance each other's demands. It is also necessary for a woman to become conscious of that *voice within herself* which belongs to the father of her youthful Athena. This is the judging voice of her animus, which so easily becomes dark, or negative. It is the part of her inner self that always holds up the *collective* standard, the voice that says "ought" and "should" and makes her feel guilty for not measuring up to the prevailing ideals of whatever collective spirit she is serving. It often speaks with the voice of a particular man in her life, usually husband, lover, father, or the animus voice of her mother. But it is not that person who is actually speaking or who has any real control over her. Rather it is an unrecognized part of her own being. When a woman can recognize that natural, instinctual, and potentially oppressive inner judge and consciously distinguish it from her true, individual self, she is ready for a healthy development of the mature Athena.

In the mature Athena, service to the collective ideal is replaced by service to the divine. The mature Athena still seeks to be a vessel of perfection, but she chooses God's perfection over man's, a perfection that is more merciful than man's because it includes the natural limitations of unfolding life on earth. In Christian imagery, this is the Virgin Mary saying yes to God, agreeing to become the physical vehicle for the manifestation of the divine in the world. The birth of Mary's son in the rough, earthy stable instead of in the well-appointed inn illustrates the difference between God's perfection and man's.

A woman's wholeness is not served, however, if she embodies only the mature Athena. The youthful Athena is always present, whether conscious or not. If the youthful Athena is unconscious, she will distort the mature Athena's service to the divine by substituting the voice of collective religion for the voice of the living spirit. If the mature Athena has not learned how to recognize and separate herself from the judging voice of her negative animus, her compulsion to perfection will enslave her to unrealistic collective standards of religion that are no less destructive than unrealistic standards of secular life.

Both the youthful and the mature aspects of Athena are needed in human life. The youthful Athena helps a woman shape herself and her surroundings into an effective vehicle for service to the human community. She accepts the training and coaching that come from the masculine ideal. The mature Athena takes the form she has gained from that training and offers it in service to the divine. In allowing the prepared vessel of her life to be filled with the living spirit of the divine for a purpose discerned by her individually through her own spiritual journey, she accepts her true vocation, rather than one placed upon her by outside expectations.

Sophia

A balance between the youthful and mature aspects of the various feminine quarters and between the quarters themselves does not come about automatically. It is Sophia, the fourth quarter in the feminine quaternity, who, like the King in the masculine quaternity, is of a different quality than the other three quarters and oversees the health and balance of the whole.

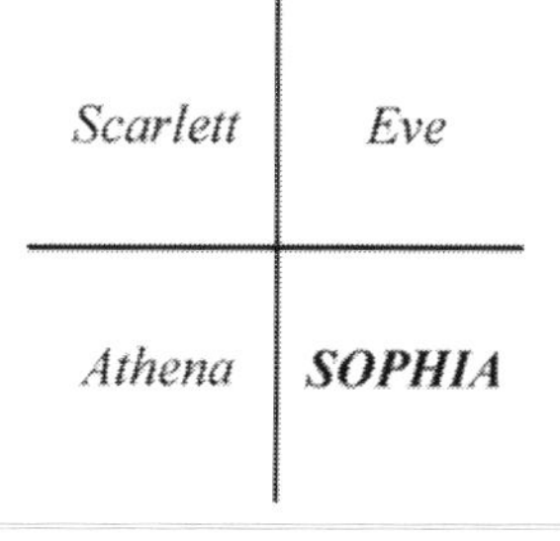

Fig 11.5. Sophia Quarter

"Sophia," wrote Carl Jung, "is the woman wisdom of God." In Greek translations of the Bible, *Sophia* is the word used to translate the Hebrew word *Chokhmah*, which refers to divine Wisdom. Both the Greek and Hebrew words are feminine in gender. This *Chokhmah*, or *Sophia*, or Wisdom, as revealed in scripture is a mysterious primeval order, a manifestation of divine meaning that is found in the heart of created life. This is not the blindness and cruelty that characterizes nature when no consciousness of the divine is present. True Wisdom is marked by her benevolence toward humankind. It is through her that the love of God flows into creation. In the following passage from Ecclesiasticus (The Wisdom of Jesus Ben Sirach), Wisdom takes on the image of a sheltering tree—protective, benevolent nature imbued with the glory of God:

> Happy is the man who meditates on Wisdom... who studies her ways in his heart, and ponders her secrets....He pitches his tent at her side, and lodges in an excellent lodging; he sets his children in her shade and camps beneath her branches; he is sheltered by her from the heat, and in her glory he makes his home.

It is this woman wisdom of God unfolding from the natural life process that brings everything in life into balance—not without pain, but always with mercy. Life provides its own corrections, but whether we are protected and aided by that process, or trammeled and crushed, depends on our relationship to Wisdom.

Sophia is the part of a woman who is the daughter of the feminine aspect of the divine. Like every daughter, she has the instinct and desire to identify with her mother. A woman who is particularly strong in the Sophia quarter will tend to identify with nature itself. She is the woman who likes things the natural way, who shuns technology and elaborate manifestations of culture. She gardens, hangs her clothes in the sun, takes walks in the woods, and says whatever comes to her mind.

It is the Sophia aspect of woman who finds interest in every twist and turn of unfolding life. She does not necessarily understand the meaning of all that happens to herself and those around her, but she senses importance in it and feels a great need to talk about it. This is the teenager spending endless hours on the telephone, the neighbors lingering at the backyard fence, and the long lunches of women who are friends. When these conversations are going well, there is an element of eternity in them—they take place in a timeless realm. Meaning constellates from them. Insights are received, and health and balance are restored. An hour flies by like a minute, and a woman comes away from them blinking her eyes as she readjusts to the here and now, her hair dripping a little with the waters of the stream of life.

When the Sophia quarter is not lived consciously, it can become more a refuge from life than a source of healing and balance. Gossip, soap operas, television talk shows, and romance novels appeal to an unconscious Sophia, as do tabloid newspapers and naively received astrological predictions and psychic readings.

In her Sophia aspect, a woman not only identifies with nature and the process of life but also with Wisdom itself. She feels that she herself is the one who knows how life should unfold and what would be best for everyone in her circle, and she tries earnestly to control things and make them come out that way. She truly thinks that she is the one who can solve the problems of all her family members, who can mend the broken hearts of her friends, and who knows which way her children's lives should go.

Sometimes she is seized with genuine intuitions, with knowing that comes to her not through her mind but through her body. She knows in her heart or in her gut or perhaps through a dream she has had. If she is unconsciously identified with the feminine side of the divine, she will think that this kind of knowing is a special power which belongs to her and which she is supposed to use to influence the course of events in her world.

The mature Sophia, like the mature King, is relatively rare. She is the woman who awakens to the fact that the wisdom of the divine does not come from her but from life itself. It is life that knows what is needed and how to bring that about. It is life that provides the answers and makes things unfold. The mature Sophia knows that although her intuition may be a gift, it is not a special power. She cannot control life. She may see wonderful possibilities, but that does not mean she has the power to bring them about. She may see disaster looming, but that does not mean she has the power to stop it. The mature Sophia knows that Wisdom gives her understanding but not power. Her task is to try to recognize as best she can the true stream of life, to trust it, and to work with it where possible to help it bring healing and wholeness to herself and the world around her.

It is the mature Sophia who understands the unconscious and feels comfortable in that realm. She presides over the inner journey. She needs a Wise Man's map, a trustworthy cultural understanding of the nature of the unconscious, to keep herself safely connected to human reality, but the territory of the unconscious itself is not strange to her. A man approaching the unconscious in his Wise Man aspect will always have an anima figure in his dreams or outer life—a Sophia—who leads him into the realm of mystery that the unconscious appears to him to be. But the Sophia part of a woman does not experience the unconscious as a mysterious realm. It feels familiar to her. She does need the help of her animus, but it is for the order and meaning he imparts, and even more it is for his watchful and protecting love, a mediation to her of the love of God.

It is in a fully developed Sophia that all the other aspects of woman come together and express themselves in the truest love of which the human heart is capable. This is a love that does not seek to control or to hold but only to know and to further the will of God as it unfolds from the process of life. Sophia accepts whatever comes, knowing with the fourteenth century anchoress Julian of Norwich that, "All shall be well, and all shall be well, and all manner of things shall be well." As with Julian, the mature Sophia's love for the divine is at the center of her being. While Athena loves the heavenly side of God as a daughter loves her father, Sophia loves the heavenly divine as a spouse, as her other half, her completion, the masculine complement of her feminine being. And because of her love for heaven, heaven's love flows through her to others, not by her design but by her faithful attention to the presence of the divine in every aspect of life's unfolding.

All four quarters of the feminine quaternity are active within every woman's personality, whether their manifestations are conscious or unconscious. It is the goal of life's journey to bring the four quarters into consciousness and balance, an end that can only be attained when life is fully lived.

Chapter Twelve

Psyche and Eros and the Feminine Quaternity

When a woman accepts the task of individuation, she enters into a conscious experience of the natural process by which the four quarters of the feminine quaternity are brought into balance in her own being, a development which readies her ultimately for conscious union with the life-sustaining love of the divine. An illustration of this process can be seen in the classical myth of Psyche and Eros.

The story of Psyche and Eros is a tale within a tale, an ancient Greek myth recounted in the *Metamorphoses* or *Golden Ass*, a novel written by Lucius Apuleius, a second-century Roman. Psyche, whose name means "Soul," is a human woman and the main protagonist of the myth. Her love involvement is with Eros, the mythical god of love (also known as Cupid or Amor), a personification of divine love.

As the story of Soul and Love, the myth of Psyche and Eros is a particularly compelling one, and a number of writers in both religion and psychology have taken their turns at wresting the meaning from it. C. S. Lewis made his contribution by transposing the story into his interpretive novel *Till We Have Faces*. Three Jungian analysts have also devoted books to it. Erich Neumann presents a particularly insightful treatment in his work, *Amor and Psyche*. Somewhat easier to approach and also containing much insight is Robert Johnson's *She. The Golden Ass of Apuleius*, by Marie-Louise von Franz, is an analysis of the entire novel within which the myth is situated. Von Franz makes a valuable contribution to the Psyche and Eros literature by looking at Psyche's story in terms of a man's anima. Psyche as anima is certainly one way in which the myth should be viewed—men should see this as the story of their own souls. And so, too, should same-sex lovers see their story in it, for it is first and foremost the story of Soul and Love. But because the soul is feminine and is usually carried more consciously by women than by men, for the purpose of analysis I will speak of the myth as a woman's tale. While my own analysis includes or shares some elements from all three of the Jungian works cited above, much of it is not found in those sources, especially the connection drawn between Psyche's four tasks and the feminine quaternity.

Psyche Is Sacrificed

The tale opens with Psyche as a maiden, one of three beautiful daughters of a king and queen. While her sisters are beautiful in an ordinary way, Psyche's beauty is of a higher order, so much so that she begins to attract the adoration and devotion that formerly was reserved for Aphrodite, the goddess of love. "Here is a *new* Aphrodite," people say, "an Aphrodite who is flesh and blood and lives among us." This, of course, excites the jealousy of Aphrodite, who determines to rid Psyche of the special quality of her beauty.

Aphrodite summons her son Eros, whose arrows inflame with love whomever they strike without regard for rules, bounds, or standards of suitability. She instructs him to make Psyche fall in love with and marry the vilest of men, the lowest of the low. Certain that this will take care of her rival, Aphrodite departs for an extended holiday in Poseidon's realm beneath the sea.

Meanwhile, Psyche's two sisters make happy marriages to kings in other lands, but no one asks for Psyche's hand. Men hold her in awe and pay homage to her beauty, but none wants to marry her. Her father becomes concerned and consults an oracle of Apollo. To his dismay, he is told that he must take Psyche to a lonely mountaintop where she will meet the one for whom she is destined. But this will be her funeral rather than her wedding, for the one who will come to claim her for his own will be a fierce, winged dragon.

As terrible as this is, the gods must be obeyed, and so, with great sorrow, Psyche's father and mother take her to her doom on the wild mountaintop. Accepting her fate, Psyche does her best to comfort her grieving parents. They leave her there, darkness falls, and she waits in fear and trembling. But no dreadful beast comes to claim her. Instead, the gentle West Wind wafts her down into a hidden paradise deep in the valley below. Here she finds a beautiful palace filled with all the treasure of the world. Disembodied servants, known to her only by their voices, minister to all her needs. Then in the darkness of night, the one to whom she has been wed enters her bridal chamber. She hears him and feels him, but she cannot see him. He is tender in his love, and though he leaves before daylight can reveal his identity, she is content to be his wife. He continues to return in the same way every night. As she settles into life in paradise, she comes to love her unseen husband, as he loves her.

Two Streams of Life and Love

This is the beginning of the tale, which we will now interrupt to look at its meaning thus far. We will interpret it as if it were a dream.

Psyche is one of three sisters. The others are ordinary, but she is extraordinary. It can be assumed that these are three parts of one woman (or of a man's anima)—the two sisters representing ordinary consciousness, perhaps mother's daughter and father's daughter, and Psyche representing the inner life of the soul.

Every woman carries the radiance of Psyche in her being. This is the pure feminine light that glows in her most noticeably when she is a young woman moving full of hope toward adult life, her dreams of love and fulfillment still intact. The radiance of Psyche comes from within and is beyond the beauty of ordinary flesh.

Although physically real, Psyche's beauty has a spiritual quality, and to those who are discerning, the presence of the divine is clearly evident in it. It can be seen in a woman at any time in her life when she is centered in herself, when her spirit, soul, and body are knit together in harmony.

Psyche's beauty calls forth from man a positive response, an admiring, adoring, even worshipful regard, but it does not call forth a physically sexual response. There are two streams of love and attraction between the masculine and the feminine, both coming from the unconscious. One is experienced at the surface of life and involves romantic fantasy and physical desire. The other comes from a deeper level where the human soul and divine love are ever drawn to each other.

It is not easy to think about these two streams of human life and love. I have had a number of dreams that shed light on this subject, three of the clearer ones coming as understanding, with no images. The first of these speaks of a split in consciousness between body and spirit. The dream said:

> *We have a body mind and a spirit mind. While we are in our body minds, absorbed in our bodies, we cannot commune with the God of heaven, the God of the Old and New Testaments.*

The dream seems to suggest that this split is general in the human condition—consciousness of one level obscures consciousness of the other.

The next dream came several years after the one above:

> *I am given the understanding that Sigmund Freud was estranged from sexuality. He did not know what it was. This was because he did not know about the deeper, truer level where real sexuality takes place.*

Freud, of course, was virtually fixated on sexuality, but the only stream of the unconscious of which he was aware was the stream of wish-fulfilling fantasy and physical desire that connects us to the surface of life. This dream makes it clear, however, that sexuality has a truer reality at a deeper, more spiritual level than the level with which Freud was concerned. What Freud failed to understand was that sexuality at the surface of life is a symbolic language that refers to our journey toward wholeness at the deeper level.

A few weeks after the dream about Freud, I received a further clarification about the two levels:

> *While dreaming deeply, I have a clear realization about the surface of life, about how limited it is. And a sense of the level below the surface where the real life is—where God is present all the time.*

This dream suggests a correspondence between the deeper level of life and what Christians call the kingdom of God, which, as Jesus pointed out, is always with us though seldom recognized. The surface of life, on the other hand, is understood in the dream to be more like what Jesus referred to as "this world," a limited reality that is not as important as it seems. One would not have to use Christian language to talk about these truths. They are universal, and other religions have their own ways of speaking about them.

These, then, are the two levels of life, each with its stream of love. The two streams tend to be experienced as mutually exclusive, especially by the focused consciousness of men, and this gives rise to the difficulty a man typically has in approaching woman on the physical level of sexuality while he is loving her for the beauty and wisdom of her soul. In our story, therefore, Psyche, who carries the beauty of the deeper stream, is loved and even worshiped by men, and yet she has no suitors and no offer of marriage.

Aphrodite symbolizes the romantic and physically sexual stream of love. This stream leads to an outer world enactment of the union of the opposites with all its joys, difficulties, and varied consequences, but it does not necessarily lead to a corresponding inner union.

Aphrodite's requirement for consciousness is minimal. Love strikes and entangles two people, and, if conditions allow, sets them on a course together. No effort by the participants is needed to assemble the components of this situation—it all happens automatically through the archetypal effect that Aphrodite symbolizes. The woman always appears beautiful, the man always appears strong and full of potential. Their love for each other always seems destined from the beginning of time and sure to last forever. Romantic fantasy and physical desire carry them forward. But after this initial experience has done its work of entangling them in a new life together, a change begins to occur: the romantic feelings dissipate and sexual desire begins to wane. If there is no *real* love coming to them from the second, deeper stream—if there is no awareness of the divine, no nourishment from the soul—then the initial love that seemed so sure and lasting takes a downward turn and may not stop in its decline until it finally turns into its opposite, hate.

The two sisters in the story carry the ordinary consciousness of the surface of life and thus make ordinary marriages in the Aphrodite way. Psyche, the soul of the woman represented by the three sisters, sinks down into the unconscious, submerged by the intensity of the early stage of ordinary love. It is as if she has died. But she has not died. She has in fact been wed to a mysterious but loving husband whose kingdom is a virtual paradise.

This tells us that a potential for deeper love exists in the Aphrodite experience. This is always true for all of us—an archetypal truth is a universal truth. In the early throes of human love one's soul is forced into the unconscious, where it finds a deeper, truer love hiding beneath the everyday reality of physical love and romantic illusion. But it is a love upon which the light of ordinary consciousness does not fall. It lives only at this deeper level, separate and apart from life on the surface. We are not disturbed by this in the beginning because deep down in ourselves we have an unconscious sense of its promise. In the early stages of romantic love our souls are content to be sheltered in paradise.

We now continue with the story.

Psyche Is Banished from Paradise

In due course Psyche's sisters hear about her supposed death and come to the mountaintop to grieve for her. Psyche's husband is distressed at this. In the darkness of his nightly visits, he warns Psyche not to reveal herself to them, for they will not rest until they have persuaded her to try to find out who he is. And if ever she looks upon him, she will lose him forever. Furthermore, the child she now carries—for she has become pregnant—will be divine if she goes along with things as they are, but if she tries to see her husband's face, the child will be born a mortal.

Psyche now falls into despair as she realizes for the first time how completely she has been cut off from human company. She wants to see her sisters. She is inconsolable until at last her husband gives in and allows the West Wind to waft the sisters down into the valley for a visit. Their grief immediately gives way to envy when they see Psyche's paradise and hear about the great love she enjoys with her husband. Their own husbands, who at first had seemed such happy matches, have turned out to be old and sickly and stingy with their money, no longer regarding their wives as lovers but as nursemaids. Why should Psyche be so happy and they so miserable?

The two sisters set about to undo Psyche's situation. They try to persuade her that her husband is an evil monster and that she should shine a light on him to see this for herself and kill him. Because Psyche has never seen him, she cannot be sure that her sisters are wrong. He may indeed be the dreadful monster to whom she was originally betrothed. So the next night as her husband sleeps, Psyche approaches him with a lamp in one hand and a knife in the other. When she holds the lamp above him, however, what she sees is not a monster but beautiful, winged Eros, the god of love himself. She drops the knife and at that same moment accidently pricks herself on one of his arrows and falls more deeply in love with him than ever.

As she swoons with this deeper love, a drop of hot oil spills from the lamp onto Eros' shoulder, wounding and awakening him.

Upon seeing her transgression—the lamp and the fallen knife—he flies away. As he rises, she catches hold of him and is carried out of paradise into the wide world, where finally she can hold on no longer and drops to earth. Eros alights in a nearby tree and speaks to her, explaining that his mother Aphrodite had told him to unite her with a foul husband, but that on seeing her, he had pricked himself with his own arrow and taken her for his wife, loving her dearly. Now, however, she has betrayed him and he must fly away from her. With this, he disappears into the heavens.

Reuniting the Two Streams of Life

Again we pause to examine the meaning of what has occurred.

The deeper love that can be sensed beneath the surface of physical and romantic love turns out to be nothing less than divine love itself, the everlasting, unfailing love for which our souls have always longed. Ordinary consciousness is responsible for bringing this to light. It is the two sisters who realize that the soul is missing and presumed dead and who go to mourn for her at the place where she was lost. Only then does the soul remember ordinary consciousness and wish to be reunited with it. It is when the effects of Aphrodite have worn off that we realize that we have lost track of the deeper, truer part of ourselves, and we begin to mourn its loss. This crisis comes at midlife, if not before, and sets in motion a response from the soul that, when given the right circumstances, can lead us into the individuation process.

The chief impediment to this development in consciousness turns out to be Eros himself. Divine love as it first arises in the unconscious cannot be lived consciously at the surface of life. It is too divine, too heavenly, too demanding that outer life be paradise. In order for the heavenly divine to live in human life, it must sacrifice some of its glory, let go of its expectation of perfect fulfillment, and accept the limitations of outer reality, which even at best can hold and express only a small portion of unfailing love. In the same way, as we shall see, the human soul must endure sacrifice and suffering in order to be integrated into ordinary life. This development of the soul is a human task, a work to be consciously engaged. Divine love, meanwhile, retreats more deeply into the unconscious, where in its own mysterious way it will be transformed in tandem with the soul's progress.

The story now continues.

Psyche Searches for Eros

With great lamentation Psyche watches Eros fly away until he is out of sight. Then in her despair, she heads straight for a nearby river and throws herself in. But the river, knowing she belongs to Eros and is under his protection, disgorges her back onto the shore. There she meets Pan, the god of nature, who comforts her, telling her not to despair but to go find Eros and address him with her prayers, for he is soft-hearted and will reconcile with her. So Psyche sets out to find him. But first, she settles the score with her sisters, whose envy broke up her paradise. She tricks them into dying of their own greed by throwing themselves headlong into the valley of paradise without waiting for the aid of the West Wind.

Meanwhile, Aphrodite returns from her holiday beneath the sea. The world has fared badly while she was playing in Poseidon's realm and while Eros was secluded in paradise with Psyche. Because of their absence, there is no longer any joy and love to be found in the world. Relationships of every kind have fallen into neglect and ruin. Hate and loathing are running rampant. The reason for Aphrodite's return, however, is not that she is particularly concerned about this. She comes back to wreak her vengeance on Psyche for stealing the heart of her son Eros, who has returned to his mother's house to recover from the wound he suffered from the hot oil. Because his love for Psyche has not abated, Aphrodite puts him under guard to keep the lovers from reuniting.

Psyche does not know where Eros has gone. She looks for him first in the temple of Demeter, the divine earth mother. There she hears that Aphrodite is after her, and she begs Demeter for refuge. The earth goddess sympathizes with her, but she fears Aphrodite and will not let Psyche stay in her temple. Psyche goes next to Hera, the wife of Zeus, but Eros is not here either, and again Psyche is refused refuge. Now she realizes that she has no choice but to go to Aphrodite and throw herself on the goddess's mercy. She hopes that at least she might find Eros at his mother's house. This decision is driven home when Aphrodite sends Hermes, the messenger of the gods, to stir up all the world in a universal search for Psyche. There is no longer any possibility for escape.

So Psyche goes to the house of Aphrodite. There she is met at the door by the servant Habit, who grabs her by her hair and drags her to the goddess of love. Aphrodite greets her with scorn and turns her over to her handmaidens Trouble and Sorrow, who whip her and torment her in various other ways. When they have finished, Aphrodite beats her some more and then assigns her an impossible task to be completed by the end of the day.

Stillness and Surrender: The Feminine Way

Before we go on with Psyche's first task, we will stop once again to examine the meaning of what has unfolded.

Psyche is desolate at the loss of Eros. Here, symbolically, is a woman whose ordinary consciousness has penetrated the depths of her own being and glimpsed the living reality of divine love. She has recognized the heavenly divine as her own inner spouse, her Beloved, her highest value. From this point on, she will allow nothing to come between herself and the fulfillment of that love. It is this, and only this, that gives her the strength and courage for a true individuation journey.

When our consciousness pierces the depths and finds the love of God within ourselves, our soul, no longer separated from consciousness, is drawn out of the paradise of the unconscious. As the soul enters the ordinary world, the surface and the depths come together, creating a new level of consciousness. But the surface and the depths, though bridged, are still very far apart. The surface of life has suffered from having lost track of its soul. Discord and difficulty have replaced the hopefulness of youth. Ordinary relationships, with their unexamined shadow sides, carry little of the tender love of the divine that the soul has come to know in her secluded paradise. Much change and transformation will be necessary in order to integrate the two worlds, each of which needs what the other has to offer. The surface of life needs the unfailing tender love and saving grace of heaven that resides in the depths of each of us, and the love of heaven needs the surface of life in order to be fully known and truly lived.

At the outset the two realities are so far apart that Psyche despairs of ever seeing Eros again. She first collapses in a fit of weeping, and then she tries to drown herself. This collapse and impulse to die is Psyche's hallmark. We will see it again and again as the story proceeds. It is the way of the soul, the feminine way of growth and change. An individuation journey that is not marked by episodes of deep weeping and the soul-felt willingness to die to one's old way of being is not a true journey of transformation. The masculine aspect of the journey involves heroic action, but the feminine aspect involves stillness and surrender in the face of the seeming impossibility of effective action. It is this feminine surrender that opens us to the depths of the spirit and to the help that is always available from that realm when our own strength is no longer enough.

The river refuses Psyche's bid for death. Because it knows that she belongs to Eros, whose power the river honors and fears, it will not drown her and instead puts her back onto the shore. This is the first of many indications in the story that although Eros is not present in an obvious way, he is in fact present insofar as nature itself has consciousness of him and of Psyche's relationship to him and gives her special aid and protection in his name. This symbolizes nothing less than natural spirituality—the Wisdom of unfolding life—as it is experienced by us when we approach it in the context of a conscious relationship with divine love.

The idea of natural spirituality is reinforced by the appearance of Pan, the god of nature. Pan, who knows Eros to be tender and forgiving, assures Psyche that she can draw him back to her with her prayers. With this encouragement, Psyche sets out to find her husband. The meeting with Pan tells us in symbolic language that the individuation journey begins when we meet the living spirit of nature and establish dialogue with it. This cinches the new level of consciousness, making permanent the connection that has been achieved between the surface of life and the spiritual depths. The center of this new consciousness is divine love, which can also be called the Self, or the God-center within, or in Christian language, the Christ. It alone can bring about the unification of the two competing streams of life.

The new, integrative consciousness brings an end to ordinary consciousness, which has the ego at its center. This is symbolized in the story by the death of the two sisters, whose tendency to envy and greed show the overriding dominance of the ego. Psyche will now be required to carry within herself the ordinary consciousness of the sisters, as well as the deep consciousness of the soul. Symbolically, this is a woman who has become one with her soul and who must now integrate the deeper awareness of her soul with the reality of everyday life and love.

For Psyche to integrate the two levels of consciousness, she must enter the world of Aphrodite and submit to the consequences of ordinary love, just as her sisters did. But resistance always accompanies any movement toward new consciousness. Psyche, who undertakes this journey as both a mother-to-be and as a wife, tries to hide from Aphrodite in the temples of Demeter and Hera, symbols of archetypal motherhood and wifehood. The call to individuation, however, is a call away from the central identification a woman has found as the mother of her children or the wife of her husband. These are important relationships, but a woman must eventually move beyond them to become, like the Virgin Mary, the spouse and mother of the living spirit of the divine, both within the depths of her own being and in a way that has reality in the ordinary world.

It is important to understand, however, that we cannot move beyond what we have never attained. Psyche's visits to Demeter and Hera might also be seen as homage paid to these instinctual realms of womanhood as she enters the individuation process. A woman who by midlife has not consciously lived as wife or mother will find as an aspect of her individuation journey that these parts of herself must come awake and gain some kind of outlet in her life, however attenuated that outlet may be. Instinctual life must be accepted and valued in its own right before it can be sacrificed and transformed into a higher reality.

A complete surrender to the individuation process can no longer be evaded when Hermes stirs up the whole world in search of Psyche. This symbolizes the point at which the unconscious breaks out in a display of synchronicity and archetypal dreams that have a powerful effect on the ego, breaking down its resistance. At this moment we realize that we have no choice but to go along with the change in consciousness that is arising in us. New life is coming, a life we cannot imagine and yet cannot refuse. With this submission of the ego, the way is open for transformation.

In the story, Psyche submits to Aphrodite. This new part of ourselves that has come into consciousness, this part of us that has been touched and loved by the divine and knows now what that feels like, must consent to enter the context of ordinary human life and love. Though we agree to this because we have no other option, we also hope that through this we will find the divine love we have lost. What we find, however, is suffering at the hands of Habit, Trouble, and Sorrow. The daily requirements of mundane life and the twists, turns, and seeming reverses of its slow development feel like torture to the soul, which longs for the fulfillment of the tender, unfailing love that it knows to be its rightful due. But that perfect love that was known in the depths lacked outer reality, and the only way to make it real is to integrate it with the surface of life. A beginning to this must be made, even though the quality of love first encountered in everyday life is so far from perfection that the soul feels nothing but torment.

It is, in the first place, life's burden of Habit, Trouble, and Sorrow that drove our ordinary consciousness to seek our soul in the hope of finding a better way to live. But reconnection with our soul brings with it the requirement to learn life all over again in a way that accords with the soul's way. This is what the individuation journey accomplishes. In the story, this relearning is symbolized by four seemingly impossible tasks imposed upon Psyche by Aphrodite. These four tasks can be correlated with the four quarters of the feminine quaternity. With each task, the soul faces the seemingly impossible challenge of living a whole and healthy feminine life in the face of the overwhelming demands of everyday reality. But where ordinary consciousness found only Habit, Trouble, and Sorrow, the soul finds a way that is eased by the love of God and that leads ever closer to the ultimate fulfillment of that love in a manifestation that is as human as it is divine.

We now return to the story.

Psyche's First Task

Aphrodite is jealous of the deep love between Psyche and Eros and resentful of their secret marriage, from which a child is soon to be born. The goddess of love considers Psyche to be an upstart, a mere mortal who is not worthy of her divine son. To prove Psyche's unworthiness, Aphrodite gives her a task that no mortal woman could accomplish. She shows her a great heap of jumbled seeds: wheat, barley, millet, poppy seeds, chickpeas, lentils, and beans. She tells Psyche that she is so low and ugly that she could only attract a lover by being his drudge, and so now it will be seen how worthy a drudge she is. Before night has fallen, she must sort all these seeds into separate piles according to their kind. Certain that she has gotten the best of Psyche, Aphrodite leaves to attend a wedding feast.

Psyche sits down in a stupor, overwhelmed by the impossibility of the task. But a little ant sees her and feels sorry for her, knowing that she is the beloved spouse of the great god Eros. The ant goes out into the fields and calls together all the other ants in the vicinity. Addressing them as nurslings of mother earth, he urges them to pity Psyche in her plight and come to her aid. So they all go in, a great host of tiny beings, and separate the seeds one by one, accomplishing the task before nightfall.

Relearning Eve's Quarter

Looking now at the meaning of Psyche's first task, we see that as the soul enters ordinary life, it comes up against the challenge of the Eve quarter of the feminine quaternity, with its requirement for the endless tending of physical life. This is the realm of the personal mother, the aspect of the feminine that is instinctual mother, or earth mother. She is symbolized in Greek mythology by Demeter, who was closely associated with grain and other cultivated fruits of the earth. The heap of seeds of cultivated food plants can be seen as an image of the many small details which accompany the living of life and require the attention of the feminine in the Eve quarter. Whether in a man or a woman, it is Eve energy that is needed for keeping a house or an office, preparing food, tending children, and in general overseeing the physical details of life.

"You are nothing but a drudge," says Aphrodite. This is true of all of us when we live the Eve quarter in a purely Aphrodite way. Earthly love begets earthly life, which must be tended. How is one to take care of all the many details of fundamental earth life? Overwhelmed by the task, Psyche cannot do a thing. She just sits there. As we have seen, this is her hallmark. When the soul is overwhelmed, her answer is to *do nothing*. But this nothing is actually something. It creates an opening for help from the spiritual depths, which is just what happens in the story. To Psyche's aid comes an army of ants—friends of Eros, nurslings of mother earth. The problem of the seeds arises from life on earth, and so does the solution. The ants symbolize little bits of earth energy, coming naturally. They are the little impulses and urges that can be felt coming to us through our bodies, saying: *Do this. Now this. Now this.*

When faced with an overwhelming task—as for example, when we have been tied up with a project at work, the house is a mess, and twenty relatives are descending the next day for Thanksgiving dinner—the answer at first is to sit down and be still. Wait. Keep waiting until a little impulse comes, a tiny jolt of energy from somewhere deep inside that says: *Go make the cranberry sauce.* The impetus, the will to engage, is only for that task and no other. And so we get up and do it. Then we clean up where the bubbling sauce has splattered on the stove. Then we feel moved to clean the entire stovetop. Then the countertops. Now we take a magazine from a countertop to the coffee table in the living room, where we do some straightening. Then take a dirty glass back to the kitchen and wash up some dishes. One task leads to another, each with its own energy that says, *Yes, do it.* The little impulses know that perfection is not the goal. *Do this. Leave that.* There is a solution that fits the time and energy available, and the ant helpers know what it is. They guide us to just the right efforts in just the right order. We need no overall plan. We simply follow the guiding impulses from within, the living spirit manifest in the earth of our being.

The answer to an overwhelming task in the Eve quarter is not one big, focused effort but a diffuse, interwoven effort from the feminine principle's diffuse, interweaving consciousness. If we were to put on a masculine mind and focus our consciousness too much into organized effort, we would lose our ant helpers. Their little impulses would be overwhelmed, unfelt. Driven by ideas of perfection, we would wear ourselves out by doing too much, or else we would give up in the face of all we think we have to do and therefore would do too little. But when the ants are helping us, we move from this to that at an even pace, taking time for ourselves and others when needed, and yet never losing our forward momentum.

With the help of the soul, Eve's realm is relearned. When Aphrodite is in charge of this quarter, we are at the mercy of our nurturing instincts, which, when unchecked by reflection and consciousness, make us feel we must give of ourselves and keep on giving until we have met all the needs and expectations, real and imagined, of those for whom we feel responsible. But when we are at one with our soul, the Eve part of us is no longer driven by unconscious instinct or the expectations of others. The living spirit of the divine, which loves us and understands us and comes to us individually from the depths of our own being, guides us in the ordering of our lives. It tells us what needs to be done, and it tells us when we have done enough, according to our particular circumstances. It frees us from drudgery and awakens us to the beauty and value of tending life in a God-centered way.

With this development, the Eve aspect of life is no longer an unwelcome chore. It becomes an important and valued part of our feminine being, fundamental to all the other parts of our feminine selves. It is especially fundamental to the Wisdom quarter of Sophia, since our willingness to tend our home can be an outward reflection of our willingness to tend our inner life, where the same never-ending attention is required.

We now continue the story.

Psyche's Second Task

In the evening the goddess of love returns from the wedding feast and finds to her dismay that all the seeds have been sorted. "This is not your work!" cries Aphrodite. "It is the work of Eros!" And so the next morning she gives Psyche a second impossible task. She tells her to go fetch some golden fleece from the terrible rams that wander in a grove beside a certain river.

Psyche knows this cannot be done, as the rams are too fierce to be approached. She goes to the river as she was told, but her intent is to throw herself into the water and drown herself. She is stopped, however, by the gentle murmur of a green reed growing at the river's edge. Like a panpipe blown upon by divine breath, the reed speaks to her and tells her not to kill herself.

It is true, the reed says, that the rams are dangerous. They draw blazing heat from the sun, which maddens them with a wild frenzy. Their horns are sharp and their foreheads are like stone, and even their bite is sometimes poisonous. If Psyche tries to approach them now, as the sun moves toward its zenith, they will kill her. But if she waits until noon has passed and the sun has begun to cool and the rams have been lulled to sleep by the soft river breeze, then she can go to the grove, where earlier the rams were charging about, and gather there the wisps of golden fleece that she will find clinging to the twigs and brambles.

So Psyche waits in the shade of a tree until the heat of the sun begins to wane. Once the rams have grown quiet, she goes out and easily gathers all the golden fleece she needs and takes it back to Aphrodite.

Relearning Scarlett's Quarter

Psyche's second task sends her to the second quarter of the feminine quaternity, to Scarlett's realm, where she must get some masculine power. Scarlett is the father's daughter at the ego level, the one who must learn how to handle herself in the competitive outside world.

Aphrodite wants to see Psyche do some work of her own. Rams, who battle each other with their heads, symbolize the effectiveness of masculine consciousness in achieving a place for oneself in the world. With their massive, spiraled horns, rams could be said to represent masculine-mindedness, man's instinctual attitude toward power and achievement. The rams' golden fleece is linked symbolically to the fiery power of the sun, the hot blaze of consciousness.

A woman needs a measure of masculine power to free herself from a one-sided, all-feminine existence. Without it she will have no life of her own in the outside world, nor will she have any basis for relating to man except as mother to son. So Psyche must go into the realm of masculine consciousness and get from it what she needs for her own wholeness and fulfillment of life. But how can she, as feminine soul, take on this dangerous masculine power, heated as it is by the energy of the sun to the point of mad frenzy? How can she hope even to approach it? Overwhelmed again, she goes to the river to kill herself, a symbolic recognition of her need to sacrifice her present state of consciousness in order to make room for a new way of understanding things.

Her surrender opens her to help from the spiritual realm. This time, it is a reed that speaks to Psyche from the shallow water at the river's edge. The river symbolizes the unconscious, the feminine counterbalance to blazing masculine consciousness. The reed is of the river, but its phallic shape and its associations with Pan and with breath, which symbolizes spirit, make it a masculine symbol. This cool and gentle masculine element from the unconscious tells Psyche how to approach hot, fierce masculine power. She is not to confront it directly. The feminine will be destroyed if it tries to seize power in a direct struggle with the masculine. A woman who takes on masculine power in this way does so at the cost of her feminine being. The threat to her is not only from masculine power in the outer world but from the fiery masculine energies within herself. If a woman identifies too strongly with her masculine side, her feminine side will be eclipsed.

The reed tells Psyche to wait until the intensity of the noon sun has passed. This means symbolically that instead of entering into a direct struggle for power, a woman should bide her time and watch for opportunities which might otherwise be overlooked, unanticipated avenues that open to her from life itself and offer all the power she needs to lead a balanced and whole feminine life. When she approaches power in this way, without direct confrontation and competition, she will find enough of it lying about the edges of things, opportunities that are hers for the taking and that fit well her need to have a satisfying life in the outside world while maintaining the essence of her feminine reality.

When living the Scarlett quarter unconsciously, in a purely Aphrodite way, we either approach it too passively and never make any legitimate bid for consciousness, identity, and power or we approach it too actively and wound our feminine being by meeting masculine consciousness and power head on. Psyche's way, the way of the soul, is supported by the love of the divine and leads our feminine selves to lives in the outside world that are balanced, healthy, and fulfilling. The masculine power that we gather in this way will be enough.

Psyche's Third Task

As we continue with the story, we find that Aphrodite is not at all pleased with Psyche's success at gathering the golden fleece. She now proposes to test whether Psyche has prudence and stoutness of heart beyond that of a mortal woman. She tells her to go to the peak of a certain high mountain, from which peak a black stream flows down a channel worn deeply into the steep and slippery rock face of the mountain. The stream is guarded by fierce dragons that never sleep, and its waters continually cry out, "Beware! Doom! Get Away!" The black water descends in an inapproachable chasm to the Stygian swamps in the valley below, where it feeds the streams of the underworld. Aphrodite gives Psyche a small crystal urn and tells her to fill it with water from the place where the stream emerges on the mountaintop.

Psyche goes to the mountain with no hope of getting water from the stream. Instead, she intends to throw herself from the high peak and put an end to her suffering. When she arrives at the foot of the mountain, however, she sees that it is impossible to even climb its steep face. This realization paralyzes her as if she were turned to stone. All her senses leave her body and she cannot even weep. But the watchful eyes of kindly Providence see the anguish of her soul, and the eagle, the royal bird of Zeus, recognizes her as the bride of Eros and flies down from the heavenly heights to give her aid.

The eagle tells Psyche that even the gods fear the Stygian waters, which are both holy and cruel. Just as mortals swear by the divinity of the gods, the gods swear by the majesty of the River Styx. But even so, the eagle knows what to do. He takes the crystal urn in his talons and flies to the peak, where he tells the guarding dragons that he comes at Aphrodite's bidding to fetch some water. The dragons grudgingly allow him to fill the urn. The eagle returns to Psyche, who receives the urn with joy and carries it back to Aphrodite.

Waiting in Athena's Quarter

With the third task, we have not only entered a new quarter of the feminine quaternity, but we have ascended to a new level of human life, one that goes beyond nature to include culture. With the first two tasks, Psyche mastered the youthful level of instinctual feminine life. All the elements in those earlier tasks were natural: seeds, ants, rams, reeds. But with the third task a cultural element—the crystal urn—is introduced, symbolizing civilization. Psyche has entered the quarter of Athena, the daughter of the spiritual father. She is now in the realm of service to life beyond her personal life, the realm of community and civilized humanity. Here Aphrodite tests her for prudence and strength of heart, qualities that are associated with the heavenly ideals of the masculine spirit.

The crystal urn represents the purified vessel of Psyche's physical being. Her completion of the first two tasks was symbolically equivalent to integrating her shadow. She is no longer an unconscious creature of nature, but instead she has transcended to a higher level of human life. She has become, like the crystal urn, a solid reality through which the light of consciousness can shine. Now the purified vessel of her being is ready to be filled with her own limited portion of the divine purpose that runs through the heart of life.

The black river represents this vital stream of the divine. It is none other than the unconscious itself. As the source of all divinity, all mystery, and all life, it is experienced as both holy and cruel. The gods and goddesses of Olympus are but archetypes produced by the unconscious, which is greater than they are. Thus even they are in awe of it.

Everything spiritual comes from the unconscious. The part of the river involved in this third task runs from the mountaintop to the valley and symbolizes the upper, or masculine, spirit. The waters that run from the swamp down into the underworld would symbolize the lower, or feminine, spirit. Psyche is told to fill her urn at the place of highest spirit. But to approach directly the living stream of the divine is dangerous to the extreme. Frail human consciousness could easily be shattered by an unmediated engagement with the unconscious. Normally it is a religious structure that provides the necessary mediation for human contact with the divine. In this task, however, Psyche is asked to seek a direct experience with the divine outside of any established structure.

What is symbolized here is a woman who has taken time out of her life to do her shadow work and purify her natural being. But for what purpose? Though she has become a new person, she does not yet know what this means for her at life's higher level. She has the feeling that she is meant to partake of the heart of life itself, that she is supposed to carry forward into the greater world something important from the divine source of things. She feels she has something of value to offer. But with her new connection to the home side of life and her understanding that competition for power is not good for her and is not her way, how is her cup of life to be filled?

Psyche does absolutely nothing to fill her cup except to go stony still and wait. As her body life shuts down, she becomes open to the upper spirit of the divine. A woman on her individuation journey must wait in this way for her assignment for the second half of life, which is not a matter of career but of vocation. Since so much of her shadow work has now been completed, her ego desires are no longer at the center of her being. She is not waiting to find out how to become rich and famous, but how to serve greater life as she was meant to serve it, however great or small that realm of service might be. The shape of this is not something she can decide for herself. It can only be discerned. It comes from the living spirit of the divine, and she must wait for it to announce itself and become apparent. Like the Virgin Mary, she awaits her annunciation.

Zeus's eagle, an image of the masculine spirit of heaven, comes and fills Psyche's urn for her. This would be the moment in a woman's journey when the way opens to her, both within herself and in the world outside. Her special value is recognized, her path is becoming clear, and she accepts her true vocation of effective service to life beyond her personal life.

We now return to the story.

Psyche's Fourth Task

Aphrodite is not pleased that Psyche has successfully accomplished the first three tasks. "You must be a great sorceress!" Aphrodite says sarcastically. And so she assigns a final task. Handing Psyche a small wooden lockbox, Aphrodite tells her to take it to Persephone, the queen of the underworld, and ask Persephone to fill it with a day's worth of beauty for Aphrodite, whose own beauty is getting worn out from all her cares.

Psyche is now sure that she is doomed. Knowing she would never survive a journey into the underworld, she heads straight for a high tower from which she plans to hurl herself to her death. But before she can throw herself down, the tower begins to speak, telling her that it makes no sense to kill herself because if she did so, she would still have to go to the underworld but with no hope of return. Instead, she should follow the tower's instructions for how to accomplish the task she has been given.

The tower tells Psyche where to find the hidden entrance to the underworld. It also tells her that she must not enter the underworld empty-handed, but rather, she must carry a barley cake in each hand and two coins in her mouth. As she proceeds along the path through the underworld, she will meet a lame man with a lame donkey loaded with wood, and the man will ask her to do him the favor of picking up some twigs that have fallen from the donkey's load. She must not help him, however, for to do so she would have to put down a barley cake. Nor must she speak, for that would mean dropping her coins. Instead, she must pass by in silence.

Then, says the tower, she will come to the river of the dead, where she must pay the boatman his toll. She is to do this by letting him take one of the coins from her mouth. As the boatman ferries her across the river, a dead man floating in the water will beseech her to pull him aboard, but she must turn a deaf ear and resist taking pity on him. Once across the river and on her way again she will encounter three old weaving women, who will ask her to lend a hand in the weaving of their web. She must refuse, lest one of the cakes fall from her hand.

The tower warns her that all these temptations to put down the barley cakes are Aphrodite's traps for her. If she is ever to see the light of day again, she must hold onto the cakes until she reaches the three-headed hound which keeps sleepless guard over the house of Persephone. The awful baying of this creature terrifies even the dead, though they are past all hurt. But a barley cake will silence him. She must throw him one of the cakes and slip past as he eats it.

Once past the dog, she will be in Persephone's hall. The queen of the underworld will welcome her and offer her a seat and a sumptuous feast. But Psyche must sit on the ground and ask for coarse bread to eat. She is to give Persephone the box, explaining why she has come, and Persephone will fill the box and return it to her. Then Psyche must retrace her steps, giving the other barley cake to the hound and paying the boatman with the last coin. Once back across the river, she must hurry out to the open world beneath the sky.

Now the tower gives Psyche a final warning. Above all, it tells her, she must not open the box to see the treasure of divine beauty that Persephone has put into it. She must instead take the box straight to Aphrodite.

Having listened carefully, Psyche proceeds on her way according to instructions. Armed with barley cakes and coins, she finds the entrance to the underworld and successfully makes her way to Persephone's hall, avoiding all temptations and pitfalls. Persephone fills the box in secret, and Psyche carries it back through the gloom of the underworld and emerges into the light of day.

Now all she has to do is take the box to Aphrodite. But as she walks along, she thinks about what she is carrying in her hands. It is nothing less than the gift of divine beauty. If she could have just one drop of this for herself, she could be sure of winning Eros back again. How could she forego such an opportunity and risk losing her Beloved? She would be a fool to pass this up. And so Psyche opens the box. But what she finds inside is a hellish sleep that rushes out and covers her like a cloud, and she falls to the ground unconscious.

The Inner Journey through Sophia's Quarter

The fourth task takes Psyche on a conscious journey into the fourth quarter of the feminine quaternity. This is Sophia's realm, the inner world of the feminine spirit, the realm of Wisdom and natural spirituality. A woman on her individuation journey has actually been engaged in this task from the beginning. Like the King quarter in the masculine quaternity, the Sophia quarter is different in quality from the first three quarters. It overarches the others, and when it is consciously lived, it coordinates them and brings them together into wholeness and balance. It is the conscious journey through the fourth quarter that has made possible the conscious journey through the other three.

That is why when Psyche completes the first three tasks, Aphrodite accuses her of being a sorceress. Sorcery, which is the shadow side of Sophia, is an attempt to use the feminine spirit for personal power. Although Psyche is not a sorceress, she is tempted in the end to try a bit of sorcery—to steal some divine beauty for her own use—and it is this that proves to be her undoing.

For the fourth task, Psyche must go into the underworld and fetch back some divine beauty from Persephone, who is the daughter of Demeter and a symbol of the eternal maiden. It was Persephone who, while picking flowers in spring, was abducted by Hades and carried down into the underworld, from which she regularly returns for half of every year. As the eternal daughter of the earth mother, Persephone symbolizes the natural beauty of young womanhood, the beauty that fuels love at the surface of life. As the wife of Hades, she is the queen of the underworld.

With this new assignment from Aphrodite, Psyche despairs, as always, and as always, help appears. A tower speaks to her. For the first time, her helper is not a natural being, like the ants, the reed, and the eagle. It is not even a divine being, like Pan or Zeus. It is an edifice built by human hands, and it symbolizes a human understanding of the journey she has to make. We can see it as a Wise Man's map, a systematized understanding of the nature of the unconscious. In our day, the tower might be Jungian psychology.

The mystical traditions of the great religions are towers that were built in the past and still stand. No one should attempt a direct experience with the depths of the unconscious without guidance from a well-constructed tower. It is the tower that can tell Psyche where to find the hidden entrance to the underworld. Jungian psychology does the same when it tells us to pay attention to dreams and synchronicity, entryways to the unconscious that are in plain sight, yet hidden to the unaware.

Psyche is told to carry two barley cakes in her hands and two coins in her teeth. (It is not explained how she carries the lockbox—perhaps tucked in her clothing.) The barley cakes and coins effectively tie up her hands and require her to keep her mouth shut. She must make the journey as one who is powerless and wordless. When we begin a conscious relationship with the unconscious, we must direct our attention to the journey. It is necessary that we allow our energy to turn inward, away from outer engagement with the world. This means pulling back from a fully active life. Furthermore, we must be quiet. In most contexts of our lives, we must refrain from trying to explain ourselves and from telling very much about what we are learning.

These requirements are difficult. Though our energy has turned inward, we continue to live in the outer world, where we must meet certain responsibilities. Most people around us are unaware of what we are going through, and yet, for the most part, we cannot explain it to them. If we should try, they would not understand. Even worse, they might think us unbalanced, which we are in a way—unbalanced toward inwardness. We are in a different place from where they are and from where we ourselves will later be. So it is best if we say nothing. This is what it means to keep the coins safe.

It is important to understand that turning inward for the inner journey does not mean a complete withdrawal from the outer world. One needs the mundane routine of daily life to balance the potentially disintegrating influence of the unconscious. As the *I Ching*, the Chinese book of wisdom, would put it, small undertakings in outer life can be accomplished at this time, but great undertakings should not be attempted.

The trials Psyche faces along the path through the underworld—the lame man and donkey, the drowning dead man, and the three old weaving women—have to do with the necessity for us, when we are individuating, to overcome our instinct to help and tend life indiscriminately. If we are to save our energy for our journey, we can no longer afford to be pulled by every need that presents itself to us. If we were not on an individuation journey, it would not necessarily be the right thing for us to refuse in this way to let our feminine nature be of general service to the world. But our journey is leading us to a new kind of usefulness, one that is uniquely our own and more precisely guided by the divine than any collective assignment could be. There is something of this in what Jesus meant when he said, "Let the dead bury the dead." In order to follow an individual call from God, we must turn a deaf ear to the collective call from the world.

When Psyche pays the boatman his coins, she symbolizes a person who, by remaining inactive and silent, has saved enough energy—symbolized by money—to meet the requirements of the inner journey. The three-headed dog that guards the halls of Persephone can be seen as a symbol of the anxiety which is normally experienced as we advance toward a true engagement with the unconscious. The dog terrifies the dead even though they are past all hurt. So, too, the anxiety which surrounds the unconscious is ultimately harmless, provided we have saved our barley cakes by keeping our conscious energy available for reflection upon our inner journey.

Psyche is told to refuse the lavish hospitality offered to her in the underworld. Accepting only the simplest food and sitting on the ground to eat it is symbolic of a balanced approach to the unconscious. When we tap the unconscious, we tap a stream of mystery and meaning that can easily carry us much further and deeper than our human life requires. Our challenge is to stay grounded in solid reality and accept only the insights that offer aid to the immediate living of our lives. If we try to take too much from the unconscious, we will lose our connection to life in the greater community, which will come to regard us as strange and incomprehensible, while we come to regard it as hopelessly shallow and benighted.

Psyche, however, follows her instructions and avoids this pitfall. Her wooden box having been filled by Persephone, she returns safely to life in the outer world. But now, after almost completing the task, Psyche inexplicably disregards the tower's final warning and opens the forbidden box. We will delay our discussion of this until after we have heard the conclusion of the story.

The Wedding of Psyche and Eros

Psyche lies unconscious on the ground, and all seems to be lost. But now Eros arises from his bed in his mother's house, his wound healed at last. No longer can he bear his separation from his beloved Psyche. His mother has posted a guard at his door, but Eros slips away through a high window and flies swiftly to Psyche's side. Kneeling beside her, he wipes off the deadly sleep and puts it back into the box. As Psyche awakens, Eros tells her to take the box to his mother and leave the rest to him.

While Psyche is taking Persephone's beauty to Aphrodite, Eros goes to his father, Zeus, to seek protection from his mother's continuing wrath. Zeus, the giver of law and civility, responds by speaking of the perpetual trouble Eros has caused him with his arrows of love that so often upset the laws of heaven and violate public order. The sky father does, however, acknowledge his love for his son, remembering how Eros grew up in his own arms and was reared by his own hands. As he listens to the story of the love between Eros and Psyche, he begins to see a solution to the problem of his troublesome son.

Zeus calls an assembly of all the gods and goddesses, including Aphrodite. He explains to them that Eros needs to be married in a public way, rather than in the secret way of his marriage in paradise. A proper marriage will settle him down, fetter his lustful boyhood spirit, and bring him into full maturity. Since Eros has chosen Psyche, he should be allowed to keep her and hold her in his arms for all eternity.

Zeus turns then to Aphrodite and assures her that this will not be an unworthy match for her son, that he will ensure that it accords with the laws of civility. With this, he sends Hermes to fetch Psyche up to heaven. When Psyche arrives, Zeus offers her a cup of ambrosia, inviting her to drink it and become immortal so that she can join with Eros in a marriage that will endure forever. Psyche accepts the cup and becomes immortal.

A grand wedding now takes place in the presence of all the company of heaven. A mollified Aphrodite provides the orchestra for the wedding feast and even joins in the dancing, while Pan plays his pipe of reeds. After the wedding Psyche and Eros make their home in the heavenly community, and before long their child is born, a daughter whose name is Pleasure.

Feminine Wholeness in the Outer World

We have seen that at the end of the fourth task, which symbolizes the inner journey, Psyche opens the box and falls into a deadly sleep, finally meeting her defeat. I once had a dream that said, in meaning with no images: *Outer life and inner life meet their limits in each other. Neither can go on and on without end.* The idea conveyed in the dream was that consciousness oriented toward inner life cannot expand indefinitely, but will eventually be brought up short by the outer world, just as the expansion of consciousness that is oriented toward outer life will be finally brought to a halt by the inner world.

This limitation of inner life by the outer world is what is symbolized by Psyche's failure at the end of the story. Psyche represents a woman who has taken the inner journey. She has learned the way of the unconscious and found healing for the four quarters of her feminine being by allowing the spiritual depths and the surface of life to become integrated in her consciousness. She has found the treasure of the inner world, the beauty of the feminine aspect of the divine. It has required the most desperate struggle of her life to gain consciousness of the unconscious and learn its value. It is, therefore, not at all obvious to her that she cannot keep that feminine spirit as a part of her outer world identity.

There is a difference, however, between *identification* and *relationship*. Although a woman can and should have a continuing relationship with the unconscious, she must guard against identifying with it. For if she tries to take even a drop of that identity for herself, she cancels out her own conscious being. She can only be a human woman, not a goddess.

When a woman turns away from the outer world and identifies herself with the feminine spirit of the inner world, she loses sight of her own humanity. The human community is an outer world community, and she cannot live in it effectively if she feels herself to be at one with the Wisdom of the inner world. The inner world of the feminine spirit is meant to heal outer life, but not to replace it. It is meant to assist it and serve it, but not to preside over it. If outer life is to thrive, it must be led by the masculine spirit of consciousness, the heavenly spirit of law and civilization. The final hurdle on a woman's individuation journey is to come to the realization of this truth: that the inner journey itself is not the goal, that the inner journey is meant to lead back to the outer world of conscious structure, order, and civilization, just as the outer journey will always lead back to the inner world of rest, healing, and transformation.

Psyche's failure is a human one, and the myth seems to suggest it is inevitable. But at the very moment when human effort and understanding meet their limit, divine love breaks free from its confinement in the unconscious and reappears in outer life. Healed of the wound it received when it first encountered consciousness, it is now ready for a higher, more developed relationship with the soul, one that is more in harmony with heavenly order and community than was the immature love that could live only in paradise.

When Eros removes Persephone's beauty from Psyche and puts it back into the box, he lets Psyche know that her own humanity is enough, that he loves her fully and completely just as she is. From the very beginning, her own beauty has been greater than that of any goddess for the very reason that it is human and real. A woman, however, cannot arrive at this truth all alone. It must be conveyed to her by a personal experience of love in her own life. Once she has experienced it and learned it, she is ready to be consciously joined to divine love forever and to live a life that reflects her experience of that love and her confidence in it.

The wedding of Psyche and Eros brings the story to a close. All the gods and goddesses are in attendance, symbolizing the state of wholeness that has been attained. This is an image of the divine marriage, the same union of opposites—of heaven and earth, of divine love and human soul—that is portrayed in the Song of Solomon and the book of Revelation. Although the divine marriage can never be fully realized within the limits of earthly life, it can be partially realized to the extent that the two streams of human life and love—the depths of the spirit and the surface of life—are brought together into one. In that union, the temporal is elevated by the eternal, and the eternal is made real by the temporal. The fruit of the divine marriage is the pleasure of the fullness of life, both in heaven and on earth.

Chapter Thirteen
Types, Quarters, and Stages of Life

THIS CHAPTER IS INCLUDED for those who want to go further into the wonders of the masculine and feminine quaternities and learn how they are reflected in the Jungian psychological types (see Chapter Three) and manifested in our stages of life. If this greater depth is not of interest to you at this time, you might wish to go on to the next chapter and save this for future study. If you do wish to continue with this material, it will be more meaningful to you if you know your Jungian psychological type. Many people know their type from having taken the Myers-Briggs Type Indicator (MBTI). There are also a number of other tools available for determining one's type, some more reliable than others. None, including the MBTI, is perfectly reliable. I myself have devised a tool, the Quickie Type Test, which you can find in Appendix A. I invite you to make use of it. You might want to do this even if you know your type, just to get back into the swing of typology talk. The Quickie Type Test contains only four questions, and yet it works surprisingly well, especially when paired with descriptions of the types (also in Appendix A) to confirm whether the type determined by the test is actually a good fit. If your first result from the test does not produce a good fit with the corresponding type description, you can keep retaking the test (it does not take long), changing the answers that are difficult to decide, until you get a fit with a type description that does feel right. It is this fit that matters most, not the test that led you there. Once you know your Jungian psychological type, you will be ready to move on into this discussion.

When I was writing about the quaternities in the late 1990s for the first edition of this book, I dreamed in words, not images: "*The quaternities are related to the Myers-Briggs.*" I awoke and thought, hmm, how might that be? The Myers-Briggs Type Indicator is a widely used diagnostic tool for determining a person's psychological type according to the relative ranking of Jung's four functions—sensing, intuition, thinking, and feeling—and the two attitudes—introversion and extraversion. In the wake of that dream, I gave a great deal of thought to how the four quarters might correlate with Jung's four functions. Did Eve/Poet correlate with feeling? Soldier/Scarlett with sensation? Sophia/Wise Man with intuition? King/Athena with thinking? Well, yes, it seemed they did a little bit. But it also seemed they did not. I could just as well link the Eve/Poet quarter with sensation, or the Soldier/Scarlett quarter with thinking, and so on. In the end, I could not make a match between the quarters and the functions. I gave up and said to the Dream Giver, "I heard what you said about my quaternities being related to the Myers-Briggs, but you didn't explain how this is so, and I can't figure it out. Sorry." So the book went to press without mention of this supposed correlation since I had no understanding of it to convey.

A few years later in the early 2000s, I heard a series of lectures on Jungian typology by John Giannini, a Jungian analyst associated with the C. G. Jung Institute in Chicago. The material in these lectures came from his about-to-be-published book *Compass of the Soul* (2004), in which he proposes a bridge between the way Jung and most Jungian analysts think about the Jungian psychological types, on the one hand, and the way the Myers-Briggs people think about them, on the other. Jung's way is to diagram each type on an equilateral cross, using one axis for the judging functions (thinking/feeling) and the other for the perceiving functions (sensation/intuition). The strongest function of the type is placed at the top of the vertical axis, and the weakest function—which will be the same in either judging or perceiving—is placed at the bottom. The second strongest function is placed on the right-hand side of the horizontal axis, and the third strongest on the left. I use this model in Chapter Three. The Myers-Briggs way of designating the types is to assign letters to each of four pairs of Jungian opposites. The first pair is made up of the two attitudes of consciousness: extraversion (E) and introversion (I). The second pair is comprised of the perceiving functions: sensation (S) and intuition (N). The third pair is the judging functions: thinking (T) and feeling (F). The fourth pair, which is original with the Myers-Briggs model, though derived from Jung, is made up of the two opposing ways of engaging the outer world: with a judging (J) function and with a perceiving (P) function. When a person's preference for one side or the other of each of these four pairs of opposites is determined, their Jungian psychological type is revealed and can be written by using the four designated letters placed in the particular order given above.

Thus an ESFJ is an *extravert* (E) who uses *sensation* (S) more readily than its opposite, intuition; who uses *feeling* (F) more readily than thinking; and who meets the outer world more readily with a *judging* (J) function than with a perceiving function. This means that sensation and feeling, indicated by the two middle letters, are an ESFJ's first two functions. But which is the primary, or strongest, function, and which is the auxiliary, or second-strongest, function? It might be assumed that sensation (S) is primary because that letter comes first, but that is not the way it works. The order of the two functions designated by those two middle letters is always the same without regard to which function is strongest: a perceiving function, S or N, is *always* the second of the four letters of the type name, and a judging function, T or F, is *always* the third. The determination of which function is stronger requires a complicated calculation having to do with the fourth letter, which is always a J or a P. Fortunately, you do not have to make this calculation for yourself. You can look at a chart like the Type Charts provided at the end of this chapter where the four functions for each type are clearly designated in their order from strongest to weakest. There is also a chart at the end of the Quickie Type Test (Appendix A) that shows each four-letter type name with the letter for the strongest function underlined. For those who would like to make this calculation for themselves, the procedure is explained in the notes for this chapter at the end of the book.

The Function Couplings and the Human-Wholeness Quarters

We return now to John Giannini's lectures. We have seen that the Jungian way of depicting a type is to put a person's four functions on an equal-armed cross in a particular order from strongest to weakest, whereas the Myers-Briggs way is simply to name each type with a sequence of four letters. With this four-letter sequence for naming the sixteen possible types, the Myers-Briggs branch of Jungian typology abandoned the mandala form of the equal-armed cross as the standard way to portray and think about the psychological types. Instead, it took up a more linear mode of thinking, using charts with rows and columns to shuffle around different combinations of types and subtypes and to correlate them with different qualities of personality. Central to the Myers-Briggs school of thinking is an emphasis on the two middle letters of the type name, which, as we have seen, indicate each type's first and second functions. People who use the Myers-Briggs model tend to think of themselves and others as being SFs, sensing feelers, or STs, sensing thinkers, or NFs, intuitive feelers, or NTs, intuitive thinkers. John Giannini calls these four pairs of primary and auxiliary functions the *function couplings*. In the Jungian model, on the other hand, with the functions at the four poles of the two axes—and with Jung having used single-function type descriptions in his seminal work, *Psychological Types*—people tend to think of themselves and others simply as thinkers, feelers, sensates, or intuitives. The qualification of introverted or extraverted is commonly added in both models. I myself was following the Jungian model, with its emphasis on single functions, when I was unable to correlate my human-wholeness quarters with Jung's typology.

From John Giannini's lectures, however, there came a great light. He proposed that there is much to be gained by putting the function couplings from the Myers-Briggs model onto the Jungian equilateral cross. The couplings would go into the quadrants between the poles of the axes. And—voila!—we have a fleshed-out quaternity. An ESFJ, for example, would look like the diagram in Figure 13.1.

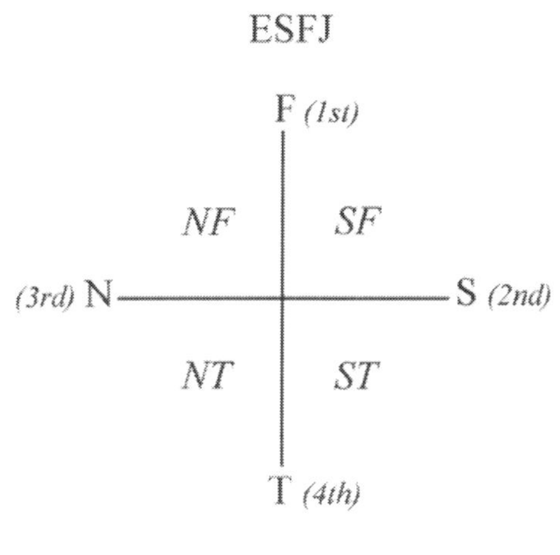

Fig 13.1 ESFJ

As Giannini unveiled for us this marvelous innovation and talked about the distinctive qualities of each of the function couplings, I immediately began to see a correlation between the couplings and the four quarters of my own human-wholeness quaternity. It quickly became apparent to me that the Eve/Poet quarter draws most strongly on the sensing function combined with the feeling function: SF. The Soldier/Scarlett quarter draws most heavily on sensing combined with thinking: ST. The Sophia/Wise Man quarter draws most heavily on intuition combined with feeling: NF. And the King/Athena quarter draws most heavily on intuition combined with thinking: NT. Or put another way, Eve/Poet energy *is* SF energy, and so on for each quarter. As we shall see in the next section, however, this correlation is not simply an equivalency. The qualities of the human-wholeness quaternity flesh out and clothe the function couplings. They also reveal a deeper, more human-life-oriented basis for the function-coupling quaternity than is evident when the quarters are viewed merely as the four possible combinations of primary and auxiliary functions of consciousness.

Giannini clearly sees the function couplings as archetypes. He sees that they belong together on a mandala of human wholeness. He sees that the function-coupling mandala, as an overarching archetype arising from the Self, must have an order and predictability that manifests in every human life. But what is that order and predictability? Giannini spent much time in his lectures, as he does in his 500-page book, correlating the function couplings with the works of several different researchers who have made some progress in this line of inquiry. He is especially impressed with the masculine quaternity of Robert Moore and Douglas Gillette. He correlates the function couplings with their four quarters and bases much of the rest of his discussion on this correlation.

As I note in Chapter Nine, my own independently derived masculine quaternity shares some features with the Moore-Gillette quaternity—primarily in the similar names we give the quarters—but it differs from it in the fundamental basis of the four-part division. My four-part division is based on a combination of two basic dualities in human life. The first division is between the mother-world and the father-world. The second is between youth and maturity. Because Moore and Gillette do not base their four-part division on these two dualities, our quaternities have major differences in the contents of their quarters, despite their shared names. Consequently, Giannini's discussion became of little use to me once he began to pair the function couplings with the Moore-Gillette quarters. I pair the couplings differently with my quarters. I see the nature of the basic contents of the paired quarters differently. I see the sequence of progression through the quarters differently. And, as we have seen, I have a different understanding of the fundamental basis of the whole business. John Giannini did provide me with two important breakthrough ideas: first, that the quarters on Jung's four-function cross can be fleshed out with the function couplings; and second, that the function couplings are rightly understood to be archetypes that fit together in a quaternity of human wholeness. But an immediate fork in the road appeared when Giannini began to incorporate the Moore-Gillette quaternity into his discussion. I took the other fork and moved on in a direction of my own.

The Four Energies of Human Wholeness

If you have read the preceding chapters on the masculine and feminine quaternities—including the material on the Beatles and on Psyche and Eros, which demonstrate a surprisingly clear order and predictability in the human-wholeness quaternity—you will find that what follows here flows naturally from the understandings that have already been established in those pages. We begin by constructing a picture of the human-wholeness quaternity of the preceding chapters, but with some new elements added to it (Fig 13.2). First of all, we add the function couplings. Then we add some symbolic imagery to help us capture and hold the essence of each of the four quarters. And finally, we add specific stages of life to indicate that each of the quarters is naturally aligned with its own twenty-year period in what we might call a universal human life. The resulting diagram contains a wealth of information that is foundational to our discussion. I invite you to take a few moments to study it. As in life, it is best absorbed by taking it quarter by quarter in the sequence indicated by the arrow.

Except for the incorporation of the function couplings and the specificity of twenty years for each of the stages of life, all aspects of this diagram have been explained in detail and illustrated by example in Chapters Nine through Twelve. While the twenty-year specificity for the stages of life is not to be regarded as absolutely exact, twenty years is, in fact, a very close approximation of the actual length of each stage. At around age twenty, most of us leave home and go to work. At around age forty, most of us begin to enter our midlife transition. And at around age sixty, most of us find ourselves in the doorway to elderhood, a time in which our perspective and activities will change in increasingly profound ways from what they were in midlife.

What the function couplings add to the human-wholeness quaternity is a clear understanding of which of the four functions of consciousness are especially needed for each quarter. The Eve/Poet quarter draws heavily on our sensing function (our perception of physical reality) combined with our feeling function. If both of these functions are naturally strong in us—that is, if we are one of the four SF psychological types—our consciousness will be quite strong in the Eve/Poet arena of life. But if either of these functions is naturally weak—that is, if our psychological type is ST, NF, or NT—then we can expect our consciousness in the Eve/Poet arena to be relatively weaker than an SF's consciousness would be. An NT, who has neither sensing nor feeling as a first or second function, will be especially weak in the Eve/Poet arena of life.

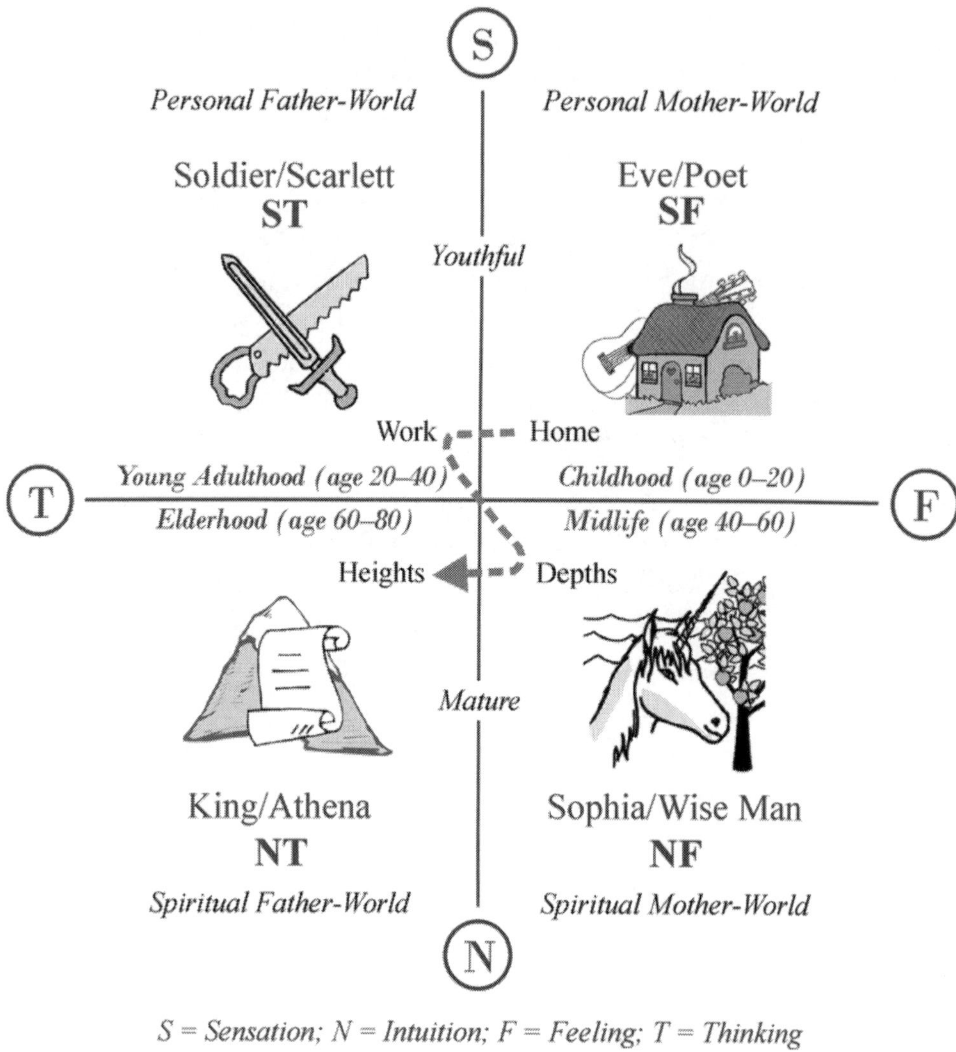

FIG 13.2. A QUATERNITY OF HUMAN WHOLENESS

This basic formula works the same for the strengths and weaknesses of all the psychological types. The consciousness of ST types is particularly strong in the Soldier/Scarlett (ST) arena of life and particularly weak in the Sophia/Wise Man (NF) arena. The consciousness of NF types is particularly strong in the Sophia/Wise Man (NF) arena and particularly weak in the Soldier/Scarlett (ST) arena. The consciousness of NT types is particularly strong in the King/Athena (NT) arena of life and particularly weak in the Eve/Poet (SF) arena. Likewise, the consciousness of SF types is particularly weak in the King/Athena (NT) arena.

While these inborn weaknesses might seem discouraging on the face of it, the good news is that these natural proclivities are simply our starting point. Life leads us naturally in twenty-year stages through the different energies of all four of the quarters and gives us ample opportunity to build up the strength of our consciousness in each one as we go through it. As we appropriate new consciousness in each quarter, we take that with us to the next, until at the end we come out well-balanced—provided we have stayed awake to what life has asked of us and fully accepted the challenges of each quarter.

Two Stage-of-Life Sequences, One Life

So far, the stages of life, once pointed out, are rather obvious. Childhood draws heavily on Eve/Poet (SF) energy. Young adulthood draws heavily on Soldier/Scarlett energy (ST). The midlife transition draws heavily on Sophia/Wise Man energy (NF). And elderhood draws heavily on King/Athena energy (NT). What is not so obvious is that most of us have a different sequence of quarters through which we also traverse our four stages of life, with the second sequence being superimposed upon the first. The underlying, foundational sequence is our passage through the quarters as a universal human being, as illustrated in Fig. 13.2, while the superimposed sequence is the one by which our particular psychological type passes through the quarters.

To approach this, let us first look more closely at the twenty-year stages for the universal human being. In the first stage, as life begins, we all face the challenge of getting our physical and emotional needs met in the Eve/Poet mother-world. Whether this goes smoothly or not, our first twenty years is the time for it. Then as young adults, we all have to go out into the Soldier/Scarlett father-world to face the challenge of establishing our own physical foundation in life. We all have to find a way to secure an income, to get a roof over our head, and to put bread on the table. Then at midlife, we all get caught up in the internal reckoning that comes with the realization that there is more life behind us than in front of us. The meaning of life begins to come to the fore. We face fading hopes, missed opportunities, the lingering impact of the wounds and mistakes of early life, and perhaps the hollowness of outer-world success. We descend, in one way or another, into the depths of the spiritual mother-world of Sophia and the Wise Man, where gradually we die to our youthful selves and are reborn as our mature selves—older and wiser, as we say. And before we know it, another twenty years have passed, and we emerge into the world of the elders where the King and Athena reign in the heights of the spiritual father-world. Our hair is turning white: an outward sign of the gradual spiritualization of our way of thinking. Our eyesight and hearing are beginning to dim, forcing us to rely more and more on inner vision, inner hearing. Our thinking and understanding, our vantage point, is moving higher with the experience of our years as if ascending a mountainside toward heaven's realm of broad vision and eternal truths.

Of course, few of us do well in all of these quarters, and none of us hits each one right on the dot of the associated decade change. But life itself is a powerful guide, and as long as we are alive in the world, we are, as universal humans, drawn inexorably through these four stages of life, no matter how ragged the process or how much we may or may not be learning from the lessons that are coming to us.

We are not only universal humans, however. We are also individuals with inborn differences that greatly affect the way our particular lives unfold. One of the more profound ways we differ from most of those around us is in our psychological type. If we each put our psychological type on an equal-armed cross in the Jungian way, with our strongest function at the top and so on, and if we put our function couplings into the quarters between the function axes, as John Giannini showed us how to do, and if we then superimpose this over the twenty-year periods of the universal human mandala, we find that, with the exception of ESFPs and ISFJs, the energies of our own function couplings are out of sync with at least two of the universal life stages, and in some cases with all four. You can see this for your own type in the Type Charts at the end of this chapter.

Let us take an INTJ as an example. Since this is my type, I can use my own life stages to illustrate how a superimposed sequence works. Figure 13.3 shows us the INTJ Type Chart.

INTJ

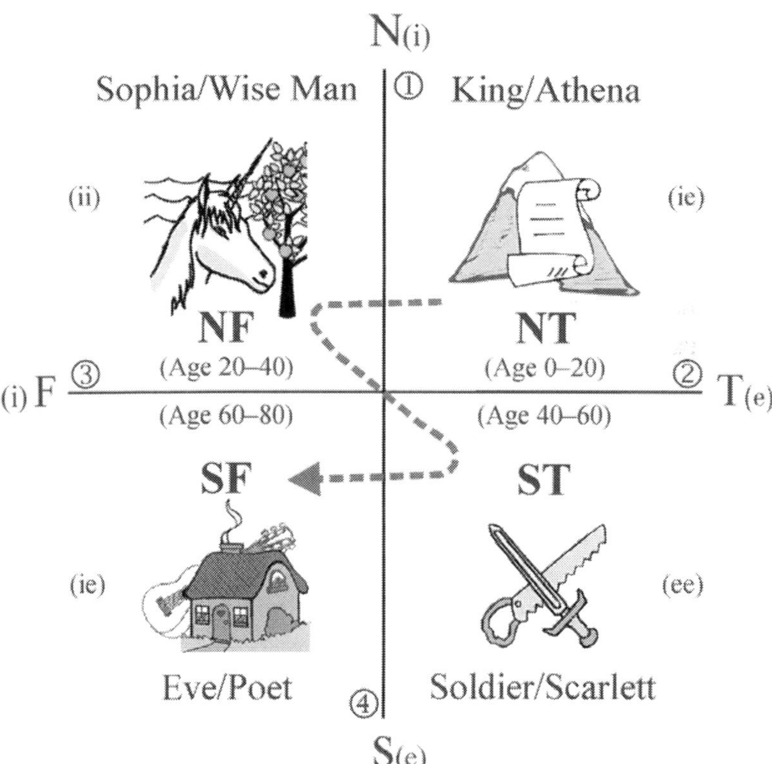

S = Sensation; N = Intuition; F = Feeling; T = Thinking
(i) = introverted; (e) = extraverted / ① = 1st function, etc.

FIG 13.3 INTJ TYPE CHART

As NTs, INTJs are natural Kings and Athenas. Because of this they often seem old as children and are less likely than other types to lose themselves easily in the carefree games of childhood. They tend to be above the fray and somewhat preoccupied with thought, and they often have suggestions for how things around them might be better managed or understood. All of this was true of my own childhood. For example, I was almost completely unconscious of the mean-girl culture of middle school and high school. Though I was vaguely aware of the dramas in which many of my friends were embroiled, I was living obliviously beyond all that in some other place in my head. If any girls were mean to me, I did not notice. I had my own more lofty concerns for the problems of community life. For example, in the ninth grade I helped get up a petition to improve conditions in our lunchroom. We wanted . . . what? Salt and pepper on the tables? I think that was it, although I cannot quite remember now. Perhaps we wanted ketchup as well. All of us who signed the petition were sent to detention hall for exercising what I felt quite strongly were our civic rights. That was in 1962, and I still feel a little indignant about it.

Age twenty to forty brought me, as an INTJ, into my NF quarter, the arena of Sophia and the Wise Man. This is the realm of Mother Nature, the great healing and nurturing container of life, the world of natural rhythms and cycles, the spiritual mother-world of the whole human family. I turned twenty in 1967, the Summer of Love, the very moment of the arrival of hippies on the mainstage of Western culture. Hippie culture is a quintessential manifestation of NF energy. I fell right into it and threw my heart and soul into the cause of Mother Nature: blue jeans, a house in the country, an organic garden, homemade whole-wheat bread, the whole bit. I graduated from college with a degree in anthropology, a quintessential NF field of study, and then I set about writing fiction, another strongly NF activity. Only toward the end of this period, in my late thirties, did I come to the heart of NF territory—the depths of the unconscious with its language of dreams and synchronicity. This deeper awakening completely captured my life, knocking out the anthropology and fiction-writing as it drew me across the forty-year divide into my ST quarter and my real mission in life, which was to help bring into our overly-masculine culture the lessons I had learned about the healing and transforming gifts of the spiritual mother-world.

Remember that I am an NT to start with. I was born first to serve the spiritual father. Only secondly, as a second-stage NF, was I born to serve the spiritual mother. So in my work to help bring awareness of the feminine divine into the consciousness of our modern world, my focus has always been as much on the masculine divine's world of organized community as it has been on the feminine divine's world of individual healing and transformation. Therefore my ST soldier work in the cause of the Great Mother took place within the church, where it also served the cause of the Sky Father. Like a good Soldier in service to the King, I turned my thinking to the practical problems that had to be solved to institute church programs in dreamwork, to be the publisher and distributor of my *Natural Spirituality* book, to give lectures and workshops on natural spirituality topics at church-oriented conferences, and to master software programs by which I could edit, illustrate, and publish a magazine for fostering dreamwork in churches.

Just when I thought this kind of work was going be my life forever, I turned sixty, and a great portion of energy for that activity simply melted away. I was entering the SF stage of my life. The up-close-and-personal world of Eve and the Poet finally began to come alive for me and to claim me. I did not completely stop what I had been doing before, but I gradually cut it back by more than half. I became much more present to the physical life that was right in front of me than I had ever been before. I was more "down in" life—in my house, in my neighborhood, and in my community. For example, as an NT my mothering instincts were not very conscious in the first half of life and I never had birth children of my own. In my sixties, however, I became a hands-on grandmother for my goddaughter's little son, to the extent of keeping him in my home several days a week for the first two years of his life. While this was not the same degree of mothering activity I would have had as a full-blown mother, it did draw on the same Eve energy and gave me my own particular portion of it.

There is one more predictive piece that comes from the life sequence of our psychological types. This has to do with introversion and extraversion. Remember that each axis in the Jungian type cross has opposite functions at its opposing poles. So if extraverted thinking is at one pole, introverted feeling will be at the other pole. Or if introverted intuition is at one pole, extraverted sensation will be at the other. It is also the case that our second function is always opposite in "version" from our first function. This means that in our first stage of life we draw our energies from both an extraverted function and an introverted function. If our first function is the introverted one, we will be a little more introverted than extraverted, but both "versions" will be evident in our personalities. In the second stage of life, however, our third function comes more into play, forming a function coupling with our first function. Both functions in this second pair carry the energy of our dominant "version"—they will both be either introverted or extraverted. So if we are extraverts, we will be more extraverted from age twenty to forty than we were in our first twenty years. And if we are introverts, we will be more introverted during this period than we were in the stage of childhood. Then in our third stage of life, from forty to sixty, the opposite happens. Both functions in our third function coupling carry the "version" energy that is opposite our dominant "version." This means that introverts are more extraverted from forty to sixty than they ever were before, and extraverts are at their most introverted during this time. Then finally, from sixty to eighty, it evens out again and we go through a function-coupling stage that draws on both an introverted and an extraverted function. Our dominant "version" will again be a little stronger since in this pairing of our third and fourth functions it is our third function—the stronger one—that carries our dominant "version." (You can see your own type's changes in introversion and extraversion in the Type Charts at the end of this chapter.)

This pattern certainly held true for me. I was extremely introverted from twenty to forty. I worked at home as a writer and seldom answered the telephone. But from forty to sixty I was propelled out into the world with all the mission activity I referred to above. Most people do not much enjoy having to operate out of their opposite "version" during this stage, and I was no exception. It was stressful. But in the course of those twenty years I did learn to be more extraverted, and for that the discomfort was worth it. So while I have been glad to get back to a more introverted time in my fourth stage of life, I am thankful that I am no longer as introverted as I was as a young adult. All in all, I am thankful for the entire process that has rounded out my energies through the course of my life. None of it came from my own doing. I simply lived into each stage of life as it arrived, always with a bit of a struggle until I caught on to the new direction.

It Works Because It Is Archetypal

I will be the first to say that if we were to approach this proposed pattern of life stages with only our sensate perception of reality, it would not be credible that our different psychological types could shape our inner and outer lives in such a predictable way. By what material mechanism could such an effect be produced? But all of us also have access to an intuitive perception of reality, whether this is strong or weak in our conscious functioning. It is our intuition that perceives the archetypal energies beneath the surface of life, and it is intuition that "gets it" when it comes to the psychological types. In his book *Compass of the Soul*, John Giannini makes a clear case for the fact that the psychological types are archetypes. As part of that discussion, he speaks of "the sudden sense of awe and excitement emanating from the unconscious that often accompanies the discovery of our own type and which is typical of an archetypal experience."

It is because of this "sudden sense of awe and excitement" that arises in most of my listeners when I present this material in a public forum that I believe these life-stage patterns to be fundamentally true. The usual reaction that people have to the sequence of quarters for their psychological type is appreciation for how it makes the broad pattern of their life make sense. Now they see why they were always weak, or strong, in this or that area of their lives. Now they see why their focus, or their circumstances, or their yearnings, changed from this to that at a certain period. Now they see why they used to feel so extraverted but have lately begun to wonder if they are actually introverted. Or vice versa. Or why in their early life they used to be so strong in thinking, but in later years feeling seemed to take over. Or why after having at first been so strongly oriented to the spiritual life, physical life began to seem more compelling at what can now be seen as a predictable point in their life sequence.

I have presented workshops on this material to hundreds of people, and there have not been more than two or three of those who have said to me, in the end, that the life-stage sequence for their type does not fit their life. In fact, I can only think of two. One was a woman in her early twenties, too young to be able to see much of a pattern, although some young people can see their patterns fairly readily. The other one, who was in midlife, was hostile to the whole idea of psychological types and could not take in much of anything I had to say. There may very well have been others along the way for whom the material did not work, but they did not let me know about it.

There are, however, always several people at every presentation who at first say that the life sequence for their type does not fit them. And so I ask them, "What type are you?" And they usually say, "Well, I'm pretty sure I'm a ____." Let's say that INFJ is in the blank. So then I ask them about their lives. "What were you doing from twenty to forty? From forty to sixty?" And so on. And indeed, their life course does not fit for an INFJ. So I scan the Type Charts for a life course of a similar type that would make a better fit. "What about INFP?" I say. "Do you think you might be that? Go read the type description and see." And when they do this—and what they are reading is the type description, not the life sequence—they almost always announce that it is true, they have finally found their true type; they had it wrong before. Similarly, it sometimes happens that from the very beginning someone cannot decide on the basis of the test and the type descriptions which of two types they are. I might add that this happens as often with the MBTI as with the Quickie Type Test. Neither can guarantee an iron-clad result, so this is not an uncommon problem. More often than not, however, when we look at how someone's life stages have unfolded, it becomes clear which of the two contending types that person is. When these three tools are used together—the type test, the type descriptions, and the stages-of-life sequence—one's psychological type can almost always be determined.

What the Quarters Might Look Like in Real Life

As you study your own type and consider your life course in terms of the quarters, questions are likely to arise about how the quarters actually look when they are lived out in real life. Here we meet the same situation we find when we ask what a mother looks like in real life. How many billion different mothers are there on the planet? Yet, beneath each one of those billions is the mother archetype, and because of that archetype certain qualities will always be present—whether conscious and positive or unconscious and negative—in every one of those mothers. This is the essential nature of archetypes, and the four quarters of the human-wholeness quaternity are archetypes, as are the sixteen types themselves. For each type, there are hundreds of millions of people who share the same sequence of energies for their stages of life, and this particular sequence is manifested in hundreds of millions of different ways. But because it is the same sequence, there are also underlying similarities that make the life course of each type different in predictable ways from the life courses of all the other types.

All four of the function-coupling energies are always present and are always being used at all times in our lives. But in each quarter through which our type passes, there will always be one of these function pairs that has extra energy behind it, and because of this, it colors that period of life as we go through it. It puts its stamp on it. If the quarter is going well, that energy engages us. We find ourselves wanting to give expression to it, even when we have no idea that it actually is a particular energy that can be named in this way. We simply live into it automatically whether we are conscious of the process or not. If the quarter is not going well, if we are somewhat, or perhaps greatly, resistant to this particular energy, it will manifest anyway, but often this will take a very literal form. For instance, we might literally move to the mountains during our NT stage, while within ourselves we experience very little in the way of higher perspective or broader vision. When we are not open to a quarter's new energy on the inside, which means we are not letting our consciousness expand to integrate it, that particular quarter of our lives is likely to be bumpier than the others. Obviously, the manifestations of the four energies are myriad in all the billions of human lives on the planet; however, since they are archetypal energies, it is possible to give at least a rough sketch of what each of the quarters might look like when lived in real life.

What does an SF quarter look like? During our SF years, the hands-on, caretaking energies of Eve and the pleasure-of-life energies of the Poet gradually come to the fore. Among the many possible forms this can take are literal or surrogate parenting; tending to needy or ill adults; taking care of animals; nest-building (making a home); taking time for the art and pleasures of sensate life (food, music, sports, painting, crafts, camping, dancing, etc.); reconnecting with childhood relationships, experiences, and/or places; spending time in relaxation and comradery with friends and family, and so on. While this list is by no means exhaustive, it conveys some idea of the special coloring that comes with an SF quarter.

For some psychological types, their SF quarter does not arrive until age forty or sixty. For those who have SF as a third quarter, there might be a delay in parenthood until the late thirties or early forties. It is not unusual for those who have it as their fourth quarter not to have children at all, although this is by no means the rule. No matter when it comes in life, the SF quarter, like all the others, sometimes does not go well. In some examples I have seen of this quarter going badly, the twists and turns of life force SF circumstances upon a person who, for reasons usually rooted in childhood wounds, is ill-equipped to embrace such situations or to handle them well. For example, a person who has SF as a second quarter might become a parent at that time, perhaps from an unwanted pregnancy, and then, because of a resistance to SF energy, might fail to engage well with parental responsibilities. When SF energy is resisted, a person's life course will almost always be rocky during the time of his or her SF quarter, though it often smooths out when the next quarter arrives.

What does an ST quarter look like? The ST energy of the Soldier/Scarlett quarter comes into play when we apply thought to concrete, practical problems. Though we need this at home when we are working on our income tax or trying to master the controls of a new television, we need it most of all for practical intercourse with the world outside the home. It is from the outside world that we derive the income that supports life at home. But ST energy is not only about making a living. It is also about mission, about making a concrete and practical contribution to the particular society in which we live. While home life is held together by love and deeply felt obligation, society is held together by systems. It has rules and regulations. It has standardized procedures. It does not make room for us because it loves who we are. It makes room for us because we have found a way to offer to it, on its own terms, something that we have that it needs. To achieve this, we have to be objective and practical. We have to put our minds to it and solve the particular, concrete problems that arise. We have to discipline ourselves to fit into the system. We have to show up on time. We have to study the manuals and practice the skills.

We all have to meet the ST challenge in one way or another when we are in the universal ST stage from age twenty to forty. But in the life sequence of many psychological types, the more personal ST quarter does not begin until the age of forty or sixty. In these cases, especially when it does not come until sixty, ST energy is more likely to be about mission—a meaningful contribution to one's particular community—than about getting a job or providing an income, although this may also be involved. For those who have deep wounds in the personal father-world, as we saw with John Lennon and the Beatles, the ST quarter is likely to be a rough ride, perhaps a time of addiction or divorce or lack of direction. But even when the going is tough, some bit of progress can usually be seen. To the degree that ST energy can be consciously integrated, it leads to competence and usefulness in the real world outside one's door.

What does an NF quarter look like? With the NF energy of Sophia and the Wise Man, we descend to the depths, to the well of mystery beneath the surface of life, where the riches of the unconscious, imperceptible to our senses, flow to us through our intuition and bring from us a response from our feelings. The healing power of this energy can be palpably felt when, for example, if we are feeling particularly frazzled, we withdraw into the solitude of nature and sit there quietly for a time. As the birds get used to us and go back to their business and the breezes ruffle the leaves around us, the divine feminine enfolds us, flows into us, calms us, centers us, deepens us, and gradually brings to us some sort of adaptive attitude or understanding that enables us to get up and go back out into life with renewed clarity and strength. NF energy heals and transforms us, both in small, daily ways and in big, life-changing ways. It is the energy of Mother God. The feeling element in it tends to be centered on the natural world and on people, although on people in general more than on the people in our face-to-face world, which is more the province of our SF energy.

NF energy is present when we open ourselves to others outside our own group and care about their well-being. It is present when we bring to light intuited human realities through such artistic expressions as acting or the writing of fiction. It is present when we delve into genealogy, which takes us into the unseen world of the unconscious, the land of the dead, and brings to life, and into connection with ourselves, people from earlier times and other places. NF energy is present when we are stricken with illness, especially when it is grave or life threatening, for illness can take us into the shadow of death and transform us into a new version of ourselves that is deeper and wiser than who we were before we became ill. NF energy is present when we develop an interest in the spiritual depths, in dreams, synchronicity, and other manifestations of the feminine divine. It is present when we take up art in a way that opens us to right-brain awareness and diffuses a one-sided orientation to the concrete and the logical. And, most characteristically, it is present when we are drawn to live closely with nature, impelled by a deeply felt intuition that our health and wholeness depend on maintaining harmony with her, both in our inner and outer lives.

An unhealthy manifestation of NF energy would be to live too literally and one-sidedly with nature and thereby lose a balanced connection with culture and civilization. Another would be to live too deeply in the world of art and lose our connection with the ordinary world of instinct and convention. Worst of all, we can lose our way in the inner world, or become overpowered by it, and suffer the effects of mental illness. But just because the NF quarter carries such dangers does not mean that we should, or even can, stay away from it. Our health, our wholeness, and our creativity—both as individuals and as the whole human race—depend on it and cannot exist without it. All of us are drawn by life to spend some time with the transforming energy of the NF quarter, whether we willingly embrace it as a life-giving adventure or unwillingly suffer it as a harrowing passage. Often, in fact, it calls both of these responses from us, for transformation requires the death of the old, and death is seldom easy. It is for this reason that the NF quarter is the most devalued and the least conscious of all the quarters—a situation in global human consciousness that very much needs to change.

What does an NT quarter look like? The NT energy of the King and Athena operates above the concrete world of particulars and is concerned with the laws and principles and good working order of the whole of the human community. It takes the view of eternity, looking back into the past and forward into the future. In an individual life, this global perspective has to be balanced with the limitations of earthly life, and this is the central challenge we face when we enter this realm of the spiritual father. As our NT selves, we have to work out the best possible compromise, for the present time, between the ideals of heaven and the realities of earth.

NT energy takes us up to that higher level of vision that sees far in all directions and recognizes the patterns and possibilities of which our present reality is but a part. It is often NT energy that sends us into further education, especially to study abstract and theoretical subjects such as law, religion, math, or astronomy. While in our NT quarter, a particular effort we have previously been making in our face-to-face world might grow into a more global enterprise. A local issue in which we have become involved might move us to a higher level of involvement at the regional or even national or international level. Our NT energy might send us out to explore the world, to travel and visit traces of other times and places in history, to help us piece together for ourselves the big picture of the human journey. Our NT energy might put us to work at a higher level in our own community in an effort to bring it just a little closer to the heavenly ideal. We might become active as a Friend of the Library or as a lay leader in our church or as a poll worker on election day. Or we might take a government job to help draw up or implement better rules and regulations for some aspect of the community as a whole. These are the kinds of things NT energy gets us into, although this list is certainly not exhaustive.

When NT energy is resisted, it might do its work more literally by sending us to climb mountains or to travel around the world just to say that we have done it. When it is overdone, it takes us too far into the heavens—into the overly-academic ivory tower, for example, or into life-denying religious ideology. But when NT energy does the work in us that it is meant to do, it broadens our vision and steadies us by helping us situate our present reality in a greater, ongoing reality that makes sense on the whole and that we know intuitively is unfolding as it should. NT energy at its best brings us the inner knowledge that we are part of eternity and that, no matter what is happening in the present moment, we are always in the safekeeping of the mystery and majesty of the power of heaven.

It is not always easy to identify which of the four energies of human wholeness is being manifested most strongly in each quarter, given that the energies of the universal human pattern are always operating underneath and that the energies we have already integrated are always influencing the way our new energies are being manifested. But there is no need to tie ourselves in knots over this. We can look at our own Type Chart and glean what understandings it might yield at the moment and be satisfied with that. It is always good to come back to this material from time to time as the years go by, for the mysteries of psychological type yield themselves slowly, and new understandings will always arise as new life unfolds and our consciousness grows.

Knowing our type and its particular life stages can give us an overall sense of what to expect as we go forward. But although we can help our own process by being more conscious of it, the process will unfold whether we are conscious of it or not. It is not incumbent upon us to *do something* about our psychological type. We can relax in the knowledge that if we simply live our lives faithfully, each of our pieces will fall into place at the right time and under the best circumstances that our lives will allow. That being said, it is also true that the unfolding of our psychological type is likely to go more smoothly if we wake up to its reality and give it our conscious cooperation.

As you study your Type Chart in the following pages and think about the stages of your life, it might help to keep in mind these core attributes of the four quarters of human wholeness.

SF takes us home and gives us warmth and pleasure.

ST takes us to work and gives us mission and security.

NF takes us to the depths and gives us healing and transformation.

NT takes us to the heights and gives us vision and equanimity.

SF Type Charts

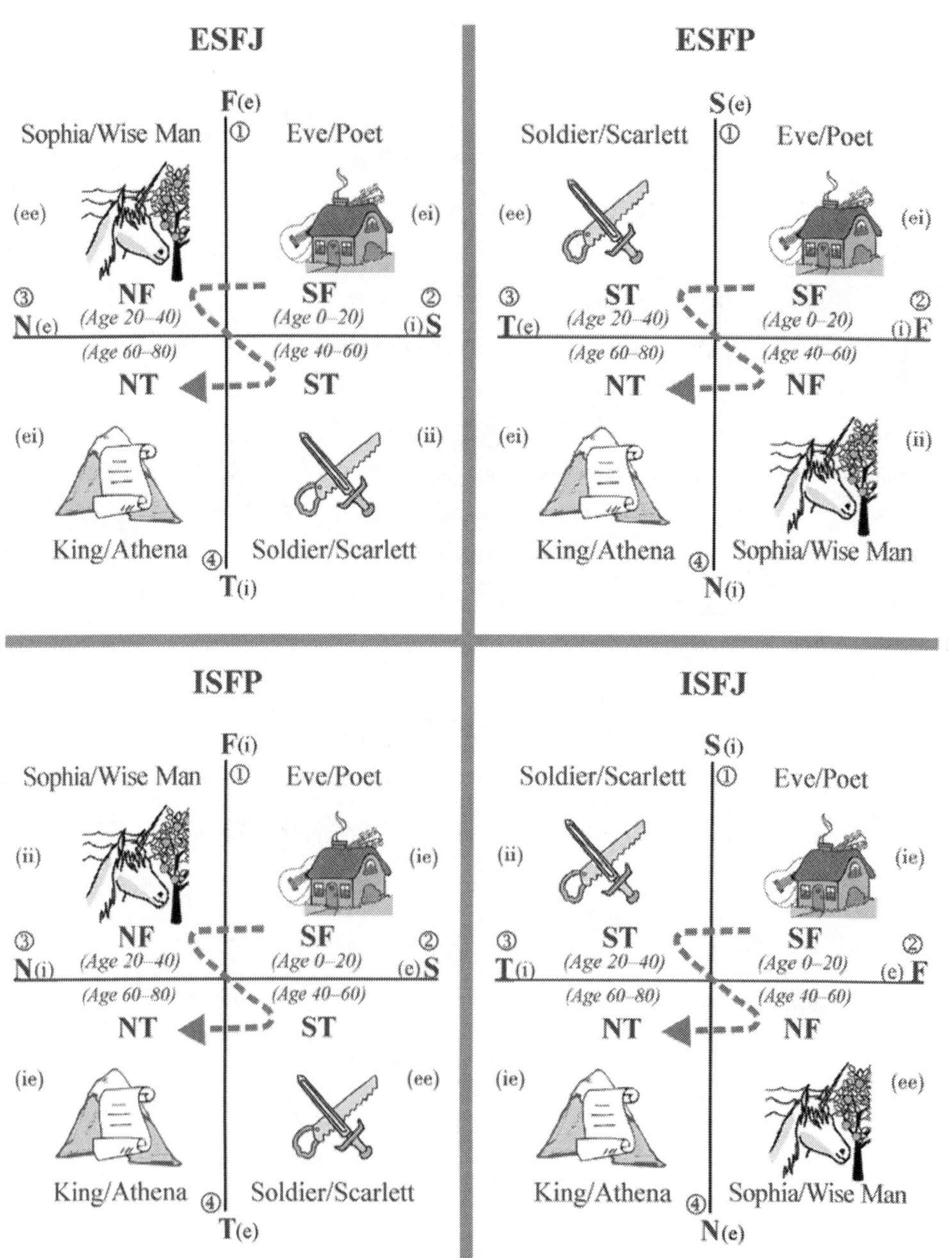

S = sensation; N = intuition; F = feeling; T = thinking
(i) = introverted; (e) = extraverted / ① = 1st function, etc.

ST Type Charts

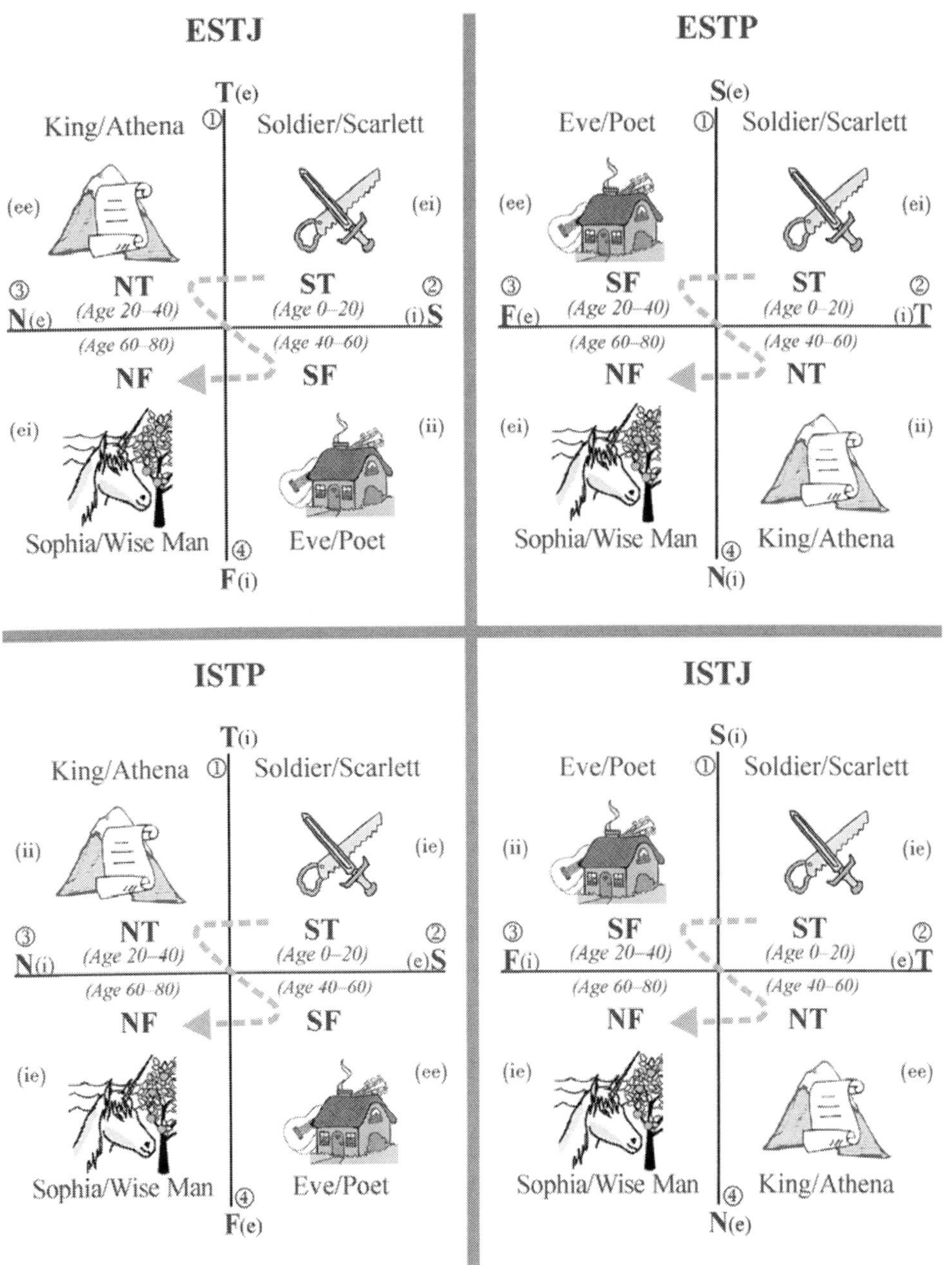

S = sensation; N = intuition; F = feeling; T = thinking
(i) = introverted; (e) = extraverted / ① = 1st function, etc.

NF Type Charts

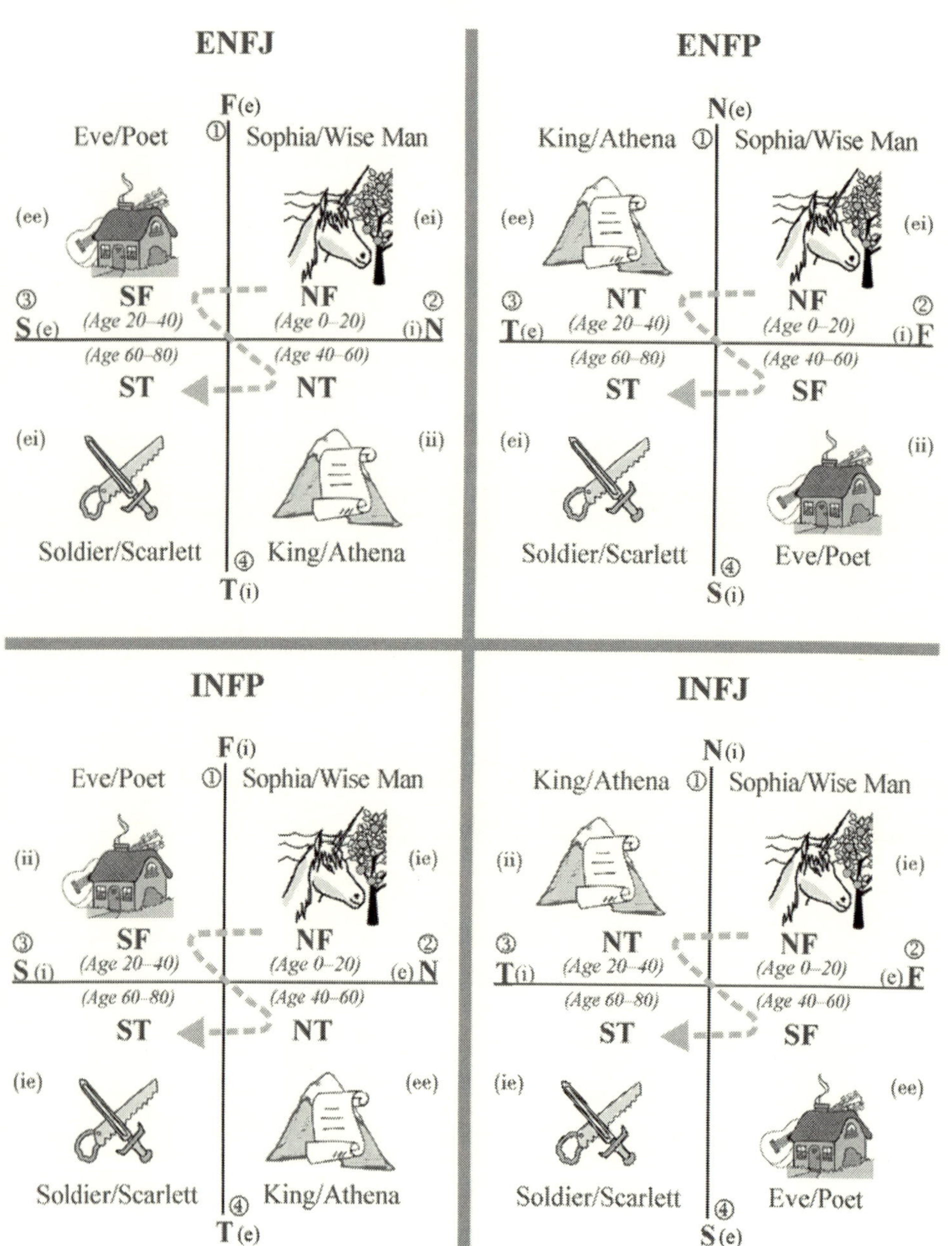

S = sensation; N = intuition; F = feeling; T = thinking
(i) = introverted; (e) = extraverted / ① = 1st function, etc.

NT Type Charts

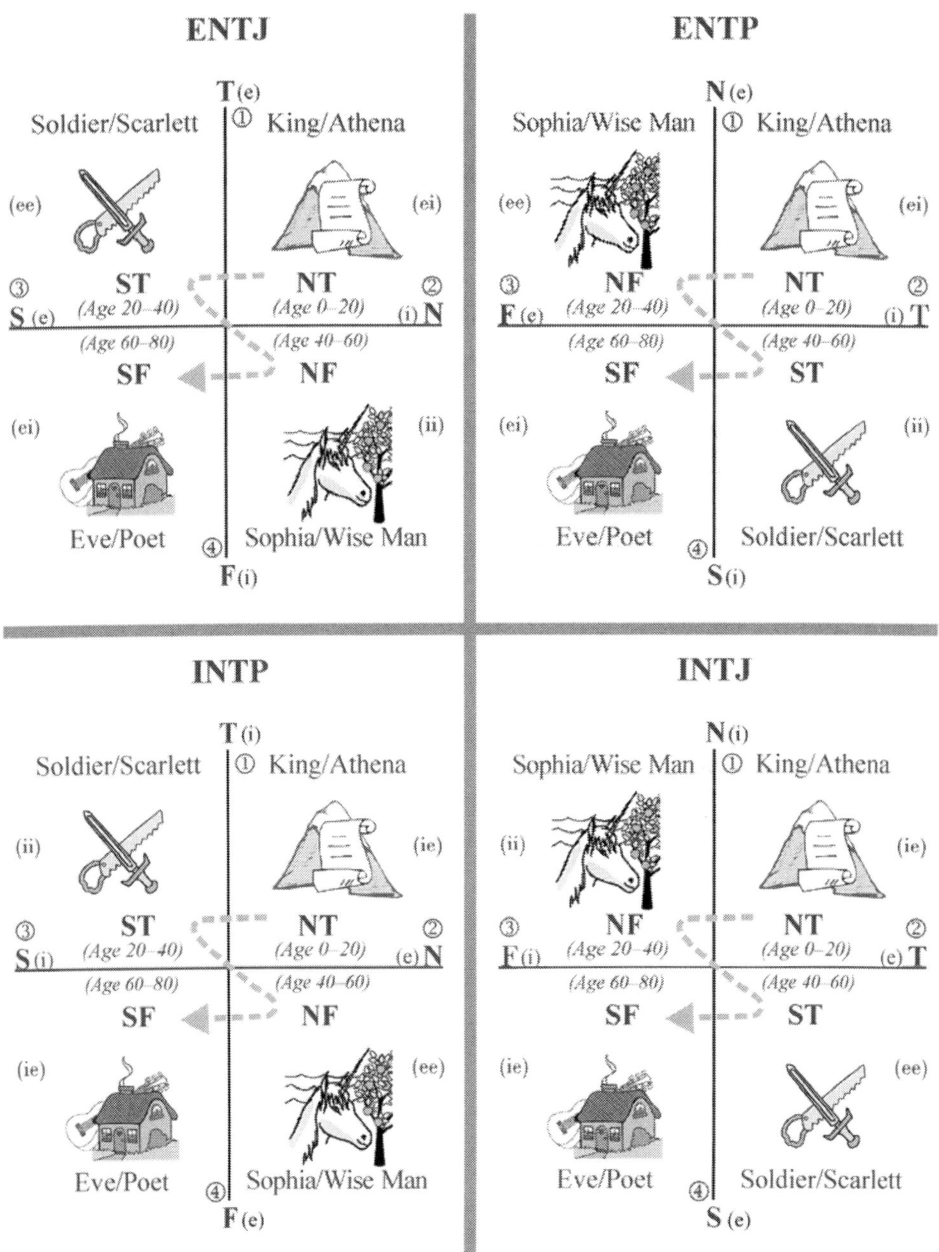

S = sensation; N = intuition; F = feeling; T = thinking
(i) = introverted; (e) = extraverted / ① = 1st function, etc.

Part Four

Inner Work in Spiritual Community

Chapter Fourteen
How To Start a Dream Group

BACK IN MY EPISCOPAL CHURCH in Georgia in 1991, as I finished teaching the first twelve-week class that contained most of the material that would become this book, a number of people who had taken the class asked me not to fold up my tent and go home when the class was done. "You have convinced us that our dreams are important," they said, "but what are we going to do now? We don't know how to interpret them." The obvious answer was that we should start a dream group, even though I was quite aware that Carl Jung had said that dreams can only be effectively analyzed on a one-to-one basis, certainly not in groups. But while that might have been true in Jung's world, my world called for giving group dreamwork a try.

So six of us began gathering weekly in one of the first church dream groups ever, stumbling forward through uncharted territory, learning by trial and error which methods and procedures were effective and which were not. Our dream group took root, grew, and kept on meeting week after week, year after year. When we were roughly ten years into it, some of us began attending events at the Haden Institute, an organization dedicated to the support of spirituality-oriented group dreamwork. There we learned the technique of projection dreamwork—"If it were my dream"—based on the pioneering work of Montague Ullman and Jeremy Taylor. Although at first we were resistant to some of its restrictions, our group gradually came to see the value of this

Haden Method, as it is now called, and we adopted it as a best practice for analyzing dreams in a group. When I left that church in 2009 to move to Kentucky, the dream group I left behind had been meeting continually for eighteen years and had grown into three groups with different meeting times. As of this writing, it is still going strong after 25 years. I know of few other weekly church programs, other than Sunday school and choir, that have such staying power.

In Kentucky, I decided to start a dream group that would not be affiliated with a church. It seemed right to try to offer this valuable inner work to spiritual seekers who no longer feel comfortable attending church-sponsored activities. For the new group, there were only three of us at first and we met in my home. Though we were small in number and were not church-affiliated, we were careful to maintain a spiritual container for our dreamwork through the use of opening and closing liturgies. The ones we used and still use are based on the liturgies I had used in my church group in Georgia, although we modified the language and included some multifaith elements in order to honor the sensibilities of the growing number of people in our world today who are spiritual but not religious (see Appendix B). I soon found that a dream group grows more quickly outside the institutional church than within it: there is a great openness to new spiritual practice among the spiritual but not religious, as well as a ready openness to the reality of the unconscious, the realm of Wisdom. Our group outgrew my home within just three years, and, as of this writing, we now meet weekly in the local Chinese medicine clinic (after clinic hours), where we use their several treatment rooms for our breakout groups.

As I enter my second quarter-century of dream-group participation, I can say unequivocally that a well-run dream group has an inherent life of its own that is stronger and more sustainable than any other group spiritual activity of which I have ever been a part, except, perhaps, for Sunday worship. This does not mean that great numbers of people flock to dream groups. They do not. But in every community there are a small but significant number of people for whom Jungian inner work in spiritual community is just what they have always been looking for, and once they find it, many of them settle in and stick with it for the long haul. Yes, it is a bit of trouble to get oneself together to go to the meetings every week, but for these people, the rewards are worth it. They have discovered the vibrant life of the divine that pulses beneath the surface of life, and they find it to be continually interesting, wondrous, and new. They enjoy the comradery of the dream-group community, a group of fellow travelers who share their interest in staying tuned to the spiritual depths. They appreciate the interactional health of the group: because people in a dream group are consciously doing their shadow work, relatively little of their shadow gets projected onto the people around them. Acrimony and factions do not arise. Dissatisfactions are easily voiced and readily addressed. And perhaps best of all, everyone in a dream group grows and deepens as time goes by. Not only can everyone see this in all the others, but they can also feel it in themselves. Real change happens. Real progress is made toward health and wholeness in both the inner worlds and outer worlds of all the people in the group. More than anything else, it is the richness of life in a dream group that brings its members back to it week after week, year after year.

I must admit, however, that when I first moved from Georgia to Kentucky, I tried doing without a dream group. In order to have one I would have to organize it, and I was tired of organizing. But then I found that it was much harder to stay in touch with my dream life without a group. When you are in a dream group, there comes a time each week when you say to yourself, "I *must* have a dream by Thursday," or whenever the meeting day is. That extra concentration, that persistent nudging of your attention, usually brings forward into the morning light at least one dream a week. Without this added pressure to pay attention to my dream world, it became easier and easier to let it slip out of sight and stay there. I also began to miss having a group of fellow travelers with whom I could talk about the deeper level of spiritual life. And so after just six months of going without a dream group, I set about organizing yet another one. This time, however, I was careful to structure it in such a way that neither I nor anyone else would have to carry very much of the burden of leadership. In this new dream-group model that my friends and I have developed over the last decade, we all carry the leadership together.

I believe this model would function well for any dream group, whether inside a church or out. It is not complicated. To describe it here as simply as possible, I will divide it into two parts. The first part covers the basic elements of the regular meetings, and the second covers the supporting elements that make a strong container for the group (Fig 14.1).

Regular Meetings of a Dream Group

1. Gather
2. Share leadership
3. Establish a spiritual container
4. Tell dreams
5. Take a break
6. Analyze dreams
7. Honor and release the spiritual container

Supporting Elements for a Dream Group

1. Educate
2. Collect resources
3. Travel
4. Grow

Fig 14.1. A Dream Group Model

Regular Meetings of a Dream Group

Gather

Before a group can gather, it must be formed, and there is no end to the different ways a group can be formed. You could start one informally among friends. Three people would be enough at first. You could probably even do it with two. But you would want to grow it to four, five, or six members as soon as possible. This is because not everyone can attend every meeting, and if there are only two or three people in all, the regular meetings will often have to be canceled due to absences. In a more organized setting, like a church or a yoga center, you can put up a sign-up sheet and gather a group of anywhere from four to twelve. Twelve active members is an ideal number—that would usually mean six to ten people at each meeting, which is perfect for group dreamwork. My own long-running group has about thirty active members, which translates into roughly twelve to twenty people at any particular meeting. As I will explain below, when the number of people present is over ten or twelve, we divide into breakout groups to do our actual dream analysis. One caveat to keep in mind in group formation is that not everyone who initially expresses interest in joining the group and attends the first few meetings will find dreamwork to be what they want or need. If you start with twelve people, you are likely to end up with six to eight who stay past the first few months. This means that if you start with significantly fewer than that, perhaps only three or four, you will need to start looking for additional members right away.

So where should a dream group meet? Anywhere that is regularly available and offers privacy for the group's conversation. A home, a church, a yoga center, a corner table in a coffee house. It is not a good idea to move the meeting place from week to week or month to month, although this could be done if necessary. The problem with a moveable meeting place is that there will always be some people who can only attend from time to time, and when the infrequent attendees suddenly find themselves free to attend, they need to have ready knowledge of where the meeting place is.

How often should a dream group meet? Every week is by far the best, though some dream groups meet every two weeks, and some meet only once a month. Weekly meetings are best suited to the day in and day out nature of our life with the feminine divine. Frequent meetings keep us tuned to the Wisdom path, prodding us to pay continual attention to our dreams and synchronicities. They help us live into the fact that attention to the unconscious is not simply an interesting enhancement that we sprinkle onto our lives from time to time. It is as integral to the daily health of our souls as exercise and wholesome food are integral to the daily health of our bodies. While it is better to have a dream group that meets every two weeks than not to have one at all, it is much better to have one that meets every week.

That being said, every week for ever and ever is likely to become burdensome for even the most dedicated dream-group members. One of our better innovations in our Kentucky group is that we take a month-long break three times a year. We do not meet during April when most people want to be outside in their gardens. We do not meet during August when many people go to the beach and others simply need a summer break. And we do not meet in December when most people are busy with the holiday season. This gives us a regular rotation throughout the year of three months on and one month off. We all look forward to the one month off, and then we all look forward to getting back to the group for the next three months. It works beautifully.

Finally, how long should a meeting last? Ideally for two hours. Ninety minutes will work if every minute is used productively, although the meeting time will feel more pressured than a more relaxed and convivial two hours would feel. A single hour is better than nothing, but much will be lost when the time frame is so short. Our Kentucky group meets late in the day on Thursdays from 5:15 to 7:15, a time slot that works well for most people. One of my church groups in Georgia meets on Sundays after church from 12:30 to 2:30. Another meets on Tuesday mornings from 10:00 to noon.

Share Leadership

The leadership model you want to avoid for your dream group would look like this. A single person who knows a lot about Jung and dreamwork convenes a group. This could be a man, but let us say she is a woman. This is her group. She has knowledge and insight to give to the people who are gathered in it. They are pleased about this and gladly regard her as their teacher, their source of wisdom about dreams and the unconscious. When they tell their dreams, they tend to look at her, as if telling them to her rather than the whole group. When they analyze dreams together in a group, they make a few contributions of their own, but mostly they wait to hear what she will say about the dream since she is the one who has the most knowledge. Because it is her group, both in her eyes and in theirs, they take it for granted that the chairs will be set up and the tea made when they get there. Nor, usually, do they stay to help clean up afterward. In fact, if they are meeting in her home, she is likely to decline help if they offer: no problem, she's got it in hand. In the days between the weekly meetings, some of them will call her to go over their dreams, since she is the one who knows best how to analyze them. All of the members are grateful to her for making the dream group available and for helping them understand their dreams. They do not know what they would do without her.

I have lived this model. It comes naturally to someone who has knowledge about Jung and dreamwork, and, at first, it feels like a good way to run a dream group. It might be a good way, or at least an okay way, if the group lasts only six weeks or so, but in a long-term dream group, the burden imposed on the leader by this model becomes heavier and heavier as time goes by until it ultimately becomes unsustainable. And this is not the worst of it. The worst of it is that it encourages the dream-group members to project onto the leader their own inner wise man or wise woman, and this greatly impedes their discovery of the presence of Wisdom within themselves.

Here we come to the most important principle of group dreamwork. *Every single one of us has the living waters of Wisdom within our own being.* The flow of Wisdom is universal, archetypal. It is an inner spiritual process available to all. All we need is a little bit of instruction about how to awaken it, how to turn it on, how to begin to notice it. Very little instruction. In fact, what we need most is simply a context that will allow the Wisdom waters to start flowing within us. This is not to say that we do not need education about Wisdom and her ways. We do, although for the most part, as I will explain below, we can and should educate ourselves. Nor is this to say that we immediately become wise as soon as we begin dreamwork. It takes time to awaken fully to the reality of the unconscious and to become familiar with its language, patterns, and principles. But after a year of healthy group dreamwork, which means that no one's hand is being held by a know-it-all leader, a growth in Wisdom is clearly perceptible both in individuals and in the group as a whole. Almost anyone who has been in a group for two years will be notably competent at dreamwork. And any dream-group members who have regularly attended for three years or more will be paddling their canoe with the best of them.

So how do you set up a dream group in such a way that the one who knows the most about Jung and dreamwork does not automatically become the leader and guru? You do it by very consciously and explicitly structuring it otherwise. First and foremost, you rotate leadership of the group meetings every week. Skill in dream analysis is not a requirement for leading the group. In the Haden Method of projection dreamwork, all members of the group participate equally in the working of a dream. There is no place in this process for a guru—be it a trained analyst or a well-read layperson—to say, "This is what it means." The leader of a dream-group meeting simply moves the group through the different parts of the meeting. That is all. Anyone can do it. The person who knows the most and who probably led the way in forming the group might naturally lead the group's first meeting, and perhaps the second and third, until everyone is settled in and fairly comfortable. Then the weekly leadership should begin to rotate, with the explicit understanding that the group belongs to everyone and everyone must help to lead it. The same goes for setting up the room for the meeting and providing refreshments and straightening up afterward. This should be a group effort from the beginning, with everyone taking a share in the tasks. The leader for each week and the people setting up and taking down can be designated beforehand using a sign-up sheet, or the roles can be taken up on an ad hoc basis as each meeting convenes.

If someone in the group has significantly more knowledge about inner work than the others, he has a special responsibility to do all he can to minimize the tendency of others in the group to make him the leader and guru. He should explain to them at the outset that we all have a universal tendency to project our inner wise person onto someone else who seems to be wiser than we are. He should acknowledge that some in the group will naturally do this with him and that this is not a bad thing. In fact, it is good. It means that their inner wise person is waking up and wants to become conscious. It is important, however, that this process not remain stuck in an unconscious state and go no further. All members of the group should try to stay awake to their own tendency to project their inner wise one. They should try to catch themselves when they are doing this and roll back their projections and claim their wise one for themselves, for all of them are capable of learning how to discern what is coming to them from the unconscious. It will take a little while, but they will learn. This brief teaching only has to be delivered once, or perhaps twice for those who were not present the first time. It almost always has a salutary effect for the simple reason that everyone in their truest selves would rather be self-empowered than led by others.

Though the goal is to have a dream group that leads itself, there is still a need for particular people to take on particular roles. My Kentucky dream group grew so fast that by the time we had been going for three years, we had to break up into two or even three groups for the part of the meeting in which we actually analyze dreams. The problem then became how to make sure that each breakout group had in it a fair share of the more seasoned members to help carry the dream analysis process along. The ones who were in their first year were still novices, and the ones who were in their second year did not yet feel confident in steering the dreamwork itself. So we gathered together a team of three-year veterans and formally named them the Dream Leader Team, with the idea that we would make sure that there would always be at least two of them in every breakout group. At first, there were six or seven on the team, including myself. The next year we added more, and so on until we had grown the team to twelve. Twelve seems like a good archetypal number for a leader group, and so we stopped there. Now we only add more members as needed to make up for natural attrition.

The Dream Leader Team meets together once during each of our three break months to share a meal and talk about issues having to do with the growth and development of the dream group. Different members of the team take responsibility for different tasks in the running of the larger group. One sends out email notices to the members on a weekly basis, reminding them of upcoming meetings and other business. One manages our library. One keeps our supply of snack food stocked. One composes our handouts and keeps them printed. Not all of the twelve have particular duties, but all of them do take a special responsibility in the running of the group. They are usually the ones who sign up to lead the weekly meetings.

The development of the twelve-person Dream Leader Team is the single most important innovation that has come out of our Kentucky dream group. Despite our mantra of leaderlessness, the team does provide a measure of leadership, which no group can do without entirely. But the leadership is spread so widely that the rest of the group feels, accurately, that it is only their fellow members taking this part or that for the moment and that the group belongs to everyone, including themselves. And the whole group does participate accordingly. Everyone, whether on the Leader Team or not, signs up for a turn each month at setting up and taking down the meeting space, and everyone participates equally in the dreamwork discussions. As for the burden imposed on the Leader Team itself, the leadership role for each person is quite small and easily sustainable.

The leader of the weekly meeting, then, can be anyone in the group. She begins the meeting by asking for announcements having to do with the business of the group. Some dream-group models follow this with a time for check-in by the individual members, letting each person tell a little about what has been going on with them since the last meeting. In our model, we do not do this, as there is no time for it. We save such catching up for informal conversation before and after the meeting and during the break. Instead, we do a different kind of catching up by letting everyone in the group tell a dream. But before we do this, we put in place our spiritual container so that we will have a healthy context for bringing out our dreams and, later, for working them.

Establish a Spiritual Container

The establishment of a spiritual container is not simply a nice thing to do, but is crucial both to the health and wholeness of the group and to the balance and inner stability of the individuals as they do their dreamwork. It is not too much to say that it makes all the difference in the effectiveness of the work. This is due to the synergy that is constellated when the masculine and feminine energies of the divine are brought together into a union. To help drive this idea home, I will relate a dream I once had about the masculine and feminine sides of our spiritual life. It went like this:

> *I am trying to explain the essence of spiritual life to some people in a church setting. "It consists of two parts," I say. The people are interested in this—they are listening. I especially notice a woman priest with short, straight hair. As I begin this presentation, we are near the end of our session and almost out of time.*
>
> *"One part is the life of faith," I say, realizing at that moment that faith is the essence of the masculine side.*
>
> *Yes, yes! They all agree with this enthusiastically. The time for the session is ending. Very happy and satisfied, they all get up to leave. They do not even notice that I have not yet had a chance to tell them about the second part. Even the woman priest cares only about the faith side of our life with God.*

> *I go out into the hall where they are now standing about. "You didn't hear the second part," I say. They have to admit they did not, and so they give me their half-hearted attention.*
>
> *"The second part is dreams," I say. I have thought this through before saying it. I have sorted through all the various elements and expressions of the divine feminine and have realized that dreams are the essence of the feminine side of spiritual life, as faith is of the masculine.*
>
> *"To live a whole religious life," I say, "you need to think about and record your dreams at least twice a week. Every day would be better, but twice a week is the minimum." I say this after thinking about it and concluding that church people, in general, can only be expected to record dreams twice a week.*

Just as church people can only be expected to record their dreams twice a week, most people engaged in group dreamwork can only be expected to spend a small amount of time with the kinds of sacred readings and prayers that would invoke their faith in the power of heaven. But if they are to lead a healthy and whole spiritual life, they must do at least that much. They must join the masculine side of their spiritual life to the feminine side. In the spiritual world as in the physical world, it is the conjunction of masculine and feminine that produces new life.

Dreamwork gives us a full and rich engagement with the feminine divine. Most of the time in the dream group is devoted to this. For the sake of spiritual balance, therefore, a natural spirituality dream group always begins and ends with brief attention to the masculine divine, invoking the power of heaven to come make a safe container for, and a synergistic union with, the divine feminine energies that come to us through our dreams. In the particular liturgy used by our group, the feminine divine is also invoked, but the balance of attention is on the masculine divine. The liturgy itself, with its formal structure, is a masculine spiritual expression.

The liturgy we use in our Kentucky dream group is included here in Appendix B for free use by any who might want to adopt it. It has been fine-tuned for the sensibilities of the spiritual but not religious, while still carrying a clear and strong expression of a balanced masculine and feminine spirituality. Though comprised to some extent of biblical passages, it also contains Hindu and Daoist texts. Most people would be surprised at how well some biblical passages support our work with dreams. Psalm 16:7, for example, declares: "I will bless the Lord who gives me counsel; my heart teaches me night after night." Also to be found in Judeo-Christian scripture are beautiful, sublimely-worded passages about the saving qualities and divine nature of Wisdom, which is explicitly recognized as feminine. Other biblical passages that we use are focused more directly on the masculine aspect of the divine. Our passages from the Bhagavad Gita and the Dao De Jing also speak of both the masculine and feminine qualities of the divine. Most of these texts appear in our liturgy as canticles—a kind of poetry fashioned from scripture. We say a canticle to Wisdom as we begin our dreamwork, for our path at this point is down into the depths of the inner world, the realm of the feminine divine. In our closing liturgy, as we come up from the depths and back to the outer world, we say a canticle to the power of heaven. Our preferred way to read the canticles is to take turns around the circle, with each person reading either a sentence or a verse.

Tell Dreams

Our dream-group model is unusual in that it includes the telling of dreams, with no analysis, by everyone present at every meeting. In fact, we consider this to be the lynchpin of our dreamwork activity. In those rare instances when our meeting time is shortened to an hour or less, we would rather spend our time letting everyone tell a dream and not analyze any of them than to let only one or two tell a dream to be analyzed. This is because the unadorned telling of dreams by everyone is a rich and satisfying experience not only for each individual in the group but for the group as a whole. For individuals, it means that each one of us has a chance every week to give voice to the wonder and mystery of our inner world. No matter what dream-group model is being followed, there will never be enough time in any single meeting to analyze more than one or two or three dreams. This means that any of us in our dream group can go for weeks on end without having one of our dreams worked by the group. Without the chance for all of us to tell a dream every time, our typical experience of a dream-group meeting would be a lot of sitting and listening and talking about the dreams of others without ever having a chance to tell a dream of our own. The tension that builds in a group under these circumstances is palpable. *Will I finally get to have a dream worked today?* most people will be thinking. According to the law of averages, the answer will likely be no, which means that another week will pass without a chance for most of these people to lay before the group an offering from their own dream life.

Until you have experienced it, you probably cannot imagine how rewarding it is to sit in a circle with ten or twelve people and listen to each of them, in turn, read or recall a recent dream they have had. This is a sharing of whole dreams, not just a title we have given to a dream or a synopsis of one, as is done in some other dream-group models. We each tell a whole dream, or if the dream is especially long, a whole section of one. No analysis is given along with the telling, and no associations are made with any of the images. Neither the dreamer nor anyone else is allowed to say anything about what they think the dream might mean. The dreamer simply tells the dream, and then we move on to the next person. And as we go around the circle, everyone in the group hangs on every word. The dreams are so interesting. So intriguing. So funny. So horrifying. So spirit-filled. So absurd. So amazing. So puzzling. So beautiful. Often we notice the appearance of interweaving themes. Look how many people are dreaming about snakes this week. Yet another really weird one: this must be weird-dream week. Three bathroom dreams this week: we have a lot of shadow work going on.

When everyone in the group tells a dream, the room fills with spirit. The group is woven together. Our minds have no idea about the meaning of any of the dreams, but our souls recognize them as interesting and valuable images of the divine life that is continually unfolding in each of us. We get it when someone is going through a dark time, or has come to a transcendent moment, or has gained more clarity and structure in their dreams than they used to have, or has moved into an especially opaque time. We do not need to know what the dreams actually mean or what is going on with that person in outer life. Just hearing each other's dreams each week keeps us bonded together as fellow journeyers in the vibrant world of unfolding life and flowing spirit.

This telling of dreams takes roughly twenty to forty minutes, depending on the size of the group. The maximum number of dreams that can be accommodated in that time frame is usually between ten and twelve. If there are a few more than ten or twelve people present, do not worry, as there will always be some people each time who will not have a dream to contribute. Either they do not remember a recent dream, or they would rather not tell any of the ones they do remember. (This is entirely appropriate when a dream deals too obviously with issues that are too personal to be shared.) So if you have up to thirteen or fourteen people present at a meeting, you can let everyone tell a dream who has one, knowing that in all there will not be more than ten or twelve dreams told. But if you have fifteen people or more, you would let every other person tell a dream. Or skip every third person. Then when this larger group breaks into smaller groups for actual dreamwork, the small groups will begin by letting those who did not get a chance to tell a dream in the larger group tell theirs now. In this way, everyone always gets a chance to tell a dream every week.

Take a Break (and Break Up the Group if Necessary)

If your group meets for ninety minutes, you do not need a break, nor do you have time for one. But if you meet for two hours, you do need a break at approximately the halfway point. Exactly where the break comes will depend on how many people are present to tell dreams during the dream-sharing time. If it only takes twenty minutes for everyone to share a dream, then you will want to analyze one of the dreams before taking a break; after the break, you will analyze others as time permits. If it has taken closer to forty minutes to share dreams, then you will be almost to the halfway point, given the inevitable five-minute delay in getting started, the group-business announcements, and the opening liturgy. Therefore, you will want to take a break here and do all your dream analysis after the break.

If there are more than ten or twelve people present, it is best to divide into two or more groups for analyzing dreams, and it is best to decide who is going to be in which breakout group before you take the break. Then after the break, everyone goes straight to their breakout group and gets to work. The primary reason for breaking into smaller groups is to let more people have a chance to get their dreams worked.

The situation in which the group is so large that it needs breakout groups for dream analysis is only likely to arise after the group has become established at a smaller size and has grown over time to this larger size. This means that the members of the group are well-bonded and are unlikely to want to break up into separate groups for the entire dream-group meeting. In our Kentucky dream group, we solve this problem by keeping the larger group together for the opening liturgy and the sharing of dreams, then splitting up for dream analysis, and then coming back together for the closing liturgy. This procedure works very well for us.

As for the break itself, ten minutes is a good length of time. Tea or coffee can be provided, though water alone is enough. Snacks are nice, but it is best not to get too fancy with them. A dream group goes on week after week, year after year, and one of the secrets of keeping it going is keeping it simple. We find that a bowl of goldfish crackers and a bowl of peanuts and raisins are all that we need.

Analyze Dreams

The ideal group size for working dreams is four to twelve, though it can also be done with three, and a group of twelve might prefer to break up into two groups of six. When breakout groups are used, it is desirable to have at least two seasoned members in each group to give confidence to the newer members as the discussion goes along. Although anyone can take the part of actually leading the group through the dreamwork process, this role tends to fall naturally to one of the more seasoned members. The dreamwork procedure that we use in our group is comprised of five simple steps:

1. The dreamer tells the dream.
2. The group asks clarifying questions.
3. The dreamer tells the dream again.
4. The group projects meaning onto the dream.
5. The dreamer makes a few final comments, or not.

The first thing the group has to do is choose a dream to analyze. There are a number of ways to do this. The worst way is to ask who wants to have their dream worked. This immediately favors the bold over the reticent, and it leaves very little room for Wisdom to have a say. Other ways are better. It can be decided on the basis of who has gone longest without having a dream worked, although this, too, is a bit rigid for Wisdom's ways. If one of the dreams is an especially disturbing one, it might be a natural pick and one in which Wisdom has had something to say by bringing it naturally to the fore. In the same vein, a dream might be chosen by the group because it is especially intriguing or puzzling. But the best way of all to choose a dream, in my opinion, is to have everyone write a title for his or her dream on a slip of paper, put the titles in a "hat," and draw one out. This puts the choice completely in the hands of Wisdom's synchronicity. Or as some of us in our group would say, "God has chosen."

It is hard for our scientific, rational minds to believe that there is anything other than blind luck involved in the drawing of lots, but after using the hat method exclusively for the last several years, I have come to have complete faith in its synchronistic wisdom. I have seen it unerringly choose the dreams of new members week after week until all of them have had a dream worked. I have seen it choose the dreams of the same person for two or three weeks in a row, to the consternation of that person, who feels he is getting more than his fair share. "But God has chosen," we say, and as we work his dreams, we receive the gift of being shown how themes unfold in our dreams week after week, while he gets special support for a passage in his journey that seems to have needed that support. Those who might not have a dream worked for a very long time under this method do not seem to mind. After all, everyone gets to tell a dream every week, and everyone gets something out of the dreamwork whether one's own dream is worked or not. The dreamwork itself gives the dreamer quite a workout, and most people are happy to have that role fall to someone else. Based on my own experience, I much prefer the drawing of lots for choosing which dream to work. It is the only method that is free of tension, and the results are always good.

Once a dream has been chosen, the leader asks the dreamer to tell the dream, which can either be read from a journal or told from memory. Then the leader asks the group for clarifying questions. Unlike the questions we should ask ourselves when we work on our own dreams, the clarification questions in this group method must always be restricted to the dream itself. They should not go beyond the dream to anything in the dreamer's outer life, including the dreamer's feelings in outer life or any associations to the dreamer's outer-life past. Only the feelings and events that were in the dream can be probed. The only exception to this is when a character in the dream is an outer-life person. Then the dreamer can be asked to say three things that come to mind when he thinks of that person. This is necessary in order to give the other group members, who probably do not know this person, something to go on when projecting their own meaning onto that dream character. The same would apply to places or specialized situations of which the others in the group have no knowledge. It would be off limits, however, to ask the dreamer to say three things about Oklahoma. Everyone would already have their own associations with Oklahoma and would not need to probe the dreamer's life to get more. Clarifying questions might ask for more details about the setting of the dream, the exact way in which particular events took place, how exactly the dreamer felt when this or that happened in the dream, and so on. Anything inside the dream is fair game. Anything outside the dream, except for the exceptions noted above, is out of bounds.

The dream does not have to be milked to the very last drop. The process can get tedious if the questions slow down to a trickle and people begin scraping the bottom of the barrel to get new ones. The leader should bring the questioning to a close when the energy for it is clearly beginning to wane. She should first ask if there are any more questions, and if not, she then asks the dreamer to tell the dream again. With this telling, it is a good idea for the group to close their eyes as they listen, for now they are really going into the dream and taking it on for themselves. When the dreamer has finished telling it, the leader asks him to turn his chair around so that he can face away from the group. This is to allow him to listen without having to make eye contact with, or any response to, those who are talking about his dream. An exception to this procedure is made when the dreamer is hard of hearing. In that case, he remains facing the group so he can hear better, and he simply keeps his eyes down. Many dreamers like to take notes on what is being said, though this is optional.

To illustrate this next part, we need the use of an actual dream. So we will use this one:

> *I open my front door to go outside and am startled to find someone right there where I am about to step out. It is an adolescent boy, about fourteen, beautiful in form and energy, dressed in camouflage, a soldier's clothing. His energy is not stiff in a soldierly way, but whole and balanced. He is delivering something to my doorstep, has just delivered it and is walking away, fully engaged with his job, moving on to the next delivery.*

In the example we are constructing here, the dreamer has told this dream, clarifying questions have been asked, and now the dream has been told again while the group has listened with their eyes closed. The dreamer now turns his chair around, and there is silence. The leader lets the silence last for as long as it needs to last until someone finally begins to speak. “In my dream,” someone might say, “I’m wondering what positive new development has taken place having to do with my masculine self. There is new, healthy soldier energy present. Has my soldier self had a wound that goes back to when I was fourteen? And has that now been healed?” Then there might be more silence, and after a time someone else will speak up. “If it were my dream, I would be thinking about what the package might be. Maybe it’s a dream that’s being delivered. It could be that my animus has brought me an important dream.” And then someone else might say, “If it were my dream, I would think the package might be something coming to me in outer life. In the dream, I am going outside of my house. I’m leaving the inner world and stepping out into the outer world. And right there on my doorstep is something new.” And then someone else might say, “In my dream, not only have I received a package, but the boy himself is something new.” Another person might say, “What about the camouflage he is wearing? It seems to me that this connects my young soldier self to nature, to the feminine divine. Maybe that’s why his energies are so balanced.”

So it would go until everyone has said all that has come up in them to say. Then the leader invites the dreamer to turn back around and to make any remarks he wishes to make, or to make none at all if he would prefer. The dreamer’s remarks bring the work on this dream to a close.

This procedure for analyzing dreams in a group is specifically designed to keep the group from prying into the dreamer’s personal life. It is not the same procedure we would use to work on our own dreams or to talk over a dream with a close friend. In both of those cases we would ask for the dreamer’s personal associations with the images in the dream, for this is the surest way to get to the specific developments in the dreamer’s life with which the dream might be concerned. A long-term dream group with no more than seven or eight people in all would be in effect a group of close friends, and personal associations might be appropriate in such groups. But in a dream group that is larger than seven or eight people, it is usually not a good idea to draw out the private material that would come with asking for associations. The larger container is not appropriate for such personal discussion. There are too many people present. The situation is too public.

Fortunately, good work can be done on the dream without going into the dreamer's personal issues. This is because the underlying currents of human life are universal. We all share in them, each with our own particular experience and understanding of them. There will always be some elements in another person's dream that strike chords in our own experience and awaken intuition from our own inner flow of Wisdom. When such a chord is struck, we speak about it by saying, "If it were my dream...," or "In my dream...," for we are not speaking about the meaning of the dream for the dreamer, but for ourselves. Because of the universal nature of the underlying currents of human life, some of what we say may in turn strike chords with the dreamer and trigger new insights for him. Some of what we say may do the same for others in the group, who have also entered into the underlying currents of the dream. The overall result is that everyone gains something of value from the discussion. New insights come to all of us about the way of Wisdom in our own lives and in human life in general. Doing group dreamwork in a strong spiritual container is, in fact, like sitting through a class in Wisdom's school.

It is important to understand, however, that it seldom happens that the meaning of a dream is completely nailed for the dreamer when using this method of dreamwork. This is because we have deliberately left out his personal associations with the images in the dream, and those associations are key for homing in on what the dream might be specifically saying about specific issues in his life. But the dreamer can do that work for himself. What the group dreamwork does is to open the dream for the dreamer and shine light on parts of it that might otherwise have remained in darkness. The approach of each commentator is different, and some of those approaches might strike the dreamer as being fruitful paths to take for himself and follow to where they might lead.

Honor and Release the Spiritual Container

In our dream-group model, we bring our dreamwork to a close five minutes before the group's official ending time in order to leave time for our closing liturgy. If we are in breakout groups, we end the dreamwork ten minutes before the final close to in order to allow us time to gather back into one group. As we go into the closing liturgy, our hearts are especially full with what we have experienced in the dreamwork we have just done. We have all gained new insights. We have realized new truths. We have witnessed the mystery of the living spirit that weaves through our lives and brings us meaning. With this fullness of heart, we easily let our spirits rise together in thanks and praise as we recite one of our canticles to the power of heaven. Thanks and praise is the most natural expression of devotion to the masculine divine and it comes to us naturally at this time. Were it not for the canticles to Wisdom in our opening liturgy, in which we have already addressed the divine as she, there might be an objection in our closing liturgy to addressing the divine as he. Instead, we are aware that we are making a balance of these two sides of our spiritual experience, an equality that does not favor one over the other but joins them together in our conscious experience of them. We ourselves are the container in which they are now joined as we set forth on our individual paths out into the world.

Supporting Elements for a Dream Group

Educate

When people come into a dream group, they need at least some explanation of what they are getting into. In my own experience, this can be handled in one of two ways. The group can begin as a book study, in which the group reads and discusses an introductory book for a number of weeks before moving into dreamwork. Alternatively, the first two or three meetings of the group can be dedicated to a formal orientation that is presented by some of the more knowledgeable members of the group. Both of these approaches give good results.

To establish a dream group in an institutional setting like a church, synagogue, or mosque, where people are accustomed to signing up for classes, it is relatively easy to start with a book study that lasts anywhere from four to twelve weeks. The book should cover the basics of Jungian inner work: consciousness and the unconscious; dreams and synchronicity; shadow and anima/animus; archetypes and the Self; and the idea of individuation. *Natural Spirituality* has been widely used for this purpose since it was first published in 1998, and in my opinion, of course, it is still a good one to use. In order to give people enough time to absorb the material it contains, a class based on this particular book works best if it runs for at least eight weeks. Alternatively, the first two parts of the book, through Chapter Seven, "Synchronicity," would be sufficient to get a dream group started, and this material could be covered in four to six weeks. Other books that could serve as introductory book studies are *Unopened Letters from God*, by Robert Haden; *Inner Work*, by Robert Johnson; and *Where People Fly and Water Runs Uphill*, by Jeremy Taylor.

It is typical that when a book study ends, only about half the participants choose to stay on for a dream group. While there could be more than half, you should be prepared for even less than half. But even if you find that only four people stay with you from a group of twelve—which has happened to me more than once—you should not feel that you have somehow failed. Intellectual curiosity does not necessarily translate into readiness for the inner journey. However, if your resulting dream group has only four or five members, it would be a good idea to offer the class again in six months. Once a strong, core group has been established, it will be enough to offer the class just once a year.

If you are not in an institutional setting and are simply gathering a group together from friends and acquaintances, it will likely to be easier if you start with a minimum of instruction and then add more education through monthly study days as the group goes along. This easy-entry method is the one our Kentucky dream group uses. For our first three meetings in September every year, we have orientation days. Prospective new members sign up for this, having heard about it from friends who are in the group. In order to keep our group from being overwhelmed by too large a wave of new members, we allow only fifteen new people to sign up for each year's orientation. We make it clear that being admitted for orientation does not obligate a person to stay on after the orientation is over. And even though the teaching content is different for each of our three orientation days, we only require a new member to attend at least one of these days in order to qualify for admittance to the dream group when orientation is over. This is because the busyness of modern life will always make it impossible for some of the new people to attend all three meetings. Our main goal is simply to give these fifteen people a chance to check out the dream group and see if they want to stay in it. Usually only about twelve of the fifteen who have signed up will attend the orientation at all, and of these, probably no more than half will choose to stay. However, all those who have attended at least one orientation day are welcome to come into the dream group at any time in the future. We put them on our email list and they receive our weekly notices forevermore unless they opt out. Likewise, anyone who attends regular dreamwork meetings for a time and then drops away is kept on our email list and is welcome to return at any time. Members who have not attended for a long while will sometimes use the orientation days as a good time to reenter the group.

Both old and new members attend orientation days. The established members help welcome and settle the new people, and everyone benefits from a yearly review of the basics. The teaching content for our three orientation days includes the basic principles of Jungian psychology, which are delivered as simply as possible, with the understanding that we are merely giving people a glimpse of the territory about which they will be learning more through experience and self-study in the months and years to come. We also explain how our dream group is organized and what to expect in a typical meeting. In the final session, we give a demonstration of our dreamwork method.

Under this orientation-days system, new members who choose to stay on in the dream group come into it with very little education under their belts. We, therefore, encourage them to begin reading for themselves immediately, and we put out on display for them the introductory-level books that we have in our library. We also help them, and ourselves, become gradually more educated through our monthly study days. For this, we take a full dream-group meeting every month to discuss a book on Jungian inner work that we all buy and read together. We take each book slowly, covering only one or two books a year, knowing that we cannot expect people to find time to read more than fifty or sixty pages in preparation for each study day. Most dream-group members like these sessions and make a special effort to attend them. Beyond introductory reading and monthly study, we encourage everyone at every level to keep reading for themselves in whatever area of inner work might currently be drawing their attention. Each of us in the group is responsible for our own self-education, and we trust the flow of Wisdom to lead us to the resources we need at each step along the way.

Collect Resources

To support dream-group members in their self-education, a library is essential. Theoretically you could do without one, letting each person find and obtain her own relevant books and perhaps swap them around with others. But it is far better for the group to have its own bookcase full of books categorized under such topics as Dreamwork, Synchronicity, Masculine and Feminine, Introduction to Jung, Authored by Jung, Personality Types, and so on. A list of the books in the library of our Kentucky dream group can be found in Appendix C. There are also many CDs and DVDs that are excellent resources for dream-group libraries, including CDs containing the major talks given at the annual Haden Institute Summer Dream and Spirituality Conference, and DVDs from the webinars of the Asheville Jung Center. The Haden Institute talks are also available on iTunes for free downloading (in the iTunes

Store search "Seedwork"). For more information on these and other resources, see Appendix C.

We pay for the library in our Kentucky dream group by collecting five dollars a month from each dream-group member. We simply put out a basket at each meeting and use the honor system; no record-keeping is involved. For checking out books, we put into each book an index card containing the title and author of the book and a place for the person checking out the book to put his name and the date. On our bookshelf, we have a holder for cards from the books that have been checked out. When a person returns a book, he retrieves the card from the stack of cards in the holder, scratches out his name, puts the card back into the book, and puts the book back on the shelf. A member of the Dream Leader Team oversees the library. She keeps an eye on the cards in the checked-out stack, and when a book has been out for more than two months, she sends an email to the person who has it out, asking him to return it or renew it. She also tries to keep the shelved books sorted into their categories, and she orders new books when needed.

Travel

It greatly strengthens a group when its members know through first-hand experience that inner work in spiritual community is a larger development in the world today than their local experience alone might suggest. Out in the greater world, there are conferences and courses of study that are aimed at supporting this growing development in human consciousness. If even a few members of a dream group can find the time and money to attend some of these conferences and perhaps enroll in some of these courses of study, the group as a whole will be energized by the reports they bring back. One's own group might be small, but to know that it is part of a world-wide movement strengthens our sense of meaning and purpose, especially in the face of the typical lack of comprehension in the larger community in which one's local group is embedded. At a Haden Institute Summer Dream and Spirituality Conference, for example, one gets to spend the better part of a week in a group of several hundred people who all speak the same inner-work language. For that brief period of time, the minority becomes the majority, and one experiences what it might be like in the future when Wisdom has gained full equality with masculine consciousness in the world at large.

Conferences and training courses not only strengthen the spirit of local dream groups, but they also further the education of its members and deepen the overall wisdom of the group. As of this writing, the programs of the Haden Institute offer the best balance of Jungian inner work and healthy spirituality. The roots of the Haden Institute are in Christianity, but it is multi-faith in its attitude and is conscientiously free of dogma and religiosity. It is oriented toward the new spirituality of the future while still retaining the deep and timeless spiritual values from the past. Smaller regional gatherings that maintain this same healthy balance of Jung and spirituality, and often involve some of the same personnel, can be found scattered here and there, sometimes as an annual gathering, sometimes as a one-time offering. A good place to find out about these is on the website of The Rose in the World (roseintheworld.org), an online magazine for natural spirituality that grew out of the dreamwork program in my church in Georgia. This website is also a good place to announce your gathering if you are planning one.

Besides these well-balanced conferences and educational offerings, there are also straight Jungian offerings from the many Jung societies around the country and the world. Most cities have a Jung society that brings in a series of speakers throughout the year. For example, members of our Kentucky dream group often drive to Cincinnati, which is not very far away, to hear Saturday lectures by Jungian analysts. More accessible to everyone are webinars of the Asheville Jung Center (ashevillejungcenter.org), as there is no traveling involved. Not only are live webinars available, but past webinars can be downloaded or purchased on DVDs. The more the members of a dream group embrace such educational opportunities, the stronger that group will become and the greater its effect will be in helping to bring in the new day when Wisdom will be granted equality in human consciousness everywhere.

For more information about conferences, training courses, and other educational opportunities, see Appendix C.

Grow

We have already talked about how to bring new members into a dream group, but we have not talked about how important it is to do this. There is a definite tendency in any established dream group to want to keep it just as it is. People in a dream group bond with each other rather strongly, and the group with its particular members takes on a particular personality. The group settles into a comfort zone. People are happy there. The idea of opening the doors and letting in new people disturbs this comfort and threatens the happiness of the merry band. But if a group resists change, it begins to ossify. It cuts off its own access to new life. Welcoming and integrating new members is the same as welcoming and integrating new parts of one's own personality. Growth is natural and necessary for ongoing life, and in the end, it inevitably feels good and right. We should always let our dream groups grow, not only so that we ourselves can have continuing life, but so that the spirit of Wisdom can spread freely to all those who want to learn how to gain access to her life-giving waters.

Chapter Fifteen
Does Jungian Inner Work Belong in Church?

THE QUESTION OF WHETHER JUNGIAN inner work belongs in church will be of little interest to some readers, while for others it is a question of great importance. Those in the former category need not feel they must stay for this chapter; nothing will be lost if they skip it and move on to the Appendices, or go start calling their friends to get up a dream group. The rest, however, are invited to join me for a discussion of what some of us consider to be the most pressing issue facing Christianity today.

The case has been made in this book that the basic elements of Jungian inner work are valuable tools with which the natural spirit can be comprehended and received into a deepening Christian life. But when Christian leaders are offered the Jungian tools, two questions naturally arise. First, is such conscious inner work the true business of Christianity? And, second, even if it is the business of Christianity, what kind of Christian was Carl Jung? Is he a person the church can trust?

We will take the second question first.

What Kind of Christian Was Carl Jung?

Midway through the writing of this book I had the following dream, which came in words with no images:

> *"The reason Christians have disdained Jung is because of his assassination on religion. But they should get from him what he has to offer before they leave him behind."*

I realize "assassination on religion" is not grammatically correct, but these are the words of the dream as best I could recall them when I awoke. If I were to change them, it would change the meaning I sensed as I dreamed. "Assassination *of* religion" would imply that in some sense Jung had actually done away with religion, but this was not what the dream was saying. "Assassination *attempt* on religion" was not the dream's wording nor quite the meaning that I understood as I dreamed. What I understood in "assassination on religion" was the hostile attitude Jung sometimes showed toward organized Christianity, which he felt ignored the gospel message that Christ is the teaching and healing spirit of God that seeks us through dialogue with the unconscious.

This is a good example of the compensatory nature of dreams, for I, myself, would never have characterized Jung's quarrelsome attitude as that of an assassin. I have always considered him to be a deeply religious man. It was not until I had this dream that I was able to look at him through the eyes of organized Christianity and see the hostility that it has with some justification perceived in him.

Although the dream led me to take a clearer view of the darker side of Jung, it has not swung me into a reversal of my previous estimation of him. Rather it has made me acknowledge and accept the paradox of Carl Jung, as the dream indicated all Christians should do. The fact is that despite his hostility to the keepers of traditional religion, Jung was at the same time a deeply religious man. Even in *Answer to Job*, the work in which his impatient attitude shows itself most clearly, Jung's concluding words are:

> [E]ven the enlightened person remains what he is, and is never more than his own limited ego before the One who dwells within him, whose form has no knowable boundaries, who encompasses him on all sides, fathomless as the abysms of the earth and vast as the sky.

Jung's hostility toward organized Christianity was not that of an avowed enemy. It was more like that of a creative son toward the traditional family from which he sprang, a genius of a son so filled with the vision of his creative contribution that he was unable at the same time to hold in full value the time-honored structure for which God intended his creativity. There is no doubt that Jung loved God and lived closely all his life with a continual, conscious experience of God; nor is there any doubt that he valued the core content of the Christian tradition in which he was deeply rooted. This is obvious in his letters as well as in his autobiography, *Memories, Dreams, Reflections*. In that he wrote:

> I falter before the task of finding the language which might adequately express the incalculable paradox of love. . . . I sometimes feel that Paul's words—'Though I speak with the tongues of men and angels, and have not love'—might well be the first condition of all cognition and the quintessence of divinity itself. . . . I have again and again been faced with the mystery of love, and have never been able to explain what it is. Like Job, I had to 'lay my hand on my mouth. I have spoken once, and I will not answer.' (Job 40:4f.) Here is the greatest and the smallest, the remotest and the nearest, the highest and the lowest. . . . Man can try to name love, showering upon it all the names at his command, and still he will involve himself in endless self-deceptions. If he possesses a grain of wisdom, he will lay down his arms and name the unknown by the more unknown, *ignotum per ignotius*—that is, by the name of God.

Of Christ, Jung said in a letter written in 1953, "The Christ image as we know it certainly did not appear as the result of human intervention, it was the transcendental ('total') Christ who created for himself a new and more specific body." To Upton Sinclair, whose book *A Personal Jesus* Jung criticized for stripping Jesus of his divinity, he wrote:

> *I have a certain picture of a personal Jesus.* It has been dimly suggested to me through certain New Testament data. Yet the strongest impression came to me from the [Shroud of] Turin. . . . Its stern and august countenance has confirmed my formerly vague expectations. I am, as a matter of fact, so profoundly impressed by the superiority of this extraordinary personality that I would not dare to reconstruct its psychology.

According to tradition, the image of Jesus was somehow imprinted on his burial shroud, which was left behind in the tomb after the resurrection. Jung had a copy of the face of Christ as it appeared on the Shroud of Turin and kept it in his study, behind a curtain.

Jung also had in his study, hanging in a window, a stained-glass image of the Crucifixion. Once when Pastor Walther Uhsadel, a theologian at the University of Hamburg, was visiting him, Jung pointed to that image and said, "You see, this is the crux for us." When Uhsadel asked what he meant, Jung replied,

> I've just got back from India, and it has struck me with renewed force. Man has to cope with the problem of suffering. The Oriental wants to get rid of suffering by casting it off. Western man tries to suppress suffering with drugs. But suffering has be to overcome, and the only way to overcome it is to endure it. We learn that only from him.

And here he pointed to the crucified Christ.

Jung's near-death experience when he suffered a heart attack at age 69 gave him certainty about the reality and desirability of the afterlife. He had experienced himself moving into the next world and then, to his dismay, being pulled back into this one through his doctor's intervention. To a friend with terminal cancer he wrote concerning what he had learned:

> On the whole my illness proved to be a most valuable experience, which gave me the inestimable opportunity of a glimpse behind the veil.

> The only difficulty is to get rid of the body, to get naked and void of the world and the ego-will. When you can give up the crazy will to live and when you seemingly fall into a bottomless mist, then the truly *real* life begins with everything which you were meant to be and never reached. It is something ineffably grand. . . . Death is the hardest thing from the outside and as long as we are outside of it. But once inside you taste of such completeness and peace and fulfillment that you don't want to return.

Because I came to Carl Jung through his autobiography, in which he speaks freely of his spiritual nature and his life-long experience of God, I have never doubted that he was in God's camp, so to speak. His difficulties with organized Christianity have not seemed problematic to me, especially considering the fact that the time during which he lived, 1875–1961, was a time when the church was especially stiff and self-satisfied. It was only in the 1960s that the church began to open up to the winds of change—to greater lay leadership and to the ministry of women—signaling an opening to the feminine side of spirituality, which has led increasingly toward a recognition of the unconscious and natural spirituality. My experience of the church in my own time has not been of a closed and unreceptive institution. Because of this difference in climate, I have been more willing than some Christians to grant Jung his gruff opinions about the church. I have never felt that I had to share all those opinions with him.

My Own Problem with Jung

While I very much trust Carl Jung as a spiritual leader and admire him as a human being, the one problem I have always had with him is that he seems to have been almost too much in love with the unconscious. The world of the unconscious is not a human realm, just as the bottom of the sea is not a human realm. I personally would not like to live in a submarine, nor would I want to live as deeply immersed in the unconscious as Jung seems to have lived. In his investigation of the unconscious he became so familiar with its archetypal language, so fascinated by it, and so much its champion, that he almost seems to have lost his full citizenship in ordinary life. At times his ideas and understandings were of such depth and couched in so arcane a language that hardly any other human being could sustain a creative dialogue with him, though he wanted dialogue and continually searched for it in both the worlds of psychology and theology.

While I find Jung's writings to be immensely valuable, I also find that if I follow him too far in his thinking, I begin to take on a conceptual framework that is more complex than my needs require and that leads me away from the heart of my own life. The world of symbol and image that comes to me through my dreams certainly does contain recognizable mythological and archetypal themes, but, on the whole, it seems closer to the world of everyday life than Jung's inner world seemed to be. This is partly due to the fact that Jung was more introverted than most of us and therefore more open to the depths of the unconscious. But I think it is also because his experience of the unconscious came to him not only through dreams and synchronicity but also in large part through a technique he named *active imagination.*

Active imagination is a process in which inner images from the unconscious enter into waking consciousness—as if one were dreaming without being asleep. There are techniques for bringing on this state, though it can also occur spontaneously. It is very close to daydreaming, the main difference being that consciousness usually manipulates daydreams to bring about scenes and images that are wish-fulfilling. In active imagination, images are allowed to arise without interference and are respected as autonomous manifestations of inner reality. One then consciously enters the fantasy material and *relates* to it in an honest way, creating a dialogue between the needs and viewpoint of consciousness on the one hand and of the unconscious on the other.

This can be as simple as a spontaneous dialogue with an unseen inner figure, or it can go much further and lead one deeply into impressive imaginative scenes full of mythological symbolism that arises from the depths and unfolds like pages of a modern fantasy novel or a medieval alchemical treatise or a Gnostic gospel from the early Christian era. Jung felt that active imagination was an especially effective way to resolve the tensions between the competing demands of consciousness and the unconscious. It was, in a way, the central religious sacrament he offered to his patients.

It seems clear that active imagination, when practiced faithfully within a grounded, moral framework, has real value for some people. The spiritual exercises of Ignatius Loyola are based on a particular version of it. However, I have found it to be of limited usefulness in my own journey. Furthermore, I have not observed it to be of long term, regular usefulness to most of the people with whom I have journeyed in my dream groups, where dreams and synchronicity seem to be the staple foods of the natural spirit. It is as if active imagination were too rich a food for most of us.

As we have seen, there is a myth that warns of the dangers of eating lavish food offered up by the unconscious. In the tale of Psyche and Eros, one of Psyche's tasks is to go to the underworld to fetch a box of beauty ointment from Persephone, the queen of the underworld. Among the many admonitions Psyche is given for surviving such a venture is that once she has entered Persephone's hall, she must decline the soft chair and rich food she is offered and instead sit on the ground and ask for common bread. If she does not, she will not be able to return to the human world.

Psyche is told to stay grounded and eat simply. This is something that introverts especially need to hear, for they are tempted by inner riches in the same way extraverts are tempted by outer ones. The lure away from authentic human life is the same in either case. All we need from the unconscious are the teachings and understandings that help us resolve the specific problems of our own lives and some of those of our own communities.

There is, however, much more than that floating around in the unconscious depths. When we tap into the unconscious, we sometimes get tantalizing glimpses of what seem to be answers to huge questions. There is a decided tendency in the unconscious for intricate systems of knowledge to try to form up into something which the human mind can comprehend, but which often, in fact, cannot be fully comprehended, at least not in our present state of being, except perhaps at a prohibitively high cost in mental energy. It is these sorts of foods from the unconscious that are so tempting and yet are too rich for human digestion. As I was struggling with this problem in my own journey, I had the following dream:

> *From the deep part of the night, no images, just this understanding: Meaning should not be sought or reached for in a big way, separate and apart from life. It should be taken in a little at a time within life itself, as life is being lived. Meaning and life should go along together, neither getting ahead of the other.*

For the most part, Carl Jung brought up from the unconscious meaning and understanding that we can use. His depth of wisdom and clarity of insight were immense, and his writings will be a valuable source for the human community for a long time to come. But in some of his writings we do find a feast too rich in meaning to be absorbed into everyday life. In a book like *Aion*, which is about the development of the symbol of the Christ through the Christian era, the many nuggets of gold which are there to be mined are buried in a difficult and not particularly useful framework of Gnostic and alchemical discourse. The point Jung seeks to make in this, and in some of his other works, is that these early, arcane systems of knowledge—Gnosticism and alchemy—refer to the basic principles of the psychology of the unconscious, which was yet undeveloped and for which these ancient authors had no other language than these raw, symbolic utterances.

I am sure he is right about this, and we should be grateful to him for having the curiosity and intellectual capacity to delve into the ancient manuscripts and make sense of them for us. But I disagree with his implied suggestion that we should retrieve the languages of alchemy and Gnosticism in order to revive the true spirit of Christianity. We can get a little help from these sources to elucidate the symbols in our dreams, but for the most part, Jung's own psychology has replaced these premature constructions. He has given us a more straightforward, more *conscious* framework, one that is hard enough to mesh with the collective discourse of our time without cluttering it with these archaic symbolic systems.

Jung and the Problem of Evil

My own problem with Carl Jung, then, is his tendency to extreme interiority, although this does not negate the overall positive value I place on his life and work. Many other Christian writers find that their greatest problem with Jung is his contention that evil is not merely the absence of God, as Christianity has sometimes defined it but is, in fact, a spiritual reality that is as much a part of God as goodness is.

Satan, Jung often pointed out, was, in the Old Testament, a member of God's court, one of God's own sons. He was thrown from heaven in a celestial event that Jung understood to have occurred alongside the incarnation of Christ. For Jung, it was self-evident that good and evil are two parts of a whole, necessary opposites in God as well as in man.

Space and time break wholeness apart into its separate, conflicting components, which human consciousness is then able to perceive and reflect upon. Therefore, it is only in this world of space and time that the problem of the opposites, including good and evil, is constellated and can be worked out. Jung felt that just as humankind needs God, God needs humankind in order to resolve the problem of the opposites: of good and evil, light and dark, masculine and feminine, spirit and nature, consciousness and unconsciousness—all the many paradoxical aspects of the unknowable, transcendent God.

This means that evil is not something *caused* by man but rather is something that *happens* to him, just as grace happens to him. It is a problem put upon him by God, not because man is bad and needs to be punished but because he is alive and must answer the challenge of a world where good and evil, light and dark, order and chaos, certainty and fear, joy and sadness are the alternating currents of life, the inhalation and exhalation of the very breath of being.

Man does not cause evil in Jung's way of thinking, but he must deal with it when it arises in him and around him, and for this, he needs all the strength and moral courage at his command. Man must realize the necessity of choosing the good and of trying to align himself with it. He must not, however, delude himself by thinking that he can banish evil, which is a part of God, a part of life itself, and is not in man's power to eradicate.

The idea that man causes evil, and, therefore, can eliminate it, inflates man to God-like status and underestimates the reality and power of evil. When man thus fails to look at evil with clear eyes, evil gains an advantage and can catch him unaware. Jung felt that Nazi Germany was a terrible, large-scale example of this.

When man knows, on the other hand, that evil is an eternal aspect of life, that it is a part of the divine drama and will always reappear as surely as night follows day, then he is ready for it. As he sees it arise, whether within himself or without, he accepts the challenge, looks to the unconscious for guidance and teaching, appeals to God for mercy and divine help, learns the lessons that proceed from the struggle, and finally transcends to a more integrated state of being. And then he waits for the next round, just as Jesus did after the temptations in the wilderness: "The devil left him, to return at the appointed time."

Many Christians have trouble thinking about evil in this way. They are unable to reconcile this presumed dark side of divine reality with their knowledge that God is the ultimate in goodness and love. They cannot accept such a paradox. The important thing to realize, however, is that it does not matter what Carl Jung has said about this. With the spiritual tools he has given us, we no longer have to depend on him or anyone else for answers to these kinds of questions.

So long as we stand within the framework of a healthy spiritual tradition, our dreams and the synchronistic events of our lives can bring us whatever further understanding we need to have about the nature of evil and other such difficult matters. Each of us can be met in the place where we are and led to the understanding that is right for us. An ultimate answer to the question of evil can probably never be given because an ultimate single viewpoint can never be reached from which to ask the question. What is important, therefore, is that each of us learns enough about evil to handle the challenge of it in our own lives.

Carl Jung had his own revelations about evil and came to his own conclusions about it. It would violate the spirit of his work, however, if we were to accept his answers for ourselves. It is to the teaching spirit of the unconscious that we each should look for answers, for it is here that we find the true teacher who gives us understanding by degrees as we are ready to receive it. Jesus said in his farewell discourses: "I still have many things to say to you but they would be too much for you now. But when the spirit of truth comes he will lead you to the complete truth." It is still true that there is much before us that is yet to be learned.

Christianity and Individuation

Carl Jung knew that he had found the spiritual tools that modern Christianity needs in order for its members to open themselves to the spirit of truth in a new and deeper way. The religious problem facing the people of the Western world, Jung felt, is the need for mature individuals to break their identity with collective consciousness and set out on the more difficult road of individuation. This, he would say, is the deepest meaning of that admonition in the Gospel of Matthew, "Enter by the narrow gate, since the road that leads to perdition is wide and spacious, and many take it; but it is a narrow gate and a hard road that leads to life, and only a few find it."

In *Aion*, Jung wrote that the Christian tradition describes the individuation process "with an exactness and impressiveness far surpassing our feeble attempts." Jung could see that the elements of Christianity symbolize at every point what life is like when, in the context of a strong moral relationship with God, one opens to the reality of the unconscious and begins to take it into account.

As Jung grew older, he turned his attention more and more to the task of illuminating the connection between the symbolic language of Christianity and the natural process of individuation, which seeks realization at some level in every human life.

Many followers of Jung feel that his analytical psychology ushers in a new level of religious life that goes beyond organized Christianity and leaves community religion behind. They see the analyst's office as a viable substitute for the house of public worship. The dream I related at the opening of this chapter suggests, however, that it is Carl Jung who will ultimately be left behind. But the dream also warns that before Christians do leave him behind, they should first accept from him the gifts he has offered them. I believe Jung would be satisfied with that, as he was first and foremost a servant of God. "I am not a Jungian," he often said. Neither do Christians have to be Jungians in order to make use of Jung's work.

The inner landscape Jung described did not belong to him, and it will not disappear with his passing. Consciousness and the unconscious are not Jungian theories—they are phenomena that simply exist. Dreams and their symbolic language did not come from him. He merely observed them in a systematic way and described their regular features. So too is synchronicity a reality that has always been present in the world and always noticed, whether by whole cultures or only by observant individuals. Jung's contribution was to describe this phenomenon and give it a name. Archetypes are universal motifs that any of us can discover for ourselves by studying the mythologies of the world. Nor did Jung conjure up the symbolic images of transcendence that come to us in dreams, visions, and life experiences. He merely took note of them, categorized them, and gave them in their many manifestations a single name—the Self. Shadow, anima, and animus are his labels, but they refer to true realities that everyone meets as dream images and as living psychological facts. Individuation, that key concept of Jungian psychology, is a true and natural process that comes to us from God. Jung merely recognized its importance and named it. These inner realities could just as well have other names, but his are the ones that have been presented most comprehensively and successfully and that are gradually becoming accepted in the educated world.

Jung's framework offers the conceptual equipment we need to discern the features of the natural landscape of our inner world. Using these tools, modern Christians can begin to decipher the language of God's feminine voice, which speaks through natural, created life to shape us into our truest forms and lead us toward oneness with God.

Is Jungian Inner Work the True Business of Christianity?

In words that exactly fit the outcome of an individuation journey, Jesus said that he had come to bring life to his followers and life to the fullest. It might be expected that a person who needed and wanted to deepen his or her life by consciously entering into the process of individuation could go to any church and find there a context and guide for the journey. But at the present time, this opportunity is offered only rarely within the domain of organized Christianity. Church-based dream groups are becoming more common, yet they still are few and far between. Jungian study groups in churches are not quite as rare, but while a study group is valuable for preparing the ground for a journey, it is not in itself a context for the journey. A study group provides what this book provides, an intellectual framework for thinking about the inner life. But ideas alone are not enough. Individuation requires a context in which a person's own dreams and synchronistic experiences can be examined for meaning on a regular basis over a long period of time. The church as a whole does not yet recognize as a part of its mission the provision of a context for individuation. Yet, if the individuation journey is God's business, it belongs in God's house, where the feminine spirit of God should be as well-tended as the masculine spirit and as freely and universally available.

Natural Spirituality in Scripture

As we saw in Chapter Two, the feminine spirit has not always been neglected by the church. Its inclusion in Christian life is strongly supported by scripture. There are several different ways in which both Hebrew and Christian scriptures include natural spirituality within their framework and assume it to be an important aspect of our life with God.

The most obvious way in which natural spirituality is carried in the Bible is *straightforwardly*. Present throughout scripture, to a much greater degree than in Christian life today, is the understanding that dreams and visions play a vital role in the human experience of God. Looking at some of the most well-known examples, we begin with Jacob on his way to the country of Laban.

"He had a dream," says the twenty-eighth chapter of Genesis. "A ladder was there, standing on the ground with its top reaching to heaven; and there were angels of God going up it and coming down. And Yahweh was there, standing over him...." In the dream God reaffirmed for Jacob the covenant God had made with Abraham, giving Jacob special assurance that God would be with him through his coming trials and would never desert him until God's promises to him had been fulfilled. The very image of angels moving up and down a ladder between heaven and earth is an image of the dialogue with God that is available to us through attention to our inner life.

The most gifted and renowned dream interpreters in Hebrew scriptures are Joseph and Daniel, both of whom are also portrayed as towering men of God. In the stories of each of these men, a clear understanding is put forward that dreams come from God and are best interpreted by persons who are especially devoted to the service of God. Soothsayers, sages, and magicians who do not know and worship Yahweh are unable to interpret adequately the images of the inner world.

In the story of Joseph, for example, which is found in the book of Genesis, we are told that the king's cup-bearer and baker, who are imprisoned with Joseph, are distressed because they have had dreams which they cannot interpret. "'Are not interpretations God's business?' Joseph asked them. 'Come, tell me.'" The point is made that because Joseph is a man of God, he can interpret their dreams.

As this story goes on, Pharaoh hears of Joseph's reputation for dream interpretation and summons him to unravel the mystery of his own troubling dreams. He says to Joseph, "I have heard it said of you that when you hear a dream you can interpret it."

Joseph answers, "I do not count. It is God who will give Pharaoh a favorable answer." In this it is made explicit that the wisdom revealed by dreams comes from God, not from the dream interpreter.

Pharaoh goes on to relate to Joseph two dreams that came to him in the same night. "Pharaoh's dreams are one and the same," says Joseph, showing us something of what he knew about the structure of the inner world—in this case, that dreams that come in the same night are often different images of the same truth. He then adds, "God has revealed to Pharaoh what God is going to do." In this Joseph makes clear his understanding that the God of Abraham, Isaac, and Jacob speaks through dreams to all persons, regardless of nationality or religious consciousness.

Much later in Jewish history, during the exile in Babylon, Daniel makes this same point when dealing with a dream that came to the Babylonian king, Nebuchadnezzar. Daniel, to whom God has given "the gift of interpreting every kind of vision and dream," explains to the king:

> O king, on your bed your thoughts turned to what would happen in the future, and the Revealer of Mysteries disclosed to you what is to take place. This mystery has been revealed to me, not that I am wiser than any other man, but for this sole purpose: that the king should learn what it means, and that you should understand your inmost thoughts.

This understanding that dreams come from God and that their interpretation is God's business is firmly embedded in the spiritual reality put forward and upheld by the Old Testament. There are places where Hebrew scripture seems to speak against dreams, but an examination of context reveals that in most cases such warnings are against dream interpretations by persons who are not devoted to God.

The firm belief that dreams and visions come from God is carried into the New Testament through the gospel story of Joseph and the Wise Men, where five different dreams were received and followed to ensure the survival of the Christ child. Jesus himself does not speak directly about dreams. However, there are many places in the Gospels where there are definite permeations of the veil between consciousness and the unconscious, as for example, when Jesus sees Nathaniel under the fig tree, when he walks on water, when he appears with Moses and Elijah in the Transfiguration, and in his resurrection appearances. Whether dream, vision, or synchronicity, experiences of inner reality are essentially the same and require the same response from us if we are to gain from them the gifts they offer. That response is to stand firmly in rational consciousness while opening to the nonrationality of the unconscious, using rationality to look for a meaning from God in nonrational events. The Gospels carry at their very heart this approach to the nonrational expression of the unconscious.

Moving on beyond the Gospels to the book of Acts, we can see that feminine spirituality was central to early Christianity's life in God. This account of the beginning years of the church was written several decades after the events portrayed, and it, therefore, has the same problem with the factuality of historical detail that all oral tradition has. But while Acts may not always be reliable for events of time and place, there is no reason to doubt that it gives us an accurate portrayal of the assumptions of spiritual reality by which the earliest Christians were guided. As I illustrated in Chapter Two with the story of Peter and Cornelius, the portrait given in this earliest account of Christianity is of a people who are intensely focused on being led and taught by God through compensatory events from the unconscious.

Natural spirituality is also straightforwardly presented in books of the Bible like Ezekiel and Revelation. Here we are given the raw material of visions and dreams, and it is left largely to the reader to interpret them. It is expected that the reader will understand that this obscure symbolic language from the inner world is the language of God and that its interpretation, as Joseph made clear in the book of Genesis, is God's business.

Wisdom Theology in Scripture

A second way in which the Hebrew and Christian scriptures support natural spirituality is *theologically* through their development of the Wisdom tradition. The books of the Bible considered to be "Wisdom" books are, from the Hebrew canon: Job, the Psalms (in part), Proverbs, Ecclesiastes, and The Song of Songs (The Song of Solomon); and, from the Apocrypha: Wisdom (The Wisdom of Solomon) and Ecclesiasticus (The Wisdom of Jesus Ben Sirach). Elements of Wisdom theology are found in the New Testament in both the Gospels and the Epistles.

Biblical scholar Gerhard von Rad has offered a definitive treatment of the Wisdom theology of the Old Testament in his book *Wisdom in Israel.* I draw heavily from this work in the summary I present here.

The earliest recorded scripture belonging to the Wisdom tradition is the proverbial wisdom that begins in the tenth chapter of the book of Proverbs. Also known as sentence wisdom or instructional wisdom, proverbial wisdom consists of such nuggets as, "The wise of heart takes orders, but a gabbling fool heads for ruin," and "Their uprightness sets the honest free, the treacherous are imprisoned by their own desires." This collection was set down around the time of David and Solomon, 1000–800 B.C.E.

Central to proverbial wisdom is the observation based on long experience that righteous behavior, which belongs to the moment and is to be found in the context of each situation, supports us in our human lives and brings us into a sphere of blessing. This basis of *experience*, rather than ideals or speculation, is characteristic of Wisdom literature. The assumption behind proverbial wisdom is that experience teaches that creation contains inherent natural laws and that one must learn about these and conform to them in order for things to go well both for the individual and the community. At the heart of these inherent laws is the fundamental principle that goodness is a life-promoting force: life thrives when goodness is done.

The Hebrew Wisdom writers found no conflict between the inherent laws in creation and the Law of Yahweh given down from above. They understood that it is Yahweh who delegates truth to creation. Faith in inherent laws and faith in Yahweh are the same thing.

By the time the book of Job was recorded, around the sixth century B.C.E, the Wisdom theologians had begun to go deeper to address the question of the nature of this inherent order that comes up out of the world. "Where does Wisdom come from?" asks the twenty-eighth chapter of Job, which puts forth the understanding that Wisdom is not a human quality, but rather is something far removed from humankind. God had to do with it at the creation of the world. From the very beginning, it has been a reality that is in the world and subject to God's ordering activity. Yet it is separate from the works of creation and cannot be acquired and possessed like the precious metals of the earth. It is something in between created life and heavenly life. Wisdom is the order given to the world by God, but the world never reveals the mystery of its order.

In the eighth chapter of Proverbs, which is believed to have been written around the fourth or third century B.C.E, the Wisdom theologians begin to personify the mysterious order of the world. Personification is a development based on the emerging understanding that Wisdom *calls* to humankind. This idea that Wisdom calls us was unique to Israel. Other ancient cultures shared the idea of an inherent order in the world, but only Israel perceived that the inherent order was turned toward humankind.

This understanding was not based on speculation but on the actual human experience of being called by Wisdom. It is something that happens to a person in the world, something that is actually brought upon us by the world. The Wisdom writers are speaking of the active influence on us of the environment itself—an ordering power which affects us and corrects us. This mysterious attribute of the world, this Wisdom, is variously characterized by Gerhard von Rad as primeval order, mysterious order, world reason, meaning, or the self-revelation of creation. Because the primeval order turns toward us and calls us, the Wisdom writers found personification to be indispensable to the expression of its reality. In Proverbs 8, we read:

> Is not Wisdom calling? Is not Understanding raising her voice? On the heights overlooking the road, at the crossways, she takes her stand; by the gates, at the entrance to the city, on the access roads, she cries out, "I am calling to you, all people, my words are addressed to all humanity."

We are told that the call of the primeval order is not hidden or esoteric. She stands on the heights, by the roadside, where the paths cross. In other words, her call is in the synchronistic events of our daily lives and in our nightly dreams. What she says is clear and precise: that people should listen to her and learn from her; that she will lead them out of ignorance and idle talk and teach them intelligence and truth; and that she will show them the way to fullness of life, to divine favor and security. "For whoever finds me finds life," she says.

Another astonishing attribute of the primeval order put forward in these later Wisdom writings is that she not only calls us, but she also *loves* us. The relationship into which she summons us is a relationship of love. "I love those who love me," she says in Proverbs. Jesus Ben Sirach, the author of Ecclesiasticus, which was written around 180 B.C.E, tells us:

> Court her with all your soul, and with all your might keep in her ways; go after her and seek her; she will reveal herself to you; once you hold her, do not let her go. For in the end you will find rest in her and she will take the form of joy for you.

Wisdom is presented as a woman who calls to men quite openly in the streets and public squares and invites them to come into her house. She is the true partner who calls men to herself—the true lover. The primeval order moves toward us and seeks our ear, loving us, endeavoring to draw us into a sublime bond of love—a bond between humankind and the divine mystery of creation.

In the book of Wisdom, which was written in the last half of the first century B.C.E, only a few decades before the birth of Jesus, a decisive step is taken in the development of Wisdom theology: Wisdom begins to move toward deification. "For within her is a spirit intelligent, holy, . . . so pure, she pervades and permeates all things. . . . She is a breath of the power of God, . . . a reflection of the eternal light."

Gerhard von Rad does not extend his discussion beyond Old Testament scriptures, nor does he look forward toward New Testament developments. And so we leave von Rad as we look at this last of the Old Testament writings in terms of the easy passage it provides to the Gospel events. "What man indeed can know the intentions of God?" asks the book of Wisdom. "It is hard enough for us to work out what is on earth. . . . Who, then, can discover what is in the heavens? As for your intention, who could have learned it, had you not granted Wisdom and sent your holy spirit from above?"

In these words, there are familiar echoes of the Gospels and the Epistles. In John's Gospel, Jesus says to Nicodemus,

> If you do not believe me when I speak about things in this world, how are you going to believe me when I speak to you about heavenly things? No one has gone up to heaven except the one who came down from heaven, the Son of man.

Over and over in the gospel story, Jesus speaks of having been sent down from above to make known the Father's will. In the eleventh chapter of Matthew, Jesus says, "No one knows the Father except the Son and those to whom the Son chooses to reveal him." Then, echoing the words of another Old Testament Wisdom writer, he says,

> Come to me, all you who labour and are overburdened, and I will give you rest. Shoulder my yoke and learn from me, for I am gentle and humble in heart, and you will find rest for your souls. Yes, my yoke is easy and my burden light.

This is an unmistakable parallel to a passage in the book of Ecclesiasticus, in which Jesus Ben Sirach writes of Wisdom,

> Put your neck under the yoke, and let your souls receive instruction; it is to be found close by. See with your eyes that I have labored little and found for myself much rest.

In the Gospels Jesus speaks as Wisdom incarnate. In him the primeval order that loves us and calls us is made flesh before our eyes. Wisdom's presence in created life is no longer partly veiled, no longer hidden and esoteric. Speaking as Wisdom, Jesus tells us that to live in the kingdom of God we have only to believe in Wisdom's reality and follow its continually revealed teachings. According to this understanding, it is not simply the teachings of the historical Jesus that we should recognize and follow but teachings of Wisdom that come to each of us through our own experience of the flow of life.

Like the authors of the Gospels, the Apostle Paul recognized Christ as the incarnate Wisdom of God. It was Paul who understood what to do with this revelation in the wake of the death, resurrection, and ascension of Jesus. He knew that we must relax our grip on the outer-world, historical Jesus and look for the eternal Christ within ourselves. "Even if we did once know Christ in the flesh," wrote Paul, "that is not how we know him now." He could see that the incarnation had made Wisdom visible as a living inner reality, present in everything and available to everyone.

According to Paul, Christ permeates all of creation, just as Wisdom was said to do in Hebrew scriptures. He spoke of the Holy Spirit in the same way. In 1 Corinthians he speaks of "a Christ who is the power and the Wisdom of God." Elaborating further, he says,

> But still we have a Wisdom to offer to those who have reached maturity. . . . The hidden Wisdom of God which we teach in our mysteries is the Wisdom that God predestined to be for our glory before the ages began. . . . These are the very things that God has revealed to us through the Spirit, for the Spirit reaches the depths of everything, even the depths of God.

Natural Spirituality as Underlying Meaning in Scripture

There is, then, a scriptural development of Wisdom theology that begins at the time of David and Solomon and extends through the Gospels and the letters of Paul. Thus does the Bible give theological as well as straightforward support to natural spirituality. Beyond this, there is a third way in which Holy Scripture lends its support, and that is that is supports it *inherently.* Reference to the spiritual realities that arise from a conscious, God-centered dialogue with the unconscious can be seen to underlie almost every aspect of both the Hebrew and Christian scriptures.

This inherent presence of natural spirituality in the Bible becomes obvious once we have a framework of understanding by which it can be perceived. Those who are able to see it in this way find themselves in something of the same position as the disciples to whom Jesus said, "To you it has been granted to know the secrets of the kingdom of God; but for others they are in parables."

This does not mean, however, that there is any competition between this deeper level of understanding the Bible and the more common level at which it is traditionally interpreted. An individuating person continues to hear scripture at both levels of meaning, sometimes drawing from the deeper level, sometimes from the "parable" level. Both ways of experiencing biblical truth have their own value and neither negates the other.

The inherent presence of natural spirituality in the Bible does not require that its authors consciously understood this deeper level in the same terms in which we understand it today. The unconscious expresses itself through human lives and human words in layers of meaning that none of us can fully fathom. Just as we could see deeper layers in the lives of the Beatles than they themselves were able to see, so can we see in scripture aspects of its truth of which its authors may not have been aware.

The deeper level that reflects natural spirituality is found virtually everywhere in the Bible. The stories in the Hebrew scriptures, for example, can be seen as stories of individuation. Abraham's call to leave the land of his fathers and follow the promise of God into a new, completely unknown world is a symbolic picture of the call to individuation. A further illustration can be seen in the story of Saul and David. Saul, in this view, symbolizes the first half of life, when the personality is centered around the ego. Like Saul's kingship, this is a state of being that is ordained by God at the outset, but which ultimately falls short of what God requires of us. David represents a new kingship that can come into being in the second half of life if one learns to put God, instead of the ego, at one's center. Like David, one's new self must refrain from seizing its day too early, but rather it must bide its time and wait for the slow but sure developments that arise from the inner journey as adult life naturally progresses. It is virtually impossible for the ego to be truly transformed before it has reached its full strength at midlife.

Besides its inherent presence in the stories of the Bible, natural spirituality can also be found underlying individual passages of scripture. For example, images of the coming of the Messiah in Hebrew scriptures, as well as depictions of Christ in Christian scriptures, can be seen as symbolic pictures of what is experienced in the life and being of a person who comes into a conscious relationship with the unconscious. The following passage in Isaiah illustrates this point:

> A shoot springs from the stock of Jesse. . . . On him the spirit of Yahweh rests, a spirit of wisdom and insight, a spirit of counsel and power, a spirit of knowledge and of the fear of Yahweh. . . . He judges

> the wretched with integrity and with equity gives a verdict for the poor of the land. His word is a rod that strikes the ruthless, his sentences bring death to the wicked. . . . The wolf lives with the lamb, the panther lies down with the kid . . . with a little boy to lead them. . . . The infant plays over the cobra's hole; into the viper's lair the young child puts his hand. They do no hurt, no harm, on all my holy mountain, for the country will be full of knowledge of Yahweh as the waters swell the sea.

When viewed through the lens of natural spirituality, these familiar words become a beautiful picture of the individuation process. They offer a symbolic description of what it is like to come to know the Wisdom of the unconscious ("a spirit of wisdom," etc.), to do shadow work ("verdict for the poor, . . . death to the wicked," etc.), and to experience the gradual transformation of the conflicting aspects of one's life into balance, wholeness, and peace ("the wolf lives with the lamb," etc.). This process is shown to spring forth from earlier faithful living ("the stock of Jesse"). The Messiah, when viewed through this lens, is understood to be the Self, the divine guidance that arises from within and becomes the new inner center to which the ego of the individuating person bows its head.

Thus it can be seen that the Bible supports natural spirituality in at least three different ways: straightforwardly, theologically, and inherently. There is no reason, therefore, why the Wisdom tradition in its modern form as Jungian inner work should not be fully incorporated into the life of the church.

Natural spirituality is in fact already coming into the church, and it will continue to come in as we move through the twenty-first century. Members of the rising generation, those born since the Beatles, are especially open to the feminine side of the spirit of God. So ready are they to understand it that they almost seem to have an inborn knowledge of it. Today's young adults are the fruit of the expansion of consciousness that took place in the chaos of the twentieth century. Those of their elders who gained a higher wisdom from that time are the ones who first began to introduce natural spirituality into the life of the church. But it is these later generations who will embrace it more fully and who, in due time, will take over and complete the work.

Appendices

Appendix A
Find Your Type

A Quickie Type Test

For each of the four questions below, choose one of the contrasting sets of personal tendencies. Inevitably, some statements in both sets will ring true for you. The question is, which set is *most basic* to you. Which set, *though it might not fit perfectly*, fits a just a little better than the other?

This test is accurate more often than not. To confirm your result, read about the indicated type in the accompanying Type Descriptions. More than 90% of those type characteristics should fit you. If not, change the hard-to-decide answers on your test and look at the new type description that produces. *A good fit with a type description is a better indicator of your type than is the test result itself.* There should be one of the sixteen type descriptions that fits better than the rest, though others might be close.

Question #1

Which set carries the most weight for you, even if only slightly?

Set A

- • Though I do need time alone, my life energy usually feels strongest and clearest when I am doing things with other people.
- •• Though I do take note of my own thoughts and feelings, I tend to be more interested in the thoughts and feelings of others and feel best when I can interact with them.
- ••• My active side tends to be stronger than my reflective side. I usually welcome stimulation from outer life and sometimes get dispirited if I am alone too long.

Set B

- • Though I do like being with other people, my life energy usually feels strongest and clearest when I am by myself following my own interests.
- •• Though I do take note of the thoughts and feelings of others, I tend to be even more aware of my own thoughts and feelings and feel best when I can honor them.
- ••• My reflective side tends to be stronger than my active side. I usually welcome privacy and am easily drained by too much stimulation from outer life.

Question #2

Which set carries the most weight for you, even if only slightly?

Set A

- When I perceive a scene, I usually first see the parts, the specific details; then I put those together to get the whole picture and perhaps to see a pattern in it.

• • Although I do have some sense of the shape of things beneath the surface of life, I tend to be more strongly attuned to what is physically real on the surface.

• • • Though I can envision new possibilities, I usually need concrete evidence before I can give them much credence. Real experience convinces me.

Set B

- When I first perceive a scene, I usually first take in the whole picture and sense a pattern in it; then I take in specific details, though many escape my notice.

• • Although I do take into account what is physically real on the surface of life, I tend to be more strongly attuned to the shape of things beneath the surface.

• • • Though I value concrete evidence, I often believe in new possibilities before concrete evidence for them has been produced. What I have seen with my inner vision convinces me.

Question #3

Which set carries the most weight for you, even if only slightly?

Set A

- I know I come more from the head than from the heart all in all, though I do have a well-functioning heart and use it often.

•• Usually, the first thing I judge in a process is whether it makes sense in terms of logic and efficiency; then I judge whether my feelings and those of others are being honored.

••• Although not always, I usually react first with objective reasoning and detachment, while my heart and feelings stay more in the background and wait their turn.

Set B

- I know I come more from the heart than from the head all in all, though I do have a well-functioning head and use it often.

•• Usually, the first thing I judge in a process is whether my feelings and those of others are being honored; then I judge whether it makes sense in terms of logic and efficiency.

••• Although not always, I usually react first with my heart and feelings, while detachment and objective reasoning stay more in the background and wait their turn.

Question #4

Which set carries the most weight for you, even if only slightly? *(This is a question about how you operate in the outer world, not the inner world, which will not be the same. It might help if you think of how you are at work rather than how you are at home.)*

Set A

- • Though I sometimes put off making decisions, it usually feels better to get things decided and settled as soon as possible, even if I might need to change my mind later.
- •• Though I sometimes pull things together at the last minute, it's not the way I work best; I usually try to look ahead and get things squared away in good time.
- ••• While I'm not as neat and organized as some, I do like for my environment to be in fairly good order—messiness is stressful for me.

Set B

- • Though I sometimes make ready decisions, I usually wish to have more information or see other possibilities before making up my mind.
- •• Though it would be great to get things done early, I usually have too much to handle in the moment to get started on something else before I have to.
- ••• A certain amount of order is good, but I can tolerate a fair amount of messiness in my environment—I see it as life in progress.

Test Results

Circle your answers, A or B:

#1 Extravert or Introvert?
A = **E** B = **I**

#2 Sensate or Intuitive?
A = **S** B = **N**

#3 Thinking or Feeling?
A = **T** B = **F**

#4 Judging or Perceiving?
A = **J** B = **P**

Put your letters in sequence to see your type:

(E or I) ______ (S or N) ______ (T or F) ______ (J or P) ______

To determine which function is first (strongest) and which is second, find your type below—the letter underlined is your first function, the other middle letter is your second function.

ESFJ	☐	ENFJ	☐
ESFP	☐	ENFP	☐
ISFJ	☐	INFJ	☐
ISFP	☐	INFP	☐
ESTJ	☐	ENTJ	☐
ESTP	☐	ENTP	☐
ISTJ	☐	INTJ	☐
ISTP	☐	INTP	☐

SF (Sensing Feeling) Type Descriptions

No description will fit perfectly, but if you are an SF, there should be one of these that fits 90% or better. A type that is only one letter off from yours will also have many characteristics that fit, but not as many as your own type has. You should view the characteristics loosely, as "tend to"/"often are"/"can be ." (Tip: You can discern a fit more easily when your mind is rested and fresh.)

ESFJ *1st: extraverted feeling; 2nd: introverted sensation*

Caring and sensitive, sociable and outgoing: •genuine concern for others •strongly value family and social ties •always doing kind and thoughtful things for their loved ones •strong desire to nurture •worry about tragic events befalling their loved ones •look for the best in others •energized by being around people •sunny, optimistic, and cheerful •quickly establish rapport •strong sense of community •inspire others with their enthusiasm •like to organize people •enjoy belonging •talkative and expressive •freely speak their minds •often fast and loud talkers, sometimes too much so.

Realistic and practical, oriented to physical life: •down to earth; great common sense •base decisions on experience and facts •dislike abstract ideas •focus on the present •enjoy creating order, structure, and schedules •get right to work on assignments and finish on time •careful and precise with details •large or complicated tasks can overwhelm them •want to provide practical and tangible help to others •strong body awareness •often athletic •competitive •like to collect things •good sense of color and fashion •tend to have expensive tastes •enjoy their possessions and take good care of them.

Strong need to feel loved and appreciated: •eager to please •need expressed affection, validation, and praise •like to have an audience •thrive on being needed •quick to volunteer •try not to offend or disappoint •concerned about the opinions and feelings of others •strong value on harmony •tend to be polite and obedient •apologize quickly •won't usually push their own opinion •but will firmly state their values if there is a need •hurt by indifference or unkindness •more attuned to others' needs than to their own •tend to look for worth too much on the outside, not enough on the inside.

Like structure and consistency: •like things to stay as they are •love tradition and rituals •want to know the rules •strong on should and ought •like schedule and routine •high regard for authority •listen well, follow directions closely •dutiful, loyal, and hardworking •good on follow-through •like things clean and neat •prefer a conventional lifestyle •direct and firm in their assertions •like things under control, with a consistent plan they can count on •hesitant to try new things—they slow down and get wary •keep an eye on the past and work to preserve existing methods and traditions.

ESFP *1st: extraverted sensation; 2nd: introverted feeling*

Take life as it is and live it to the fullest: •like to be busy, moving about, doing things with others •exuberant lovers of life •need physical exertion •love going places •observant •notice the beauty of the world •like to go with the flow •respond quickly to the needs of others •adapt easily to changes in plans •like trying new things •plunge in and learn as they go •upbeat and optimistic •eager and expressive •can seem vulnerable and naive •find it hard to be still for long •live completely in the moment •want things *now* •can be irritable if delayed from doing something fun.

Gentle, friendly, fun, and highly social: •care deeply about family and friends •warm, generous, and kind •witty and charming •eager to please •like physical closeness and open affection •enjoy people •initiate conversation •need to know they are liked •like attention •pleased and proud of what they have done •like buying things for others •love animals •disturbed by meanness or cruelty •withdraw if scolded •quick to apologize and to forgive •readily express appreciation •skillful at handling conflict and easing tensions •loyal friends •can get overly involved in helping others.

Realistic and literal: •good common sense •like practical, useful activities •easily learn physical skills •notice and remember visual details •attuned to what is trendy and popular •like beautiful things •like spending money •take pleasure in their possessions •collect things •have packrat tendencies •will spend money on travel to fun places •like tangible rewards •like giving tangible help to others •learn by doing •dislike abstract explanations •would rather do than talk •express themselves through action •impressed with superficial attributes; may trust people not worthy of trust.

Spontaneous, adaptable, and comfortable with chaos: •live always in the moment •bold and fearless •quickly size up a situation and act creatively •good in a crisis •often act before thinking •not planners •can be impulsive and disorganized •easily disregard rules •find it hard to stay on schedule and comply with structure •have to cultivate self-imposed limits •have trouble saving money •impatient to get on with the next fun thing •easily distracted and can fail to follow-through •have to learn to think ahead to avoid getting behind in things •have to learn not to get distracted and forget commitments.

ISFJ *1st: introverted sensation; 2nd: extraverted feeling*

Strong awareness of the present moment: •literal experience of life •very observant •focus on physical surroundings •especially notice beautiful or pleasant details •have a rich, accurate memory of their observations •like outdoors and being physical •accurate and thorough with facts •realistic and practical •more concerned with what is than what might be •like tangible results of their efforts •like simple pleasures •like nice clothes •like having creative projects •make quick, critical judgments, but try not to hurt others with them •pay more attention to the surface than to what is going on underneath.

Warm and gentle, loving and loyal: •great desire to keep loved ones close •form deep bonds with parents and family •accepting, trusting, and affectionate, once they know you •sweet and unassuming •a bit reserved •sensitive and emotional •upset by aggression or rudeness •easily hurt by criticism •find it hard to hide or even control their upset reactions •need private time and rest •like the intimacy of one to one •don't like the limelight •love animals •comfortable being alone •strong need to be accepted and liked •need personal feedback •tend to overestimate the expectations of others.

Strong attachment to what is familiar: •strongly guided by previous experience •like routine and knowing what to expect •convention and tradition give them comfort and security •hang back in new situations •upset or frightened by sudden change •sometimes see only the negative possibilities •easily cry if worried or afraid •not very flexible •can remain a long time with one activity •good with repeated, sequential procedures •usually have one best friend at a time •not adventurous by nature •the more experiences they have to draw on, the more confident they become.

Like order and structure: •respect established procedures and authority •strong desire to do what they are supposed to do •expect praise for being good •strongly opposed to what they dislike •don't compromise easily •listen carefully to instruction •would rather follow than lead •don't like open-ended plans or projects •like focused and structured lifestyle •faithful in their responsibilities •strong work ethic •would rather do things themselves •organized and self-disciplined •careful and deliberate in their spending •firm in their decisions •perfectionists •small mistakes weigh heavily.

ISFP *1st: introverted feeling; 2nd: extraverted sensation*

Accept the world at face value: •very much in the here and now •easygoing and yielding •will not be hurried or rushed •earthy and literal •realistic and practical •don't mind dirt and messiness •usually identify strongly with nature •see beauty in all living things •appreciate simple things •can't pretend to feel what they do not •can be hard to motivate •optimistic and easily satisfied with life •often do just what is required and no more •don't plan ahead •accident-prone because they are so much in the moment they don't imagine consequences •deal well with needs of the moment •good in a crisis.

Sensitive and loving, with strong inner values: •feel everything personally and deeply •attuned to the feelings and needs of others •easygoing and likeable •loyal and trustworthy •sympathetic listeners •good social and communication skills •often the peacemaker or mediator •love animals •want to contribute to the well-being of others •need to feel safe and secure before they share their feelings •don't want people they don't like getting too close to them •don't want people they do like invading their privacy •sensitive to criticism and sharp words •their deep emotions can come out dramatically.

Like hands-on activity: •like to investigate things by taking them apart •learn by doing more than by hearing or reading •like doing arts, crafts, and such •like their cherished possessions spread out around them •comfortable with their bodies •good dexterity, balance, and coordination •often are good athletes •good physical energy and stamina •prefer action to words; tend to express feelings that way •like to be useful •good at day-to-day caretaking •enjoy helping people develop practical skills •very dedicated to their work when it engages their feelings •want their lives to reflect their values.

Playful and curious free spirits: •explore their world without judgment or plan of action •highly observant •free-flowing, relaxed style •often hum to themselves •inquisitive and spontaneous •don't like to be bossed •like a cooperative, egalitarian environment •might enjoy sports for the camaraderie, but not competitive •enjoy physical adventures like hiking and biking •try things just to see what will happen •don't like limits on their freedom •will learn if curious, but not simply for learning's sake •can be impulsive •weak at managing money •like to keep their options open; put off decisions.

ST (Sensing Thinking) Type Descriptions

No description will fit perfectly, but if you are an ST, there should be one of these that fits 90% or better. A type that is only one letter off from yours will also have many characteristics that fit, but not as many as your own type has. You should view the characteristics loosely, as "tend to"/"often are"/"can be ." (Tip: You can discern a fit more easily when your mind is rested and fresh.)

ESTJ *1st: extraverted thinking; 2nd: introverted sensation*

Logical and practical; decisive, clear, and assertive: •analytical and objectively critical •literal and matter-of-fact •good at analyzing and correcting problems •competent and efficient •convinced only by reason and logic •require hard evidence as proof •can accept cold, hard truth •incisive understanding of order and complexity •good at devising systems and procedures •don't understand feelings very well •can be honest to the point of bluntness •can be impatient and abrupt •can have difficulty hearing other points of view •can be stubborn once they make up their minds.

Friendly, outgoing, and active: •like to stay busy •make friends easily •like physical activity •like to please others by helping out •like to be outdoors •enjoy structured group activities •innately competitive •like being center of attention •often well-liked by peers •natural good sense of humor •don't take offense easily •usually verbal and talkative •like to talk about the work they do •easily express needs and frustrations •impatient with delays •can be bossy, stubborn, and aggressive •their anger can be explosive •after venting they return to equilibrium •can be tender with those they trust.

Fair-minded and responsible: •thorough and efficient •want to achieve goals and meet commitments •strive to be reliable and competent •can be workaholics •willingly follow rules and expect the same of others •have clear standards and beliefs •like to be the leader •peers are willing to follow them •are convinced their way is best •like to advise others on procedures •don't like confusion, inefficiency, or halfway measures •take constructive criticism well, often after bristling first •get angry if they perceive unfairness •careful and safety-minded •responsible in relationships •thrifty •good providers.

Rely on first-hand experience: •like activities that engage their senses •great memory for facts and details •quick learners of physical skills •like solving known problems with proven techniques •like to know what to expect •comfortable with past experience: like to apply and adapt it •like for traditions to be preserved in detail •like repeated activities •like habit and routine •hate feeling out of control •unsettled by novelty and uncertainty •impatient with abstractions •can get upset and angry at small changes •first reaction to anything new is usually negative •often love new things after trying them.

ESTP *1st: extraverted sensation; 2nd: introverted thinking*

Active, adventurous, and freedom-loving: •live in the present moment •need hands-on experience •very dexterous •prefer actions to words •intensely curious and naturally impulsive •great need for physical freedom •love the natural world •don't mind getting dirty •lack a sense of moderation •fearless •seek risk-taking adventures •don't think of consequences •never assume the worst might happen •rarely take anything very seriously •roll with the punches •always pushing limits •tend to brush off criticism •don't like to be controlled •feel trapped by pressure, obligation, and commitment.

Logical, resourceful, and practical: •realists of the first order •active and creative problem solvers •like tests and challenges •task oriented •mechanically inclined •care little for standard rules or procedures •find new ways to use existing systems •devise easy ways to do difficult things •quick learners of physical skills •notice tiny details •don't like abstract learning •impatient with discussion or waiting around •naturally direct and honest •can be blunt and even outrageous •find it hard to understand hurt or shocked reaction of others •need logical explanations of why others feel as they do.

Gregarious, fun-loving, and charming: •funny and delightful •talkative •quick to make friends •life of the party •affable and personable •like attention and applause •casual and easy-going style •rarely intimidated by public speaking •practical jokers •don't take themselves or anything else very seriously •will ignore or walk away from conflict •tend to express themselves in action rather than words •people pleasers in public but independent and aloof in private •unpredictable and freedom-loving in relationships •like being with others who share their sense of adventure •very loyal to friends.

Like the good things in life: •like to accumulate possessions •find it hard to delay gratification •impressed by superficial measures of worth, like clothes or money •generous with material things •care a lot about their reputations and social standing •take their social obligations seriously •always aware of the impression they are making •try to dress and act right for public respect •take pride in how they look •usually have a great sense of fashion •attuned to the trendy and the popular •can schmooze when needed for their public image •promote themselves well •try to win others with charisma and success.

ISTJ *1st: introverted sensation; 2nd: extraverted thinking*

Logical, analytical, tough-minded and practical: •extremely pragmatic •down-to-earth, sensible, and matter-of-fact •profound respect for facts •systematic •tend to make quick, critical judgments •clear and steadfast in their opinions •literal and precise •ask very specific questions and want explicit answers •love to learn facts and then share them with others •want to be trusted and respected for what they know to be true •fairly competitive academically •balk at doing what doesn't make sense to them •can be honest to the point of bluntness •their compliment is high praise.

Loyal and dependable, hard-working and steady: •high value on competence and responsibility •fulfill commitments on time •work slowly and steadily until job is done •well organized, efficient, and careful •expect rules and orders to be followed •devoted friends and companions •their affections run deep •show love through doing practical things and by being loyal •maintain close relationships for years •tend to be frugal •quite safety-conscious •amazing powers of concentration •will work and move at their own pace, unaffected by bustle around them •tend to find it hard to relax.

Private and self-contained: •persons of few words •like to work alone •dislike distractions and interruptions •can be impatient with people •dry, understated wit •modest, unassuming, and down-to-earth •pensive •enjoy being in nature and notice many details •prefer simplicity to extravagance •calm, reserved, and serious •have difficulty understanding needs different from their own •hard to engage them in any discussion or activity in which they are not interested •will not be pushed into interacting •often prefer the sidelines •must meet them in their world •affectionate in private.

Rely on past experience or else clear direction and guidance: •know and trust those things they have personally experienced •uncomfortable with the unfamiliar and unpredictable •trust standard procedures •value traditions •like consistency, order, and routine •confused by ambiguity and frustrated by contradictions •skeptical of new ideas •resistant to change •persist in the beliefs and worldview with which they start out •have clear likes and dislikes •can be quite particular about smells, tastes, and textures •not big risk-takers •physically and socially cautious •don't like open-ended plans or activities.

ISTP *1st: introverted thinking; 2nd: extraverted sensation*

Active, hands-on engagement with life: •action-oriented and challenge-loving •focus on tangible reality •learn best through direct perceptual experience •skilled and precise with tools •high level of physical energy and stamina •don't like to be bored •some like to take physical risks •calm and resourceful in a crisis •very observant •attuned to popular trends •like high-quality, high-status goods •appreciate excellent food •accept life as it is •generous and fun-loving •like to explore nature •like to keep options open •often will not complete tasks or follow through on commitments.

Logical, analytical, practical problem-solvers: •enjoy troubleshooting concrete problems •factual and pragmatic •objective and honest •efficient, systematic, and expedient •curious •look for the essential structure beneath the facts •dislike ambiguity, abstractions, and unnecessary details •great memory for details and facts •organized in their area of interest, but otherwise disorganized •only follow a rule if they understand the reason for it •find it hard to compromise if they don't see the logic of it.

Quiet, reserved, independent, and difficult to read: •strongly individualistic •self-contained and even-tempered •not guided by convention or others' expectations •unpredictable and challenging to live with •their focus on facts and logic can seem critical and insensitive •if not "with" a situation, won't pretend they are •if too much is asked, will walk away •not very verbal •would rather share experience than thoughts and feelings •can be talkative in areas they know a lot about •show love in practical ways by doing favors or fixing things •often enjoy mixing with people •can be affable and personable •a bit disconnected from their emotions •hard for them to process disappointment and hurt •very private about their sad and hurt feelings, making it hard to experience close connection with them.

Focused and self-disciplined, confident and self-determined: •don't like to supervise or be supervised •take life seriously •rely on their own internal standards and work on their own terms •will bypass rules and policies if they are in the way •not naturally impressed by people in authority—respect has to be earned •like to demonstrate competence—more to themselves than to others •focus on results •do only what is needed •change course easily if they see a better way •hate being told what to do.

NF (Intuiting Feeling) Type Descriptions

No description will fit perfectly, but if you are an NF, there should be one of these that fits 90% or better. A type that is only one letter off from yours will also have many characteristics that fit, but not as many as your own type has. You should view the characteristics loosely, as "tend to"/"often are"/"can be ." (Tip: You can discern a fit more easily when your mind is rested and fresh.)

ENFJ *1st: extraverted feeling; 2nd: introverted intuition*

Friendly persuaders, charismatic leaders: •natural leaders •ambitious and willing to work hard toward their ideals •creative problem solvers •curious about new and different ideas •great power to inspire and persuade others •can be manipulators and politickers •excellent communicators •good with an audience •perform with charm and warmth •prize harmony and cooperation •good at networking •can be loyal followers as well as inspiring leaders •feel validated by the esteem and admiration of others •don't naturally focus on realities or logical outcomes •accept setbacks as new challenges.

Warm and engaging, socially adept: •love people •socially confident •personable, congenial, and gracious •radiate warmth and energy •very verbal; love to talk •highly receptive listeners •diplomatic and tactful by nature •highly empathetic •quick to comfort and try to cheer the other up •physically affectionate •focus on people's most admirable qualities •above all, need harmony in relationships •are loyal and involved friends •bring enthusiasm and intensity to intimate relationships •need love, acceptance, and support more than most—they *have* to have it •supersensitive to criticism •wither and withdraw if don't feel liked •forgive easily but need apology, then cheer up quickly.

See meaningful connections; like to help people grow: •bright and enthusiastic learners •grasp global concepts and see connections between things •tend toward imaginative, less obvious interpretations of material •have a psychological turn of mind •good insight into people •see potential for growth in others and work to help them achieve it •can become overly involved in friends' problems •well-developed spiritual side •sometimes philosophical •want to make a contribution to humanity •often good writers and editors •need time alone to tend their inner lives and express their creativity.

Goal-oriented and conscientious, orderly and decisive: •motivated by personal excellence and self-mastery •want control of their own projects •active lifestyle •like organized lives •want to cooperate and follow rules; but put people over schedules and rules •good with routine •need to know what is expected of them •like to get things decided; can rush it and make poor decisions •tend to be time-conscious and in a hurry •have and will express definite opinions and values •can confront when necessary.

ENFP *1st: extraverted intuition; 2nd: introverted feeling*

Outgoing and lively, dynamic and charismatic: •contagious enthusiasm and joy for life •always looking for new people, ideas, and possibilities •exuberant, optimistic idealists •unconventional and open-minded •initiate projects and invest great energy in getting them going •natural leaders •good at understanding how people and groups work •care about humanitarian concerns •highly sociable and gregarious •wide circle of friends •good sense of humor •enjoy telling stories and being center stage •can be unnerving to be around—too loud, too fast, too messy •hard for them to know if their energy is too much for the situation •fear boredom and stagnation •can be restless, anxious, and sleepless.

Rich imagination and active mind: •given to reflection as well as to action •readily see meaning, significance, and connections—big picture people •strong value system •want to understand themselves and the meaning of life •like reading, writing, and creative projects •appreciate and participate in arts and culture •verbally fluent •need to talk about their many original ideas •great problem-solving and creative-thinking skills •easily see alternatives •their minds can move at a frenetic pace •thoughts often wander and moods quickly change—on one track one minute, on another the next.

Strong value on closeness and intimacy: •relate with warmth and affection to many people •good at establishing rapport and making others feel comfortable •keenly perceptive •friendly, caring, and supportive •listen well to friends' problems •peers seek their counsel •value depth and authenticity in their close relationships •can make others feel unconditionally loved •like meaningful conversations •need to express their wide range of feelings and have them honored and understood •get their feelings hurt easily and have difficulty moving past it •tend to feel emotionally abandoned when criticized.

Dislike routine, structure, and factual details: •like a casual, relaxed atmosphere •like to work at their own pace with little structure or supervision •adaptable •value process more than finished product •prefer to leave follow-up to others •question rules and limits •have difficulty eliminating options •wait until the last minute •can lose focus •can forget to eat or sleep when fully engaged •can seem random and scattered, messy and chaotic •see mess and chaos as activity and possibility.

INFJ *1st: introverted intuition; 2nd: extraverted feeling*

Gentle and tenderhearted; compassionate, concerned, and accommodating: •cheerful and warm at home; serious and quiet out in the world •have a soft and gentle quality that lasts all their lives •others find it pleasant to be in their company •highly sensitive to how others are feeling •perceptive, empathetic understanding of people •hate to disappoint others •deeply attached to family and close friends and like spending time with them •easily share feelings, emotions, and affections in private •quietly nurturing •can lose themselves in the needs of a loved one •have difficulty saying goodbye or separating •need harmony; get tense and frustrated when it is lacking •deeply hurt when not understood.

Complex and deep; rich imagination and inner life: •intuitively understand complex meanings and human relationships •see patterns and connections •good with symbolism and metaphor •love to read •interested in big issues, like meaning of life and death •insightful and visionary •have a beautiful view of the world •like to advise and counsel friends and family members •tire from too much interaction •need lots of time alone •spend much of their time inside their own heads •keep their intuitions private; can be difficult to know •once they trust you, they will share ideas, visions, and dreams quite freely •often disconnected from the external world •hard to get and hold their attention.

Committed to their inspirations and ideals: •highly developed sense of what is good and right, based on a very personal set of values •usually reserved, but will assert themselves when their values are threatened •loyal to people and institutions that exemplify their values •have a visionary grasp of human possibilities that can elevate and inspire others •want meaning and purpose in all areas of their lives •can struggle with depression from being chronically unheard and misunderstood.

Comfortable with routine and like order around them: •need to know what is expected of them •appreciate rules •want options settled •strong nesting instinct; like a comfortable, orderly, aesthetically pleasing home •like to work in a quiet, organized setting •work best alone •work toward long-range goals •follow through on commitments •concentrate well and think things through •rework, adjust, correct, refigure •dislike interruptions •self-impose a lot of work; can exhaust themselves.

INFP *1st: introverted feeling; 2nd: extraverted intuition*

Primarily oriented by strong personal values and deep feeling: •values are central to all they do •trust their own unique view and perception of the world •try to clarify their values and live in congruence with them •idealistic and humane •tend to take up causes that have affected them personally •often work at helping the sick, disabled, or disenfranchised •often are determined achievers who proceed in a quiet, inconspicuous way •measure themselves against high standards •their emotions are deep, intense, and personal •can be inflexible if one of their core values feels violated •take everything personally •strong need to feel understood and accepted •become moody, pessimistic, and negative when feeling offended or dismissed •can wear out loved ones with need to be handled with kid gloves.

Gentle, calm, and easygoing; private and reserved: •keep what is most important to them private; can be hard to understand •to reveal their feelings, must feel safe and trust the other completely •need a best friend close by •retreat or withdraw in large groups •value authenticity and depth in relationships •loyal, devoted, and committed to family and friends •good at nurturing, encouraging, validating, and affirming others •can be entertaining and whimsical when they feel comfortable •dry, witty, subtle humor •don't like to impose their values; prefer to gently persuade, influence, and inspire.

Highly reflective; like to contemplate the mysteries and meaning of life: •strong inner life and complex feelings •often artistic or creative •love books •eager to discover and relate what they are learning to what they already know •vivid imaginations •often lost in their private thoughts •can seem cool and aloof •happiest when alone •often sensitive about their environments •dislike interruptions, loud noises, and loud people •often conflicted between the need for solitude and a desire for connection.

Value autonomy and new ideas; dislike rules and schedules: •original and individual •want options open •curious and creative •like learning and researching •dislike competitive environments •unconcerned with order; not very aware of time •make designs and use materials in unconventional and unusual ways •often earthy in appearance and way of living •can be content with a rather meager or Bohemian lifestyle •see possibilities everywhere, so sometimes see betrayal and deception where it is not.

NT (Intuiting Thinking) Type Descriptions

No description will fit perfectly, but if you are an NT, there should be one of these that fits 90% or better. A type that is only one letter off from yours will also have many characteristics that fit, but not as many as your own type has. You should view the characteristics loosely, as "tend to"/"often are"/"can be." (Tip: You can discern a fit more easily when your mind is rested and fresh.)

ENTJ *1st: extraverted thinking; 2nd: introverted intuition*

Confident, competent leaders with high personal standards: •intellectual, strategic visionaries •have an abiding sense of their own authority •calm, collected, and happy to take charge, even in the face of chaos •decisive, clear, and assertive •like to organize people and get them moving in the right direction •always see possibilities of improvement •well-developed ability to read between the lines •think ahead to anticipate problems and plan for future needs •focus on resolving problems, reaching conclusions, and moving ahead •often admired by their peers •can be tough •tend to hide their soft, sentimental side •can be inwardly insecure •when stressed can have explosive outbursts of judgment on themselves and others.

Live life with gusto and enthusiasm: •active, busy, and very physical •stimulated and inspired by things out of the ordinary •like any kind of creative activity or project •tend to be gregarious and fun-loving as well as serious and driven •socially adaptable; make friends quickly •energized by stimulating interactions with others •like to work with strong-minded, independent, results-oriented people •very goal directed •willing to sacrifice everything for the realization of a plan •tend to brush off constructive criticism or words of caution •can be workaholics •value prestige and status •love worldly things.

Knowledgeable, logical, and intellectually curious: •love gaining knowledge •always seeking to understand why the world operates as it does •have an extraordinary ability to see all sides of an issue •like to engage in intellectually stimulating exchanges •like and respect people who challenge them on solid ground •feel compelled to point out an illogical premise or unjustified conclusion •can have a know-it-all attitude •don't want to risk looking stupid or inept •keep their emotional lives private.

Value order, rationality, and efficiency: •comfortable with order and structure; like to have a plan •need to be prepared; not good at improvising •want to do things perfectly the first time •like clear and definite guidelines •hold themselves and others to the rules •demand fairness •dislike inefficiency, incompetence, and indecisiveness •alert to aspects of a system that have no functional purpose and driven to rid the system of them •like to get things done ahead of schedule •don't like changes in a plan.

ENTP *1st: extraverted intuition; 2nd: introverted thinking*

Active, energetic, and adventurous; clever, creative, and fun: •eager to learn new things and explore •bored if not allowed variety and innovation •constantly toying with new ideas and scanning for possibilities •imaginative, enterprising, and resourceful •don't like to be limited or trapped •have an urgency to push forward •their interests can seem limitless •like companions who are mentally stimulating and enjoy new adventures •mobilize people with their energy and enthusiasm •will tune out and become restless if they lose interest •can be exhausting to have around •can wear out their own bodies.

Theoretical and curious, logical and analytical: •innovative and ingenious •innate love of learning •resourceful in solving challenging problems •assertive and questioning •see patterns and connections not obvious to others •clear and organized thinking; understand how systems work •their intelligence is fluid, unpredictable, and given to idealism •develop their own theories about the world and human nature •often enjoy metaphysical speculations •enjoy debate •can usually see the big picture in any issue or discussion •can become self-absorbed with their ideas and keep relationships distant.

Outgoing and confident; charming, quick-witted, and friendly: •gregarious •energized by being around others •well-liked by peers •don't like to be alone for long; seek constant interaction and engagement •love to delight others with their long and engaging stories •often have a knack for making people laugh •can quickly size up a situation and see the humorous patterns •value honesty and tend to be very direct •can be charismatic leaders, inspiring others with their eloquence and lightning-quick minds •verbally fluent •can wear others out with their talking •good at convincing others of their point of view •good at understanding people and their underlying motivations •clever in their dealings with others.

Adaptable, freedom-loving, and unconventional: •strong-willed and independent •have confidence in their ideas and insist on doing things their way •relaxed and casual style •don't like highly structured systems and organizations •don't mind disorganized or chaotic surroundings •ignore traditional ways of doing things •will challenge authority •like to improvise and figure it out as they go •tend to procrastinate •constantly test boundaries •so individualistic they may be entirely unique.

INTJ *1st: introverted intuition; 2nd: extraverted thinking*

Strong sense of themselves; confident in their intuitive insights: •always guided by intuition •deep perception •highly developed imagination •unique perspective on the world •trust their insightful connections regardless of established authority or popular opinion •have a clear vision of what they are trying to do and are dissatisfied with less •independent in the highest degree •unaffected by the outside world •unusually strong strength of will •there is little that upsets or intimidates them •can be intractable •have the drive and organizing skills to implement their ideas •their rich inner life is a source of great joy and satisfaction to them •until experience teaches them otherwise, they think they know everything •can be unaware of the negative effect on others of their belief they have the absolute truth.

Intellectually engaging big-picture thinkers: •rational, detached, and objectively critical •innovators in the field of ideas •naturally see things from a different perspective •can't help but see how everything is interconnected •easily see possibilities and underlying principles •driven to pull unexpressed possibilities into the existing framework •love learning •read voraciously •study a variety of subjects in great depth •curious about big questions like death and God •insightful, creative synthesizers; clear and concise •don't like center stage unless completely prepared and feeling highly competent.

Private, reserved, hard to know: •find energy in solitude •very internal; need lots of time alone •tend to be more passive than active in their engagement with life •like low-key, one-on-one social time •dislike small talk •quite talkative about topics that interest them •calm and even-tempered •honest and direct •dry, wry humor •more light and playful inwardly than they seem from outside •very loyal •emotionally contained •don't want to be fussed over •sensitive to rejection but hide their hurt •can be aloof •can be blunt •can neglect relationships because so absorbed in their work.

Dislike confusion, mess, and inefficiency: •like structure and routine, but not dull routine •like to know in advance what's going to happen •make logical decisions based on gathered information •want no one in their workspace •low threshold for outside stimulation •impatient with wasted motion, words, and emotion •value elegance of form and subtlety of expression •can be perfectionists.

INTP *1st: introverted thinking; 2nd: extraverted intuition*

Great focus and intensity of thought, attuned to patterns and possibilities: •logical, analytical, and objectively critical •take intellectual matters seriously •lifelong learners •avid readers

•want clear and complete answers for why things are as they are •see possibilities and connections beyond the present and obvious •creative and original thinkers •bring great energy, intensity, and focus to researching and analyzing complex problems •naturally build complex theoretical systems to explain the realities they see •can find solutions that run counter to prevailing wisdom or knowledge •their thinking can seem scattered and hard to follow •more interested in pure knowledge than in practical use.

Highly self-contained; keep much of their thinking to themselves: •very autonomous •quiet, contained, calm, and detached •like one-on-one interaction •slow to disclose their thoughts in conversation •will argue and raise issues only when they think it reasonable to do so •prize precision in communication •their precision of thought may be too complex for others to understand •need a lot of time alone •favorite activities are fairly intellectual, solitary, and internal •tend to give more attention to interests and hobbies than to people •can become cynical or depressed without an outlet for their abilities.

Quietly warm and engaging, witty and quirky: •charming, approachable, and congenial •stimulating conversationalists, easily connecting one topic to another •dry wit and rich sense of humor •dislike protracted small talk •prefer to discuss ideas •will not jump in and talk—need to be asked and then listened to with patience and interest •easily drained by too much contact with others •sometimes display nervous habits or signs they are not at ease •honest, even blunt •not easily offended •loyal to those important to them •very private about matters of the heart •show their feelings in subtle ways.

Like a flexible, unstructured environment: •naturally nonconforming, skeptical, even disdainful of rules •live in a casual way, unaffected or uninvolved with the world and people around them •like a calm, conflict-free atmosphere •move at their own pace, unaware and unconcerned about time, structure, or inconvenience to others •innate spirit of wanderlust •can be fearless about taking on physical challenges •have a quiet confidence •so unique and different, they often have a hard road.

Appendix B A Liturgy for Dream Groups

This material may be copied and distributed freely

Opening

The God of all faiths tells us in Hindu scripture: By whichever way you approach me, so I receive you. All paths lead to me.
Come then, and let us walk in the light of the Way.

[Here may be said a canticle to Wisdom]

[Then one or two of the following:]

- I will bless the Holy One who gives me counsel; my heart teaches me night after night. *Ps 16*
- Without going outside, one can know the whole world. Without looking out the window, one can see the ways of heaven. *Dao De Jing 47*
- Darkness is not dark to you, O Giver of Life; the night is as bright as the day; darkness and light to you are both alike. *Ps 139*

O Giver of Life, we praise you for the universe which you have been evolving through time, vitalizing matter with energy, bringing forth all things as an expression of your creating Wisdom, permeating your creation with love. As your Wisdom reawakens our souls to the Eternal Mysteries that surround us, may we be led with courage through darkness and light to the fullness of life for which we were created. With that fullness of life may we better serve you, our loved ones, and the communities of which we are a part. *Amen.*

Adapted from a prayer by Teilhard de Chardin

Closing

Glory to the Holy One whose power, working in us, does infinitely more than we can ask or imagine:
Glory to the Mystery of Being from generation to generation.

[Here may be said a canticle to the Power of Heaven]

Accept, O Giver of Life, our thanks and praise for all that you have done for us. We thank you for the splendor of the whole creation, for the beauty of this world, for the wonder of life and the mystery of love. Grant us the gift of your Spirit, that we may know it and make it known, and through it, at all times and in all places, may give thanks to you in all things. *Amen.*

[Special intercessions and thanksgivings]

May the Holy One bless us and keep us. May grace flow to us and through us. May Wisdom and Love light our way and give us peace, this day and evermore. *Amen.*

Canticles to Wisdom

[Canticles are read by all in turn, by sentence or by verse]

A Song to Wisdom

Wisdom 7:21–8.1

All we have come to know, hidden and plain, we have been taught by Wisdom, who designed them all.

For within her is a spirit intelligent and holy, unique and manifold, benevolent and humane, steadfast and calm, almighty and all-surveying.
Wisdom is quicker to move than any motion, so pure, she pervades and permeates all things.

She is a breath of the power of God, pure emanation of the glory of the Almighty, and nothing impure can enter her.
She is a reflection of the eternal light, untarnished mirror of the working of God, image of his goodness.

Although alone, she can do all; herself unchanging, she makes all things new.
In each generation she passes into holy souls and makes them friends of God, and prophets; for God loves none so much as those who live with Wisdom.

She is more splendid than the sun.
She outshines the constellations.
She reaches mightily to the ends of the earth.
And she orders all things well.

Weaving of the Dao

Dao De Jing 14

One looks at it but it cannot be seen; it is called Yi, "balanced within and permeating all things."
One listens to it but it cannot be heard; it is called Xi, "woven into the fabric of all things."
One grasps it but it cannot be obtained; it is called Wei, "moving hidden within all things."

These three aspects cannot be physically examined, as they blend in as one with everything.

Its rising does not bring brightness, its sinking does not bring darkness.
Unending, unending it cannot be named, always able to rise again because it has no form.

It is the shape of that without shape, the image of that without form; it is the obscure and unconscious.
One can open and receive it but will not see its beginning; one can follow it but will not see its end.

Keep disciplined to the primordial Dao, so as to navigate all that modern day holds.
It is possible to know the primordial beginnings: it is called Dao Ji, "weaving of the Dao throughout space and time."

Translated by Joseph Fiala

Wisdom's Gift

Wisdom 7:7–15

I called on God, and the spirit of Wisdom came to me.

I preferred her to scepters and thrones, and I accounted wealth as nothing in comparison with her.
Neither did I liken to her any priceless gem, because all gold is but a little sand in her sight, and silver will be accounted as clay before her.

I loved her more than health and beauty, and I chose to have her rather than light, because her radiance never ceases.
All good things came to me along with her, and in her hands uncounted wealth.

I rejoiced in them all, because Wisdom leads them; but I did not know
that she was their mother.

I learned without guile, and I impart without grudging.
I do not hide her wealth, for it is an unfailing treasure for mortals.
Those who get it obtain friendship with God, commended for the gifts
that come from instruction.

May God grant me to speak with judgment, and to have thoughts
worthy of what I have received.
For he is the guide even of Wisdom and the corrector of the wise.

Canticles to the Power of Heaven

[*Canticles are read by all in turn, by sentence or by verse*]

The Profound Mystery

Dao De Jing 1

Dao can be spoken of, but not the constant, eternal Dao.
Its name can be named, but not the constant, eternal name.

The nameless is the origin of heaven and earth.
The named is the mother of the ten thousand things.

Therefore a constancy without desire is the means to contemplate its
deep wonders.
A constancy with desire is the means to contemplate its manifestations.

These two arise together but differ in name.
Together call them Xuan, "the profound mystery."

Inside this mystery lies more and more mystery; it is the door to many
deep wonders.

Translated by Joseph Fiala

Jubilate Deo

Psalm 100

Be joyful in the Lord, all ye lands.
Serve the Lord with gladness and come before his presence with a song.

Be ye sure that the Lord he is God.
It is he that hath made us and not we ourselves.
We are his people and the sheep of his pasture.
O go your way into his gates with thanksgiving and into his courts
with praise.
Be thankful unto him and speak good of his Name.

For the Lord is gracious.
His mercy is everlasting.
And his truth endureth from generation to generation.

I Permeate the Universe

Bhagavad Gita 9:4–34

Thus says the Holy One: I permeate the universe with my unmanifest form; all beings are brought forth and sustained by me.

All creation exists within me, yet my inconceivable vastness extends beyond it.
Nature and her laws proceed under my guidance, bringing forth all created things, animate and inanimate.

To those who follow the path of Wisdom, I am known as the many and the One.
Behind the faces of all gods, they recognize my face.

I am the father and mother of the universe, and its grandparent, too.
I am the sum of all knowledge and the bringer and refiner of new understanding.
I am the beginning and the end, the way and the goal of life; it is I who reign over life and I who support it.

I am insight, I am home and shelter, I am the heart's true friend and lover.
I am the heat of the day; I bring the rain and I hold it back.
I am death and immortality; I am all that is and all that is not.

I favor all beings equally—none are more dear or less dear to me.
But those who love me with devotion live within me, and I live within them.

Keep your mind on me always; feel me with your heart; love me, serve me, and acknowledge me with reverence.
In turning to me, you will find me, and we will be together forever.

English rendering by J. R. Hudson

Domine, probasti

Psalm 139, 1–17

Lord, you have searched me out and known me.
You know my sitting down and my rising up; you discern my thoughts from afar.

You trace my journeys and my resting-places and are acquainted with all my ways.
Indeed, there is not a word on my lips, but you, O Lord, know it altogether.

You press upon me behind and before and lay your hand upon me.
Such knowledge is too wonderful for me; it is so high that I cannot attain to it.

Where can I go then from your Spirit? Where can I flee from your presence?
If I climb up to heaven, you are there; if I make the grave my bed, you are there also.

If I take the wings of the morning and dwell in the uttermost parts of the sea, even there your hand will lead me and your right hand will hold me fast.
If I say, "Surely the darkness will cover me, and the light around me turn to night," darkness is not dark to you; the night is as bright as the day; darkness and light to you are both alike.

For you yourself created my inmost parts; you knit me together in my mother's womb.
I will thank you because I am marvelously made; your works are wonderful, and I know it well.

My body was not hidden from you while I was being made in secret and woven in the depths of the earth.
Your eyes beheld my limbs, yet unfinished in the womb; all of them were written in your book; they were fashioned day by day, when as yet there was none of them.

How deep I find your thoughts, O God!-How great is the sum of them!
If I were to count them, they would be more in number than the sand.
To count them all, my life span would need to be like yours.

Appendix C
Natural Spirituality Resources

THE INNER JOURNEY cannot be taken without maps, charts, and accounts by earlier travelers. Study is required to gain competency in the inner world just as it is required for the outer world. Concern about the inner world, however, usually comes at midlife, when a potential journeyer has enough capability and self-discipline to educate himself. Indeed, the most effective study for the individuation journey is individual study, for it is then that one's inner guide has the greatest freedom to steer a person to the book or tape that he or she needs next, according to that person's individual development.

The following natural spirituality resources are arranged in categories which move from entry-level material to long-range, continuing education. A library containing a large selection of these books and audio-visual media would be an important supporting element for any natural spirituality dream group. Also listed here are opportunities for conferences, training programs, and online seminars as of the time of publication. The lists given here are by no means exhaustive and are meant only to be a starting point.

Selected Books for Building a Strong Foundation

The following are basic, entry-level books that are especially effective in presenting the central themes of natural spirituality. Taken all together they offer a solid foundation for the early stages of the individuation process.

Works by C. G. Jung

Jung's writings can be difficult, but they are important for a well-grounded orientation to the unconscious. More than any of his followers, Jung understood the serious, God-centered nature of the individuation journey. The works of later Jungian writers are usually helpful and worthwhile, but not uniformly so. By beginning at the source—with Jung himself—one becomes better equipped to judge the value of the works of later Jungians.

When reading Jung, one must not expect to understand everything. The reader must take from it what he can and leave the rest for return readings. The further along one goes on one's individuation journey, the more comprehensible Jung becomes. The following works have been chosen for their ease of entry, as well as for the thorough grounding they offer in Jungian thought when taken all together.

C. G. Jung. *Memories, Dreams, Reflections.* Recorded and edited by Aniela Jaffé. Translated by Richard and Clara Winston. Reissue. New York: Vintage Books, 1989. Jung's autobiography, as told to his trusted assistant Aniela Jaffé in the last years of his life. Free of scientific language, it tells as much about Jung's inner journey as about his outer one.

________. *Analytical Psychology: Its Theory and Practice.* The Tavistock Lectures. New York: Pantheon Books, 1968. A series of lectures delivered by Jung in his sixtieth year to a group of physicians in London. A clear and lively exposition of his basic ideas in nontechnical language.

This book goes in and out of print, but used copies are available from Amazon and other online booksellers. It is also contained in its entirety in Jung's *Collected Works,* Vol. 18, which is always in print. And thanks to the C. G. Jung Center of Boulder, it can be read online (but not copied) at this URL: www.jungboulder.org/tavistock-lectures-from-the-symbolic-life-cw-18.

________. *The Portable Jung.* Edited by Joseph Campbell. Translated by R. F. C. Hull. Reprint. New York: Penguin Books, 1976. A collection of Jung's more accessible scientific writings. A comprehensive overview of his life's work.

Dreams

Robert A. Johnson. *Inner Work: Using Dreams and Active Imagination for Personal Growth.* Reprint. San Francisco: Harper and Row, 2009. An easy, readable introduction to Jungian dreamwork.

Candy Smith. *Beginning Dreamwork: How To Have a Conversation with Your Soul.* Foreword by Joyce Rockwood Hudson. Orlando: SPC Books, 2011. This is a narrative of one person's unusually self-aware experience of feeling her way into dreamwork. Beautifully written, accessible and compelling, it lays out in non-technical language the universal process that is set in motion when dreamwork is effectively engaged, It demonstrates rather than explains dreamwork's essential nature.

C. G. Jung. *Dreams: (From Volumes 4, 8, 12, and 16 of the Collected Works of C. G. Jung).* Translated by R. F. C. Hull. Reprint. Princeton, NJ: Princeton University Press, 2010. A collection of Jung's scientific writings on dreams. What is most valuable in this collection is Part IV, "Individual Dream Symbolism in Relation to Alchemy," which occupies two-thirds of the book's 300 pages and examines the archetypal elements in one person's dreams over a long period of time. This same dream series is included in *The Portable Jung,* but without the accompanying illustrations. Jung always makes for dense reading, but this work is invaluable for gaining a foundation in the archetypal elements of dreams.

Synchronicity

Robert Aziz. *C. G. Jung's Psychology of Religion and Synchronicity.* Albany, NY: State University of New York Press, 1990. An excellent systematic, scholarly study of synchronicity in terms of Jung's psychological framework. Looks at synchronicity in both scientific and religious terms.

Jean Shinoda Bolen. *The Tao of Psychology: Synchronicity and the Self.* Reprint. San Francisco: Harper and Row, 2005. A short, easy introduction to synchronicity by a Jungian analyst.

Masculine and Feminine

Irene Claremont de Castillejo. *Knowing Woman: A Feminine Psychology.* Reprint. Boston: Shambhala, 1997. A classic work of high quality. Topics covered include masculine focused versus feminine diffused consciousness, the animus, love, and older women.

James Hollis. *Under Saturn's Shadow: The Wounding and Healing of Men.* Toronto: Inner City Books, 1994. Accessible and clearly written. Includes such topics as the anima, the mother complex, and father hunger.

John A. Sanford. *The Invisible Partners: How the Male and Female in Each of Us Affects Our Relationships.* Mahwah, NJ: Paulist Press, 1980. A clear introduction to the problem of anima and animus in human psychology.

Natural Spirituality and the Traditional Religions

Christianity

Morton T. Kelsey. *Dreams: A Way to Listen to God.* Mahwah, NJ: Paulist Press, 1978. A short, comprehensive, easy introduction to the world of dreams. Written from a Christian perspective.

John A. Sanford. *The Kingdom Within: The Inner Meaning of Jesus's Sayings.* Revised edition. New York: HarperOne, 2009. A readable book that explores the teachings of Jesus in terms of inner life and growth. By a Jungian analyst who is also an ordained clergyman.

Robert L. Haden, Jr. *Unopened Letters from God: A Workbook for Individuals and Groups.* Flat Rock, NC: Haden Institute Publishing, 2010. Uses biblical stories to provide a bridge to dreamwork for practicing Christians. Author is a Jungian therapist and ordained clergyman.

C. G. Jung. *Jung on Christianity.* Selected and introduced by Murray Stein. Princeton, NJ: Princeton University Press, 1999. A good selection of Jung's writings on Christianity.

Judaism

Joel Covitz. *Visions in the Night: Jungian and Ancient Dream Interpretation.* Toronto: Inner City Books, 2000. By an ordained rabbi and Jungian analyst, this book examines ancient, medieval, and modern literature for insights into the nature of dreams.

Gustav Dreifuss and Judith Reimer. *Abraham, the Man and the Symbol: A Jungian Interpretation of the Biblical Story.* Asheville, NC: Chiron Publications, 1995. The Israeli authors' application of Jungian thought adds to a deeper understanding of the father of Israel and Judaism.

Buddhism

Radmila Moacanin. *The Essence of Jung's Psychology and Tibetan Buddhism: Western and Eastern Paths to the Heart.* Second edition. Somerville, MA: Wisdom Publications, 2002. Covers much about the commonalities between Jungian psychology and Buddhist philosophy.

Sufism

Llewellyn Vaughan-Lee. *Catching the Thread: Sufism, Dreamwork, and Jungian Psychology.* Inverness, CA: The Golden Sufi Center, 1998. Integrates the wisdom of the Sufis with the insights of Jungian psychology.

Books for a Natural Spirituality Library

In addition to the basic resources given above, a traveler on the path of individuation should read widely and continually. A well-stocked library for a natural spirituality dream group would include the following books and more. Most of these have been written with the layperson in mind.

Reference Books

Boris Matthews, trans. *The Herder Dictionary of Symbols: Symbols from Art, Archaeology, Mythology, Literature, and Religion*. Reprint. Asheville, NC: Chiron Publications, 1993.

J. E. Cirlot. *A Dictionary of Symbols*. Reprint. New York: Welcome Rain Publishers, 2014.

Robert H. Hopcke. *A Guided Tour of the Collected Works of C. G. Jung*. Reprint. Boston: Shambhala, 1999.

Works by C. G. Jung

C. G. Jung. *Analytical Psychology: Its Theory and Practice*. The Tavistock Lectures. New York: Pantheon Books, 1968.

_________. *C. G. Jung: Psychological Reflections: A New Anthology of His Writings, 1905-1961*. Selected and edited by Jolande Jacobi. Reprint. Princeton, NJ: Princeton University Press, 1978.

_________. *C. G. Jung Speaking: Interviews and Encounters*. Edited by William McGuire and R. F. C. Hull. Reprint. Princeton, NJ: Princeton University Press, 1987.

_________. *Dream Analysis: Notes of the Seminar Given in 1928-1930 by C. G. Jung*. Edited by William McGuire. Princeton, NJ: Princeton University Press, 1984.

_________. *Dreams: (From Volumes 4, 8, 12, and 16 of the Collected Works of C. G. Jung)*. Translated by R. F. C. Hull. Reprint. Princeton, NJ: Princeton University Press, 2010.

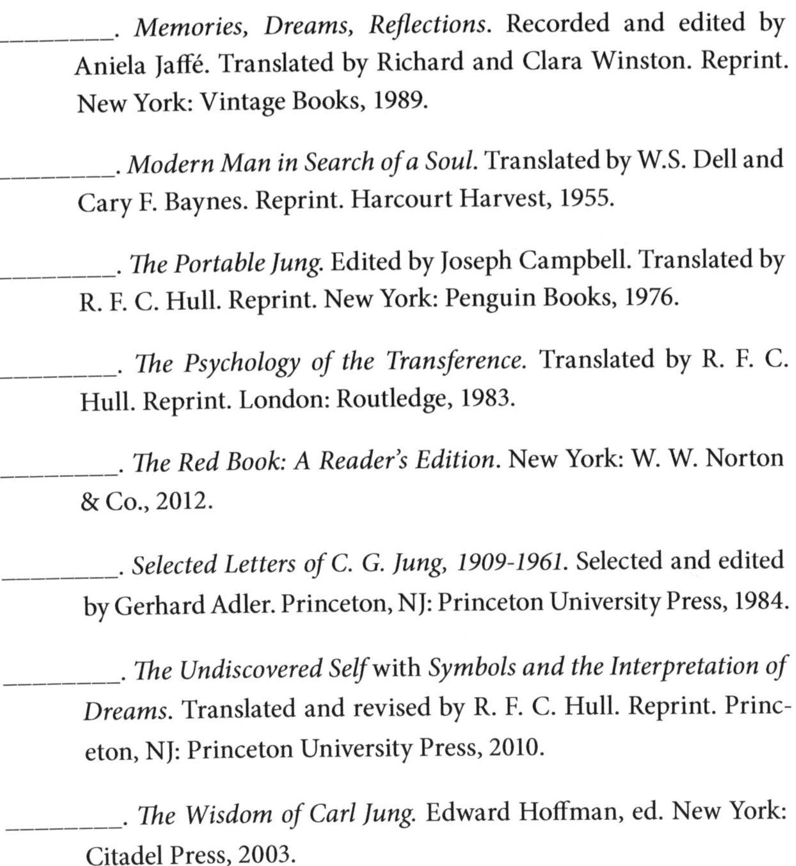

_________. *Memories, Dreams, Reflections*. Recorded and edited by Aniela Jaffé. Translated by Richard and Clara Winston. Reprint. New York: Vintage Books, 1989.

_________. *Modern Man in Search of a Soul*. Translated by W.S. Dell and Cary F. Baynes. Reprint. Harcourt Harvest, 1955.

_________. *The Portable Jung*. Edited by Joseph Campbell. Translated by R. F. C. Hull. Reprint. New York: Penguin Books, 1976.

_________. *The Psychology of the Transference*. Translated by R. F. C. Hull. Reprint. London: Routledge, 1983.

_________. *The Red Book: A Reader's Edition*. New York: W. W. Norton & Co., 2012.

_________. *Selected Letters of C. G. Jung, 1909-1961*. Selected and edited by Gerhard Adler. Princeton, NJ: Princeton University Press, 1984.

_________. *The Undiscovered Self* with *Symbols and the Interpretation of Dreams*. Translated and revised by R. F. C. Hull. Reprint. Princeton, NJ: Princeton University Press, 2010.

_________. *The Wisdom of Carl Jung*. Edward Hoffman, ed. New York: Citadel Press, 2003.

Overviews of Jungian Psychology

E.A. Bennet. *Meetings with Jung*. Zürich: Daimon, 1985.

Barbara Hannah. *Jung: His Life and Work*. Wilmette, IL: Chiron Publications, 1997.

M. Esther Harding. *The 'I' and the 'Not I': A Study in the Development of Consciousness*. Bollingen Series LXXIX. Princeton, NJ: Princeton University Press, 1965.

Carl G. Jung, and M.-L. von Franz, Joseph L. Henderson, Jolande Jacobi, and Aniela Jaffé. *Man and his Symbols*. New York: Dell Publishing, 1964.

Mary Ann Mattoon. *Jung and the Human Psyche: An Understandable Introduction*. London: Routledge, 2005.

Robin Robertson. *Beginners Guide to Jungian Psychology.* York Beach, ME: Nicholas-Hays, 1992.

Daryl Sharp. *Digesting Jung: Food for the Journey.* Toronto: Inner City Books, 2001.

Murray Stein. *Jung's Map of the Soul: An Introduction.* Chicago: Open Court, 1998.

Marie-Louise von Franz. *C. G. Jung: His Myth in Our Time.* Toronto: Inner City Books, 1998.

Dreams

Fraser Boa. *The Way of the Dream: Conversations on Jungian Dream Interpretation with Marie-Louise von Franz.* Boston: Shambala, 1994.

Greg Bogart. *Dreamwork and Self-Healing: Unfolding the Symbols of the Unconscious.* London: Karnac Books, 2009.

Kathrin Asper. *The Inner Child in Dreams.* Translated by Sharon E. Rooks. Boston: Shambhala, 1992.

Edward F. Edinger. *The Living Psyche: A Jungian Analysis in Pictures.* Asheville, NC: Chiron Publications, 1990.

Robert L. Haden, Jr. *Unopened Letters from God: A Workbook for Individuals and Groups.* Flat Rock, NC: Haden Institute Publishing, 2010.

Robert A. Johnson. *Inner Work: Using Dreams and Active Imagination for Personal Growth.* San Francisco: Harper and Row, 1986.

Morton T. Kelsey. *Dreams: A Way to Listen to God.* Mahwah, NJ: Paulist Press, 1978.

James Kirsch. *The Reluctant Prophet.* Einseideln, Switzerland: Daimon Verlag, 1973.

John Layard. *Lady of the Hare: A Study in the Healing Power of Dreams.* Boston: Shambhala, 1988.

John A. Sanford. *Dreams: God's Forgotten Language*. 1968. Reprint. New York: HarperOne, 1989.

________. *Dreams and Healing: A Succinct and Lively Interpretation of Dreams*. Mahwah, NJ: Paulist Press, 1978.

Louis M. Savary, et al. *Dreams and Spiritual Growth: A Judeo-Christian Way of Dreamwork*. Mahwah, NJ: Paulist Press, 1984.

Candy Smith. *Beginning Dreamwork: How To Have a Conversation with Your Soul*. Foreword by Joyce Rockwood Hudson. Orlando: SPC Books, 2011.

Jeremy Taylor. *Dream Work: Techniques for Discovering the Creative Power in Dreams*. Mahwah, NJ: Paulist Press, 1983.

________. *Where People Fly and Water Runs Uphill: Using Dreams to Tap the Wisdom of the Unconscious*. New York: Warner Books, 1992.

Marie-Louise von Franz. *Dreams: A Study of the Dreams of Jung, Descartes, Socrates, and Other Historical Figures*. Boston: Shambhala, 1998.

Synchronicity

Robert Aziz. *C. G. Jung's Psychology of Religion and Synchronicity*. Albany, NY: State University of New York Press, 1990.

Deike Begg. *Synchronicity: The Promise of Coincidence*. Asheville, NC: Chiron, 2001.

Jean Shinoda Bolen. *The Tao of Psychology: Synchronicity and the Self*. Reprint. San Francisco: Harper and Row, 2005.

Joseph Cambray. *Synchronicity: Nature and Psyche in an Interconnected Universe*. Reprint. College Station, TX: Texas A&M University Press, 2012.

Allan Combs and Mark Holland. *Synchronicity: Science, Myth, and the Trickster*. New York: Paragon House, 1990.

Marie-Louise von Franz. *On Divination and Synchronicity: The Psychology of Meaningful Chance*. Toronto: Inner City Books, 1980.

Personality Types

Renee Baron. *What Type Am I: Discover Who You Really Are*. New York: Penguin Books, 1998.

A. J. Drenth. *The 16 Personality Types: Profiles, Theory, and Type Development*. Inquire Books, 2013.

Isabel Briggs Myers. *Introduction to Type: A Guide to Understanding Your Results on the MBTI Instrument*. Revised by Linda K. Kirby and Katharine D. Myers. Mountain View, CA: CPP, Inc., 1998.

________, with Peter B. Myers. *Gifts Differing: Understanding Personality Type*. 1980. Reprint. Palo Alto, CA: CCP Books, 1993.

Daryl Sharp. *Personality Types: Jung's Model of Typology*. Toronto: Inner City Books, 1987.

Paul D. Tieger and Barbara Barron-Tieger. *Nurture by Nature: Understand Your Child's Personality Type—And Become a Better Parent*. Boston: Little, Brown and Co., 1997.

Lenore Thomson. *Personality Type: An Owner's Manual*. Boston: Shambhala, 1998.

Marie-Louise von Franz and James Hillman. *Lectures on Jung's Typology*. 1971. Reprint. Dallas, TX: Spring Publications, 1986.

The Shadow and Evil

Robert Bly. *A Little Book on the Human Shadow*. New York: HarperOne, 1988.

Mario Jacoby, Verena Kast, and Ingrid Riedel. *Witches, Ogres, and the Devil's Daughter: Encounters with Evil in Fairy Tales*. Translated by Michael H. Kohn. Boston: Shambhala, 1992.

Robert A. Johnson. *Owning Your Own Shadow: Understanding the Dark Side of the Psyche*. HarperSanFrancisco, 1994.

C. G. Jung. *Jung on Evil*. Selected and Introduced by Murray Stein. Princeton, NJ: Princeton University Press, 1995.

Marie-Louise von Franz. *Shadow and Evil in Fairy Tales*. Boston: Shambhala, 1995.

Connie Zweig and Jeremiah Abrams, eds. *Meeting the Shadow: The Hidden Power of the Dark Side of Human Nature*. New York: Tarcher, 1991.

Masculine and Feminine

Robert Bly. *Iron John: A Book about Men*. Reprint. Cambridge, MA: Da Capo Press, 2004.

Jean Shinoda Bolen. *Goddesses in Everywoman: Powerful Archetypes in Women's Lives*. Reprint. New York: Harper and Row, 2014.

________. *Gods in Everyman: Archetypes that Shape Men's Lives*. Reprint. New York: Harper and Row, 1989.

Irene Claremont de Castillejo. *Knowing Woman: A Feminine Psychology*. Reprint. Boston: Shambhala, 1997.

M. Esther Harding. *The Way of All Women*. Reprint. Boston: Shambhala, 2001.

James Hollis. *Under Saturn's Shadow: The Wounding and Healing of Men*. Toronto: Inner City Books, 1994.

Robert A. Johnson. *He: Understanding Masculine Psychology*. Rev. ed. New York: Harper Perennial, 1989.

________. *Lying with the Heavenly Woman: Understanding and Integrating the Feminine Archetypes in Men's Lives*. HarperSanFrancisco, 1994.

________. *She: Understanding Feminine Psychology*. Rev. ed. New York: Harper Perennial, 1989.

________. *Transformation: Understanding the Three Levels of Masculine Consciousness*. New York: HarperOne, 1993.

________. *We: Understanding the Psychology of Romantic Love*. New York: HarperOne, 2009.

Linda Schierse Leonard. *Meeting the Madwoman: An Inner Challenge for Feminine Spirit*. New York: Bantam Books, 1993.

________. *The Wounded Woman: Healing the Father-Daughter Relationship*. 1982. Reprint. Boston: Shambhala, 1985.

Helen M. Luke. *The Way of Woman: Awakening the Perennial Feminine*. New York: Doubleday, 1995.

Robert Moore and Douglas Gillette. *King, Warrior, Magician, Lover: Rediscovering the Archetypes of the Mature Masculine*. New York: HarperOne, 1991.

Gertrud Mueller Nelson. *Here All Dwell Free: Stories to Heal the Wounded Feminine*. Reprint. Eugene, OR: Wipf and Stock Publishers, 2006.

Erich Neumann. *The Great Mother: An Analysis of the Archetype*. Translated by Ralph Manheim. New edition. Princeton, NJ: Princeton University Press, 2015

John A. Sanford. *The Invisible Partners: How the Male and Female in Each of Us Affects Our Relationships*. Mahwah, NJ: Paulist Press, 1979.

Ann Belford Ulanov. *Receiving Woman: Studies in the Psychology and Theology of the Feminine*. Philadelphia: Westminster Press, 1981.

Marie-Louise von Franz. *The Feminine in Fairy Tales*. Rev. ed. Boston: Shambhala, 2001.

________. *The Problem of the Puer Aeternus*. Reprint. Toronto: Inner City Books, 2000.

Marion Woodman. *Addiction to Perfection: The Still Unravished Bride*. Toronto: Inner City Books, 1982.

Stages of Life, Aspects of Wholeness

Allan B. Chinen. *Once Upon a Midlife: Classic Stories and Mythic Tales to Illuminate the Middle Years*. Reprint. Xlibris: 2003.

Imelda Gaudissart. *Love and Sacrifice: The Life of Emma Jung*. Trans. Kathleen Llanwarne. Asheville, NC: Chiron Publications, 2014.

Barbara Hannah. *The Archetypal Symbolism of Animals: Lectures Given at the C. G. Jung Institute, Zurich, 1954-1958*. Asheville, NC: Chiron Publications, 2005.

James Hollis. *Finding Meaning in the Second Half of Life: How to Finally, Really Grow Up*. New York: Gotham Books, 2006.

_________. *Hauntings: Dispelling the Ghosts Who Run Our Lives*. Asheville, NC: Chiron Publications, 2013.

Mario Jacoby. *Longing for Paradise: Psychological Perspectives on an Archetype*. Toronto: Inner City Books, 2006.

Robert Johnson. *Balancing Heaven and Earth: A Memoir of Visions, Dreams, and Realizations*. New York: HarperOne, 1998.

Verena Kast. *A Time to Mourn: Growing through the Grief Process*. Einsiedeln, Switzerland: Daimon Verlag, 1993.

Linda Schierse Leonard. *Witness to the Fire: Creativity and the Veil of Addiction*. Reprint. Boston: Shambhala, 2001.

Helen M. Luke. *Old Age*. Gt. Barrington, MA: Lindisfarne Books, 2010.

Carol S. Pearson. *The Hero Within: Six Archetypes We Live By*. Rev. ed. New York: HarperCollins, 1998.

Murray Stein. *In Midlife: A Jungian Perspective*. Woodstock, CT: Spring Publications, 1998.

_________. *Minding the Self: Jungian Meditations on Contemporary Spirituality*. London: Routledge, 2014.

_________. *The Principle of Individuation: Toward the Development of Human Consciousness*. Asheville, NC: Chiron Publications, 2006.

Marie-Louise von Franz. *Individuation in Fairy Tales*. Rev. ed. Boston: Shambhala, 2001.

_________. *The Interpretation of Fairy Tales*. Boston: Shambhala, 1996.

_________. *The Psychological Meaning of Redemption Motifs in Fairytales*. Toronto: Inner City Books, 1980.

Audio-Visual Media for a Natural Spirituality Library

DVDs

C. G. Jung: The Wisdom of the Dream. A three-part series about the life of Jung and his understanding of dreams, mythology, and the depths of the human psyche. Includes a major English-language interview with Jung recorded in 1956. Three discs. Total running time: 159 minutes.

The World Within: C.G Jung in His Own Words. Rarely seen footage of Jung himself interviewed in Switzerland. He talks at length about his work on dreams, memory, archetypal figures and the importance of ritual and fantasy (60 minutes). Also includes this Special Feature: *Remembering Jung—Interview Excerpts with Jung's Associates*: Sir Laurens van der Post offers a candid description of Jung's discovery of the need to heal the 'rejected feminine' aspect in men and women and how this contributes to the positive evolution of modern culture (20 minutes). Gerhard Adler (30 minutes). Liliane Frey-Rohn (27 minutes).

A Matter of Heart: The Extraordinary Journey of C. G. Jung into the Soul of Man. A film portrait of Jung. More than a linear biography, the film presents a full perspective through the skillful interweaving of rare home movies, valuable archival footage, and a wealth of interviews with such notables as Sir Laurens van der Post, Marie-Louise von Franz, and Joseph Henderson, M.D. (107 minutes). Also includes these Special Features: *Face to Face: Professor Jung, 1959*—C. G. Jung interviewed on the BBC's popular 1960's TV chat show (30 minutes). *C. G. Jung at Bollingen Tower Retreat, 1951*—excerpts from an uncompleted documentary about Jung (21 minutes).

Appointment with the Wise Old Dog: Dream Images in a Time of Crisis. This beautiful film speaks deeply of the value of dreams for healing the soul and illuminating life's difficult passages with wonder and meaning. David Blum, internationally known music conductor, shares on film his paintings of dream images and the guidance they gave him as he approached death from cancer. A powerful, moving film that should be in every dream group's library. Introduction by Yo-Yo Ma. (30 minutes.) Available from the David Blum website: davidblummusiciananddreamer.com.

The *Remembering Jung* series. Filmed interviews with noted Jungian analysts who were in direct relationship with Jung. Taken altogether this series offers a wealth of insights and stories illustrating the depth of Jung's discoveries and their significance in our lives, individually and collectively. Especially noteworthy are interviews with Marie-Louise von Franz, Joseph Henderson, Sir Laurens van der Post, James Kirsch, and Jung's grandsons Dieter Baumann and Rudi Niehus. Available from the bookstore of the C. G. Jung Institute of Los Angeles: junginla.org.

Seminars from the Asheville Jung Center. Video recordings of online seminars by some of the world's leading Jungian thinkers, on such topics as Jung's *Red Book*, psychology and spirituality, art and the psyche, and the shadow and evil. Available on DVDs and as downloads from the Center's website: ashevillejungcenter.org.

CDs and MP3 Downloads

The Golden World: Our Search for Meaning, Fulfillment, and Divine Beauty, Robert Johnson. In this intimate audio encounter, Jungian analyst and teacher Robert Johnson shares his fascinating memories of the defining moments of his 86 years as a spiritual seeker. From a childhood near-death experience to the chance encounter that leads him to first explore Jungian study, Johnson illustrates the essential concepts that have become the cornerstones of his acclaimed work.

Lectures from the Haden Institute Summer Dream and Spirituality Conferences. An annual conference centered on Jungian dreamwork in a spiritual context. Ten major lectures a year from 2003 to present. Available for *free downloading* on iTunes. In the iTunes store search "seedwork." On the page you reach, click "See All" in upper right corner to see the complete offering of lectures.

Archetypal Experiences Surrounding Death, Marie-Louise von Franz. A recorded lecture, with excellent audio quality (100 minutes).

Available from the bookstore of the C. G. Jung Institute of Los Angeles: junginla.org.

Reminiscences of C. G. Jung and his Influences Today, Laurens van der Post. A recorded lecture, with excellent audio quality (57 minutes). Available from the bookstore of the C. G. Jung Institute of Los Angeles: junginla.org.

Classes from The Jung Center, Houston, Texas. A rich treasury of audio recordings of classes in depth psychology that have been taught at The Jung Center by Pittman McGehee, James Hollis, Jerry Ruhl, and others. Available from The Jung Center Bookstore: junghouston.org.

Lectures from Journey Into Wholeness. Journey Into Wholeness sponsored multiple conferences a year from 1978 to 2006, exploring ourselves and our world through the psychology of C. G. Jung. Many of these lectures are available from The Jung Center Bookstore: junghouston.org.

Conferences, Training Programs, and Online Seminars

Haden Institute Summer Dream and Spirituality Conference. An annual five-day conference centered on Jungian dreamwork in a spiritual context. 10 major lectures, 30 practical workshops, four dream group sessions. Held at Kanuga Conference Center near Henderson, NC. For information and registration: hadeninstitute.com.

Haden Institute Dream Leader Training Program. A two-year course for individuals who want to enhance their skills in working with dreams. This program has great value not only for those who want to lead dream groups or offer dreamwork coaching, but also for those who simply want to deepen their own personal journeys with dreams. It is of great benefit to any dream group to have several members who have attended this program. The more the better. For information and registration: hadeninstitute.com.

Asheville Jung Center. The Center's primary focus is to offer world-class Jungian seminars through internet technology. During these live seminars, international participants can ask questions of the speakers from live audio-video connections, e-mail, or online chat. Seminars can be watched live or recorded. Individuals without high speed internet can also participate by watching recorded DVD's of the seminars, usually available a few months later. Continuing Education credits for professionals are also available. Many of the seminars are presented from leading Jungian academic centers such as the International School Of Analytical Psychology Zurich (ISAP), the C. G. Jung Institute of San Francisco, the Tavistock Clinic of London, the C. G. Jung Institute of Chicago, and other sites. The Center's website is ashevillejungcenter.org.

Acknowledgments

For help with the original edition of this book, I thank Miriam Chaikin for the close reading she gave to the work in manuscript form and for the benefit of her editorial wisdom. Likewise, I thank Karen Orchard for her editorial advice and for her encouragement and support for the project from the beginning. I am grateful to Charles Hudson, Martha Harris, Gabriel Clark, and Ann Clark for reading the original manuscript and offering helpful suggestions and reactions.

The vision of natural spirituality as a church program was developed in the 1990s in joint enterprise with the members of the Natural Spirituality Program of Emmanuel Episcopal Church in Athens, Georgia, and together we worked out many details over the course of several years. I thank them every one for their enthusiastic participation in this pioneering effort. I especially thank Agnes Parker, Frank Farrar, and Heidi Simmonds for their steady companionship during that formative period. I also thank the past members of the clergy of Emmanuel Church who gave our natural spirituality program such a receptive and supportive environment, especially Jim Yeary, Barry Griffin, and Eddie Ard. I will be ever thankful to two other men of the church, Nick Johnson and Cecil Hudson, for crucial early support in my journey, before its destination was clear and its fruit had been born. And I offer deep gratitude to Mary Jo Brown, whose companionship was crucial in those early years when there was no program, nor any thought of one, but only the two of us struggling together to make sense of our inner experience within the context of our life with God.

I am grateful to Robert Johnson and John Sanford for their attention to the original edition of this book in its preliminary form and for their much appreciated words of encouragement. I also thank the leaders of Journey Into Wholeness for their offer of newsletter space when the original copy-shop edition of this book was published in 1998. That support led to sufficient sales to justify the publication of the first trade paperback edition in 2000. To Sandy Hudson, I will be ever thankful for her beautiful design work for the 2000 edition, the high quality of which added to its success.

Soon after the 2000 edition was published, the Reverend Susan Sims Smith, Canon for Special Ministries in the Episcopal Diocese of Arkansas, began an effort, with the encouragement of Bishop Larry Maze, to establish dream groups in parishes throughout their diocese. Just as she was embarking on this quest, Susan discovered *Natural Spirituality* and began to recommend it as a handbook for those fledgling dream groups. For a short period in those early days, the Amazon page for *Natural Spirituality* proclaimed it to be the #1 Best Seller in Arkansas! That initial boost was crucial for setting the book on a successful course and bringing it to the attention of the greater world. Though each of us have shifted our places in the world since then, the partnership that Larry, Susan, and I forged at that time is still ongoing, and I am deeply grateful for their continuing companionship and support in this work.

I offer deep gratitude to the Reverend Bob Haden, who reached out to me in 2003 and made me a colleague in his work at the Haden Institute. For more than a decade, we and others working with us have produced the annual Summer Dream and Spirituality Conference under the aegis of his institute. From the time of our first meeting, Bob has included me on the faculty of the institute's Dream Leader Training Program and has made *Natural Spirituality* required reading for its students. The role of the Haden Institute in spreading *Natural Spirituality* across the country and around the world cannot be overstated. I thank Bob for his early and ongoing friendship and support.

I am deeply grateful to Murray Stein for his early and continuing support for *Natural Spirituality.* As soon as he saw the book, which was soon after it was published, he offered to carry it in the catalog of Chiron Publications, for which he was at that time the publisher. Because the book already had its own publisher, Chiron took it on as a distributor. This distinction, however, was barely noticeable in the catalog. In effect, Chiron adopted *Natural Spirituality* right out of the cradle and claimed it as its own. I can never thank Murray enough for stepping up and doing that. Now I am also grateful to Steve Buser and Len Cruz, the present publisher and editor, respectively, of Chiron, for taking on this revised edition as an official Chiron publication. I am thrilled that Chiron's imprint will now be on the spine. I thank both Steve and Len for their strong and steadfast support.

Last but not least, I am grateful to my Kentucky dream group for their ongoing companionship on this journey we all share, and especially for helping me develop a new and effective model for how to start and run a dream group. For reading the manuscript for this new edition and giving me helpful suggestions—from alerts about typos to refinements of ideas—I thank Nash Cox, Fonda McWilliams, and Mary Frank Slaughter. For allowing me to use his wonderful translations from the Dao De Jing in the liturgy in Appendix B, I thank Joseph Fiala. And for the beautiful painting, "Inner Wilderness," on the cover of this edition, I thank Betty Beshoar. All are members of our dream group.

June 2016

Frankfort, Kentucky

Notes

Scripture quotations, unless otherwise noted, are from *The Jerusalem Bible* (New York: Doubleday, 1968)

Chapter One - Beginnings

p.26 "I don't need to believe...": *C. G. Jung Speaking: Interviews and Encounters*, William McGuire and R. F. C. Hull, eds. (Princeton, NJ: Princeton University Press, 1977), 428.

Chapter Two - Do We Really Need Inner Work?

p.38 Peter and Cornelius: Acts 10:1–11:18

p.41 "Even if we did once know...": 2 Corinthians 5:16.

"There is only Christ...": Colossians 3:11.

"The Spirit reaches the depths...": 1 Corinthians 2:10.

"fills the whole creation": Ephesians 1:23.

Chapter Three - Consciousness

p.51 "Our consciousness...": C. G. Jung, "The Psychology of Eastern Meditation," in *Collected Works*, vol. 11 (Princeton, NJ: Princeton University Press, 1958), par. 935.

Chapter Four - The Unconscious

p.71 "Just as conscious contents...": C. G. Jung, "Approaching the Unconscious," in *Man and His Symbols*, C. G. Jung, ed. (London and New York: Dell Publishing, 1964), 37.

p.81 "The Father is greater...": John 14:28.

"If you know me...": John 14:7.

p.82 "I am the Way": John 14:6.

"I am the gate": John 10:9.

"come…through me": John 14:6.

"believe in me": John 10:38.

p.84 "We know that the mask…": C. G. Jung, *Psychology and Alchemy*, *Collected Works*, vol. 12 (Princeton, NJ: Princeton University Press, 1944), par. 29.

p.85 "'Speak to us yourself'…": Exodus 20:19.

Chapter Five - The Language of the Unconscious

p.87 "The unconscious is the only…": C. G. Jung, "The Undiscovered Self," in *Collected Works*, vol. 10 (Princeton, NJ: Princeton University Press, 1954), par. 565.

p.88 Lincoln's inauguration: Carl Sandburg, *Abraham Lincoln: The War Years*, vol. 4 (New York: Harcourt, Brace, and World, 1939), 91-94.

Lincoln's last dream: Ibid, 265-66.

p.89 "old women and by young men and maidens…": Ibid, 244.

Chapter Six - Dreams

p.105 "The dream is often occupied…": C. G. Jung, "On the Psychology of the Unconscious," in *Collected Works*, vol. 7 (Princeton, NJ: Princeton University Press, 1953), par. 24.

Nativity story: Matthew 1:18-2:23.

p.108 "Every night a Eucharist...": Anthony Storr, *Feet of Clay: A Study of Gurus* (New York: Free Press Paperbacks, 1997), 97.

Chapter Seven - Synchronicity

p.127 "Since psyche and matter…": C. G. Jung, "On the Nature of the Psyche," in *Collected Works*, vol. 8 (Princeton: NJ: Princeton

University Press, 1960), par. 418.

p.135 "She is so pure...": Wisdom 7:24-25.

p.136 "The Spirit's power...": *The Hymnal 1982: according to the use of The Episcopal Church* (New York: The Church Hymnal Corp., 1985), Hymn 296.

p.137 "river of life...": Revelation 22:1.

Chapter Eight - The Opposites

p.141 "Alleluia! The reign of the Lord...": *Revelation,* chapters 19-22.

p.148 I thank Heidi Simmonds for the idea that the sun is flaring and outer and the moon pocked and inner. *Personal communication.*

Chapter Nine - Masculine Wholeness

p.157 Toni Wolff's feminine quaternity: Toni Wolff, *Structural Forms of the Feminine Psyche*, trans. Paul Watzlawik, privately printed for the Students Association, C. G. Jung Institute, Zurich, July 1956. Available online from University of Florida Digital Collections: http://ufdc.ufl.edu//AA00001582/00001.

Jung's four stages of the anima: C. G. Jung, *Psychology of the Transference*, in *Collected Works*, vol. 16 (Princeton, NJ: Princeton University Press, 1954), par. 361. These ideas are recapitulated by Marie-Louise von Franz in C. G. Jung, et al, *Man and His Symbols* (New York: Dell, 1968), 195.

p.158 Robert Moore and Douglas Gillette's version of the masculine quaternity is laid out in their book, *King, Warrior, Magician, Lover: Rediscovering the Archetypes of the Mature Masculine* (Harper SanFrancisco, 1990). It is elaborated in four further volumes, each of which is devoted to one of the quarters: *The King Within: Accessing the King in the Male Psyche* (New York: Avon Books, 1992); *The Warrior Within: Accessing the Knight in the Male Psyche* (Avon, 1992); *The Magician Within: Accessing the Shaman in the Male Psyche* (Avon, 1993); and *The Lover Within: Accessing the Lover in the Male Psyche* (Avon, 1993).

Chapter Ten - The Beatles and the Masculine Quaternity

p.177 "The thing is, we're all really the same person....": Hunter Davies, *The Beatles: The Authorized Biography* (New York: McGraw-Hill, 1968), 322.

p.183 Jung on psychedelic drugs: Marie-Louise von Franz, *Psychotherapy* (Boston: Shambhala, 1993), 297.

p.187 "There's four of us...": *The Lost Beatle Interviews*, Geoffrey Giuliano and Brenda Giuliano, eds. (New York: Dutton, 1994), 41.

p.205 Jung's Liverpool dream: C. G. Jung, *Memories, Dreams, Reflections*, 197–199.

Chapter Eleven - Feminine Wholeness

p.219 "Sophia is the woman wisdom of God": C. G. Jung, *Jung on Alchemy*, ed Nathan Schwartz-Salant (Princeton, NJ: Princeton University Press, 1995), 148.

"Happy is the man...": Ecclesiasticus 14:20-27.

Chapter Twelve - Psyche and Eros and the Feminine Quaternity

p.224 C. S. Lewis, *Till We Have Faces* (New York: Harcourt Brace, 1957); Erich Neumann, *Amor and Psyche: The Psychic Development of the Feminine* (Princeton, NJ: Princeton University Press, 1956); Robert Johnson, *She: Understanding Feminine Psychology*, revised edition (New York: Harper and Row, 1989); Marie-Louise von Franz, *The Golden Ass of Apuleius: The Liberation of the Feminine in Man* (Boston: Shambhala, 1992).

Chapter Thirteen - Types, Quarters, and Stages of Life

p.257 To calculate the first and second functions in the four-letter names of the Jungian psychological types, we start with the fact that any *extravert's* first function is by definition extraverted. That is, it is more directed toward the outer world than toward the inner world. For any extravert, then, the fourth letter in the four-letter sequence—the J or the P—indicates which of the two functions named in the middle of the four-letter sequence is the first function. (One of them, remember, is a perceiving function and the other one is a judging function.) In the case of an ESFJ, the fourth letter is J, indicating that an ESFJ meets the outer world with a judging function. This means that of the two functions signified by the two middle letters—sensing (S) and feeling (F)—feeling is an ESFJ's first function, since feeling is the one that is a judging function. The other function, sensation (S), which is a perceiving function, is, by default, an ESFJ's second function. One further point: because everyone's second function is opposite in "version" from his or her first function, an ESFJ's sensation function is introverted, directed more toward his or her inner world than toward the outer world.

A different calculation is required to determine an *introvert's* first function in the Myers-Briggs four-letter type name. This is because the first function of an introvert is by definition introverted. It is directed more toward his or her inner world than toward the outer world. For introverts, it is their *second* function that is turned toward the outer world, not their first. This means that the J or P, which tells us whether they tend to meet the outer world with a judging or perceiving function, indicates which of the two middle letters in their type name is their *second* function, the other middle letter being, by default, their first function. So an INTP would be an *introvert* (I) whose first function is *thinking* (T) and whose second function is *intuition* (N). We know this because the P tells us that an INTP meets the outer world with a perceiving function, and we know that all introverts meet the outer world with their second function. Of the two functions signified by the two middle letters, intuition (N) and thinking (T), intuition is the one that is a perceiving function and is therefore the INTP's second function. This means that, by default, thinking is the first function. A mnemonic device that some people use in making this calculation (whether for an extravert or an introvert) is that J indicates that the letter *just* next to it is extraverted, and P indicates that the *previous* letter is extraverted. This can make the calculation a little easier by eliminating the need to remember which of the functions, overall, are perceiving and which are judging.

p.269 "the sudden sense of awe…": John Giannini, *Compass of the Soul*, pg. 89.

Chapter Fifteen - Does Jungian Inner Work Belong in Church?

p.314 "Even the enlightened person…": C. G. Jung, *Answer to Job*, in *The Portable Jung*, Joseph Campbell, ed., (New York: Penguin Books, 1976), 650.

p.315 "I falter before the task…": C. G. Jung, *Memories, Dreams, Reflections* (New York: Pantheon Books, 1961), 353-54.

"The Christ image as we know it…": C. G. Jung, *Letters*, vol. 2 (Princeton, NJ: Princeton University Press, 1975), 121.

"I have a certain picture…": Ibid, 94.

p.316 "You see, this is the crux…": C. G. Jung, *Letters*, vol. 1 (Princeton, NJ: Princeton University Press, 1973), 236n.

"On the whole my illness…": Ibid, 357-58.

p.322 "the devil left him…": Luke 4:13.

p.323 "I still have many things to say…": John 16:12-13.

"Enter by the narrow gate…": Matthew 7:13-14.

"with an exactness…": C. G. Jung, *Aion*, *Collected Works*, vol. 9, pt. 2 (Princeton, NJ: Princeton University Press, 1959), par. 79.

p.326 "A ladder was there…": Genesis 28:12-13.

p.327 "Are not interpretations…": Genesis 40:8.

"I have heard it said…": Genesis 41:15-16.

"Pharaoh's dreams…": Genesis 41:25a.

"God has revealed…": Genesis 42:25b.

"the gift of interpreting…": Daniel 1:17.

"O king…": Daniel 2:29-30.

p.329 Gerhard von Rad, *Wisdom in Israel* (Valley Forge, PA: Trinity Press International, 1972).

"The wise of heart…": Proverbs 10:8, *The New Jerusalem Bible* (New York: Doubleday, 1985).

"Their uprightness…": Proverbs 11:6, *The New Jerusalem Bible* (New York: Doubleday, 1985).

p.330 "Where does wisdom…": Job 28:12.

p.331 "Is not Wisdom calling…": Proverbs 8:1-4, *The New Jerusalem Bible* (New York: Doubleday, 1985).

"For whoever finds me…": Proverbs 8:35, *The New Jerusalem Bible* (New York: Doubleday, 1985).

"I love those who love me…": Proverbs 8:17.

"Court her…": Ecclesiasticus 6:26-28.

p.332 "For within her…": Wisdom 7:22, 24-26.

"What man can know…": Wisdom 9:13.

"It is hard enough…": Wisdom 9:16-17.

"If you do not believe me…": John 3:12-13.

"No one knows the Father…": Matthew 11:27.

p.333 "Come to me…": Matthew 11:28-30.

"Put your neck under the yoke…": Sirach 51:26-27, *The New English Bible* (Oxford: Oxford University Press, 1970).

"Even if we did once know…": 2 Corinthians 5:16.

"a Christ who is the power…": 1 Corinthians 1:24

p.334 "But still we have a wisdom…": 1 Corinthians 2:6,7,10.

"To you it has been granted…": Luke 8:10, *The New English Bible* (Oxford: Oxford University Press, 1970).

p.335 "A shoot springs…": Isaiah 11:1-9.

Appendix A - Find Your Type

p.347 The sources used for these Type Descriptions are as follows: Renee Baron, *What Type Am I: Discover Who You Really Are* (New York: Penguin Books, 1998); A. J. Drenth, *The 16 Personality Types: Profiles, Theory, and Type Development*, (Inquire Books, 2013); Isabel Briggs Myers, *Introduction to Type: A Guide to Understanding Your Results on the MBTI Instrument*, Revised by Linda K. Kirby and Katharine D. Myers (Mountain View, CA: CPP, Inc., 1998); Paul D. Tieger and Barbara Barron-Tieger, *Nurture by Nature: Understand Your Child's Personality Type—And Become a Better Parent* (Boston: Little, Brown and Co., 1997); Lenore Thomson, *Personality Type: An Owner's Manual* (Boston: Shambhala, 1998).

Index

C

D

E

F

G

H

I

J

K

L

M

N

O

T

U

V

Made in the USA
Lexington, KY
05 September 2018

98171142R00242

Made in the USA
Lexington, KY
05 September 2018